T0139789

Social Media for Government Services

Surya Nepal · Cécile Paris
Dimitrios Georgakopoulos
Editors

Social Media for Government Services

 Springer

Editors
Surya Nepal
CSIRO Data61
Sydney
Australia

Dimitrios Georgakopoulos
RMIT University
Melbourne, VIC
Australia

Cécile Paris
CSIRO Data61
Sydney
Australia

ISBN 978-3-319-80098-1   ISBN 978-3-319-27237-5   (eBook)
DOI 10.1007/978-3-319-27237-5

Cover image: Screenshots of systems developed by Data61 at CSIRO This image is taken with the permission of CSIRO Data61 and contains images from the following social media systems:Emergency Situation Awareness (ESA), the Next Step Online Community and Vizie, a social media monitoring tool.

Printed on acid-free paper

This Springer imprint is published by SpringerNature
The registered company is Springer International Publishing AG Switzerland

Preface

Governments at all levels (local, state or federal) are seeking better communication means, greater transparency, more participation from and collaboration with citizens in a range of government activities, ranging from disseminating information to formulating policies and delivering services. In addition, governments are under constant pressure to deliver more with less. In recent times, social media has been particularly appealing to advance these goals because of the increased participation of the population on sites like Facebook, Twitter, YouTube and Flickr. As a result, increasing numbers of government departments and agencies have started using social media as part of their channels of interactions with citizens. Although the use of social media has been increasing rapidly in recent times, there are still a number of significant challenges associated with it regarding citizens' privacy, veracity of content, governance policies and framework, the integration of social media with organisational business processes and risk management plans, to name a few.

Aim and Scope

In this book, we bring together researchers and practitioners and present the state-of-the-art research, development and deployment of social media use by governments through a number of case studies and systems descriptions.

The book covers many research activities CSIRO has done in social media for Australian government agencies, more specifically for the Department of Human Services under the $16 million 5-year "CSIRO-Centrelink Human Services

Delivery Research Alliance (HSDRA)".[1] Chapters "Social Media for Government Services: A Case Study of Human Services", "*Next Step*: An Online Community for Delivering Human Services" through to "Improving Situation Awareness and Reporting Using the Emergency Response Intelligence Capability Tool" report on different activities that were undertaken under HSDRA. In addition, the book contains invited and peer-reviewed chapters from both academic researchers and industry practitioners.

The book is useful and of interest to a wide range of people, including academic researchers, IT industries, developers of government policies and decision makers, communication staff in government departments and agencies, and anyone in the government sector interested in making use of this communication transforming medium of interaction: social media.

Organisation

The book is organised into two parts, namely Part I: Introduction and Case Studies and Part II: Systems and Applications. The book is composed of 17 chapters. Part I contains 8 chapters and Part II contains 9 chapters.

The first chapter, "Social Media in Government Services: An Introduction", provides a basic introduction to social media such as a definition, the origin of the term, and the types of social media prevalent in the Internet. In addition, the chapter focuses on the adoption of social media for government services, introducing a number of popular application scenarios. The chapter also describes a few key challenges and issues that must be addressed, and a framework to define guidelines and policies to overcome those challenges. The chapter is then followed by a case study from the Australian Government Department of Human Services. The chapter, "Social Media for Government Services: A Case Study of Human Services", illustrates how that department is making use of social media to support its customers and improve service delivery. It provides illustrative examples of some success stories, together with the challenges they had to face. The chapter also presents a governance framework and touches one of the difficult questions to be answered: how to measure the success of social media engagement?

---

[1] See information about HSDRA and its outcomes in the following websites, all accessed September 29th, 2015:[1] http://www.csiro.au/en/Research/DPF/Areas/The-digital-economy/Digital-service-delivery.[1] https://publications.csiro.au/rpr/download?pid=csiro:EP149489&dsid=DS1.[1] https://www.youtube.com/watch?v=lZgwyaOSMsw.[1] https://www.youtube.com/watch?v=CEQX_rGLkKM.[1] https://www.youtube.com/watch?v=zrMy450eriw.[1] https://www.youtube.com/watch?v=caK2bRHcOEs.[1] http://www.technologydecisions.com.au/content/gov-tech-review/article/reinventing-government-customer-service-the-social-way-625131602.

The third chapter, "Use of Social Media for Internal Communication: A Case Study in a Government Organisation", provides a case study of using Yammer for internal communication by VicRoads, a Victorian state government authority. The chapter explains the end-to-end processes of establishing social media for internal use, including choosing the right Yammer components, gaining adoption by users, developing the network with the guidance of a community manager, and continuing the growth of the network through engagement strategies. This is followed by a case study from Dubai's public sector. The chapter, "The Role of Political Leadership in Driving Citizens' Engagement Through Social Media: The Case of Dubai's Public Sector", examines the use of social media in Dubai's government from a public policy perspective. The chapter argues that political leadership was found to be a major factor in the successful use of social media in the public sector.

The fifth chapter, "Social Media Policy in Turkish Municipalities: Disparity Between Awareness and Implementation", aims to analyse the present state of social media policy implementation and evaluation in Turkish municipalities in the Marmara region. The key message from the chapter is that, although there is an increasing rate of awareness of the benefits of social media use, there is a clear deficiency with regard to implementing and evaluating a social media policy. This chapter is followed by a chapter entitled "From Social Media to GeoSocial Intelligence: Crowdsourcing Civic Co-management for Flood Response in Jakarta, Indonesia" that describes a use case in the context of flood disaster management. This chapter provides a review of PetaJakarta.org, a system designed to harness social media use in Jakarta for the purpose of exchanging information amongst citizens and between citizens and emergency management agencies about floods.

The seventh chapter, "Detecting Bursty Topics of Correlated News and Twitter for Government Services", presents a framework of detecting bursty topics of correlated news and Twitter posts. The authors also explain how the proposed framework can be integrated into government services using the 2012 London Olympic games as an example.

It is well known that all governments are under pressure to deliver better services with reduced costs. The next chapter, "Webcare in Public Services: Deliver Better with Less?", describes a case study around webcare, a form of social media that uses online communication with citizens to address client feedback in Dutch public organisations.

The next five chapters, from "*Next Step*: An Online Community for Delivering Human Services" through to "Improving Situation Awareness and Reporting Using the Emergency Response Intelligence Capability Tool", are drawn from different activities at Data61 within CSIRO. Chapter "*Next Step*: An Online Community for Delivering Human Services" presents an online community developed as part of HSDRA. The aim of the community was to provide informational and emotional support to a specific group of welfare recipients. The paper describes the design, development, deployment, trial and results of the community. The success of any online community lies in the engagement of the citizens. In *Next Step*, several techniques were employed for this purpose, including recommenders, which have been widely used to increase the engagement. Another approach to boost engagement is gamification, the topic of the following chapter "Gamification on the Social Web". It provides a brief introduction to gamification and how it has been used in game dynamics. The chapter then presents the experience and observations on using gamification techniques in *Next Step*.

The eleventh chapter, "Improving Government Services Using Social Media Feedback", describes a social media monitoring tool, called Vizie. The tool was designed as part of an HSDRA project[2] to help analysts identify how current government services could be improved by drawing on the commentary and feedback provided in a variety of social media including Twitter and Facebook. This is followed by another chapter from CSIRO on Emergency Situation Awareness (ESA). The chapter "Using Crowd Sourced Content to Help Manage Emergency Events" presents the ESA platform, which collects tweets from Australia and New Zealand and processes them to identify unexpected incidents. The ESA platform has been trialled by numerous emergency services organisations throughout Australia. Three case studies are outlined in the chapter to explain how ESA is being used as an earthquake, bushfire events and a general all-hazard monitoring tool. This chapter is followed by a chapter entitled "Improving Situation Awareness and Reporting Using the Emergency Response Intelligence Capability Tool". It describes the Emergency Response Intelligence Capability (ERIC) tool,[3] also developed as part of HSDRA for the Australian Government Department of Human Services. The tool automatically gathers data about emergency events from authoritative web sources, integrates them and presents them on an interactive map. Emergency management teams can use ERIC for intelligence gathering and situation reporting during emergency events.

The fourteenth chapter, "A Lexical Resource for Identifying Public Services Names on the Social Web", describes an approach for developing a Lexical Resource for Public Services Names, and how it could be exploited to collect data-related government services. The chapter employs the British and Irish government websites to demonstrate the use of the developed technology, which uses the identified names to track messages in Twitter related to governments. This is followed by chapter "Transport Policy: Social Media and User-Generated Content in a Changing Information Paradigm". The chapter describes the challenges in using social media in the transport sector and demonstrates that social media provides a complementary channel for collecting transport data.

The sixteenth chapter, entitled "'Garbage Let's Take Away': Producing Understandable and Translatable Government Documents: A Case Study from Japan", describes how a government department can use a technique to produce

---

[2] https://www.youtube.com/watch?v=CEQX_rGLkKM.

[3] https://www.youtube.com/watch?v=lZgwyaOSMsw.

documents that can be automatically translated to different languages such that the resulting text is understandable. This is important in countries where the society is homogeneous and minority people do not have access to government information in an understandable form. The chapter describes the proposed technique and demonstrates its effectiveness through a case study for Japan. The tool has application beyond Japan, as many countries are encountering similar issues due to globalisation. Finally, the last chapter, "Multi-hazard Detection by Integrating Social Media and Physical Sensors", describes a tool called LITMUS. It combines social media data with data from multiple physical sensors to handle the inherent varied origins and composition of multi-hazards. The results demonstrate that LITMUS detects more landslides than the ones reported by an authoritative source.

Acknowledgement

This book was possible due to the direct and indirect involvement of many researchers, industry practitioners and academics. We acknowledge and thank the contributing authors and their research institutions or government agencies. We offer our special appreciation to Springer and its publishing editor, Dr. Christoph Baumann, and project coordinator Mr. Ravi Vengadachalam, for helping us to bring this book out on time.

Prior technical sources are acknowledged through citations at the appropriate places in each chapter of the book. In case of any errors, we would like to receive feedback so that it could be corrected in the next edition.

We sincerely hope that this book will serve as a valuable source to government agencies who would like to use social media. In addition, we also hope that it will be a valuable reference text for undergraduate and graduate studies, and researchers in this area.

Surya Nepal
Cécile Paris
Dimitrios Georgakopoulos

Contents

Part I
Introduction and Case Studies

Social Media for Government Services: An Introduction

Surya Nepal, Cecile Paris and Dimitrios Georgeakopoulos

Abstract Government agencies and departments all over the world have started using various forms of social media for different purposes. Though the use of social media in public sectors is increasing, the adoption path is not easy and straightforward. Furthermore, in many situations, the use is still in an infancy stage when it is measured against pre-set objectives. The aim of this chapter is multiple folds. The chapter first provides a brief introduction of social media and types of social media. It then describes the adoption process in government. This is followed by some example applications where social media has been successfully used. A few key challenges that are proven to be difficult in adopting social media are given. Finally, the chapter provides a framework to define guidelines and policies to overcome these challenges.

Keywords Social media · Social networks · Government services · Social web

1 Social Media

What is Social Media? There are many definitions of social media in the literature. In essence, social media is an online communication tool that enables people to create, share, interact, collaborate and exchange multi-media information with

S. Nepal (✉) · C. Paris
CSIRO Data61, Sydney, Australia
e-mail: surya.nepal@csiro.au

C. Paris
e-mail: cecile.paris@csiro.au

D. Georgeakopoulos
RMIT University, Melbourne, VIC, Australia
e-mail: dimitrios.georgakopoulos@rmit.edu.au

© Springer International Publishing Switzerland 2015
S. Nepal et al. (eds.), *Social Media for Government Services*,
DOI 10.1007/978-3-319-27237-5_1

other people in virtual communities [1]. Social media tools are built using technologies based on the Web 2.0 [2].

Who coined the term social media? The term emerged in 1990s, but it is in the early 2000s that it gained significant popularity. Jeff Bercovici from Forbes did some investigations to determine who coined the term first, which he reported in his blog in 2010 [3]. He found four key contenders: Tina Sharkey, Ted Leonsis, Darrel Berry and Chris Shipley. All claimed that they were unaware of the use of term when they first used it.

In the technology landscape, social media is a product of the evolution of the Web. Figure 1 shows the evolution of the Web and where social media stands. The first generation web (Web 1.0) was the Web of Content, where static information was shared between web users and web sites. Most users were *consumers* of information. This Web of Content lacked active interactions between information providers and information consumers (users), and amongst the users. A large number of web sites were created during this time. At the beginning of the 21st century, the web evolved from the Web of Content to the Web of Communication (Web 2.0). This provided interactive platforms, like blogs, enabling non-technical users to interact with the web, create content and share with other users. Internet users became both providers and consumers of information, a state sometimes referred as "*prosumers*". Social media (e.g., Twitter, Facebook, YouTube, etc.) is an example platform developed in this period. Around 2008, we started to see the emergence of semantic web (Web 3.0), or the Web of Context. We are now in the mobile web era (2012–2019), the Web of Things or Internet of Things (IoT). This

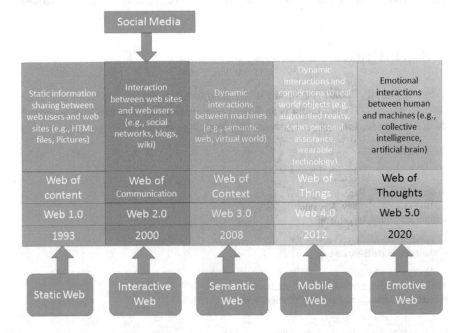

Fig. 1 Social media in the evolution of the web

era is not different than the previous ones, except that the web now has to connect all devices in the real world and the virtual world, in real time. The next web is the emotive web that supports emotional and intelligent interactions between users and the web. This is also called the Web of Thoughts, where human nature meets artificial intelligence [4].

The Federal Web Managers Council has developed the following definition of social media: "Social media and Web 2.0 are umbrella terms that encompass the various activities that integrate technology, social interaction, and content creation. Social media use many technologies and forms, such as blogs, wikis, photo and video sharing, podcasts, social networking, mashups, and virtual worlds" [5].

In terms of functionality, Kietzmann and colleagues defined social media using a honeycomb framework of seven functional building blocks: identity, conversations, sharing, presence, relationships, reputation and groups [6]. Identity represents the way users define, reveal and use their identity in social media. Conversations denote how users communicate with each other on a social media site; for example, conversations could be between individuals (i.e., peer-to-peer) or from an individual to a group. Sharing refers to how users change, distribute and receive social media content. Presence denotes the way a user can make others aware of their availability. Relationships refer to the ways users can relate to each other on social media (e.g., friend, circle, etc.). Reputation is about the way to make users aware of each other's standing in the community. Finally, groups relate to the way users form communities in a social media site. It is important to note that not all social media supports all seven functional blocks.

2 Social Media Types

Social media is still evolving. There are different types of social media prevalent today. In the following, we briefly describe some popular types of social media.

Social Networks: Social networks are the most popular social media tools. Ellison defines social networks as "web-based services that allow individuals to (1) construct a public or semi-public profile within a bounded system, (2) articulate a list of other users with whom they share a connection, and (3) view and traverse their list of connections and those made by others within the system" [7]. Example social networks include MySpace, Facebook and Google+. Social networks can be based around friendship, interest (e.g., people sharing a passion for sports), circumstances (e.g., new parents, students, or people with a specific illness) or based on a professional network.

Bookmarking Sites: Social bookmarking sites are online services that enable users to store and share internet bookmarks. In addition to simple store and browse, these sites also provide management tools such as annotations, categorisations, the ability to comment, etc. Examples of popular bookmarking sites include CiteULike [8], BibSonomy [9], Digg [10], Delicious [11], etc.

Social News: Social news websites enable user to post stories, comment and rank the posts, and view the posts based on their popularity. Slashdot [12] and Reddit are examples of such sites.

Media Sharing: Media sharing sites enable users to share media (e.g., pictures, videos) with each other. YouTube [13] and Flickr [14] are currently amongst the most popular examples of media sharing sites.

Microblogging: Microblogging enables a short message to be sent amongst users. Twitter is the most popular microblogging social media platform [15]. Other popular microblogging sites include Tumblr [16] and Weibo [17].

Online Reviews: An online review site is a website that enables users to post reviews on services, businesses, products, or people. One of the most popular review site for consumers is Epinions [18]. There is now a large number of review sites for different domains; for example, TripAdvisor for travel, WebMD for health, etc.

Question Answering sites: these are dedicated websites where users can pose a question that is answered by another member of the public. For example, Yahoo! Answers is a question answering site. The question-answers pairs present on these websites can be later found by other users with similar questions.

3 Social Media Adoption Process

Governments at all level are increasingly adopting social media for a variety of purposes, ranging from providing accurate information to citizens to participation of citizens in policy formulation and improving internal communications. In this section, we briefly discuss the drivers, approaches and phases of social media adoption reported in the literature.

The adoption of social media in government services passes through similar phases that all new information and communication technologies go through when they are introduced. Mergel and Bretschneider provided a three stages process for social media adoption as shown in Fig. 2 [19]: Experimentation, Constructive Chaos and Institutionalisation. We explain these three phases briefly below.

Experimentation: In this early phase, government agencies use social media as an informal experimentation. This normally starts with someone who likes to explore new technologies, is forward thinking and ready to be a champion for its adoption. In this case, social media use does not necessarily go through the

Fig. 2 Social media adoption process

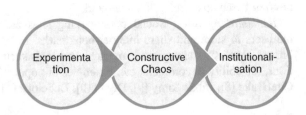

Experimentation → Constructive Chaos → Institutionalisation

standard internal processes, and social media is trialled for a specific purpose, for example for a particular service or product. The activities in this phase include information dissemination and collecting feedback on services. In many situations, the agencies run trial projects.

Coordinated chaos: This phase involves developing a business case for social media. Since the use of social media started in an informal way, there will be many accounts in different platforms without proper policies and guidelines developed. At this phase, the agencies see the benefits of using social media. However, they also potentially encounter a number of unintended consequences, such as receiving negative coverage in the press, or a discrepancy between the dissemination of information on its official channels and on social media. In this phase, a solid business case is built to use social media with benefits outweighing the negative consequences. This leads to the third phase.

Institutionalisation: This phase involves developing standard policies and guidelines for the use of social media. In this phase, social media becomes one of the official channels of communication between the agency and citizens, and of delivery for services and products. Typically, at this point, a special team is appointed to look after the social media engagement and issues.

During the institutionalisation phase, agencies can use the honeycomb framework discussed earlier to understand and develop their presence on social media platforms. Along with their framework, Kietzmann and colleagues presented guidelines for developing strategies using 4C: Cognize (recognise and understand the social media landscape), Congruity (suited to different social media functionalities and goals), Curate (how often to chime into the conversation and who should represent the agency) and Chase (understanding the velocity and flow of information) [6].

Mergel studied the adoption of social media in the US federal government and reported his observations in [20]. There are two different approaches prevalent in adopting social media: top-down and bottom up. In the top-down approach, the social media initiative comes from the executive managers to staff. In this approach, the social media enters the institutionalisation phase quite early. In the bottom-up approach, the use of social media comes from the staff at the experimental phase. Mergel also found the following factors played a role in the adoption of social media: drive from stakeholders, need for bi-directional interactions, desire for knowledge sharing, having a presence in social media, better engagement, networking and data mining.

4 Social Media Applications in Government Services

Social media has been used in government services in recent times, and its adoption continues to grow. Magro reviewed social media use in e-government in 2012 [21]. He surveyed the literature from 2007 to 2011 and categorised them in different themes such as disaster management, strategy and policy, citizen trust, and participation and digital divide. Similarly but more recently, Mainka and colleagues provided an overview of use of social media in the government sector, based on a case study of 31 international cities [22]. They found that Twitter was the most popular platform used by government, followed by YouTube and Facebook. Abdelsalam and colleagues studied the use of social media by the Egyptian government through their websites [23]. The study shows that 23.2 % of the government agencies have a Facebook link in their websites (considering the active websites only). This is followed by Twitter (13.4 %) and YouTube (11.2 %).

There is still scope for more usage of social media in government sector. The study by Kuzma in 2010 found that only 30 % of Asian governments make full use of social media technology to communicate and disseminate information to their citizens [24].

In the following, we present some example applications of social media in the government sectors, in a variety of domains.

4.1 Human Services

The Australian Government Department of Human Services (also referred to as "Human Services") has been an early adopter of social media, thanks to innovative and forward thinking communication staff and managers who recognised as early as 2009 the potential of social media to support their customers and improve service delivery.

Human Services uses social media to listen to and engage with their customers. They do so through both Twitter and Facebook (where they have their own accounts) as well as joining online communities where appropriate. They have found that social media provides an opportunity to build relationships with citizens online, increasing trust.

Since 2009, Human Services has appointed and trained a (growing) team of communication staff to engage on social media. They have also developed processes and policies to ensure good governance and mitigate the risks inherent to a government engagement on social media. (We refer the interested reader to Chap. 2 for more details.)

4.2 Disaster Management

Disaster management is probably the most highly publicised domain when we consider the use of social media. A large number of scientific literature, news reports and case studies can be found about this topic. Social media was, for example, used extensively in the Taiwan Typhoon Disaster in 2009, during the earthquake in Haiti in 2010, the Queensland floods in 2012, the Boston Bombing in 2013,[1] and, more recently the earthquake in Nepal, to name a few instances [25–27]. We briefly describe its use in the Taiwan Typhoon and the Haitian earthquake disasters below.

The Taiwan Morakot Typhoon Disaster—Huang and colleagues presented a case study on typhoon Morakot which occurred during 8–10 August 2009 in Taiwan [28]. The typhoon caused widespread damage, leaving 600 people dead and 24,950 people displaced. As soon as the typhoon started to hit Taiwan, people reported information about the real-time situation in the forum PTT,[2] one of the most popular social networks in Taiwan, which has more than 1.2 million registered users. Concerned PTT users created an unofficial Disaster Report Center, where people from affected areas could not only report the situation in real-time but also request assistance. While this is not an example of social media use by a government agency, it is an interesting case of social media being used in emergency management, complementing government activity. During the initial hours of the disaster, when the government services were overloaded, this unofficial center helped to co-ordinate the activities using local volunteers. The web site was integrated later into the local government's communication system to provide an official response to the people.

Haitian Earthquake—Yates and Paquette present a case study of the 2010 Haitian Earthquake to understand the role of social media in emergency knowledge management in [26]. The US took a lead in the rescue efforts after the 2010 Haiti Earthquake involving the United Nations, US agencies and many other countries. This was the first time the US government used social media technologies such as wiki and collaborative workspaces as the main tools for sharing information and knowledge. A SharePoint system was used for knowledge sharing across the traditional boundaries and helped create a transient collaborative space.

4.3 Beyond Disaster Management: Building Disaster Resilience

Government agencies also use social media to build disaster resilient communities. Three core elements form disaster resilience, as shown in Fig. 3 taken from [29]: Emergency Management is one element, but Disaster Risk Reduction and Community Development are also required. Social media can be used as a tool to achieve goals in these three elements.

Emergency management: one of the goals for disaster resilience is to build safe communities through shared responsibility. Social media can help in different

---

[1]http://www.govtech.com/public-safety/Social-Media-Big-Lessons-from-the-Boston-Marathon-Bombing.html.

[2]http://pttemergency.pixnet.net/blog.

Fig. 3 Three elements of
disaster resilience

ways. For example, it can be used to *generate alerts* by listening to social media
and detecting potential emergencies (e.g., the ESA system described in Chap. 12);
to *disseminate information* about disaster *preparedness* to the targeted communities, to *coordinate community responses and recovery* by creating social media
sites targeted for an event (e.g., Nepal Earthquake[3]).

Disaster risk reduction: the goal here is to minimise the residual risk. The
social media's capability to disseminate information can be used to achieve this
goal by providing information about disaster risks, supporting discussions on
forums on ways of minimising risk, providing post-event information about the
lessons learned and improving the resilience capacity, etc.

Community development: this is about building a community, so that it can provide informational and emotion support during and after disaster. The core idea
behind this is to increase the social capital. The *Next Step* online community,
described as part of Chap. 2 and more fully in Chap. 9, is an example of how government agencies can build a targetted community to increase social capital [30].

4.4 Transport

In general, social media is used quite heavily in the transport sector. Social media
applications are helping users in a range of activities from finding the best route
to travel from point A to point B, navigating through cities, to finding interesting
places. It is worth noting that public transport is itself the third highest location
(26 %) where social media is used after home (93 %) and work (32 %) [31]. A
comprehensive study of the use of social media in transportation is presented in
[32]. The study reported the results of the survey done for 34 transit operators in

---

[3]See, for example: http://social-media-for-development.org/nepal-earthquake-how-social-media-
has-been-used-in-the-aftermath/.

USA and Canada. 85 % of these agencies are using social media to increase customer satisfaction and 76 % to increase the image of the agency. They use social media in a wide range of activities, such as posting agency news, providing real time service alerts, service information, and meetings and event notices. The report also identified some of the barriers in adopting social media. Two key barriers reported are: lack of staff to look after the social media activities and the use of social media by customers to vent their frustration and anger (i.e., criticising the agency).

Another comprehensive work on the use of social media for transport sector is presented in [33]. It provides numerous case examples of how social media has been used by agencies for various purposes, including how to develop policies and procedures, drawn from industry practices. The case examples include all modes of transportation, such as mass transit, highways, aviation, ferries, bicycling, and walking. Similarly, the use of Twitter messages based tools to move people in New York City is reported in [34]. The use of social media tools in the transport sector is getting popular for a number of reasons: (a) social media platforms are free, (b) their reach and coverage are very wide, i.e., the message can cover the wide area and reach a large number of people, (c) the platforms provide near real time delivery of messages, which is helpful to convey alerts and thus direct traffic appropriately, and (d) social media provides a platform for crowdsourcing (citizens can create share content—e.g., show pictures of a problem in situ).

Government agencies also often exploit social media to communicate with their customers, for example to provide real-time road closures and traffic alerts, to disseminate information on planned roads closures and events, or to give road safety messages. For example, the state of NSW in Australia uses a social media page to inform, motivate and engage citizens through a number of social media platforms (http://www.transportnsw.info/en/travelling-with-us/keep-updated/social.page) such as Twitter, Facebook and YouTube. They have different accounts for different modes of transports as well as different geographical regions. There are nearly 34K people following the metro traffic in the Twitter. Similarly, VicRoads (the transport authority in Victoria, Australia) uses social media extensively—see https://www.vicroads.vic.gov.au/about-vicroads/how-we-use-social-media. In a nutshell, the goals of social media in transportation are to inform, motivate, and engage citizens in real time to improve transportation services.

4.5 Policy and Planning

Social media has also been used in the *planning* of government activities: from seeking new ideas for developments to seeking feedback on existing government activities. For example, the Obama administration used social media (change.gov) to inform policy through the participation of citizens during the transition phase from November 2008 to January 2009 [35]. In Australia, ACT Senator Kate Lundley launched "Public Sphere"[4] in 2009 to encourage public debate and solicit comments, as a step towards an open government through Gov 2.0. A "Public Sphere", according to Habermas [36], is a space that "...through the vehicle of public opinion it puts the state in touch with the needs of society".

The use of social media is not limited to federal/central governments. Local governments are also using social media to provide more engaging planning experience to citizens. For example, Future Melbourne[5] engaged people in the design and strategy of the future shape of their city. The city of Wellington in New Zealand introduced E-petitions to improve citizen participation [37]. In these initiatives, citizens are encouraged to contribute to the design of government policies and have a voice. Fredericks and Forth presented the study of participatory planning in the four local government areas of Brisbane City Council, Gold Coast City Council, Redland City Council and Toowoomba Regional Council in South East Queensland, Australia [38]. They also observed that the use of social media can avoid political backlash of policies by giving ownership to the citizens through active participation in the planning process. Though social media does not replace physical settings like town hall meetings, it creates avenues for participation that complement existing participatory planning processes.

One interesting example of people's participation in economic activity through social media technology is the Italian project Kublai [39]. Kublai is a small online community that provides people in creative industries an opportunity to develop projects by discussing them with like-minded people. The project had over 1600 registered users discussing 250 creative projects of which 60 have produced written documents. The main tool in the project was developed using Ning.[6]

We have so far discussed in this section how social media platforms can be used to engage citizens to help with planning and with the development of policies, and to obtain feedback on current policies. In these approaches, governments initiate the discussion topics and motivate citizen to participate. A different approach is to collect content from different social media about a certain topic (e.g., "listening to social media"), analysing the content, performing analyses to extract useful information to formulate policy. One such approach is proposed by Charalabidis et al. [40]. This is a bottom-up approach, consisting of four stages: Listen, Analyse, Receive and Act as shown in Fig. 4. In the listen phase, the policy makers listen to different social media and monitor what citizens are discussing on a certain topic. The analyse phase involves extracting positions and opinions. The receive phase deals with getting all relevant data and displaying it for effective use and exploitation. The final phase is to act on it by posting relevant policies

---

[4]http://cpd.org.au/2009/09/case-study-public-sphere-as-a-gov-2-0-example-of-open-government/—accessed September 29th, 2015.

[5]http://www.futuremelbourne.com.au/wiki/view/FMPlan.

[6]http://www.ning.com/.

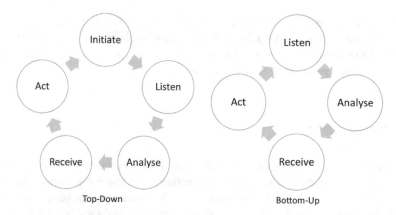

Fig. 4 Two approaches on using social media for policy formulation

and initiating discussions to collect feedback. The first three steps are called passive crowdsourcing, whereas the final step is active crowdsourcing on a particular topic or policy. When a government agency listens to its citizenry by listening to social media, it essentially performs the first three phases of this approach (see, for example, this use of social media by the Australian Government Department of Human Services in Chap. 2, facilitated by the tool presented in Chap. 11).

The second approach is a top-down approach, as shown in Fig. 4, where the process starts with active crowdsourcing on a specific topic. Staff at a government agency may probe the public by posing questions on social media. They then listen to the on-going discussions, analyse them and act on the content by formulating the policy. The formulated policy is then fed back to the citizens to get feedback. The process continues until the policy decision is made.

4.6 Government Transformation

Social media has a big impact not only in government sectors, but also on governments themselves. The impact of social media in transforming governments in North Africa and Middle East from Autocracy to Democracy in 2011 has been well recognised and noted in the literature as Arab Spring [41]. According to Ghannam [42], social media played a vital role in informing, mobilising and creating communities, increasing transparency and seeking to hold government accountable. As social media is used by millions of people, it becomes a tool for raising public awareness as well as gathering public opinion. The expectation is that there would be more than 100 million Arab users soon who are engaging on the Internet. In addition to popular global social media, people are using and engaging in locally created social media sites such as NowLebanon.com based in Beirut, and Aramram.com, 7iber.com, Ammannet.net, and AmmonNews.net, all based in Amman. Social media has also been used in activism and war. Some examples noted in the literature includes the use of social media to make the world aware of the shooting of Neda in Tehran in June 2009; and its use by Hezbollah in 2006 to create a perception of failure for Israel, etc. [43].

4.7 Campaigning

Finally, social media can of course be used by individuals in government, to inform citizens of their whereabouts and actions, and for campaigning purposes. Politicians now use Twitter, Facebook and other social media platforms extensively to keep the public informed and to connect with their constituency. They also use these platforms for campaigning purposes. The use of the social media to interact with citizens during Obama's first election in 2008 was unprecedented. He established the Barackobama.com site in which every page had links to social media sites like Facebook, MySpace, YouTube, Flickr, Digg, Twitter, Eventful, Linkedin, Blackplanet, Faitbase, Eons, Glee, MiGente, MyBatanga, AsianAve and DNC Partybuilder [44]. Other examples of the use of social media for campaigning and elections are discussed in [45–48].

5 Challenges in Using Social Media Government Services

Social media has not always been used to its fullest potential in governments. Sobaci and Karkin studied whether the use of Twitter by mayors in Turkey provided better public services [49]. They observed that Twitter was largely used for information sharing and personal messages, and that its use for transparent, participatory and citizen-oriented public service delivery was not common. This is potentially problematic, as the use of social media can set expectations of a two-way communication and of being listened to. This brings us to the challenges of employing social media in the government sector. Some of these have been identified by government agencies who trialled the use of social media for some specific purposes,[7] others have been pointed out by researchers who studied the use of social media in the government sector. Issues include privacy, security, data management, accessibility, social inclusion and governance [50]. Challenges include resourcing the social media activities, acting on the insights gained, setting up

---

[7]See, for example, "lessons learnt" from the FutureMelbourne experiment: http://www. futuremelbourne.com.au/wiki/pub/FMPlan/WebHome/Future_Melbourne_Wiki_Post_ Implementation_.pdf— accessed September 29th, 2015, or the experience of the Australian Department for Human Services in Chap. 2.

guidelines and policies, and evaluating success. We now briefly describe some of these issues and challenges.

5.1 Privacy, Security and Data Management

The privacy of an individual has become one of the critical challenges in the use of social media in general. The issue is even more important in government services as governments have a duty of care towards their citizens. Both social media providers and users, whether individuals or organisations, are struggling to deal with the privacy issues.

There are typically two views on the privacy issue in social media. Some people think that individual privacy is not an issue as people are willingly sharing information on social media [51]. This argument is led by Facebook founder Mark Zuckerberg and other social media service providers. The argument is that, if sensitive and private data is easily accessible in social media, it is because users have voluntarily submitted it, and thus it is not an issue. For example, people share their physical location, photos of family holidays and children, intimate details of their struggle and triumphs. This suggests that social media users are not concerned about individual privacy. There is also a widespread perception and belief that the new "digital generation" is not concerned about privacy.

In contrast, some believe that privacy is even more important than before. Some users are deeply concerned about personal information being easily accessible and shared on social media [52]. Users do not know where the information is stored, who can access it for what purpose, and what the rules and laws govern the information. Research also shows that a significant portion of users who share personal information on social media regrets it later [53], as sometimes the disclosure of information carries significant consequences such as losing a relationship or a job [54].

The privacy setting in social media is typically left to the users, who often struggle to understand the privacy setting in the social media sites like Facebook and their consequences [55]. Addressing this issue requires a better privacy-aware interface design, where users are visually aware of what they are sharing with whom. In addition, many social media platforms like Facebook and Twitter support a large number of third party applications. These third party applications can extract identifiable information from Facebook and share it with advertisers [56]. The protection of users' privacy from third party is tricky and often difficult to control.

Governments around the world have tightened their privacy laws to protect individual privacy. For example, the Australian Privacy Principle (APP) 11 in the Australian Privacy Act 2012 deals with data breaches that requires organisations that hold personal information to take reasonable steps to protect the information from misuse, interference and loss, and from unauthorised access, modification or disclosure. However, voluntarily submitted citizens' data is not directly protected by APPs; this thus includes the publicly available social media data (such as

Twitter, Facebook, etc.) and data stored by overseas companies. In the USA, there are a number of acts that cover the privacy of individuals, such as the Children's Online Privacy Protection Act (COPPA) and the Federal Information Security Management Act (FISMA) [50]. Yet, privacy issues are still challenging.

Security and data management are issues related to privacy. Having collected data from the public through listening to social media passively or through active crowd sourcing, how is the data securely managed and stored, if it is considered to potentially contain sensitive data? Finally, the large volume of data that might be acquired can compound the problem of storing it securely and managing it efficiently.

5.2 Resourcing Social Media Engagement

When an agency decides to engage with the public on social media, it must resource the activity(ies) appropriately. People who participate in social media conversations typically expect a prompt response to a question, regular updates, etc. An agency engaging in social media is expected to behave in the same way: in particular, it is expected to engage frequently and answer questions rapidly. It is also expected to provide useful and accurate information. This requires the agency to make the resources available for these tasks (e.g., not treat the task as an add-on to someone's existing job), and potentially train staff on how to engage in social media and behave appropriately. Some staff might find it difficult to engage with new technologies and processes, or be fearful of public failure. This must be handled with care and sensitivity.

Many government departments have policies which prevent their staff from using social media at work. As a result, staff do not have access to the internet and to social media through their normal IT systems. This clearly poses a challenge to enable some staff to access social media for the purpose of having the agency engaging in social media.

Policies and processes must be in place, for example to ensure the accuracy of the information provided, or to govern and mediate the many voices that provide input into a crowd sourcing activity.

None of these tasks are straightforward. We discuss the issues and challenges of establishing guidelines, policies and processes below. The Australian Department of Human Services also discuss these issues in their context in Chap. 2.

Finally, when engaging in social media, one needs to deal with potentially very large volume of information ("big data"). This clearly poses the challenges of processing it efficiently and effectively in order to gain the insights that were sought and to properly engage with the public. Computational tools must be employed to help with this task. While there are a number of commercial and research tools available to help with the task of dealing with social media, choosing a tool to use is not easy, as tools typically support different tasks to various degrees.

5.3 Having Patience and Establishing Trust

Developing a social media presence takes both resources and time. There is a need to recognise that an online community develops overtime, through constant engagement and care. As an example, one does not get a large number of followers immediately upon setting up a Twitter account of a Facebook page. This occurs when people realise that it is worth following the account.

Government agencies who want to use social media not only as a way to disseminate information but also as a way to listen to citizens must build a trust relationship with the public (to avoid being seen as "big brother"). Once trust is established, and an online community has formed, there is a need to protect it or the investment that was made might be lost.

5.4 Understanding the Reach of Social Media Engagement: Inclusion

While many people are now using social media, one must be aware that not everyone will obtain their information from social media and engage with it, if only because of access issues (e.g., not everyone one might have access to the internet, or know how to engage with social media). It is thus important to recognise that social media is one channel of communication amongst others, and try to reach people who might not be included in the social media engagement through other means. Especially for a government, inclusion is key.

5.5 Acting upon the Information Gathered

When an agency engages with the public to obtain ideas for or feedback on policies, it must do justice to people's time, effort and expertise, and act on the ideas and feedback received. This should be done in a transparent manner, or it will be at risk of a backlash from the public.

This is potentially a challenge for a government agency, if it had an a priori idea of what it wanted to implement and was not totally open to new ideas, or if it received many different opinions. In the latter case, processes must be in place to be able to decide how to bring all the ideas into a coherent whole, or which idea to favour (if it is not based purely through a democratic process), and to be able to explain to the public how the decision was made.

6 Guidelines and Policies

A large number of governments departments and agencies have started using social media as a medium to disseminate information to citizens and interact with them. As the social media tools are evolving, there are many unknowns about the effect of social media including reputation of the departments or even governments when things go astray or wrongly. In the early days of social media adoption by governments, social media was used without the development of guidelines or policies specific to social media use. As it was recognised that traditional communication policies are not always applicable to this new medium, new policies and guidelines started to be established. These are still evolving, as public sector staff obtain more experience with this new communication medium.

A large number of government organisations have developed the policies and have made them publicly available. The Center for Technology in Government has reviewed the publically available policies and guidelines and identified eight essential elements [57], as shown in Fig. 5: (1) employee access, (2) account management, (3) acceptable use, (4) employee conduct, (5) content, (6) security, (7) legal issues, (8) citizen conduct. We explain them briefly below:

Employee access: this element covers who can access which sites. Though the access to social media was denied to employees at the beginning, when it was feared that social media would be used for personal reasons rather than work-related, this is no longer valid when social media access becomes a part of someone's work. A social media policy must thus clearly state which social media sites can be accessed by whom and for what in the workplace.

Fig. 5 Eight essential elements for developing social media guidelines and policies

Account management: this element covers all aspects of social media accounts under the name of the agencies, including who can create, maintain and post from these accounts. It is important to keep track of all social media accounts and make them publicly available. It is also important to record the purpose of each account.

Acceptable use: this elements covers the circumstances under which an employee can use office resources for personal and private usage, and penalties for violating the policies. Clear boundaries between personal and professional uses need to be drawn so that employees know what is expected from them.

Employee conduct: this element covers the ethical code of conduct for the employee and sets out policies on what are the right and wrong behaviours of employees when engaging on social media. Most organisations have existing policies on ethical behaviour and use them as guidelines. In some cases, new guidelines needs to be developed to target social media specific cases such as online bullying.

Content: this element deals with content: who is allowed to post content in the official social media sites, who is responsible for content creation, verification (i.e., ensure its accuracy) and production, etc. Depending on the nature of the work and the sensitivity of the content, different government department and agencies may choose different strategies from minimum editorial control to assigned editorial person.

Security: this element deals with the security issues related to using social media. It covers two aspects of security: technical and behavioural. The technical aspect deals with the policies of managing user names and passwords of different social media accounts. The behaviour aspect deals with threats pertaining to certain type of behaviours by users in social media, more specifically spear phishing and social engineering.

Legal Issues: this element deals with policies to ensure that all activities in social media are following existing laws and regulations such as privacy, freedom of information, public disclosure and accessibility. For example, posts in social media site should be accompanied by relevant disclaimers.

Citizen conduct: this element deals with policies and guidelines related to citizen's participation on social media sites. As social media provides a two way communication between the government agencies and citizens, agencies should have a clear policy about whether citizen can participate, whether what they contribute is moderated or not. There is also a need for clear instructions for citizens regarding their behaviour on the agency social media site, etc.

Developing the policies for the use of social media in public sector within existing rules and regulation poses many challenges. There is a need to harmonise the policies. Consider for example engaging in social media in the process of formulating a policy. An agency might be soliciting comments on the new emerging policy. Citizens thus engage with the agency, and, through this engagement, they might ask specific questions about the policy, which the agency cannot answer due to laws preventing it from responding to questions during the notice and comment period. This is clearly problematic, as the expectation of citizens using social media is to get the response immediately. Unless such policies are harmonised, citizens may feel ignored during a critical time. Jaeger et al. also identified accessibility and equity of access as key issues in the context of social media [58]. Social media platforms may not comply with the governments accessibility policies as many social media platforms are not built for disabled people.

6.1 Maturity

The use of social media in government services has been reported many times in the literature, with a key aspect being citizen participation and transparency (and openness) of government. However, various studies report that this is still in the infancy level [59]. In their work, Lee and Kwak present an open government maturity model for social media in [60].

6.2 Cost of Democratisation

There are costs associated with the adoption of social media in government services, as has already been pointed out above (e.g., resources required). Modelling that cost is a challenge. Bryer has presented a way of modelling cost in social media [61]. We briefly describe his model below.

As social media is about the participation of citizens using information and communication technology (ICT), there are four costs associated with public participation as shown in Fig. 6: production cost, participation cost, ICT cost and the democratisation cost.

The production cost refers to the cost to the agency related to development and implementation of the social media activities. This includes staff cost, facility use, cost for generating content and verifying it, etc. The participation cost is the cost that has to be borne by the citizens to participate in social media activities. This includes internet, computer or mobile device costs. The third cost is the ICT cost. This includes ICT support cost related to the implementation, deployment and

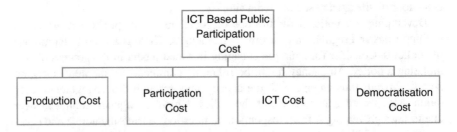

Fig. 6 Cost of adopting the ICT based public participation technology like social media

maintenance of social media activities. The fourth cost is the democratisation cost, which is a challenge to measure, but very important for the success of social media activities.

The cost of democratisation is related to building social capital. If we raise citizens' expectations and do not meet those expectations, there will be lost trust between the agencies and citizens. For example, citizens may expect that the governments will listen to them and incorporate their suggestions. However, it is impossible to incorporate suggestions from all, and some are bound to get disappointed and refuse to participate in future. Similarly, the voices of the citizens may have a negative impact on public servants, who then become less responsive. Understanding these issues is necessary to eventually be able to measure the success of social media use in government services.

7 Measuring Success

We have touched on the costs of using social media. A major challenge faced by organisations is to measure the success of employing social media: Do benefits outweigh the costs? What is the return on investment? These are difficult questions. We have outlined a model to start to think about costs above. Similarly, benefits can be multi-faceted and difficult to measure quantitatively: benefits can include, for example, "better" dissemination of information (where "better" can also mean several things: faster, wider reach, more impact, more accurate, etc.); "better" policies; a more trusted relationship between government and citizens; etc. It is clear that designing metrics is difficult, and these will depend on the original objective for engaging with social media.

8 Concluding Remarks

This chapter provided a brief introduction of social media, types of social media, social media adoption process in government, a number of unique challenges faced by government agencies and a number of example applications where social media has been used by the government agencies and departments. Though this chapter is not a comprehensive review of use of social media in public sector, it covers some important aspects of adopting social media. The following chapters in this book revisit some of the challenges and applications discussed in this chapter through case studies and applications from practitioners as well as industry and academic researchers.

References

1. Leonardi, P. M., Huysman, M., & Steinfield, C. (2013). Enterprise social media: Definition, history, and prospects for the study of social technologies in organizations. *Journal of Computer-Mediated Communication, 19*, 1–19.
2. Kamel Boulos, M. N., & Wheeler, S. (2007). The emerging web 2.0 social software: An enabling suite of sociable technologies in health and health care education1. *Health Information and Libraries Journal, 24*, 2–23.
3. Bercovici, J. (2010). Who coined "social media"? Web pioneers compete for credit,". Forbes. Disponível.
4. Aghaei, S., Nematbakhsh, M. A., & Farsani, H. K. (2012). Evolution of the world wide web: from Web 1.0 to Web 4.0. *International Journal of Web and Semantic Technology, 3*, 1–10.
5. Administration U.S.G.S. (2009). GSA social media policy. GSA Publication no. CIO 2106.1.
6. Kietzmann, J. H., Hermkens, K., McCarthy, I. P., & Silvestre, B. S. (2011). Social media? Get serious! Understanding the functional building blocks of social media. *Business Horizons, 54*, 241–251.
7. Ellison, N. B. (2007). Social network sites: Definition, history, and scholarship. *Journal of Computer-Mediated Communication, 13*, 210–230.
8. Zlatić, V., Ghoshal, G., & Caldarelli, G. (2009). Hypergraph topological quantities for tagged social networks. *Physical Review E, 80*, 036118.
9. Hotho, A., Jäschke, R., Schmitz, C., & Stumme, G. (2006). BibSonomy: A social bookmark and publication sharing system. In *Proceedings of the Conceptual Structures Tool Interoperability Workshop at the 14th International Conference on Conceptual Structures* (pp. 87–102).
10. Lerman, K. (2007). User participation in social media: Digg study. In *IEEE/WIC/ACM International Conferences on Web Intelligence and Intelligent Agent Technology Workshops* (pp. 255–258). IEEE.
11. Wetzker, R., Zimmermann, C., & Bauckhage, C. (2008). Analyzing social bookmarking systems: A del. icio. us cookbook. In *Proceedings of the ECAI 2008 Mining Social Data Workshop* (pp. 26–30).
12. Chan, A. J. (2002). *Collaborative news networks: Distributed editing, collective action, and the construction of online news on Slashdot. org.* Massachusetts Institute of Technology.
13. Davidson, J., Liebald, B., Liu, J., Nandy, P., Van Vleet, T., & Gargi, U. et al. (2010). The YouTube video recommendation system. In *Proceedings of the Fourth ACM Conference on Recommender Systems* (pp. 293–296). ACM.
14. Sigurbjörnsson, B., & Van Zwol, R. (2008). Flickr tag recommendation based on collective knowledge. In *Proceedings of the 17th International Conference on World Wide Web* (pp. 327–336). ACM.
15. Java, A., Song, X., Finin, T., & Tseng, B. (2007). Why we twitter: understanding microblogging usage and communities. In *Proceedings of the 9th WebKDD and 1st SNA-KDD 2007 Workshop on Web Mining and Social Network Analysis* (pp. 56–65). ACM.
16. Chang, Y., Tang, L., Inagaki, Y., & Liu, Y. (2014). What is tumblr: A statistical overview and comparison. *ACM SIGKDD Explorations Newsletter, 16*, 21–29.
17. Bei, J. (2013). *How Chinese journalists use Weibo microblogging for investigative reporting.* Reuters Institute Fellowship Paper, University of Oxford.
18. Regan, K. (2002). Epinions: An E-commerce Success that Almost Wasn't'. *E-commerce Times, 29*.
19. Mergel, I., & Bretschneider, S. I. (2013). A three-stage adoption process for social media use in government. *Public Administration Review, 73*, 390–400.
20. Mergel, I. (2013). Social media adoption and resulting tactics in the US federal government. *Government Information Quarterly, 30*, 123–130.
21. Magro, M. J. (2012). A review of social media use in e-government. *Administrative Sciences, 2*, 148–161.

22. Mainka, A., Hartmann, S., Stock, W. G., & Peters, I. (2014). Government and social media: A case study of 31 informational world cities. In *47th Hawaii International Conference on System Sciences (HICSS)* (pp. 1715–1724). IEEE.
23. Abdelsalam, H. M., Reddick, C. G., Gamal, S., & Al-shaar, A. (2013). Social media in Egyptian government websites: Presence, usage, and effectiveness. *Government Information Quarterly, 30*, 406–416.
24. Kuzma, J. (2010). Asian government usage of Web 2.0 social media. *European Journal of ePractice* 1–13.
25. Bird, D., Ling, M., & Haynes, K. (2012). *Flooding Facebook-the use of social media during the Queensland and Victorian floods.*
26. Yates, D., & Paquette, S. (2011). Emergency knowledge management and social media technologies: A case study of the 2010 Haitian earthquake. *International Journal of Information Management, 31*, 6–13.
27. Gao, H., Barbier, G., & Goolsby, R. (2011). Harnessing the crowdsourcing power of social media for disaster relief. *IEEE Intelligent Systems* 10–14.
28. Huang, C.-M., Chan, E., & Hyder, A. A. (2010). Web 2.0 and internet social networking: A new tool for disaster management? Lessons from Taiwan. *BMC Medical Informatics and Decision Making, 10*, 57.
29. Dufty, N. (2012). Using social media to build community disaster resilience. *The Australian Journal of Emergency Management (peer reviewed), 27*, 40–45.
30. Valenzuela, S., Park, N., & Kee, K. F. (2009). Is there social capital in a social network site?: Facebook use and college students' life satisfaction, trust, and participation. *Journal of Computer-Mediated Communication, 14*, 875–901.
31. Sensis: Sensis Social Media Report. (2015). *How Australian People and Businesses are Using Social Media.* https://www.sensis.com.au/content/dam/sas/PDFdirectory/Sensis_Social_Media_Report_2015.pdf
32. Bregman, S. (2012). *Uses of social media in public transportation.* Transportation Research Board. http://onlinepubs.trb.org/onlinepubs/tcrp/tcrp_syn_99.pdf
33. Bregman, S., & Watkins, K. E. (2013). *Best practices for transportation agency use of social media.* Boca Raton: CRC Press.
34. Kaufman, S. M. (2012). *How social media moves New York: Twitter use by transportation providers in the New York region.* http://wagner.nyu.edu/rudincenter/publication/how-social-media-moves-new-york-twitter-use-by-transportation-providers-in-the-new-york-region-2/
35. Bittle, S., Haller, C., & Kadlec, A. (2009). *Promising practices in online engagement.* Occasional paper. http://www.publicagenda.org/files/PA_CAPE_Paper3_Promising_Mech2.pdf
36. Habermas, J. (1991). *The structural transformation of the public sphere: An inquiry into a category of bourgeois society.* Cambridge: MIT press.
37. Toland, J. (2011). E-petitions in local government: The case of Wellington city council. *International Reports on Socio-Informatics (IRSI).* Bodker et al. (eds), *Proceedings of the 2011 Community and Technology (C&T 2011) Workshop on Government and Citizen Engagement 8*(2) (pp. 15–22).
38. Fredericks, J., & Foth, M. (2013). Augmenting public participation: Enhancing planning outcomes through the use of social media and web 2.0. *Australian Planner, 50*, 244–256.
39. Cottica, A., & Bianchi, T. (2010). Harnessing the unexpected: A public administration interacts with creatives on the web. *European Journal of ePractice, 9*, 82–90.
40. Charalabidis, Y., Triantafillou, A., Karkaletsis, V., & Loukis, E. (2012). Public policy formulation through non moderated crowdsourcing in social media. In *Electronic participation* (pp. 156–169). Berlin: Springer.
41. Danju, I., Maasoglu, Y., & Maasoglu, N. (2013). From autocracy to democracy: The impact of social media on the transformation process in North Africa and Middle East. *Procedia-Social and Behavioral Sciences, 81*, 678–681.

42. Ghannam, J. (2011). *Social media in the Arab world: Leading up to the uprisings of 2011*. Center for International Media Assistance 3. http://www.cima.ned.org/wp-content/uploads/2015/02/CIMA-Arab_Social_Media-Report-10-25-11.pdf
43. Mayfield III, T. D. (2011). *A commander's strategy for social media*. DTIC Document. http://www.dtic.mil/docs/citations/ADA535374
44. Kes-Erkul, A., & Erkul, R. E. (2009). *Web 2.0 in the process of e-participation: The case of organizing for America and the Obama administration*. University of Massachusetts-Amherst, National Center for Digital Government. http://scholarworks.umass.edu/cgi/viewcontent.cgi?article=1031&context=ncdg
45. Sweetser, K. D., & Lariscy, W. (2008). Candidates make good friends: An analysis of candidates' uses of Facebook. *International Journal of Strategic Communication, 2*, 175–198.
46. The Washington Post. http://voices.washingtonpost.com/44/2008/11/obama-raised-half-a-billion-on.html
47. Williams, C., & Gulati, G. J. (2009). Facebook grows up: An empirical assessment of its role in the 2008 congressional elections. In *Proceedings of Midwest Political Science Association*.
48. Mascaro, C. M., & Goggins, S. P. (2011). Challenges for national civic engagement in the United States. *International Reports on Socio-Informatics (IRSI)*. Bodker et al. (eds), *Proceedings of the 2011 Community and Technology (C&T 2011) Workshop on Government and Citizen Engagement 8*(2).
49. Sobaci, M. Z., & Karkin, N. (2013). The use of twitter by mayors in Turkey: Tweets for better public services? *Government Information Quarterly, 30*, 417–425.
50. Bertot, J. C., Jaeger, P. T., & Hansen, D. (2012). The impact of polices on government social media usage: Issues, challenges, and recommendations. *Government Information Quarterly, 29*, 30–40.
51. Kirkpatrick, M. (2010). *Facebook's Zuckerberg says the age of privacy is over*. http://readwrite.com/2010/01/09/facebooks_zuckerberg_says_the_age_of_privacy_is_ov
52. Madden, M. (2012). *Privacy management on social media sites*. Pew Internet Report 1–20.
53. Wang, Y., Leon, P. G., Scott, K., Chen, X., Acquisti, A., & Cranor, L. F. (2013). Privacy nudges for social media: an exploratory Facebook study. In *Proceedings of the 22nd International Conference on World Wide Web Companion* (pp. 763–770). International World Wide Web Conferences Steering Committee.
54. Wang, Y., Norcie, G., Komanduri, S., Acquisti, A., Leon, P. G., & Cranor, L. F. (2011). I regretted the minute I pressed share: A qualitative study of regrets on Facebook. In *Proceedings of the Seventh Symposium on Usable Privacy and Security* (p. 10). ACM.
55. Lipford, H. R., Besmer, A., & Watson, J. (2008). Understanding privacy settings in Facebook with an audience view. *UPSEC, 8*, 1–8.
56. Wang, N., Xu, H., & Grossklags, J. (2011). Third-party apps on Facebook: Privacy and the illusion of control. In *Proceedings of the 5th ACM Symposium on Computer Human Interaction for Management of Information Technology* (p. 4). ACM.
57. Hrdinová, J., Helbig, N., & Peters, C. S. (2010). *Designing social media policy for government: Eight essential elements*. Center for Technology in Government, University at Albany (2010).
58. Jaeger, P. T., Bertot, J. C., & Shilton, K. (2012). Information policy and social media: Framing government—citizen web 2.0 interactions. In *Web 2.0 technologies and democratic governance* (pp. 11–25). Berlin: Springer.
59. Bonsón, E., Torres, L., Royo, S., & Flores, F. (2012). Local e-government 2.0: Social media and corporate transparency in municipalities. *Government information quarterly, 29*, 123–132.
60. Lee, G., & Kwak, Y. H. (2012). An open government maturity model for social media-based public engagement. *Government Information Quarterly, 29*, 492–503.
61. Bryer, T. A. (2011). The costs of democratization: Social media adaptation challenges within government agencies. *Administrative Theory and Praxis, 33*, 341–361.

Social Media for Government Services:
A Case Study of Human Services

Gina Ciancio and Amanda Dennett

Abstract The Australian Government Department of Human Services has been using social media since 2009 to support its customers and improve service delivery. It has done so in a number of ways: by monitoring social media to listen to citizens, establishing Facebook and Twitter accounts to engage with the public, and creating online communities. In this chapter, we present how we have been using social media, some success stories together with the challenges we had to face. We also briefly describe our governance framework and how we might measure success.

Keywords Social media · Facebook · Twitter · Online community · Citizen engagement · Emergency management · Risk management · Health · Social services

1 Introduction

The Australian Government Department of Human Services[1] uses social media technologies to support its customers and improve service delivery. Since 2009, the department has been using social media to engage with customers, staff and stakeholders [1]. It is responsible for delivering Medicare,[2] Centrelink[3] and Child Support[4] services to 23.8 million Australians.[5]

---

[1] http://www.humanservices.gov.au/.
[2] http://www.humanservices.gov.au/customer/dhs/medicare.
[3] http://www.humanservices.gov.au/customer/dhs/centrelink.
[4] http://www.humanservices.gov.au/customer/dhs/child-support.
[5] Australian Government Department of Human Services Annual Report 2013–14.

G. Ciancio · A. Dennett (✉)
Department of Human Services, Canberra, Australia
e-mail: Amanda.Dennett@humanservices.gov.au

G. Ciancio
e-mail: Gina.Ciancio@humanservices.gov.au

© Springer International Publishing Switzerland 2015
S. Nepal et al. (eds.), *Social Media for Government Services*,
DOI 10.1007/978-3-319-27237-5_2

The work has been led by the department's Communication Division, by staff with a background in communication strategy, journalism and media, public relations, and customer service. This provides the essential mix of skills needed for government to effectively engage with citizens online.

The department's social media presence has grown from one Facebook and one Twitter account, to over a dozen official social media accounts across Facebook, Twitter, Google+, YouTube and LinkedIn. A small team of specialist Social Media Advisers manage these accounts, and also participate in a range of third party online communities, such as Whirlpool and Yahoo Answers, where our customers congregate to respond to enquiries or provide information.

In addition, the team has worked on social media research projects, such as the Next Step online community [6] (see Chap. 9), with the Commonwealth Scientific and Industrial Research Organisation (CSIRO) under the Human Services Delivery Research Alliance [3].

All of this social media engagement is governed by robust processes and policies, including a social media risk management plan [2].

In this chapter, we will cover topics such as social media monitoring and listening to citizen needs online to find issues and help resolve them, engaging in meaningful conversations with citizens online and correcting misinformation about government payments and services. We discuss managing risk and privacy, along with ideas and methods for measuring success in social media engagement projects. We present clear examples of our various experiences in adopting social media to engage with the public to achieve business objectives, and discuss the Australian Government Department of Human Services' experiences in establishing mutually beneficial relationships with citizens through social media.

2 Listening to Citizens

For the Department of Human Services, entering into the world of social media began with monitoring mentions of keywords like 'Centrelink' and 'Youth Allowance' (a specific payment type) to find what citizens were saying about the department online. As was the experience for many other government and non-government organisations, this low-risk beginning allowed the department to gather information and understand customer needs before implementing a proactive social media strategy.

2.1 Listening and Learning

We started out using freely available tools such as Google Alerts[6] and social search websites such as socialmention[7] to gain an insight into customer sentiment

---

[6]https://www.google.com.au/alerts.

[7]http://www.socialmention.com/.

about the department and the services it provides. This information provided some surprises—for example, that social media wasn't simply another avenue for complaint. Rather, posts showed that people wanted the opportunity to seek out information about health and social services and ask questions about their eligibility for payments and support. Figure 1 shows an example post from Google Alert.

In addition, we discovered that social media was not used exclusively by young people, and the places our customers were choosing to congregate online were not always where we expected it to be. While Facebook and Twitter continue to be the leading social media platforms used by Australians,[8] our customers were often choosing other platforms to share their questions and comments about Centrelink, Medicare and child support issues. Some niche online communities of interest provided an avenue for our customers to share their concerns with other people who already had their trust.

> **Example**: A discussion thread from the 'grey nomads'[9] online community, a caravan enthusiast forum for older Australians, appeared in the department's social media search results. Community members were sharing their experiences of travelling around Australia in their retirement. Some were receiving Age Pension and doing occasional casual work. There were discussions about whether customers had to visit the Centrelink Service Centre nearest their permanent home, or if they could visit any location around Australia to report their income and other changes in their circumstances. Having found these questions, the department was able to clarify that customers can visit any office, and that online and phone self service options are also available, meaning that grey nomads can update their changes in circumstances while they are on the road – news that was gratefully received!

2.2 Dealing with Volume

The results from our early social media searches were overwhelming. There were thousands of mentions daily, making it impossible for staff to manually sort through and prioritise. The problem to be resolved was how to find important mentions amongst the noise created by millions of social media posts every day—complaints that could help the department improve its services, or questions from individuals that the department could help answer online.

The department partnered with CSIRO to develop Vizie, a social media monitoring tool to address this need [4; see also Chap. 11 in this book]. Vizie automates the social media monitoring work previously undertaken by the department's social media staff and keeps records of online interactions to ensure the department meets its record keeping requirements. At a glance, social media staff can see what issues are trending, which customer posts require more immediate attention, and the words people are using to describe their interactions with the department.

---

[8]https://www.sensis.com.au/about/our-reports/sensis-social-media-report.

[9]http://thegreynomads.com.au/.

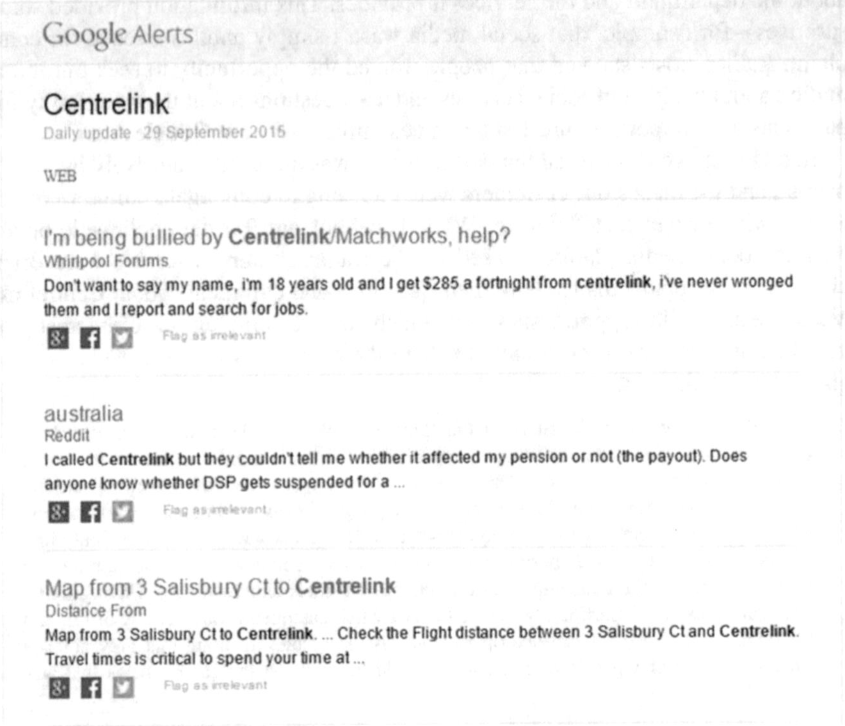

Fig. 1 An example post relevant to human services from Google alert

One of the key differences between Vizie and other social media monitoring tools is that customer issues are prioritised above popular posts or those made by online influencers, to ensure people in need get help quickly. This work changed the traditional view of what is considered an important social media post to suit the government service delivery context that we work in.

Example: Using Vizie, social media staff identified a discussion thread in a niche online forum for overclocking enthusiasts[10] where a member has asked his online network for advice about how to support his father who lived with mental health issues. He was working but that meant he couldn't provide the care he believed his father needed, and was considering whether Centrelink payments may be an option. Many of the responses he received were negative about the idea of leaving a job to receive Centrelink payments, even if the reason was to support a father with disability, and an adversarial discussion thread resulted. To avoid inflaming the conversation further, the department posted a private message in response to the individual with information about payments for people with disability and their carers, along with information about how much a person can work and earn before payments are affected.

---

[10]Overclocking is the process of forcing a computer or hardware component to operate faster than the manufacturer-specified clock frequency. Source Wikipedia: https://en.wikipedia.org/wiki/Overclocking.

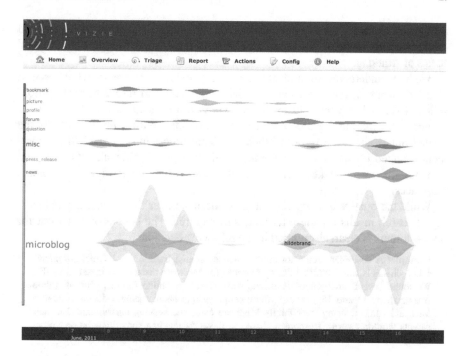

Fig. 2 A Vizie visualisation and interface

The department would not have found this individual's question by tracking only popular social media sites. By offering information to help his family's situation, we ensured an individual received the help they needed, through the medium in which they had gone searching for it.

Figure 2 shows one of the dashboards Vizie offers to view and explore social media. Vizie offers an integrated interface to numerous social media platforms. As shown in the figure, the visualisation presents the posts separated by platform, and grouped per topic. The analyst can interact with this visualisation to access the specific posts.

2.3 Crafting Keywords

To obtain the relevant social media posts, there is a need to define keywords. Establishing and refining appropriate keywords is critical for successful social media monitoring. We started out with a simple list of payments and services to monitor, then refined these over time to improve the relevancy of search results.

The department is fortunate that the names of many of its payments and programmes are unique—such as 'Austudy', 'Newstart Allowance' and 'Centrelink'—making social search easier for some topics. However there are still difficulties capturing all relevant information for keywords such as 'Medicare' and 'child support' as these are terms also used in the United Kingdom and United States of America.

We have undertaken significant work testing and refining the keywords used in Vizie, drawing on the expertise of social media staff and researchers at CSIRO. A lot of effort has gone into excluding words from results in order to limit the number of irrelevant results returned. For example, during discussions in the United States about the future of their Medicare programme in 2012, the department changed its search to exclude the words 'Congress', 'Barack', 'Obama' and 'Obamacare' to try to keep the focus of search results on Australian Medicare references.

While the quality of search results has improved over time, some manual sorting of search results for these terms is still required. The benefit of this work for our customers is clear, as outlined in the following example.

> **Example**: A customer group not easily reached through traditional or direct communication channels was identified during searches for Medicare discussions in social media. We found several anonymous questions were posted in online forums, such as Yahoo Answers!, by 14 and 15 year old young people asking about seeing a doctor without a Medicare card, or using their family Medicare card, and seeking reassurance that their parents wouldn't know. Responses shared in those forums can sometimes be unsympathetic, or contain inaccurate information for a customer's individual circumstances.
>
> To counter this and help increase the chances that the young people would see the doctor, the department responded publicly to let the young person know that doctor visits are private and also provided information for young people wishing to get their own Medicare card.

3 Changing Perceptions Through Engaging with Citizens

Social media provides a key opportunity for governments to build relationship with citizens online, develop trust and collaborate to co-design the future of public services. In the years since the Department of Human Services established its social media monitoring processes, work has expanded to include online customer and community engagement. This work has allowed customers to participate in customer service and co-design discussions anonymously, creating an environment where they feel comfortable sharing honest feedback.

3.1 Joining Online Communities

Where the department has differed from most other government agencies in Australia and overseas is its work in online communities. As referenced in some of the examples above, we have sought out, joined and actively contributed to numerous online communities. The aim is to reach our customers in the online spaces they prefer to use.

Not only has this work expanded the reach of our information online, but it has helped change community perceptions and build improve the department's reputation as a progressive and transparent government agency.

Example: The department's social media monitoring work uncovered a lively discussion thread about government payments for student in the Whirlpool online discussion forum.[11] While it was exciting to see young people sharing links to the Human Services website, policy documents and asking clarifying questions about their eligibility for student payments, some of the responses shared by fellow Whirlpool members offered information that may have mislead people about what the support they could receive. As you would expect, member responses related to each individuals' own experience in applying for payments.

The department decided to join Whirlpool to participate in the discussion, to let students know that eligibility for payments depends on a person's own circumstances – just because another student in their class does or does not receive payments, doesn't mean they will be in the same situation. At first, posts by the department were not well received. Students wanted to know why we had entered the conversation and whether we were watching their conversations 'big brother' style. We answered their questions honestly, explaining our aims of making ourselves available to answer their questions online, saving them a phone call, and correcting misinformation where needed. This eventually won them over. In the past 5 years the relationship has changed to one where members now defer to our staff to answer questions when they don't know the answer themselves, often saying 'Flick from Human Services should be on here soon, she'll know'. For the department, this type of acceptance and change in sentiment has been a key measure in the success of our social media outreach work.

3.2 Human Services on Facebook and Twitter

Alongside our social media monitoring and work in online communities, the department created official accounts on Facebook and Twitter to allow customers to find credible Australian Government information on the social media platforms they preferred most.

The first accounts were created for the General Manager and media spokesperson, Hank Jongen, and launched in 2010. This was chosen as a natural evolution to the work Mr. Jongen already did in engaging with customers through talkback radio interviews by taking those conversations online. Mr. Jongen answers customer questions posted on his Facebook and Twitter accounts (see Figs. 3 and 4) and has participated in Facebook live Q&A events for Older Australians to answer their questions about retirement, Age Pension and Concession Cards.

To help present the human side of our department, the Hank Jongen Facebook page (shown in Fig. 3) regularly shares good news stories to highlight the work

---

[11]http://whirlpool.net.au/.

Fig. 3 A snapshot of Hank Jongen Facebook page

our staff do in their local communities. The popular #giftofgiving series on his accounts demonstrate the contributions our staff make to charities.

Over time, the department expanded its approach by creating social media accounts to support various customer audiences, in line with the department's strategic priorities.

Our Student Update Facebook and Twitter accounts launched in 2011 (see Figs. 5 and 6), targeting a young audience we knew were already active on social media. The accounts share information for high school, university and TAFE[12] students with an audience of 18,000.

The department built on this experience, launching the Family Update Facebook and Twitter accounts in 2013 (see Fig. 7) to engage with one of its

---

[12]TAFE is a vocational education and training provider in Australia.

Fig. 4 A snapshot of Hank Jongen Twitter account

largest customer groups. The aim is to educate and inform customers about the online services and mobile apps available to help them claim and manage family payments while they are already in the digital channel. Our Family Update accounts are still our fastest-growing online community, gathering more than 30,000 likes and followers in the first 18 months.

The accounts have helped influence customer behaviours from always calling the department or visiting an office to ask us a question or update changes to their circumstances. Now, customers ask us approximately 1500 questions per month on social media and use digital services to most transactions, saving phone calls and visits for more sensitive or urgent issues.

Over time the department has expanded its official social media accounts further, to include YouTube, Google+ and Instagram.[13]

---

[13]www.humanservices.gov.au/socialmedia.

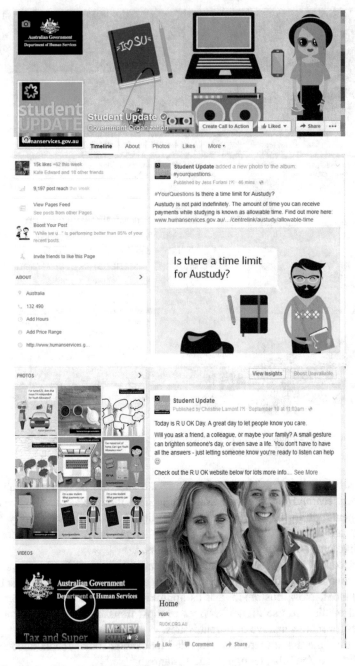

Fig. 5 Snapshots of the student update Facebook page

Fig. 6 Snapshot of the student update Twitter account

Fig. 7 Snapshot of the family update Twitter account

3.2.1 Creating Content

A solid schedule of relevant and helpful content has been critical to the success of these accounts. An average of 2–4 proactive messages are shared each week, with a focus on helping customers to access services for which they are eligible, keep payments by accurately reporting changes in their income and circumstances, and supporting them in the move to self-sufficiency with tips on training and looking for work.

The department's social media staff use an online calendar to plan content several months in advance and clearly show what content is planned for publication across accounts on any given day. There are robust clearance processes in place to ensure that published content is accurate and supports the department's current service focus.

Proactive messages also aim to generate engagement with our customers, encouraging them to post questions or share their experiences in dealing with the department. This approach helps build the department's reputation by ensuring we are open to receiving feedback and are transparent in our responses, while also helping keep our content in the Facebook news feeds of customers who follow our accounts and their friends.

3.3 Social Media Engagement During Emergencies

In a disaster event, such as flood or fire, social media is increasingly vital in delivering information to communities and strengthening relationships between emergency services and Australian communities.

During these emergencies, the Department of Human Services plays a critical role to support affected Australians—in the physical world and the virtual world. Our Service Officers, along with our specialist staff such as social workers, are some of the first to arrive in disaster-affected communities during the recovery effort. Teams set up temporary offices in Community Recovery Centres to help affected families access Disaster Recovery Payment and other support.

The first time the department tweeted during an emergency was for the floods in Victoria in September 2010 [5]. Since then, we have harnessed our strong social media presence to effectively support customers during and after a disaster—providing timely information about office closures, emergency service centres, and government disaster support.

3.3.1 Our Approach

In establishing our Emergencies Social Media Strategy, we considered the need to share critical payment and service information with citizens after an emergency with the need to ensure we are not contributing unnecessarily to the large volume of social media noise that occurs during and after an emergency.

Our approach recognises the differences between the work the police and State Emergency Services do during an emergency, and the financial aid and social work support that we are responsible for. While police and emergency services are needed immediately during a disaster, people often come to us days and weeks later for information and financial support, once they've dealt with the initial impact.

The department posts proactive messages on its official social media accounts to reach existing customers. The types of content shared include: information about Centrelink and Medicare Service Centre closures in affected areas, links to claim information for Disaster Recovery Payment on the humanservices.gov.au website, videos on how to claim and answering common claim questions, and photos and stories from staff who are working on the ground to support people in need.

Wherever possible the department also leverages trending hashtags on Twitter and share posts on community Facebook pages to ensure our emergency information is seen by people in affected communities.

Our proactive social media messages are generally timed in the following way:

1. **During event**: Only critical messages shared, for example if a Service Centre is closed due to an emergency we post messages to offer alternative access to services.
2. **Days after event**: Proactive messages about Disaster Recovery Payment amounts and eligibility, our free Social Work Service, as well as messages identifying which Community Recovery Centres our staff are located at to help access payments and other support.
3. **2–3 weeks after event**: Reminders about financial assistance and social work support, as well as stories and photos provided by our staff about their experiences helping in disaster-affected communities.
4. **6 months after event**: Proactive messages shared with information about the upcoming deadline for claiming Disaster Recovery Payment for the event.

4 Facilitating Online Communities

The department has established a range of online communities including *Next Step*, a research partnership with CSIRO [6] (see also Chap. 9 in this book).

Next Step was a closed community for parents transitioning between welfare payments and returning to work. Its objectives were to:

- provide informational and emotional support to parents;
- explore if novel technologies could help parents achieve better outcomes for themselves and their families; and
- measure social trust in the community.

Members could access tailored information—videos, resources and podcasts—and discussion forums and live Q&A events where they could ask questions and receive meaningful answers, as well as engage with other community members [7].

This case study will explore how moderators, staff in the Department of Human Services Social Media Team, managed the community and what tactics they used to bootstrap engagement. Firstly, we will provide more detailed information about the community.

4.1 Overview of the Community

4.1.1 Aim

The aim of *Next Step* was to explore if using social networking technologies could help customers achieve better outcomes for themselves by having access to informational and emotional support. Informational support was provided by having access to tailored resources and Human Services policy experts who could answer their specific questions. Emotional support was provided by having a shared space where members in similar situations could connect and share experiences and knowledge.

A unique aspect of the project was also examining social trust—exploring if trust between members and moderators developed over the life of the community and what could have attributed to these findings [8].

The main activities members could do in the community included:

- **completing member profiles** and finding buddies to work with on activities;
- **completing weekly activities** to help build their skills and confidence to return to work, including how to prepare for a job interview, identifying strengths and weaknesses, and searching for employment opportunities;
- **participating in live Q&A events** with experts to understand the transition process and have their questions answered;
- **participating in discussion forums** about their hopes, fears, concerns and aspirations during this life stage, as well as seeking information about the transition and maintaining welfare payments; and
- **reading, listening and watching content** in the resource section about the transition process, and become prepared to return to work.

4.1.2 Audience

Parents with young children who received a parenting payment (Parenting Payment) and would need to transition onto a parenting allowance (Newstart Allowance) when their youngest child turned 6 or 8 years, or transitioned in the past three months, were invited to join the community.

This niche audience was selected because of the complex transition process, and the impact it has on other aspects of a parent's life including the need to become job ready.

We conducted preliminary research, including focus groups and an online survey, with this audience group before the community began to gain an understanding of the issues they face, and to identify if there would be value in establishing the community [12, 13]. Key findings included:

- for many there was no clear understanding of the transition process or what was expected of them *"I am unclear about the process.... The lack of communication is the biggest issue... how does the whole process work? ... I am in the dark"*;
- lack of understanding led to feelings of stress and anxiousness *"Definitely stressful and overwhelming"* and *"I felt daunted"*;
- frustration with policy requiring them to transition or perceiving it as a punitive measure *"Why do we cease to be parents when our children turn 8?"*;
- feelings of anxiousness about returning to work; and
- most parents would be open to trying an online community once the concept was explained to them.

The research findings were used to design the community, develop tailored content, and manage the community once live.

As *Next Step* was a research project, only parents in the niche audience group could be invited to join. This limited the ability to recruit new community members and prevented organic growth from members through word of mouth.

Members were invited by letter of invitation via Secure Online Mail with a unique registration token. The double blind recruitment process meant community members could remain anonymous and participate freely in the community [9].

Over the twelve months the community was open, we conducted four recruitment rounds and welcomed hundreds of members to the community.

Figure 8 shows the activity page of the *Next Step* where members perform different activities to enhance their skills.

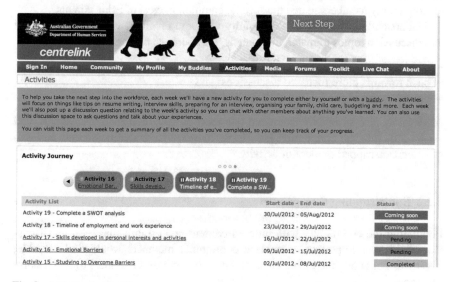

Fig. 8 Activities in NextStep

4.2 Lessons in Building Engagement

Being a new online community, the biggest challenge moderators faced when the community launched was engagement—overcoming what is often referred to as the 'cold start'.

As there were restrictions on inviting new community members, moderators focussed their attention on converting as many newcomers to regular members as possible to achieve 'critical mass', i.e., the state where the community can sustain itself through member activity.

4.2.1 Understanding Community Purpose and Value

To create a community that members would want to return to, and engage with, we needed to understand what type of community we were building and where we could offer members value.

Online communities often fall into one of five types:

1. Place—where members share a geographic region.
2. Practice—where members undertake the same activity.
3. Interest—where members share a specific interest.
4. Action—where members are dedicated to making change in the world.
5. Circumstance—where members have a situation thrust upon them.

We identified *Next Step* was a hybrid community of circumstance and interest. Parents told us during the research focus groups that they felt thrust into this situation of needing to claim Centrelink payments and felt the situation was out of their control. And all community members shared the specific common interest of being parents.

Understanding the type of community we were creating, we designed content and discussion topics to match their needs. We focussed on content that would:

– bond parents;
– push towards more focussed discussions; and
– provide support for dealing with the situation.

Moderators also strongly encouraged members to start their own discussions, and six months into the community launching, member-generated comments and discussions outstripped moderator activity.

4.2.2 Bootstrapping Engagement

Populating the community with tailored content and establishing relevant discussion topics was important to create a community members would find valuable, but it was not enough to create engagement—this required members to feel a sense of connection and belonging in the community.

Establishing Member Connections

The first step to create a sense of belonging was to establish member connections. Each member was asked to complete a 'profile' including public and private information. Public information, such as number of children, could be seen by all members and was a way for members to get to know each other without having to actively engage. Private information was used to 'match' buddies (people who members would work with to complete group activities) [10].

On the 'Community' section of *Next Step*, several member profiles were displayed to encourage all community members to get to know them. At first, this section displayed moderator profiles (see Fig. 9), but once members completed their own profiles, they were invited to feature in this section.

Providing Different Ways to Engage

The second step in the engagement process was offering different ways for members to engage. According to Jakob Nielson's rule for participation inequality in online communities [14], 90 % of people are 'lurkers', 9 % are 'intermittent contributors' and 1 % are 'heavy contributors'.

Knowing that not all members would be open to commenting and joining discussions about their personal situation, we offered a range of ways for people to passively engage—rating other people's comments, watching videos, listening to podcasts, reading resources, and completing activities. Having a broad range of ways for people to engage meant that each time 'lurkers' visited the community, they could still participate in the community and be rewarded with fresh content [11].

Giving Social Proof[14]

We used social proof—evidence from other community members—to persuade more members to model their behaviours or take certain actions. This included mentioning the number of people who completed their weekly activities to encourage more members to do their activities, and talking about comments members had posted to drive more members to read and contribute to those discussions.

---

[14]Social proof, also known as informational social influence, is a psychological phenomenon where people assume the actions of others in an attempt to reflect correct behaviour for a given situation. This effect is prominent in ambiguous social situations where people are unable to determine the appropriate mode of behaviour, and is driven by the assumption that surrounding people possess more knowledge about the situation. Source: https://en.wikipedia.org/wiki/Social_proof.

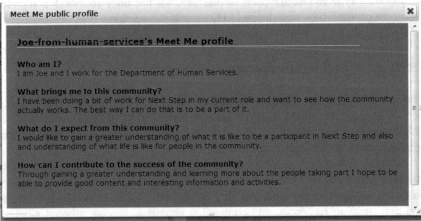

Fig. 9 Displaying a profile to encourage people to know each other

When the community first launched and we lacked the above social proof because members were not yet confident to contribute to the community, we used evidence from the preliminary research to build our credibility and foster trust. In preparing to establish an online community we held focus groups with parents who were going to make the transition back into work to ask them about the worries and opportunities they identified, and to determine how an online community would best support them. We posted messages about the focus group process and findings to explain to community members that other parents in a similar situation to them had said that they wanted this community and that their feedback was used to shape the content and the way it was delivered. For example, parents in focus groups identified that going back to work after years out of the workforce while trying to arrange childcare is stressful, so we created discussion threads to allow people to share tips and experiences on this topic, as well as several activities aimed at minimising stress.

This technique of using social proof was highly valuable in making a low level of engagement seem more meaningful and to quickly build upon it—it helped to cultivate a community of regular contributors.

Being Responsive and Setting the Tone

Underpinning these three key tactics to bootstrap engagement was the warm and inclusive welcome of moderators, and our ongoing responsiveness during the community. Our role was to set the tone of the community as a safe and helpful space where parents would be supported.

From the preliminary research, we understood members felt anxious, stressed and overwhelmed. We encouraged them to speak openly about their experiences even if they were not necessarily related to transitioning between payments or finding work. In the beginning, members would ask if they could talk about certain topics and we reassured them they could discuss anything so long as it was within the community's Terms of Use, which mainly covered being respectful to all members. This opened up discussions that bonded members and allowed them to emotionally support each other.

Moderators also actively responded to all comments and questions as quickly as possible (generally within half an hour and always same day) to demonstrate we were listening and there to support members. We proved ourselves to be helpful and caring. When members saw we could offer accurate and clear advice to support them, they were encouraged to return for ongoing assistance. Analysis by the CSIRO indicated our moderation approach was the biggest influence in establishing social trust with members.

Figure 10 shows a snapshot of discussion forum in Next Step, where members discussed various issues relevant to them.

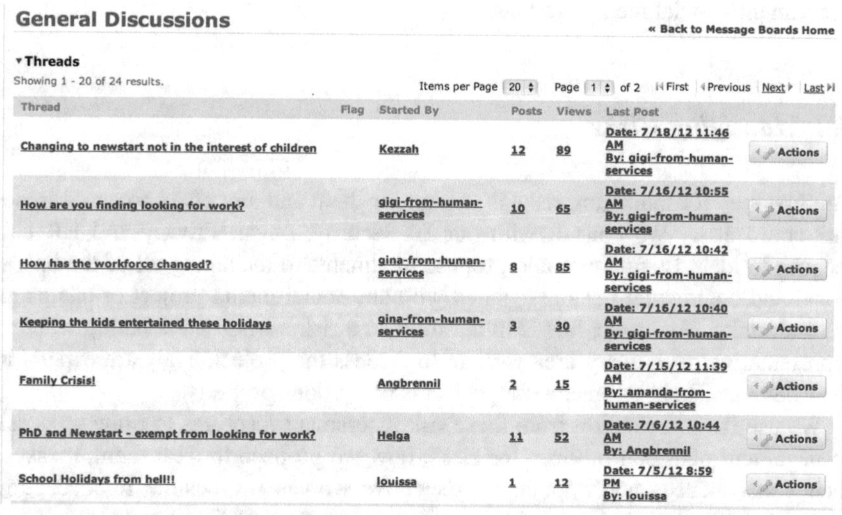

General Discussions   « Back to Message Boards Home

▼ Threads
Showing 1 - 20 of 24 results.   Items per Page [20 ♦]   Page [1 ♦] of 2   ⊩ First ◄ Previous Next ▶ Last ▶|

Thread	Flag	Started By	Posts	Views	Last Post	
Changing to newstart not in the interest of children		Kezzah	12	89	Date: 7/18/12 11:46 AM By: gigi-from-human-services	Actions
How are you finding looking for work?		gigi-from-human-services	10	65	Date: 7/16/12 10:55 AM By: gigi-from-human-services	Actions
How has the workforce changed?		gina-from-human-services	8	85	Date: 7/16/12 10:42 AM By: gigi-from-human-services	Actions
Keeping the kids entertained these holidays		gina-from-human-services	3	30	Date: 7/16/12 10:40 AM By: gigi-from-human-services	Actions
Family Crisis!		Angbrennil	2	15	Date: 7/15/12 11:39 AM By: amanda-from-human-services	Actions
PhD and Newstart - exempt from looking for work?		Helga	11	52	Date: 7/6/12 10:44 AM By: Angbrennil	Actions
School Holidays from hell!!		louissa	1	12	Date: 7/5/12 8:59 PM By: louissa	Actions

Fig. 10 Discussion forum in *Next Step*

5 Strong Governance

Engaging in social media presents risks, particularly for a government department that operates in a challenging and risk averse environment. While many of these risks are not new, the risk level, consequences or proposed treatments may differ on social media that in other situations.

Undertaking risk assessments with key stakeholders, planning for issues and having escalation processes in place has won us the support of our Executive and given permission for us to grow our social media work. Importantly, it has ensured we deliver this work in a controlled, transparent and accountable manner—serving our customers efficiently and effectively in social media.

This section provides an overview of how we govern our social media activities.

5.1 Governance Framework

Our Governance Framework tells the story of how we manage social media and includes information such as roles and responsibilities, clearance processes, constraints, risk assessment and management, corporate identity, legal and other mandatories.

We also include all of the documents our team uses, such as the moderator guidelines and Acceptable Use Policies, in the attachments.

This framework has also helped build confidence amongst stakeholders and senior executives by demonstrating we take a proactive approach to managing the department's social media presence.

5.2 Managing Risks

The first step for managing risks is to plan for them and any other potential issues that could arise. We consult with our IT Security, Legal, Privacy and HR colleagues to identify, measure and propose treatments to managing all of the operational and contractual risks associated with any social media project or campaign we undertake. Generally, this is in the form of a risk assessment meeting where a representative from every area is there to discuss the project. They are experts in their fields and help us ensure our project is being done properly.

We use the information from these risk assessment meetings to draw up a risk management plan that outlines the risks, how we propose to treat them, measure their consequences and appoint an Executive who is responsible for accepting each risk. This plan is circulated to all relevant stakeholders for approval.

While these risk plans can take time to negotiate, they enable our team to understand potential risks and plan ways to manage them before they arise.

For many years we wrote individual risk plans for every project but found this presented the potential for us to not manage risks consistently. We now have an overarching risk plan and whenever we create a new project, an individual risk schedule that only outlines the specific operational or contractual risks for that project is created.

Some of the main ways we treat risks include:

- ongoing training on security measures and escalation processes
- ongoing training for social media moderators in communicating with vulnerable customers
- having Acceptable Use Policies for all of our social media accounts to be transparent and consistent about we moderate
- moderator guidelines for our team—describing a range of issues that could arise and how to manage them—like what teams to escalate issues to and other steps to take
- seven day moderation from 9 am to 5 pm
- regularly changing passwords for our accounts and having banned words lists
- regularly reminding our audience not to share their personal information
- annual reviews of our social media risk management plan
- annual crises management simulation with our media team that crosses over media and social media risk management
- an overarching social media governance framework.

These treatment measures have helped build the skills of our staff and provide confidence in managing the worst-case scenario. The annual training in particular ensures our work is always being led by current policies and best practice.

6 Measuring Success

It is much more difficult to measure return on investment when you're not selling anything. Public sector agencies across Australia and the world are seeing benefit results in their social media work but are still looking for the best ways to measure and report on its value in dollar terms.

To help measure the value of the department's social media work, we are working on a model that tracks the cost of the social media engagement and customer service, alongside the return on reputation that results.

This section provides an overview of our current work on measuring return on reputation.

6.1 The Cost of Social Media Engagement and Customer Service

Over time, customer demand for information about social and health services on social media has been increasing. From sharing proactive messages in 2010 that received less than a dozen likes or comments, the department has an active social media following of 100,000 and now responds to approximately 1500 customer questions on social media every month. That growth requires additional staff and technology resources to monitor and respond to questions.

The department is setting new Key Performance Indicators for answering customer questions, modelled on measurements used by our call and face-to-face service channels. These include speed of answer, response accuracy and ability to answer on first query. This will allow for a cost comparison with other service channels.

The following is a list of considerations the department is tackling in this work, however measuring some of these impacts using anonymous social media data is very difficult.

Costs:

- Many social networking sites are free to establish, but over time the department has had to invest in technologies for social media monitoring and queuing social media customer questions, to make this work more efficient.
- Staff resources may need to grow over time to support increased social media demand, but this can be expensive.
- How long does the average social media response take? And is it more efficient to answer questions on Facebook and Twitter than over the phone? A social media response has the potential to benefit many customers who can see the post, however customers can't get personalised service through social media because the privacy of their personal information cannot be assured.

Savings:

- Providing information and support to customers when they are already online makes it easier for them to remain there and complete many of the transactions they can do themselves using their online accounts. This means our staff complete fewer basic transactions for customers and can spend time working on complex customer cases instead.
- The department gets an early heads-up on potential issues through social media, such as when content on the humanservices.gov.au website could be made easier to understand. This means issues can be addressed earlier also, before they have the capacity to result in numerous phone calls to the department because people don't understand the eligibility information on our website.
- If more timely, efficient and accurate social media work results in fewer calls, does that save money? It will likely result in customers being able to access more personalised phone service from our Service Officers, who have the time to complete multiple services for a customer in the one interaction, reducing the need for staff re-work or future customer contact.

6.2 Return on Reputation

Reputation management is critical for government agencies so citizens have faith in the services and support they deliver. Using social media we aim to demonstrate transparency in government communication, build trust, and create a more agile and responsive organisation.

We can readily see the impact of some of our proactive social media messages, for example our weekly Facebook and Twitter posts about our Mobile Service Centre[15] visits to regional communities have directly resulted in people visiting the buses in their town.

In addition, giving customers a heads-up about planned maintenance for online services, and responding to their complaints about service issues quickly, has greatly improved our social media following and reputation.

But when citizens can choose to interact with governments anonymously through social media, how can you track whether an individual's query was resolved? Did their dealings with government end on Facebook, or did the citizen make a phone call, email a complaint, then visit an office in person to seek a resolution?

The department is working on analysing a range of data sources to answer these questions, including sentiment analysis, and call demand and social media comparison data.

6.2.1 Comparing Call Centre and Social Media Data

The department forecasts demand for its services to ensure adequate resources are allocated to areas where demand may peak.

We are currently exploring whether our proactive social media campaigns have an impact on call demand by measuring the reach of social media messages as well as whether actual demand for phone services was greater or less than the forecast. This is measured on particular dates that correspond with proactive social media messages being published and shared.

Where the department can demonstrate a reduction in call demand compared to what was forecast, it is difficult to attribute all credit to social media activity. This is because online anonymity means there is no way for us to track that all customers who interacted with the department on social media did not call us because they already got the information they needed. This is an issue we will continue to work on as we evolve in our return on investment work.

6.2.2 Sentiment Analysis

Tracking customer sentiment about their social media interactions with us is one way, however automated sentiment provided by some social media monitoring platforms is inaccurate and has particularly difficulty dealing appropriately with sarcasm. Our social customer service staff required to manually attribute sentiment to social media posts made by our customers on the department's official social media accounts.

---

[15]http://www.humanservices.gov.au/mobileoffice.

Early data shows that often when customers write to us online their posts are negative or neutral in sentiment, but after we respond the sentiment of their replies often changes to neutral and positive respectively.

While not an accurate measure of effective social customer service on its own, when tracked against call and social media demand data, sentiment analysis provides a snapshot of how well the department is managing reputation and meeting the needs of citizens through social media.

7 Conclusion

We have been using social media since 2009 in our efforts to support the Australian Government Department of Human Services improve service delivery. This work was led by the department's Communication Division and has evolved from monitoring social media and engaging with citizens in discussion forums, to creating our own social media accounts and online communities. Along the way, we helped build new tools to monitor social media and developed a strong governance framework to better manage the risks involved. Our use of social media has enabled us to share health and social security information in an efficient and effective manner, respond to citizen questions quickly, and build trust with the Australian public. Our work continues to evolve as we explore new ways to engage and collaborate with citizens through social media. We are also now focussed on ways to measure success (or return on investment). In this chapter, we described our engagement with social media, including specific examples of projects we delivered. We also discussed some of the challenges for government in social media engagement and how we dealt with them.

References

1. Department of Human Services (2015). *How we use social media*. http://www.humanservi ces.gov.au/corporate/publications-and-resources/social-media/how-we-use-social-media. Accessed on September 11, 2015.
2. Department of Human Services (2015). *Policies on our social media accounts*. http://www. humanservices.gov.au/corporate/publications-and-resources/social-media/policies-on-our-social-media-accounts. Accessed on September 11, 2015.
3. CSIRO (2015). Transforming Human Services for the Digital Era. https://publications.csiro. au/rpr/download?pid=csiro:EP149489&dsid=DS2. Accessed on September 11, 2015.
4. Wan, S., & Paris, C. (2014) Improving government services with social media feedback. In *Proceedings of the 19th international conference on Intelligent User Interfaces* (pp. 27–36).
5. State Government Victoria (2015). Victorian Floods 2010–11 Recovery Progress Report. http://www.dhs.vic.gov.au/__data/assets/pdf_file/0011/678188/9426DHH-Report_WEB.pdf. Accessed on September 11, 2015.
6. Bista, S. K., Colineau, N., Nepal, S., & Paris, C. (2013). Next step: an online community to support parents in their transition to work. In *Proceedings of the 2013 Conference on Computer Supported Cooperative Work Companion* (pp. 5–10).

7. Bista, S. K., Colineau, N., Nepal, S., & Paris, C. (2012). The design of an online community for welfare recipients. In *Proceedings of the 24th Australian Computer-Human Interaction Conference* (pp. 38–41).
8. Bista, S. K., Nepal, S., & Paris, C. (2013). Know your members' trust. In *UMAP Workshops*.
9. Paris, C., Colineau, N., Nepal, S., Bista, S. K., & Beschorner, G. (2013). Ethical considerations in an online community: The balancing act. *Ethics and Information Technology, 15*(4), 301–316.
10. Colineau, N. (2012). A buddy matching program to help build an online support network. In *Proceedings of the 24th Australian Computer-Human Interaction Conference* (pp. 85–88).
11. Bista, S. K., Nepal, S., Colineau, N., & Paris, C. (2012). Using gamification in an online community. In *8th International Conference on Collaborative Computing: Networking, Applications and Worksharing (CollaborateCom)* (pp. 611–618).
12. Colineau, N., Paris, C., & Dennett, A. (2011). Capitalising on the potential of online communities to help welfare recipients. In *The Government and Citizen Engagement Workshop, in Conjunction with the 5th International Conference on Communities and Technologies (C&T 2011)*, June 29–July 2, 2011, Brisbane, Australia. (Proceedings published in the International Reports on Socio-Informatics).
13. Colineau, N., Paris, C., & Dennett, A. (2011). Exploring the use of an online community in welfare transition programs. In *The Proceedings of the 25th BCS Conference on Human Computer Interaction (HCI 2011)*—Extended Abstract, July 4–8, 2011. Newcastle Upon Tyne, UK.
14. Nielsen Norman Group (2015). http://www.nngroup.com/articles/participation-inequality/. Accessed September 14, 2015.

Use of Social Media for Internal Communication: A Case Study in a Government Organisation

Merrin Fabre

Abstract Enterprise social media is evolving internal communication in organisations. The networks produced by such technologies enable employees to communicate with a large number of people simultaneously across an organisation and conduct a number of activities; organising meetings and projects, sharing ideas, problem solving, creating awareness of work taking place in the organisation, and building social capital between work colleagues. This chapter will look at the main features of enterprise social media platforms, in particular Microsoft's Yammer, and the implementation of Yammer as an internal communication tool at VicRoads, a Victorian state government authority. The main components to consider when adopting a Yammer network will be examined including network setup and gaining initial users, network development with the guidance of a community manager, and continued network growth through the use of engagement strategies. Examples are provided where VicRoads has used Yammer to enable communication between employees leading to improvements in communication, culture and business practices.

Keywords Enterprise social media · Yammer · Employee engagement · Internal communication · Cultural change

1 Introduction

Social media technologies have revolutionised the way government departments and agencies engage and interact with their publics. For some, using social media has allowed them to develop new and trusted relationships with the Australian public as well as to promote the work that they do. In 2011, the Australian Bureau

M. Fabre (✉)
Internal Communications Manager, Melbourne, Australia
e-mail: merrin.fabre@gmail.com

© Springer International Publishing Switzerland 2015
S. Nepal et al. (eds.), *Social Media for Government Services*,
DOI 10.1007/978-3-319-27237-5_3

51

of Statistics (ABS) used Twitter to promote the upcoming national census. The ABS combined data from the 2006 census with popular culture references in tweet form to make the national census more current and engaging to the Australian people. Commentators considered it a novel way for a government agency to behave [2] and the pop culture tweets successfully generated interest in the census with the ABS Twitter account receiving 10,774 new followers on census night [17]. Similarly, the Queensland Police Service (QPS) used social technologies, this time Twitter and Facebook, to build a trusted relationship with its audience during widespread flooding in Queensland. Using these platforms they updated citizens with real time emergency information such as instructing people to evacuate their properties and addressed misinformation from the media by posting messages to Twitter and Facebook with the correct information and using the hashtag 'myth-buster' [13]. The QPS's quick response times to emerging events and their efforts to correct misinformation showed them to be a source of accurate, trusted information during the state emergency [1, 16]. This was reflected in the significant increase in traffic to their social media sites during the emergency period: QPS's likes on their Facebook page increased from 6400 to 165,000 and their Twitter followers increased from 1200 to 11,000 [16].

Social media use by organisations in the past few years has steadily been growing. The McKinsey Global Institute [10] conducts an annual survey on social technology adoption and use within enterprises. It reported that the use of Web 2.0 technologies (such as blogs, microblogging, online videoconferencing, podcasts, video sharing and social networking) by organisations increased from 50 to 68 % between 2007 and 2013. In particular, social networking technology use, which this chapter will focus on, increased in the surveyed organisations from 19 to 58 % between 2009 and 2013. Some companies who have chosen to invest in these products have seen positive benefits. For example, a study conducted by Reimer et al. [15] on firm Deloitte Australia's employees' use of enterprise social networking platform Yammer found that employees used Yammer to brainstorm ideas for products and projects and facilitate the creation of new employee knowledge. In addition, through Yammer's question and answer capability, the platform also helped Deloitte employees access existing expertise within the company [15]; here employees who used the social platform put forward questions, their colleagues responded and transferred their knowledge to the questioner and other employees using the platform. How companies use enterprise social media platforms and the resulting outcomes can vary. Like Deloitte, Westfield shopping centres have benefitted from using Yammer but they use the technology for another purpose, to minimise 'exceptions' [18]. Exceptions are tasks that employees need to attend to but are not part of their main duties [4]. When issues have been identified in Westfield stores, store managers and retailers have discussed the problem on the Yammer platform with each other and Westfield's support office. This interaction has led to solutions being developed to on-the-ground issues in a manner faster than business processes would allow [18].

This chapter will focus on the social networking platform Yammer, the implementation of this platform into a state government authority VicRoads and the benefits gained from its use. It will look at the main components to consider when implementing a Yammer network: its setup, development and growth. First, the chapter will briefly explore what enterprise social media is and how Yammer itself operates.

2 Enterprise Social Media

Enterprise social media is evolving internal communication in organisations. The networks produced by such technologies give employees the capacity to communicate with a large number of people across an organisation, irrespective of hierarchy, time and space.

In a review of enterprise social media, researchers Leonardi et al. [5] provided an expansive definition of the technology as "web-based platforms that allow workers to:

- communicate messages with specific coworkers or broadcast messages to everyone in the organisation
- explicitly indicate or implicitly reveal particular coworkers as communication partners
- post, edit, and sort text and files linked to themselves or others
- view the messages, connections, text and files communicated, posted edited and sorted by anyone else in the organisation at any time of their choosing".

The main format these technologies take are microblogging sites where employees write short messages about themselves and their interests [14]. A range of other tools such as wikis, document sharing and blogs can be integrated into the technology to form a social platform [12]. The platforms enable many-to-many communication where each person using the tool can send and receive messages. This is a different form of communication for organisations where one-to-many communication tools, such as email, dominate. In one-to-many communication one person is the sender who delivers a message to a set of known recipients. In many-to-many communication when a person sends a message it will be sent to a number of recipients and the sender does not know who will receive it and the recipients of the message may not know who the sender is [3], or their role or hierarchy in the organisation. The message is broadcast out to recipients where it can be seen at the time of sending or at a future time as the message is stored in the platform and can be retrieved at any time by platform users.

Reimer and Richter [14] have reviewed and compared how organisations benefit from using enterprise social media. They consider the tools to be flexible, nonprescriptive and used for a range of different communication purposes. Riemer and Richter [14] cite that for an organisation, the main purpose for the platform may best be determined over time and through employee experimentation, as the employees need to make sense of the tool and find ways to integrate use of the platform into their daily work procedures and practices. This would then lead to each organisation benefitting from the tool in different ways. Through studying how enterprise social media platforms have been adopted by organisations they have identified six categories of benefits: socialising, organising, crowdsourcing, information sharing, awareness creation, and learning and linkages [14]. Since each company is different in how it adopts its enterprise social media platform, the extent to which an organisation will realise each of these benefits may also be different.

There are a number of commercial enterprise social media platforms available for an organisation to purchase and adopt, such as Jive and Saleforce's Chatter. One of the world's most popular enterprise social media platforms, which this chapter will look into further, is Yammer.

2.1 Yammer

Yammer was developed as an internal communication tool for genealogy company Geni before being launched as a social media product in 2008. In 2012, Yammer Inc. was purchased by Microsoft and is currently being used by over eight million people and accessed by over 500,000 companies worldwide [7, 11].

In the Yammer platform, each organisation has their own private network. Basic access to a Yammer network is through a freemium model; users sign up for free using their organisational email address, which also serves as the user's unique identifier. When the first user from an organisation signs up, a network is created on Yammer for that organisation, and as more users from the same organisation sign up they are joined to this network. The network grows organically as users join and start to communicate and interact with each other. Yammer also offers a premium network for a fee, usually paid as a monthly subscription for each user. A premium network has the same features as the freemium network but with additional administrative control. This includes being able to:

- customise a network by adding company branding and usage policies
- control user management by adding, blocking and removing users
- export data from the network for analysis and record keeping
- integrate Yammer with other enterprise systems.

A Yammer network primarily functions as a microblogging site where users are prompted to answer the question 'What are you working on?'
Within the site, users are able to:

- broadcast messages (including text, images, video files and web links) across the network or send private messages to select users
- 'like', share and comment on other users' messages
- create groups that segregate discussions (groups are based on a subject, work team or project)

- seek and share knowledge by sharing files, creating shared documents, conducting polls and asking questions.

Users can access Yammer from computer-mediated devices that are connected to the Internet allowing users to create and retrieve information at any time and location.

The features displayed in Yammer are similar to those of other social networking sites. When a user signs into their Yammer network they see an interface that resembles social media site Facebook where a central feed collates posted messages. Similar to social sites Twitter and Instagram, Yammer works on a 'follower' principle. Users follow their colleagues and join groups and the messages posted by and in these will appear in their central feed. This helps users personally curate the information that they see. Regardless of who they choose to follow, users always have the option to see all messages broadcast across the network and can view the most popular messages as determined by Yammer algorithms.

Messages in Yammer are posted into groups, which compartmentalise the messages. Groups are set up by users and can be based on a specific topic, such as a business area or project. They can be open to the whole organisation or restricted to select membership. All groups have their own news feed where users' messages appear. The default group in Yammer is the 'All Company' group; messages posted into this group can be seen by everyone in the network.

An organisation's Yammer network is not necessarily isolated from the outside world. While its main 'home' network is accessible only to people within the organisation, 'external' Yammer networks can be created where employees can communicate with select customers or clients. Additional third-party applications can also be added to a Yammer network, including features such as analytics tools, calendar and scheduling tools and enterprise system integration.

As previously mentioned, enterprise social media platforms like Yammer are flexible technologies allowing them to be used for a range of different communication purposes. Employees have used these platforms to facilitate new ways to solve problems and generate ideas [15], resolve 'exceptions' that usually detract from normal business activities [18] and build social capital leading to increased motivation to share information with colleagues [19]. For Victorian government authority VicRoads the use of Yammer has enabled employees to communicate with each other in a way that has led to positive changes in their company culture. The rest of this chapter will explore how VicRoads integrated Yammer into the organisation to improve internal communication and promote cultural change.

3 Yammer at VicRoads

VicRoads is a Victorian Government authority that operates and maintains the Victorian road system. The organisation of approximately 3500 people has used social media for internal communication since 2009. Their implementation of

Yammer as a legitimate internal communication tool took a number of years and multiple engagement strategies. The stages involved in the implementation process include setting up the network and gaining initial users, developing the network with the guidance of a community manager, and continuing the growth of the network through engagement strategies.

3.1 Setting up the Network

The set up process for a Yammer network is an easy and quick one. An organisation's Yammer network is created after the first user from that organisation signs up. If an organisation has paid for the subscription-based premium version of Yammer it has access to a number of features that provide greater control of the operation of the Yammer network. VicRoads has had a premium Yammer network since 2009. With access to the full suite of Yammer features, VicRoads was able to personalise their network through adding a company logo (see Fig. 1) and assigning administrators to the network who can access a range of regulatory options such as data and user management features.

Once the network is acquired, employees can use it to broadcast messages and engage with one another almost instantly. Every user that signs up has their own user profile where they can upload an image of themselves, follow people, post messages, 'like' content, create groups and perform other functions in the network.

Fig. 1 Screenshot of VicRoads' Yammer network

To promote the use of the network within the organisation, formal or informal launch events and activities can be held. At VicRoads, they informally launched Yammer in 2010, which began the organic growth of the network; 1686 accounts were activated. In mid-2011 formal launch of the network was undertaken, which led to further growth and increased the number of activated accounts to 1851 out of a potential 3500 people in the organisation. Launching and promoting use of Yammer created awareness of the network and some people started experimenting with how to use the platform. However, Yammer developed a reputation for being 'Facebook for work'. In late 2011, Jacqueline Shields, a member if the VicRoads internal communication team, was made community manager of the Yammer network in order to develop the use of Yammer into a key corporate communications tool.

3.2 Developing the Network: The Role of the Community Manager

Community management of social networks is becoming a significant part of internal communication roles. Community managers help develop and maintain engagement in the network, they advise users on how to use the platforms and help employees build relationships with other users. They also monitor the activity within the social network and mitigate risks that may arise.

For VicRoads, the community manager Jacqueline performed a number of tasks in her role, which included:

- developing an usage policy outlining appropriate employee behaviour within the network
- tracking user behaviour, reviewing content being posted by employees and advising people on inappropriate use (usually offline)
- showing employees how to use Yammer's features
- conducting engagement activities that make using Yammer a positive and fun experience
- measuring the network's usage and growth, including tracking the number of users and groups, top posts and influential users of the network
- auditing and cleaning up the network through removing old or redundant groups
- seeking out and recruiting leaders in the organisation to use the network
- advising business areas on how to use Yammer to benefit their business goals and objectives and assisting them with developing a presence on the network.

Jacqueline provided three examples of how she and others in her internal communication team developed and managed the VicRoads' Yammer network through mitigating the risks of using Yammer, building employee engagement in the network, and helping business areas use Yammer to improve their reputation and engagement with employees.

3.2.1 Example 1: Mitigating Risk Through Social Media Policies

Although there are many communication benefits to using social media within an organisation, there are a number of risks associated with giving people use of these technologies. Some of the major risks considered by internal communicators include disclosure of sensitive information, copyright infringement, violation of privacy and inappropriate use of the platform [9, 18]. One way to mitigate inappropriate use of a social network is to implement policies that provide guidance to employees on how to and how not to use the network.

Organisations tend to have policies for social media networks used to communicate with external clients and customers, but not necessarily for internal networks. If an organisation uses social media for internal communication, their social media policies also need to include the expected and appropriate use of these internal networks by their employees. Further, the social media policies should be aligned with other relevant organisational policies, such as codes of conduct and IT usage policies and, where necessary, legislation such as the *Privacy Act 1988*, *Copyright Act 1968*, and in particular for government organisations, *Freedom of Information Act 1982* (FOI Act).

Jacqueline developed a usage policy for the VicRoads Yammer network. It introduces the purpose of Yammer and outlines the behaviours expected of employees, their responsibilities, and their obligations under the FOI Act.

For Jacqueline, the VicRoads' usage policy guides the behavioural expectations of the network. It has an educational role by stating which employee behaviours are condoned and how employees should use the network, for example the policy states that the organisation expects that posts in the network should be "informative, interesting and relevant" (see example VicRoads usage policy). The policy also has a risk management role; it outlines an employee's responsibility to comply with copyright legislation, to prevent disclosure of sensitive organisational information, and refrain from making comments that may damage VicRoads' reputation. It also informs employees that the information in the internal Yammer network can be made public. This may occur when a member of the public requests to access information posted on Yammer through the FOI Act.

The policy provides employees with a common understanding of behavioural expectations and the community manager with appropriate governance documentation. When undertaking her management role, if Jacqueline had to advise people on what was appropriate use of the Yammer network, the usage policy guided and supported her decisions on what was considered appropriate.

Within a premium network, such as VicRoads', a usage policy can be added directly to the network and is available for users to view at any time from their Yammer home page. Once in place, when users sign up they are required to accept the policy before they are admitted to the network.

VicRoads usage policy

Welcome to the VicRoads Yammer network.

Yammer gives all staff a voice. It provides the opportunity to share, collaborate and innovate right across all VicRoads offices.

Not all staff have ready access to VicRoads computers i.e., Customer Service Staff, Sprayline Road Service staff, Project Office staff and staff on leave. However all have access to Yammer via downloading the Yammer app on their Smartphones/tablets.

Yammer enables all staff with a VicRoads email address equal ability to check in, ask a question, be heard and follow what is going on across the organisation.

Your contribution is actively encouraged at all times.

You are not expected to be a social media expert. Enjoy learning and exploring how Yammer can be an effective communication tool for you. If you are not sure, ask a colleague, ask on Yammer in the Yammer Help group. Over time it will become second nature.

It is important to be mindful of Yammer etiquette:

- Be respectful to other users. Maintain a supportive, positive and productive work environment, free from intimidating, humiliating or offensive comments.
- Your posts in the All Company feed should be work-related. Exceptions are posts in non-work focused Groups i.e. the Book Club.
- It is your responsibility to ensure compliance with intellectual property laws and not upload material onto Yammer that could infringe copyright.
- Your posts should be informative, interesting and relevant.
- Check that the information you share is factual and accurate.
- Consider whether your comments are damaging to VicRoads' reputation, interests and could bring VicRoads or the Victorian government into disrepute.
- Be aware that the Victorian Freedom of Information Act (FOI) 1982 gives members of the public the right to access information posted on Yammer about the activities of VicRoads.
- As you are using a VicRoads' IT system take into account the Acceptable Use policy.
- Avoid disclosing information that has been collected for official VicRoads purposes only, without the appropriate authorisation to do so.
- When you express an opinion, make it clear that this is your personal opinion and not reflective of the views of VicRoads or the Victorian government.

- The VicRoads Yammer Network is not a vehicle for selling personal products and services unless in the Group: VicRoads Swap, Buy Sell.
- Use your correct name and your photograph in your Profile.

3.2.2 Example 2: Maintaining Employee Engagement in the Network

A community manager performs a number of activities to help maintain engagement, demonstrate behavioural expectations for sharing information, and promote socialisation within the network. For example, a common use for Yammer is for people to share information by asking and responding to questions. At VicRoads, when a person asks a question in Yammer and gets a response, Jacqueline tags the conversation with the topic #Yammerwin to highlight to users the action of seeking or providing answers was a good use of the network. It also allows her to collate all messages tagged with #Yammerwin to have a record of conversations that resulted in a positive outcomes within the network.

A community manager can conduct regular fun activities to encourage socialising and common connections between network users. Actions like these that build social capital can be precursors to information sharing between employees [19]. For example, VicRoads has a regular post called 'throwback Thursday' where archival images of work conducted at the organisation are posted on Thursdays to generate interest and to give employees an insight to the VicRoads history. The community manager normally performs this task but employees have voluntarily participated in the activity by posting their own throwback images on Thursdays. 'Friday funny' is also a regular activity where the community manager posts a link to a humorous article related to the workplace (see Fig. 2).

To increase participation in the network and decrease the number of lurkers, people who watch the action but do not post messages or engage with the network, the VicRoads' communication team created an avatar called 'Frog And Toad' (see Fig. 3). Frog and Toad is the name of VicRoads' corporate magazine, the avatar has the same name and posts messages on the network. The messages are tongue in cheek and are designed to show people that the network, although a work communication tool, is a place where people can be relaxed and their posts can be casual in nature and do not have to be written in a professional tone. Creating a less formal culture has helped encourage people who are uncomfortable about participating in the network to give it a go. It has also differentiated the communication channel from other channels within the organisation such as VNet, VicRoads' intranet. VNet is considered the organisations key communication tool and the source of truth for organisational information, whereas, Yammer is positioned to support discussion and engagement in the organisation.

Fig. 2 Screenshot of Friday funny post

3.2.3 Example 3: Finding Areas of Business Improvement

One of the roles of the community manager is to regularly monitor their social networks. They therefore have a reasonable view of:

- the types of messages and conversations taking place in the network
- which users regularly communicate with each other
- employee sentiment towards issues raised in the organisation
- where any gaps in employee knowledge or communication flow may exist.

This knowledge puts community managers in a good position to enable network-informed associating. This occurs when, through observing connections in the network, an individual can see where holes may exist, not only in the network but also in the organisation, with the view to bridging the gap [8]. For VicRoads, through Jacqueline's knowledge of the network plus the advantage of being part of the internal communication team she was able to identify gaps in people's knowledge and develop strategies to improve the reputation and operation of business groups in the organisation.

| All Company

Frog Andtoad
August 18 at 2:49pm

Follow

The F&T August edition is now available in sweet sweet hard copy. If you love the smell of freshly printed ink or you're worried about catching cooties from your colleagues, let me know and I'll send you out your very own germ-free hard copy. Booyah!

Like · Reply · Share · More

👍   and 3 others like this

August 18 at 3:03pm

Thanks Frog Andtoad - I would love a crisp hard copy! Also, if you have a July edition lying around, I would like one of those, too. Thanks!!

cc: Frog Andtoad
Like · Reply · Share · More

August 18 at 3:07pm

raises hand I'll take a hard copy! :-D
Like · Reply · Share · More

August 18 at 3:11pm

If you send one out to Spring St we'll leave it in the tea room
Like · Reply · Share · More
👍   likes this

August 18 at 3:25pm

Can we please get few copies for the KEW contact center :)
Like · Reply · Share · More

Frog Andtoad
August 18 at 4:10pm

Free copies for all! Yep, I'm just an all round good guy. What I lack in humility, I make up for in generosity.
Like · Reply · Share · More
👍   and   like this

Fig. 3 Screenshot of Frog and toad avatar

VicRoads' Facilities Management group has used Yammer to improve their reputation and engagement with employees. Previously the group had an image problem; their reputation was not positive in the organisation. Jacqueline believed there was a gap in employee understanding of the work the group undertook and a solution could be found using Yammer.

Jacqueline's first step was to meet with Facilities Management leaders and openly discuss the issue. She alerted them to their reputational problem and suggested that they could benefit from using Yammer. She highlighted that Yammer could give them a voice in the organisation allowing them to quickly and easily let people know what they do and get recognition for their efforts.

Facilities Management undertook a series of activities with Jacqueline's support. She helped them create an avatar that represented their group so they could post under the one name (see Fig. 4). The group then took pictures of the jobs they were undertaking, such as window and carpet cleaning, and posted them as updates to the network. If maintenance issues were raised by employees, Jacqueline would privately message the group to ask them to address the issue on Yammer—allowing the Facilities Management team's responses to be seen by everyone in the network, promoting transparency of the team across Yammer and positively increasing their profile.

Initially, the use of Yammer by Facilities Management was guarded. Response to employee questions on the network was slow due to the Facilities Management

Fig. 4 Screenshot of VicRoads' facilities management avatar

leadership wanting to have approval of all responses before they were posted. Jacqueline's encouragement allowed their confidence to grow and their capacity to answer questions quickly increased. This also required trust to be placed in Facilities Management employees to answer questions appropriately without a heavy reliance on leader approvals.

As a result of using Yammer to communicate with employees, the Facilities Management group saw a positive change in their reputation within VicRoads and Jacqueline reported employees now have a greater understanding of what the group does. Today, Facilities Management effectively uses Yammer as a quick and easy way to update employees on their activities and also post their participation in initiatives such as Earth Hour to promote their corporate citizenships efforts. Further, the group has incorporated the use of Yammer into their future communication strategies.

Developing governance policies, maintaining user engagement and encouraging business area participation in Yammer are three significant tasks that a community manager needs to undertake. These tasks also promote some of Reimer and Richter's [14] determined benefits of enterprise social media: socialising, information sharing and awareness creation. For VicRoads maintaining user engagement through conducting regular activities enabled socialisation and further information sharing, while creating awareness of the a team's work improved the reputation of VicRoads' business area Facilities Management.

3.3 Growing the network

Implementing an engagement strategy is also an important activity for the long-term growth and maintenance of the network. During the initial stages of Yammer use in VicRoads, Jacqueline recalls that the sentiment from employees was that it was 'Facebook for work' implying that participating on Yammer was a frivolous, social activity. Her appointment to community manager in late 2011 was to focus on improving employee engagement with Yammer and its business value to the organisation. One of the first roles for Jacqueline was to develop an engagement strategy to change the employee mindset towards Yammer to be a genuine communication tool. This engagement strategy was implemented in two stages between 2012 and 2014.

3.3.1 Stage 1: Moving Mindsets

The first stage, implemented in 2012, focused on changing the perception of Yammer from a social tool to a communication and business tool. This was a two-phase approached: identifying key Yammer users and addressing barriers to use of the network, and educating employees on Yammer use.

Phase 1: Identifying Key Users and Addressing Barriers to Use

The first phase was to identify people within the network who could use Yammer effectively (e.g., for discussing business activities) and who would encourage others to use it too. Key Yammer users were identified by:

- their position in the organisation, such as senior staff members
- their influence on the network, such as subject matter experts of key business areas
- their current contribution to Yammer, popular users on Yammer can display informal leadership and influence the network.

To enable this, an education process was undertaken to teach key users how to participate in the network. The process also addressed their concerns on risks of using the network and encouraged subject matter experts to respond to questions on Yammer increasing the usefulness of the tool for employees looking for organisational information.

Phase 2: Educating Employees on Yammer Use

The second phase focused on educating employees on how to use the network. This included identifying what business groups in the organisation could benefit from using it for communication and collaboration.

For a community manager like Jacqueline, to implement this strategy involved a lot of behind the scenes work, including:

- meeting with senior leaders to explain why it was important for them to contribute to the network
- contacting people in the organisation to respond to questions being posted on the network
- updating education materials for people to learn about the technology
- providing employees with additional information on how Yammer was being used in the organisation through other communication channels.

After implementing the two-phase engagement strategy in 2012, Jacqueline reported there was a high level of Yammer use across VicRoads and some business areas also reported benefits to their work practices. For example, the VicRoads Service Desk team increased their use of Yammer to communicate to employees the status of important IT system changes or outages. They requested an avatar to be developed for their group and they used it to post their updates (see Fig. 5). Since using Yammer the Service Desk has reported that they had an improvement in their operations; during system changes and outages, they have seen a reduction in phone calls and unnecessary enquiries from employees to them allowing them time to complete other necessary work. Jacqueline reported that employees now know Yammer is the quickest way to find out what is happening with IT if there is a problem. The just-in-time communication of short but relevant organisational

Fig. 5 Screenshot of VicRoads' service desk avatar

messages that can be delivered on Yammer has helped improved its reputation in VicRoads where it is now being considered a key communication tool.

3.4 Stage 2: Filling in the Gaps of When to Use Yammer

Building on previous success, the second stage of the engagement strategy focused on improving the use of Yammer through education of why, how and when people should use Yammer. The strategy ran for six months between April and September 2014 and involved:

- The why: Demonstrating the value of Yammer to organisational leaders to improve communication with their business area.
- The how: Forming communities of practice to show employees how to use the network as a business tool, as well as educating employees on the technology through usage tips.
- The when: Repositioning the use of internal communication tools within the organisation to help employees understand when they needed to use Yammer compared to other options like the intranet or face-to-face communication.

Following the two engagement strategies, Jacqueline reported that VicRoads Yammer usage has increased significantly with the vast majority of employees now signed into the network. In 2014, on average 79 employees per month created a Yammer account. The activity on the network also increased: between June and December 2014, on average 1300 messages were posted each month, double the number of messages posted in the previous six months at an average of 661 messages per month (see Fig. 6).

The perception of Yammer has also changed, Jacqueline elaborates, "There is no more resistance; some people do not find it valuable but they won't say that it is a waste of time. It's definitely a work tool and it is included in people's communication plans now. It is part of the fabric of the organisation".

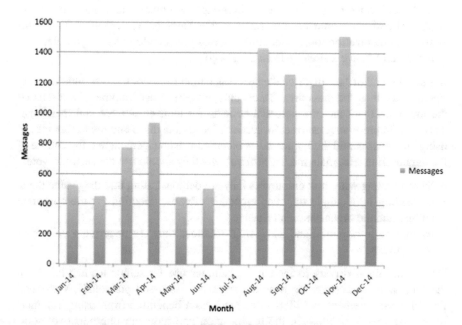

Fig. 6 Messages posted per month on the VicRoads' Yammer network

4 Lessons Learnt by a Community Manager

As VicRoads' community manager, between 2011 and 2015, Jacqueline guided the network to its current maturity level. For future community managers, some of Jacqueline's key lessons when developing VicRoads' enterprise social network community included:

- **Educate the community on how they can use the technology.** Jacqueline found that people wanted to be 'shown' how to use the tool. Being shown the tool's features and how to use them gave users greater confidence in using it and engaging with the network.
- **Partner with IT.** As a web-based platform, access to Yammer can be easily done without IT support, but Jacqueline found working with IT strengthened the development of the network. Assistance from the IT department helped her better understand the functionality of the technology and supported her management of the network when Yammer Inc. added new features to the enterprise tool.
- **Target stakeholders to develop the network.** In Jacqueline's strategies, senior leaders of different business areas were targeted to help them understand the value of the technology in their operational area.
- **Have a strategy.** Growth of the VicRoads network did not happen overnight. Dedicated strategies were the key in building user numbers and engagement levels and shifting employee mindset to where Yammer was regarded as a valuable communication tool. Jacqueline believes you should not start your network organically, "have a strategy from the get go".

In her role, one of her major challenges was helping leaders see the value in using Yammer for their business area. To encourage them to use Yammer she discussed the tool with them and the potential benefits for their employees and their business area. In presentations to senior leaders, Jacqueline discussed the advantages of using the network and the impact it has on employee engagement and the culture of the organisation. Her main messages about why they should use the network were:

- by connecting with their employees they are demonstrating that they value them
- by leading by example they can embed VicRoads' direction for the corporate culture and the organisation's values
- by sharing information and answering questions they are fostering a culture of transparency.

One of the main drivers to increasing Yammer use by senior leaders has been the success of early-adopting business areas. As discussed previously, VicRoads' Facilities Management and IT Service Desk both benefitted from using Yammer: improving their reputation in the organisation and reducing unproductive work. These early case studies, when highlighted by Jacqueline to senior leaders have led to more business areas in the organisation wanting to use the network to communicate to employees and promote their work.

A major success story for senior leadership engagement with employees at VicRoads was the use of Yammer by their Chief Executive (CE). Participation in the network by the CE has helped VicRoads achieve a positive cultural shift in transparency and trust within the organisation. The VicRoads' strategic commitment is to 'Care, Share and Dare': care about people, share to achieve better outcomes together and be daring by seizing opportunities and taking on challenges. This commitment was important to the organisation as it represents VicRoads' cultural goal and previous to this employees had felt that they weren't allowed to question and address issues concerning them. Open question and answer sessions on Yammer between employees and the CE, called Yammer Chats, has been one way in which VicRoads has changed this sentiment and allowed people to have a voice and feel comfortable speaking up and asking questions.

VicRoads introduced Yammer Chats in 2011 were its Chief Executive leads a live question and answer session on Yammer with employees about organisational developments and changes. Employees are notified by email of the time the Yammer Chat will take place and, depending on the topic, the CE may be supported by a subject matter expert or a member of the internal communication team. VicRoads have used Yammer Chats to assist with crisis management and to build on its strategic commitments. In 2014, the Victorian government announced that VicRoads would be relocating select jobs to the town of Ballarat [6]. This development naturally upset employees as no internal announcement had yet been made. A Yammer Chat was quickly organised in the following days to discuss the announcement and allow employees to ask questions and alleviate their concerns directly to the CE. Feedback about the session was that employees appreciated the time that the CE took to address the issue and giving them an opportunity to raise any questions they had.

Undertaking a Yammer Chat takes advantage of Yammer's capacity to enable many-to-many communication. The questions directed to the Chief Executive could be seen by everyone logged into Yammer, not just the person asking the question and the CE. The conversation could be viewed live by users as it took place or at later date and time, allowing people to read and participate in the conversations at a more appropriate time for them.

Today, Yammer Chats are regularly used by VicRoads as a way to communicate with employees when there is a need to discuss an issue or an organisational initiative. In April 2015, it was used to discuss VicRoads' new strategic commitment (see Fig. 7). Jacqueline believes that the effect of initiatives such as Yammer Chats on VicRoads employees is that they now feel that they have a voice, she remarks, "Previous to Yammer people thought they weren't able to ask questions; people now feel comfortable asking any question, even about the elephant in the room".

The change in culture is one of the main benefits that Yammer has provided VicRoads. The open two-way communication between senior leadership and employees has been facilitated by Yammer. However, it has been the work conducted by the community manager that has helped foster the appropriate behaviours to guide the cultural change.

Fig. 7 Screenshot of a Yammer Chat discussing VicRoads' strategic commitment

5 What's Next for VicRoads? Further Integration

Technology analysts from professional services firm Price Waterhouse Coopers believe social media technologies are advanced to the point where organisations are embedding the software into other enterprise systems and tools for greater integration of social interaction and processes within the enterprise [12]. VicRoads' use aligns with this finding, as it has now started to integrate Yammer into other platforms.

In February 2015, the organisation launched a new intranet. As part of the new design, the Yammer All Company feed is now accessible from the intranet home page (see Fig. 8). Employees no longer need to access a separate web interface to see the conversations happening within the network. Within two weeks of this change VicRoads saw 400 new members signed up (see Fig. 9). The number of employee accounts the organisation now has totals 3166 out of a potential 3500.

Fig. 8 Screenshot of VNet, VicRoads' intranet homepage with Yammer integration

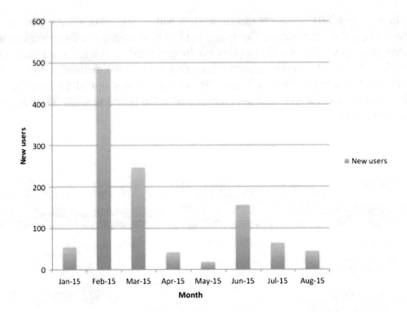

Fig. 9 New users on the VicRoads' Yammer network after integration with the VNet intranet

6 Conclusion

At its essence, social media is simply another way for people to communicate with each other. For some organisations, introducing a tool like Yammer may do no more than impose another communication tool on employees that they may or may not use. However, for business areas in VicRoads, communicating with employees through Yammer has brought about a sense of openness and transparency that has led to improved employee understanding and trust as well as a reduction in unproductive work. Through the simple act of sharing images of their work activities, VicRoads Facilities Management were able improve their reputation in the organisation. And by posting messages on Yammer about disruptions to the IT service, VicRoads' Service Desk were able to reduce the number of unproductive enquiries they received, freeing up employees to perform necessary tasks. Using Yammer allowed the business areas to share information in a different, more responsive way and by choosing to share openly they have been able to affect change in their own business operations.

The Chief Executive helped change the culture of the organisation; moving from a 'no questions asked' culture to a 'care, dare and share' culture where people felt comfortable enough to ask questions of anyone in the organisation. Yammer was able to help facilitate the transition. The platform enabled people to ask questions in an easy way to the CE, increasing employees access the CE's opinions and direction for the organisation. It also allowed people in the network to view the conversations between the CE and other employees regardless of whether or not they chose to participate in the discussion. The open and accessible nature of the tool has reflected the open and accessible intent of the CE and the new culture that needed to be implemented in VicRoads.

For Facilities Management, the Service Desk and the CE, the business benefit they needed from Yammer was different but the tool was able to address all needs. The community manager was the facilitator between them and the tool. This role helped build the network and inform employees on how to use it. It was also the community manager who helped determine the gaps in understanding between them and employees and facilitate closing those gaps through engagement with the network. Through appropriate resourcing, strategic engagement and senior leadership participation, VicRoads have been able to develop a mature social network within their organisation that has led to improved employee engagement, employee behaviour change and integration of Yammer into the organisation as highly regarded communication and business tool.

Acknowledgements Thanks to Jacqueline Shields and Dave Jacobson from VicRoads Internal Communication as well as Michelle Lambert for their support of this case study and help in collecting data.

References

1. Bird, D., Ling, M., & Haynes, Katharine. (2012). Flooding Facebook—the use of social media during the Queensland and Victorian floods. *The Australian Journal of Emergency Management, 27*(1), 27–33.
2. Jamieson, A. (2011). The Government Department with a census of humour. *Crikey,* August 10. http://www.crikey.com.au/2011/08/10/the-govt-department-with-a-census-of-humour. Accessed 25 June 2015.
3. Kimmerle, J., & Cress, U. (2008). Knowledge communication with shared databases. In S. Kelsey, & K. St.Amant (Eds.), *Handbook of research on computer mediated communication* (pp. 424–435). Hershey: IGI Global. doi:10.4018/978-1-59904-863-5
4. Kiron, D. (2012). How finding "Exceptions" can jump start your social initiative. *MIT Sloan Management Review,* September 5. http://sloanreview.mit.edu/article/how-finding-exceptions-can-jump-start-your-social-initiative/. Accessed 29 August 2015.
5. Leonardi, P. M., Huysman, M., & Steinfield, C. (2013). Enterprise social media: Definition, history and prospects for the study of social technologies in organisations. *Journal of Computer-Mediated Communication, 19*, 1–19.
6. Lillebuen, S. (2014). VicRoads headquarters to move to Ballarat. *The Age.* March 30. http://www.theage.com.au/victoria/vicroads-headquarters-to-move-to-ballarat-20140330-35rjl.html. Accessed 27 July 2015.
7. Lunden, I. (2013). A year after Microsoft bought it, Yammer nears 8M users, deeper MSFT integration… and Klout. *TechCrunch,* June 25. http://techcrunch.com/2013/06/25/a-year-after-microsoft-bought-it-yammer-nears-8m-users-plans-for-deeper-integration-and-a-new-klout-partnership. Accessed 19 July 2015.
8. Majchrzak, A., Faraj, S., Kane, G. C., & Azad, B. (2013). The contradictory influence of social media affordances on online communal knowledge Sharing. *Journal of Computer-Mediated Communication, 19*, 38–55.

9. Manchester, A. (2010). *How to use social media to solve critical internal communication issues*. London, UK: Melcrum Publishing Limited.
10. McKinsey Global Institute. (2013). Business and Web 2.0: An interactive feature. http://www.mckinsey.com/insights/business_technology/business_and_web_20_an_interactive_feature. Accessed 29 May 2015.
11. Microsoft News. (2014). Yammer co-founder David Sacks is leaving Microsoft, Yammer team is now under Office 365 organisation. http://microsoft-news.com/yammer-co-founder-david-sacks-is-leaving-microsoft-yammer-team-is-now-under-office-365-organisation/. Accessed 19 July 2015.
12. Morrison, A., & Parker, B. (2011). The collaboration paradox. *Technology Forecast, 3*, 7–17.
13. Queensland Police Service. (2011). *Disaster management and social media—a case study*. Brisbane: Queensland Police Service.
14. Reimer, K., & Richter, A. (2012). *SOCIAL—emergent enterprise social networking use cases: A multi case study comparison*. Sydney: University of Sydney Business School.
15. Riemer, K., Scifleet, P., & Reddig, R. (2012). *Powercrowd: Enterprise social networking in professional service work: A case study of Yammer in deloitte Australia*. Sydney: University of Sydney Business School.
16. Riordan, K. (2011). Police tweet on the beat during flood crisis. *ABC,* January 20 January. http://www.abc.net.au/news/2011-01-20/police-tweet-on-the-beat-during-flood-crisis/1912328. Accessed 25 June 2015.
17. Schmidtchen, D., Sturrock, A., Rowles, M., Mao, Q., Paton, E., Cotton, T., et al. (2013). *State of the service report—State of the service series 2012–13*. Canberra: Australian Public Service Commission.
18. Willimas, P., & Hill, A. (2013). *Rethinking social media: Building the social organisation through HR*. Sydney: Deloitte Centre for the Edge.
19. Yuan, Y. Connie., Zhao, Xuan., Liao, Q., & Chi, C. (2013). The use of different information and communication technologies to support knowledge in organisations: From e-mail to micro-blogging. *Journal of the American Society for Information Science and Technology, 64*, 1659–1670. doi:10.1002/asi.22863

The Role of Political Leadership in Driving Citizens' Engagement Through Social Media: The Case of Dubai's Public Sector

Mhamed Biygautane and May Al-Taee

Abstract This chapter examines the use of social media in Dubai's government from a public policy perspective. It traces its development and the intrinsic role of political leadership in encouraging and creating a virtual space for brainstorming important policy matters with a wider public audience. The chapter argues that the technological advancement Dubai and the United Arab Emirates (UAE) (Dubai is one of the seven Emirates that form the United Arab Emirates. Other Emirates in alphabetical order are Abu Dhabi (which serves as the capital), Ajman, Dubai, Fujairah, Ras al-Khaimah, Sharjah, and Umm al-Quwain.) achieved in the past few decades, has facilitated the exploitation of social media tools and allowed the engagement of the public in policy making. This is a result of the political leadership's firm willingness to modernize its public administration and involve the public in shaping public policy. Dubai currently serves as a catalyst for other governments of the Gulf and the wider Middle East and North Africa (MENA) region to utilize social media to formulate public policies that are supported and co-formed by the public.

Keywords Social media · Public policy and administration · E-government · Dubai · Gulf cooperation council · Middle East and North Africa

M. Biygautane (✉) · M. Al-Taee
Center for Commercial Law and Regulatory Studies, Faculty of Law,
Clayton Campus, Monash University, 3800 Victoria, Australia
e-mail: mhamed.biygautane@monash.edu

M. Al-Taee
Zayed University, Dubai, UAE

© Springer International Publishing Switzerland 2015
S. Nepal et al. (eds.), *Social Media for Government Services*,
DOI 10.1007/978-3-319-27237-5_4

1 Introduction

The purpose of this chapter is to analyse the utilization of social media in Dubai's government to connect and interact with the public. It traces the development of e-government in Dubai and assesses its information and communications technology (ICT) readiness to effectively communicate with the public. More importantly, the chapter sheds light on the influential role of Dubai's political leadership in fostering a culture of virtual communication with the public. While other developing countries of the Middle East and North Africa (MENA) region find it difficult to adopt and implement effective e-government programs due to financial constraints [4], [43], Dubai has successfully utilized its financial resources to build a state-of-the-art ICT infrastructure.

This chapter is organized as follows. After this introduction, Sect. 2 examines the evolution of the World Wide Web and social media tools. Section 3 briefly revisits the existing literature on engaging citizens in policy-making through the use of social media and its impact on public administration. It discusses the positive impact that social media have on citizens' trust in their government. Section 3 assesses Dubai's e-government infrastructure and technological readiness to communicate with citizens through social media platforms. It compares the United Arab Emirates (UAE) with other states of the Gulf Cooperation Council (GCC)[1] and finds that the UAE and Dubai have topped most international rankings in terms of information and communications technology (ICT) readiness and sophistication. Section 4 illustrates the role of Dubai's political leadership in encouraging the use of social media to communicate directly with the public. It also presents findings from a comprehensive survey tool that was distributed to all government entities in Dubai in order to understand their motivation for relying on social media platforms for internal communications, the rationale for using social media channels to include citizens in policy and decision making, and key challenges that they face [7]. Moreover, it discusses some of the issues that government entities in Dubai must tackle in order to better utilize social media networks. Questions on the use of social media were part of a larger pool of inquiries that investigated knowledge management practices within Dubai's public sector [7].

2 The Evolution of the Web and Social Media

One of the most popular services on the Internet is the World Wide Web, a worldwide library of information that is made available to anyone connected to the Internet [42]. The existence of the Web has thus transformed the practice of information sharing, retrieval, and communication. Up until recently, however, the

---

[1]Gulf Cooperation Council is made of six oil exporting states of Bahrain, Kuwait, Oman, Qatar, Saudi Arabia, and the United Arab Emirates.

potential of web technologies for socialization and interaction had not been fully realized [13].

Originally, the Web was designed to be a repository of texts and information for human use. However, its significant growth has now initiated a considerable increase in the expectations for web-based information retrieval, knowledge sharing, and collaborative work [12]. Although the Web has not undergone an update in its technical specifications, it has undergone collective changes in the ways in which end-users make use of it. In the past, the Web connected people to a public and shared environment; however, it did not allow direct communication between Web readers and writers unless the writers made their contact information readily available [13]. A huge number of people globally use the Web as a means of sharing personal information, videos, and photos. Making a web page available or publishing it for all people on the Internet to explore is a service available to all, and in some cases incurs no costs [42]. The second evolution of the Web (social media) is being witnessed currently, in which individuals are not only connected to the Web, but also connected together through a web platform. This solves the previous gap existing between web readers and writers [13]. The combined set of tools used to underline activities of collaboration and sharing among end-users are called "social media" or "social networking tools" [12]. Millions of people are joining worldwide online communities known as "social media" websites. These websites encourage members to share their ideas, interests, studies, photos, videos, and music with other registered users. Now, millions of people publish their thoughts on the web by utilizing blogs, which are informal websites similar to a diary or journal [42]. A popular way of verbally sharing information on the Web is podcasts. In recent times, with the evolution of the Web and the development of social media tools, such as blogs, a more amorphous, self-governing approach to the creation, capture, and transfer of information is being offered.

Adding "SLATES" features can enhance existing information and communication technology channels and platforms. "SLATES" is an acronym for Search, Links, Authoring, Tags, Extensions, and Signal introduced by McAfee [29] to distinguish the key features of these new social media technologies and their potentials in corporate contexts.

- Search: Refers to the efficiency of users to locate dispersed information on the internet
- Links: Refers to the use of links to build thorough information content interconnections among collaborating enterprises
- Authoring: Refers to the user-driven content development and publishing across an organization
- Tags: Refers to the establishment of peer-driven classification and validation of online content among collaborating enterprises
- Extensions: Involves drawing out information from previously gathered data on user activities to enable users to received advice on initiating other valuable activities. For instance, Amazon.com offers an option indicating, "Customers who bought this item also bought…"

Table 1 Social media technologies

Technology	Description
Blogging (blogs)	A blog is a self-publishing tool that resembles an online journal, in which an owner can periodically post messages. Readers can subscribe to a blog, link to it, share links, post comments in an interactive format, and indicate their social relationship to other bloggers who read the particular blog
Wikis	A wiki is a website that facilitates online collaboration by allowing multiple users to add, remove, edit, and change content. It also allows linking among any number of pages
Social bookmarking	Social bookmarking allows users to post their lists of bookmarks or favourite websites for other users to search and view
Tagging	Tagging is the use of keywords to track content on websites. It can be used as a form of social bookmarking, where a user can gain access to all of the content identified by other users and linked to a specific keyword
Really simple syndication (RSS)	RSS is a web feed format used to publish frequently updated content. It allows users to subscribe to their favorite "feeds" and receive automatic updates
Collaborative real-time editors	A collaborative real-time editor is an application that allows simultaneous editing of a text or media file by different participants in a network

Source Van Zyl [55]

- Signal: Refers to sending alerts to users about the changing state of an element of interest, such as the online status of other users in instant messaging clients

Table 1 highlights the most popular types of social media technologies currently implemented in organizations. The descriptions emphasize their online collaborative nature and the platforms they provide for user-generated content sharing.

One cannot be sure what the next stage of Web evolution or social media will be; nonetheless, it is safe to say that there is a movement toward a semantic Web. Once it has matured, the semantic Web aims to connect virtual representatives of real people using the Web [44]. This will result in maximization of the exploration of Web resources [13].

3 Engaging Citizens Through the Use of Social Media: Impact on Public Administration

Information and communication technology advancements have introduced unprecedented channels of communication that defy notions of space and time. Social media tools provide innovative platforms for fast, effective, and direct interpersonal and group communications among individuals regardless of their geographic locations [5]. Bertot et al. [6] classify social media tools into those for microblogging (Twitter), social sharing (YouTube, Flickr, and StumbleUpon), text messaging and discussions (wikis), virtual worlds (Second Life), and social networking services (Facebook and MySpace). Social media applications are primarily designed to facilitate social connectivity among people, and while they have been widely used among friends and families to communicate and share images and documents, they have begun to form official communication channels between the public and governments [22]. Government officials are increasingly relying on social media sources to gather data, exchange views and opinions, and hold discussions with their citizenry regarding what policy options they think would best serve their needs. Moreover, social media offer the opportunity to include segments of society that have not previously been involved in policy-making processes [6].

Social media applications offer numerous opportunities for governments to interact with their stakeholders in a more informal manner, and are considered extensions of traditional e-government or Web 2.0 tools [26]. The literature sometimes uses social media and Web 2.0 interchangeably [21], yet these two concepts differ quite significantly in their functions. Web 2.0 encourages the sharing of web content, while social media allow the "creation and exchange of user-generated content [37]. Mergel [30] states that the key distinction between social media and e-government services is that the former is provided by third parties and lies outside the direct control of government organizations. Social media allow "many-to-many" communication and user-generated content [38, 53]. Moreover, social media applications allow multiple contributors and active, live discussions. They have not necessarily replaced the e-government channels, but rather have complemented and reinforced their use. Kholidy et al. [23] argue that social media represent a transformational movement from e-government, with its focus on "efficiency and service delivery to integration and participation of citizens in government" (p. 406). In a similar vein, Linders [25] asserts that there has been a gradual shift from e-government, which treats citizens as "customers," to "we-government," in which citizens are no longer considered customers of government services, but rather partners in crafting and designing public policies. This partnership serves the public sector better by allowing it to benefit from the "wisdom of the crowds" [33] and get invaluable primary data directly from citizens. Kholidy et al. [23] stresses the benefits that policy makers can harvest from data mined from Facebook and Twitter pages concerning ways that they can deliver policies that are more focused, well-targeted, and better formulated. This has the potential to enhance the credibility and legitimacy of the government [10].

Van Zyl [55] highlights the criteria of social media that may enable the engagement of citizens. First is their capability to support social networking, namely, the discovery of potential relationships and the transformation of potential ties into weak and strong ties. This leads to the second criterion of social media: their capability to enable social feedback. For instance, a citizen can determine whether he or she wishes to establish a connection with another citizen needed for some form of social feedback, or a "digital reputation" can be formed that enables other citizens to rate the contributions of others. A digital reputation is a useful feature, as it allows citizens to identify whether or not a person holds the knowledge, expertise, and experience he or she claims to have, and then decide whether establishment of a strong or weak tie with that person would provide added value. Lastly, Van Zyl [55] highlights the capabilities of social media to support two or more of the following modes of computer-mediated communication in order to facilitate citizens' engagement process: one-to-one communications, such as instant messaging services, one-to-many communications, such as blogs, and many-to-many communications, such as wikis. Hence, contrary to the traditional information and communication methods that were more top-down or one-sided, the emphasis of social media is on conversations in which the platform is open for all participants to share knowledge and opinions.

McAfee [29] focuses on the social aspects of social media that enable tools to enrich citizens' interactions. They are social:

- In the way the way they are conceived—bringing together connected tools for users in a networked approach;
- In their purpose—encouraging mutual understanding by augmenting and expanding online and offline social interaction; and
- In the way they behave—instead of forcing the user to adapt to the tools, they adapt to the user. The tools emerge as a form of ameliorating under-representation, thereby expanding human interaction rather than limiting it [8].

Similarly, Coakes [11] suggests that the ways in which social media allow knowledge exchange and "sense-making" for tools depend mostly on social aspects of everyday life, and not technological ones. Thus, social media facilitate the emergence and discussion of a diverse range of topics. Additionally, Tredinnick [54] suggests that the potential for innovation of social media in government organizations does not emerge from technological breakthroughs; instead, it emerges from the potential to change the roles of social actors and constructs (for instance individuals, teams, departments, and citizens). Particularly, Tredinnick [54] highlights the special characteristics of social media (such as their openness and self-organized information structures) that allow governments to take advantage of the collective experience of users.

In light of the above, the two main benefits that social media can provide to public administration are their capabilities to enhance transparency and to increase citizen partnership [34]. Social media have enabled citizen-created content that enriches discussions, diversity of opinions, and free flow of information. They are used to engage citizens, exchange a variety of opinions, and share information. In addition, public administrators can benefit from the formation of the participative culture that is instilled in many citizens to bring their attention to the area of municipal management, connect them in the process of local public decision-making, and, as a result, enhance the government-to-citizen relationship [34].

Since social media tools enrich government communication with external stakeholders and increase internal knowledge management, their impact on the public sector can be perceived in four areas [32, 34]. Firstly, public sector transparency can be enhanced by bringing citizens together with the public sector agenda and activities, and providing updates and information on them using the platform preferred by citizens. Secondly, policy-making can be enhanced by using new ways of participation that improve citizen engagement and social consciousness. Thirdly, public services can be enhanced as a result of creative means for service delivery. Lastly, knowledge management can be enhanced through the closer relationships among governments and various public entities [32]. Thus, social media can be used in governments for mass redistribution of contents and opening of corporate dialogues between government officials and individual citizens [39].

Bertot et al. [6], highlights the opportunities that social media provide to governments, including the facilitation of democratic participation and engagement. This is achieved by allowing the participation of the public in government discussions and by giving the public a voice in policy formulation. Another opportunity is in the coproduction of content between the government and the public, in which they collectively work on establishing and delivering government services to enhance government performance and quality [6]. Also, social media provide an opportunity for crowdsourcing solutions and innovations, in which creativity is sought through public knowledge and skills to develop solutions. This is achieved by the government sharing information so that the public has a basis on which to provide such innovations and solutions. However, it has been observed that most social media initiatives are currently used for their educational and informational value rather than for direct interactions with the citizenry [30, 53]. This is largely due to governments' regulations and restrictions regarding the extent to which government officials can share information and interact with the public. Thus, social media have become a "central component of e-government in a very short period of time" [6].

Naturally, while these opportunities present a promising platform, they present new challenges in the transformation of government community interaction [6]. For instance, Van Zyl [55] explains how social media can be counterproductive by highlighting that the same perceived positives could turn into perceived negatives, i.e., employees may spend too much time posting and networking so instead of the tools increasing productivity they may lead to a decrease in productivity. On a similar note, McAfee [8] explains that there is a threat that knowledge workers will either not use these technologies due to their demanding, busy schedules or use them but they do not produce the intended outcomes. In addition, the reliability of the content is questionable, while user generated content could be an advantage, the content published in social media platforms is not guaranteed [55]. Furthermore, the efficiency of the social media platform is questionable, in relation to the bandwidth and server required and network utilisation [55]. Finally, issues of security, privacy and trust, knowing what, how much, when and how to share arise [16, 24, 31].

Martin et al. [28] discusses the challenges of implementing social media in government organizations, highlighting the need for policies and procedures to govern the use of social media. The policies and procedures can be laid out lightly such as the case of Microsoft ('do not write anything on blogs that would get you into trouble'), in a formal manner or some social computing guidelines that encourage the use of social media. Given the novelty of social media tools and their recent emergence in the public sector, there is a gap in the literature in terms of standardized policies and procedures to use. Nonetheless, there is a consensus that for organisations to succeed in adopting these tools there should be some guidelines [28, 46]. Moreover, to ensure the successful application of social media tools in government organizations there are number of factors that need to be present. Firstly, managerial support is essential when introducing these new set of tools [28, 29, 36, 41]. Although previous tools such as emails did not need managers to encourage the use of, they cannot also look into people's shoulders and tell them 'tag this or make a link or now blog about what you just did' [8]. As easy to use and intuitive [29] the social media tools are, they depend mainly on the decisions and actions taken by managers [29]. A study implemented by Paroutis and Saleh [36] of key determinants of knowledge sharing using social media tools showed that the managerial role in adopting these technologies is remarkable. They conclude that managers should be an active role in supporting social media tools, considering it as a strategic communication and interaction initiative. As a result, showcasing its benefits to employees, training and equipping them with the necessary set of skills and rewarding them for adopting the tools, for instance the "top rated blog" award or the "most active blog" or "best wiki contribution".

Schneckenberg [41] (p. 509), highlights the opportunity of social media to facilitate the process of organisational learning and knowledge exchange in public organizations but identifies that this depends on the "openness, freedom and employee empowerment in corporate environments". He enlists empowerment to be a key challenge for corporate innovation and for the use of social to enable collaboration, interaction and ideas exchange. He highlights that the main challenge is "the managerial task of balancing those inherent process inconsistencies that evolve between top down control and bottom up empowerment in period of intense organisational change" [41] (p. 517). Similarly, providing a receptive culture [41] one that encourages new collaboration practices and having a common platform is important. For instance one large wiki is better than many unconnected ones, for a common platform encourages collaboration and knowledge sharing [29]. These design and implementation lessons can be learned from government social media initiatives launched.

4 Readiness of Dubai to Engage Citizens Through Social Media Channels

4.1 Regional Comparisons and Perspectives

Dubai believes that building the necessary institutional and organizational support for e-government is essential to transform the government's bureaucratic apparatus into one that is digitalized, efficient, and smooth. Hence, Mohammed Bin Rashid Al-Maktoum, the Ruler of Dubai, created the E-government Department

Table 2 Demographic and internet usage information in the GCC states

GCC states	Population (2014 Est.)	Users Dec-00	Internet usage 30-Jun-14	% Population (penetration)
Bahrain	1,314,089	40,000	1,297,500	98.70
Kuwait	3,268,431	150,000	3,022,010	92.50
Oman	3,219,775	90,000	2,584,316	80.30
Qatar	2,123,160	30,000	2,016,400	95.00
Saudi Arabia	27,345,986	200,000	18,300,000	66.90
United Arab Emirates	9,206,000	735,000	8,807,226	95.70 %

Source www.Worldinternet.com

in 2001 within the Ruler's Court. The Department's main mission is to "direct and supervise the implementation of e-transformation in the Dubai Government" [14]. It plays the role of a central unit with the direct political support of the Ruler to ensure that all governmental entities within Dubai's government align their e-government strategies with that of the central government. Since its inception, its goal has been to "achieve a virtual government through the provision of high-quality, customer-focused e-services for individuals, businesses, and government departments, and to promote e-service adoption through customer management." [16]. It has achieved remarkable success in ensuring that all government entities in Dubai have operational websites that provide high-quality services online. Around 2000 government services, from car registration to utility bill payment, are currently offered online without the need for the public to visit any branches in person [27]. In 2013, the name of the department was changed to the Smart Government Department to inaugurate a new phase in digital government development. This was aligned with the mobile government (m-government) initiative that the Ruler of Dubai announced, which aims to provide all government services via mobile phone. The motivation behind this initiative is the incredibly high level of mobile phone penetration that has exceeded 100 % of the overall population of the UAE. Each individual person has at least two smart phones in the UAE if not more [18]. Table 2 shows Internet usage in the UAE and other GCC states, demonstrating that more than 95 % of the UAE's residents used the Internet in 2014. Providing government services through mobile phones is expected to effectively increase people's satisfaction with these services and government effectiveness as a whole.

Building the physical ICT infrastructure is equally important to deliver high-quality e-government services and bring the government closer to the public. The UAE's government believes that promoting digital transformation is pivotal to creating an effective environment for citizens and businesses [16]. The UAE has succeeded in building the required technological tools for e-government, and this is proven by its high rankings in major international reports on innovation, education, and ICT. According to recent reports by the World Economic Forum and World Bank (Table 3), the UAE achieved the 46th rank globally in innovation, 55th in education, and 12th in ICT readiness. This makes the UAE one of the leading

Table 3 GCC states' rankings in innovation, education, and ICT

Innovation			Education			ICT		
Rank	Country	Score	Rank	Country	Score	Rank	Country	Score
46	**UAE**	**6.6**	45	Bahrain	6.78	1	Bahrain	9.54
49	Qatar	6.42	55	**UAE**	**5.8**	12	**UAE**	**8.88**
57	Oman	5.88	58	Saudi Arabia	5.65	21	Saudi Arabia	8.37
64	Kuwait	5.22	63	Oman	5.23	79	Qatar	6.65
75	Bahrain	4.61	74	Kuwait	3.7	89	Kuwait	6.53
84	Saudi Arabia	4.14	89	Qatar	3.41	90	Oman	6.49

Sources World Bank (2014), World Economic Forum's competitiveness report (2014)
*Bold representation in table entries show where the UAE stands when compared to the other countries

states of the GCC in terms of its physical ICT infrastructure and readiness. It currently tops most of the other GCC states in the majority of these rankings.

These achievements are the result of well-guided government strategies. The UAE has developed both federal and local strategies that have clear guidelines and objectives. For example, the UAE's e-Government Strategic Framework's (2012–2014) vision is to "advance the competitiveness of the UAE through the application of world class practices in all areas of e-government." As Al-Khouri [1] states, this strategy is a roadmap that will guide the work of all government entities toward an effective e-transformation of all of their services. The timeframe to transform the government into paperless administrative system is three years [27]. The detailed Framework also stresses the importance of an ICT-enabling environment that covers the policies and legislation necessary to carry out the e-government initiatives.

Table 4 illustrates the rankings of the UAE in the World Economic Forum's 2014 Global Information Technology Report. The report ranks around 148 countries based on their readiness in terms of several ICT indicators. As the table shows, the UAE tops the ten best performing countries in a select range of indicators. For example, among the GCC states it ranked 8th globally in availability of latest technologies, followed by Bahrain at 26th and Kuwait at 64th. In foreign direct investment (FDI) and technology transfer, it ranked 2nd globally, followed by Qatar in 4th place and Kuwait lagging behind with a global score of 144. It ranked 9th to tie with Bahrain in the Global Government Online Services Index, and scored 1st place in global importance of ICT to government vision. The UAE ranked 2nd in global impact of ICT on access to basic services and in global ICT use and government efficiency. These rankings are a reflection of the maturity of both the ICT infrastructure in the UAE and the capacity of its citizens and residents to use those technologies.

The United Nations' E-government Development Index is another reliable source that ranks the e-readiness of governments worldwide. In 2014, the UAE ranked second among the GCC states in this indicator with a score of 0.71. This is far ahead of the world average, which is currently around 0.47, and also ahead of other GCC states such as Kuwait, which scored only 0.62. Compared to ten years earlier, the UAE has made substantial progress from its previous score of 0.47. Saudi Arabia has also made a significant jump from a low score of 0.38 to a high

Table 4 ICT-faculty of law, clayton campus, Monash university indices in the GCC states

Global ranking out of 148 countries	Availability of latest technologies	FDI and technology transfer	Global government online services index	Global importance of ICT to government vision	Global impact of ICT on access to basic services	Global ICT use and government efficiency
Bahrain	26	10	9	14	18	13
Saudi Arabia	32	8	19	8	16	7
Kuwait	64	144	47	126	78	111
Oman	56	48	35	13	34	18
Qatar	20	4	27	2	1	3
UAE	**8**	**2**	**9**	**1**	**2**	**2**

Source World Economic Forum: the global information technology report (2014)

*Bold representation in table entries show where the UAE stands when compared to the other countries

Table 5 E-government development index in the GCC states

	2004 index	2014 index
Bahrain	0.53	0.80
United Arab Emirates	0.47	0.71
Qatar	0.40	0.63
Saudi Arabia	0.38	0.69
Kuwait	0.36	0.62
Oman	0.28	0.62

Source http://unpan3.un.org (2004–2014)

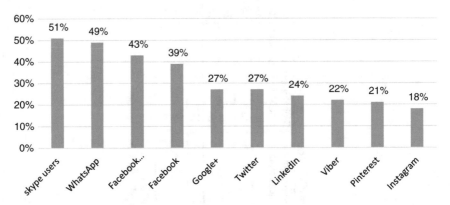

Fig. 1 Leading social networks in the UAE, *Source* http://www.statista.com/statistics/284504/united-arab-emirates-social-network-penetration/

0.69, while countries like Kuwait and Oman are now closer to Qatar's score of 0.63 (Table 5).

The availability of both a solid ICT infrastructure, and a population that highly relies on and utilizes the Internet make the government of the UAE one of the readiest in the world to embrace social media and communicate with its citizens through electronic channels. Since more than 100 % of the population utilizes smartphones (at least two smartphones in average), the governments of Dubai and the UAE are now striving to provide all services through mobile phones. Recent statistical data (Fig. 1) show that more than 40 % of Internet users in the UAE use Facebook messenger, and 39 % use Facebook to communicate with their friends and families. Moreover, around 27 % use Twitter and Google+. These positive numbers indicate that the government's investment in the needed infrastructure to communicate with citizens through social media outlets will be fruitful.

4.2 Political Leadership of the UAE and Dubai as Drivers for the Use of Social Media

The government of Dubai is among the few pioneers in the region to adopt social media networks as vehicles for service delivery and citizen engagement. The political leadership of Dubai represented by its Ruler, Mohammed Bin Rashid Al-Maktoum, believes that effective service delivery and communication with the public are strong pillars for sustained public trust in government. He is considered among the top ten global leaders in terms of numbers of followers on Facebook and Twitter, and was followed by more than 6 million users of social media in 2014 [47]. He actively uses Facebook and other social media channels to deliver messages to the public, ask for their opinions about new initiatives, and even to announce new policies and laws [32, 48].

Other influential political leaders in the UAE, such as the Crown Prince of Dubai, the Minister of State for Foreign Affairs, and other high level officials, are following his lead and harnessing the powers of social media to create direct and virtual bridges with the public. To further promote the healthy use of social media outlets, the Ruler of Dubai announced the "Arab Social Media Award," which aims to recognize and award the most influential and innovative users of social media in the Arab world. The awards are judged based on the three criteria of communication, creativity and impact, and have twenty categories ranging from government and media to the private sector and civil society [49]. This annual award will encourage public sector organizations to further innovate the ways in which they use social media to communicate and connect with people, and also motivate young people to use social media for constructive and positive purposes.

5 Engaging Citizens Through Social Media: The Role of Political Leadership in Driving Use

Since the political leadership of Dubai's government strongly encourages the utilization of social media to communicate with the public, it has not kept this posture only in its rhetoric, but has also translated it into action. In the past, the leaders of Dubai communicated with their citizens through what is known in Arabic as the *Majlis* (meeting Council) that was open for all citizens who had issues to report to their rulers. These open meetings with the public were held on a regular basis and have historically ensured the loyalty of people to their tribal leaders. Now, with the significant technological transformation witnessed by the Gulf region, this *Majlis* has been altered to a virtual one in which citizens' voice their concerns to their political leaders not through face-to-face informal meetings, but through social media channels that also ensure anonymity [20, 50]. YouTube is also used as an official platform to announce new policy decisions and to inform the public about policy-making mechanisms and the ways in which they can participate and voice their ideas to the government [48–50]. Saeed Al-Dhaheri, a UAE social media expert, emphasizes the role of social media in engaging citizens with policy makers to generate more effective and efficient public policies that can potentially serve the public good, saying that it is important to make it "so social media can become the channel of choice for the citizen to engage with the government and to have their voice reach their government. The purpose in the end is to improve the quality of services" [1].

Another important transformation that is taking place in Dubai and the UAE at large is that policy makers are reaching out to the public for their input regarding policy-making decisions through Twitter and Facebook. Nationwide brainstorming sessions via Twitter, in which policy makers gather suggestions and input from the public regarding local issues, have become the norm in the UAE [1]. The Ruler of Dubai and other high level officials have mined through all of the data gathered to gain innovative ideas from the public and take them into consideration while drafting new policies and legislation. In December 2013, the Prime Minister of the UAE called his citizens to participate in one of the largest online brainstorming sessions yet to discuss the most pressing issues facing health and education policies [49–51]. This brainstorming session attracted 41,000 tweets in English and 2700 in Arabic, and resulted in 81,000 new ideas that were sifted through and scrutinized carefully by analysts and government officials [10]. This brainstorming session resulted in some significant policy changes related to healthcare, such as the creation of a specialized medical board in the UAE. Also, most members of the Federal National Council communicate with the public through social media and pass their concerns on to the Ministers and policy makers in the government.

Government entities in Dubai have demonstrated their commitment to communication with the public through social media outlets. Currently, all 46 government entities in Dubai have social media accounts that are regularly updated and receive feedback from the public [14]. As a case in point, the Road and Transport Authority (RTA) of Dubai urges the public to publish their complaints through the Authority's Twitter and Facebook accounts. This helps the Authority become responsive to the public and more effective in handling their queries and issues. A spokesman of the Authority said, "Social media have changed the way we operate, and they are a very important tool for the RTA…We ensure that all of our employees know how to deal with social media, and this allows us to use them to their full potential" [45]. The same spokesperson was quoted saying, "Listening to them [the public] makes life easier for us—if we know what people are complaining about then we can solve it… We are hearing the public and listening very carefully to their suggestions. Managing the service is a real challenge, but for people it is easier to tweet us than call a call centre, and we are confident that we now have a clear policy and procedure to deal with these requests and are ready to respond." [45]. Posting complaints on social media channels allows other members to also voice their concerns and experiences and to provide the authorities with suggestions on how to improve their services. The Dubai Police Force is another key government entity that is adopting social media to enhance its service delivery. They publish quality insurance surveys through Twitter and ask the public for suggestions on how to enhance the quality of their services. They welcome the public's ideas, which are then sifted through by analysts and communicated to the responsible teams within the Dubai Police [51]. These are only two cases of how social media are becoming vital to the relationship between the governments and its people. Other entities are also following these examples and competing to demonstrate their commitment to citizen engagement in policy-making and also in improving the quality of services delivered to the public.

5.1 Dubai Government Entities' Motivations for Using Social Media

The Dubai School of Government distributed a long survey on knowledge management and the use of social media to communicate information among employees within government entities and the public in 2012. The surveys were filled out by HR, IT, and strategy directors of 19 key government entities in Dubai. The results of the survey offer important findings regarding the motivations for using social media within the government of Dubai [7].

When asked why government employees use social media internally, more than 70 % agreed that they use them to improve the transparency of knowledge and decision-making, and to enhance collaboration and knowledge-sharing. Social media create collaborative platforms that enable government officials to transparently and openly write their opinions and concerns and discuss them interactively. Moreover, as Table 6 illustrates, 70 % of respondents indicated that social media connect employees, consequently improving the efficiency of internal operations and innovation. Rather than using personal or group emails to communicate, government entities in Dubai are utilizing the faster method of internal groups on Facebook or WhatsApp to share ideas and news and to communicate in a more effective manner.

Table 6 Dubai public sector entities' motivations for using social media outlets

	Strongly agree	Agree	Neither agree or disagree	Disagree	Strongly disagree
Improving transparency of knowledge, information, and decision-making	41.9	32.6	11.6	0	0
Enhancing collaboration and knowledge-sharing	41.9	34.9	14.0	9.3	0
Stimulating innovation in organization processes	48.8	20.9	16.3	14.0	0
Increasing efficiency of operations by connecting staff	39.5	30.2	18.3	12	0

Table 7 Dubai public sector entities' motivations for using social media

	Strongly agree	Agree	Neither agree or disagree	Disagree	Strongly disagree
Raising citizens' awareness/ knowledge of government processes	37.2	37.2	14.0	11.6	0
Increasing citizens' trust in government	32	35.4	18.6	14.0	0
Engaging with citizens to inform and improve policy-making	30.2	37.2	16.3	16.3	0
Engaging with citizens to enhance service design and delivery	34.9	37.2	14.0	14.0	0

5.2 Using Social Media to Engage Citizens in Decision-Making and Service Delivery

The survey results also found strong approval from government officials regarding the importance of engaging the public in policy-making through social media platforms. As presented in Table 7, 74 % of respondents agreed that raising citizens' awareness of government processes was one of their main motivations for utilizing social media to connect with the public. People are usually unaware of the facilities and services that government entities can offer them. However, with the advent of social media networks, the public can ask their questions on Twitter or Facebook and receive a prompt reply from the entity concerned. Moreover, 67 % agreed that it was essential to use social media to engage with citizens in order to inform and improve policy-making processes. A total of 72 % indicated that they use social media to engage with the public so that they can enhance service design and delivery. Overall, there is a strong emphasis on involving the public in decision-making and gaining their feedback on the quality of government services.

5.3 Challenges of Using Social Media in Dubai's Public Sector

There is a myriad of challenges that come with the utilization of social media, especially in the government sector. The survey questions addressed some of these challenges and made some interesting findings. For example, only 34 % responded "yes" when they were asked if a lack of appropriate skills to use social media outlets for communicating with the public was an issue for them. However, 65 % answered "yes" when asked if they needed proper training to utilize and integrate other Web 2.0 tools for communication with the public. Most of them found the basic social media tools, such as Facebook and Twitter, to be handy, but were not

Table 8 Challenges of using social media to communicate with the public

	Yes	No
Lack of appropriate skills	34.9	65.1
Proper training to utilize and integrate Web 2.0 tools	65.1	34.9
Concerns about privacy and security when sharing personal and/or government information	58.1	41.9
Concerns that using Web 2.0 tools might have a negative impact on one's reputation	16.3	83.7
Centralized and standard tools for social media functionalities	60.5	39.5
Internal policies put on the use of Web 2.0	44.2	55.8
Official organizational policy that covers the use of Web 2.0	34.3	65.7
Misuse of working hours	25.6	74.4
Concerns about validity/usefulness of citizens' input	27.9	72.1

familiar with other tools that could serve the same purpose. A total of 58 % of the respondents viewed privacy and security when sharing personal or government information as a source of concern, especially now that the number of government Twitter and Facebook accounts are on the rise. When asked if using social media to communicate with the public constituted misuse of working hours, 72.1 % answered "no" and only 27.9 % answered "yes" to this question. To some extent, this demonstrates the seriousness of government entities in establishing new communication channels that go beyond conventional ones such as calling or emailing. Moreover, 72 % of the respondents were not worried about the validity or usefulness of citizens' input, as they usually have analysts who sift through all of the input and consider only the serious and pertinent comments from the public.

The existence of proper organizational policies is essential to organize and formalize the use of social media in the public sector. As illustrated in Table 8, the vast majority of Dubai's government entities still lack internal policies that could shape the use of social media. A total of 55.8 % of respondents answered "no" when asked if they had internal policies put into place on the use of Web 2.0, and 65.7 % answered "no" when asked if their organizations had an official organizational policy that covers the use of Web 2.0.

5.4 Policies and Legislation to Ensure Safe Use of Social Media in Dubai

While social media platforms offer an unprecedented opportunity for the public to communicate with their government and share news and opinions, when they are misused they have the potential to harm both individuals and institutions. The governments of Dubai and the UAE have put in place strict laws that aim to protect society against the misuse of social media. Spreading defamatory rumours about individuals or organizations in the UAE is considered a serious criminal act under Federal Legal Decree No. 5 of 2012 on combating cybercrimes. This Decree was issued in response to the growing number of rumours circulating in Dubai, and also the violation of people's privacy when private photos were published online without the consent of their owners. Lt. Colonel Awadh Saleh Al Kindi, Editor-in-Chief of the UAE's Ministry of Interior 999 Magazine, explained the rationale behind the introduction of the new law, saying, "We encourage UAE residents to educate themselves first and verify any information that they receive. To safeguard the country's safety and security, the UAE has put in place strict laws, which include criminal charges and/or fines for damaging social peace and public order. These laws are a deterrent to the spread of rumours or false information on social media and the Internet." [19]. Sinclair [45] has pointed out that the Telecommunications Regulatory Authority introduced new privacy laws that criminalize the breach of people's privacy by posting videos or photos that do not respect the religion of Islam or include material that is disrespectful to the religious beliefs of all residents of Dubai and the UAE. Furthermore, the Dubai Police Force shut down 15 Facebook and Twitter accounts that they found to be in violation of the laws of Dubai [20]. The Dubai Police Force affirms that while it respects people's freedom to express their opinions and concerns through social media, they have firm policies regarding the spread of rumours, hate messages, and disrespect toward the religious and cultural norms of the UAE.

6 Conclusion

This chapter has examined the importance of using social media platforms to create dynamic links between the government of Dubai and its citizens in the UAE. Technological readiness and the motivation of Dubai's political leadership have been instrumental in successfully pushing for effective communication with the wider public. Using social media outlets such as twitter and facebook have enabled the UAE's citizens and residents alike to have direct and unrestricted access to key policy makers. Voicing their concerns publically increases the likelihood of addressing them by the concerned government entities. The lessons learned from the case of Dubai can be useful for other states of the GCC and the wider MENA region. However, more research is needed regarding the restrictions on expressing political and ideological believes through social media. Cases of arrest and trial for expressing political and religious commentaries are numerous in the GCC region.

References

1. Al-Amiri, K. (2014). *Social media is helping good governments to get better*. The National, March 29, 2014. Accessible from: http://www.thenational.ae/thenationalconversation/comment/social-media-is-helping-good-governments-to-get-better/. Accessed February 20, 2015.

2. Al-Khouri, A. M. (2012, September 17) eGovernment strategies: The case of the United Arab Emirates (UAE). *European Journal of ePractice*. www.epracticejournal.eu
3. Al-Saggaf, Y., & Simmons, P. (2014). Social media in Saudi Arabia: Exploring its use during two natural disasters. *Technological Forecasting and Social Change*. Available at: http://linkinghub.elsevier.com/retrieve/pii/S0040162514002522
4. Ayish, M. I. (2005). Virtual public relations in the United Arab Emirates: A case study of 20 UAE organizations' use of the internet. *Public Relations Review, 31*(3), 381–388.
5. Benkler, Y. (2002). Coase's penguin, or, linux and "The Nature of the Firm". *The Yale Law Journal, 112*(3), 369.
6. Bertot, J. C., Jaeger, P. T., & Hansen, D. (2012). The impact of polices on government social media usage: Issues, challenges, and recommendations. *Government Information Quarterly, 29*(1), 30–40. Available at: http://dx.doi.org/10.1016/j.giq.2011.04.004
7. Biygautane, M., & Al-Yahya, K. (2012). Knowledge management in UAE's public sector: The case of Dubai. Working paper 12–01. Dubai School of Government. Accessible on: http://www.dsg.ae/en/publication/Description.aspx?PubID=299&PrimenuID=11&mnu=Pri
8. Bryant, L. (2004). Informal, joined up knowledge sharing using connected weblogs in pursuit of Mental Health service improvement [online], *Headshift*. http://headshift.com/archives/blogtalk/blogtalk_web.htm. Accessed February 20, 2015.
9. Caroll, L. (2014). *Majlis to hashtag: New source of good ideas*. Accessible from: http://www.thenational.ae/uae/technology/majlis-to-hashtag-new-source-of-good-ideas
10. Chang, A., & Kannan, P. K. (2008). Leveraging web 2.0 in government. *Washington, DC: IBM Center for the Business of Government*.
11. Coakes, E. (2006). Storing and sharing knowledge: Supporting the management of knowledge made explicit in transnational organisations. *The Learning Organization, 13*(6), 579–593.
12. Dotsika, F., & Patrick, K. (2006). Towards the new generation of web knowledge. *VINE, 36*(4), 406–422.
13. Ding, Y. (2007). Web 2.0 Explorer. *ZDNET* [online]. Available from: http://blogs.zdnet.com/web2explorer/?p=408. Accessed January 7, 2015.
14. Dubai's Smart Government Portal. Accessible from: http://www.dsg.gov.ae/en/pages/default.aspx/. Accessed January 7, 2015.
15. Dubai e-government portal. Accessible from: http://dubai.ae/en/AboutDubaieGovernment/Pages/Vision.aspx/. Accessed January 7, 2015.
16. Dzamic, L. (2009). Listen to users to make web 2.0 work for you. *Admap, 44*(501), 45–47.
17. Emirates 24/7 (2014). Two mobiles for everyone in UAE. Accessible from: http://www.emirates247.com/news/emirates/two-mobiles-for-everyone-in-uae-2014-05-26-1.550297/. Accessed January 7, 2015.
18. Emirates 24/7 (2014). UAE residents warned over social media rumours. Accessible from: http://www.emirates247.com/news/emirates/uae-residents-warned-over-social-media-rumours-2014-05-18-1.549457/. Accessed January 7, 2015.
19. Emirates 24/7 (2012). Dubai police shut 15 twitter, facebook accounts. Accessible from: http://www.emirates247.com/news/emirates/dubai-police-shut-15-twitter-facebook-accounts-2012-05-20-1.459493/. Accessed January 7, 2015.
20. Hanif, N. (2014). Social media has transformed the way people view news and governments. *The National*, [online] p. 1. Available at: http://www.thenational.ae/uae/technology/social-media-has-transformed-the-way-people-view-news-and-governments. Accessed 2015.
21. Kaplan, A., & Haenlein, M. (2010). Users of the world, unite! The challenges and opportunities of social media. *Business Horizons, 53*(1), 59–68.
22. Kavanaugh, A., Fox, E., Sheetz, S., Yang, S., Li, L., Shoemaker, D., et al. (2012). Social media use by government: From the routine to the critical. *Government Information Quarterly, 29*(4), 480–491.
23. Kholidy, H., Erradi, A., Abdelwahed, S., & Baiardi, F. (2013). HA-CIDS: A hierarchical and autonomous IDS for cloud systems. *2013 Fifth International Conference on Computational Intelligence, Communication Systems and Networks*.

24. Lavenda, D. (2008, April 1–5). The irreversible social networking revolution. *Information Management Technology.*
25. Linders, D. (2012). From e-government to we-government: Defining a typology for citizen coproduction in the age of social media. *Government Information Quarterly, 29*(4), 446–454.
26. Lindgren, I., & Jansson, G. (2013). Electronic services in the public sector: A conceptual framework. *Government Information Quarterly, 30*(2), 163–172.
27. Mansour, A. M. E. (2014). Wiki-Government as coproduction of public policies and services: Is it a feasible tool for coproduction of public services in the United Arab Emirates. *Forthcoming in Australian Journal of ICT Research.*
28. Martin, G., Reddington, M., & Kneafsey, M. et al. (2009). Scenarios and strategies for Web 2.0. *Emerald, 51*(5): 370–380.
29. McAfee, A. (2006). Enterprise 2.0: The dawn of emergent collaboration. *MIT Sloan Management Review, 4*(3), 21–28.
30. Mergel, I. (2013). A framework for interpreting social media interactions in the public sector. *Government Information Quarterly, 30*(4), 327–334.
31. Middleton, C. (2008). The social side of business. *Computer Weekly, 2*(8), 26–27.
32. Moukhallati, D. (2014). UAE leaders harness the power of social media to deliver their message. *The National*, [online] p. 1. Available at: http://www.thenational.ae/uae/government/uae-leaders-harness-the-power-of-social-media-to-deliver-their-message. Accessed 2015.
33. Nam, T. (2012). Suggesting frameworks of citizen-sourcing via government 2.0. *Government Information Quarterly, 29*(1), 12–20.
34. OECD. (2007). *Participative web and user-created content*. Paris: OECD.
35. OECD. (2009). *Focus on citizens*. Public Engagement for better policy and services. Paris: OECD.
36. Paroutis, S., & Saleh, A. (2009). Determinants of knowledge sharing using web 2.0 technologies. *Journal of Knowledge Management, 13*(4), 52–63.
37. Picazo-Vela, S., Gutiérrez-Martínez, I., & Luna-Reyes, L. F. (2012). Understanding risks, benefits, and strategic alternatives of social media applications in the public sector. *Government Information Quarterly, 29*(4), 504–511. Available at: http://dx.doi.org/10.1016/j.giq.2012.07.002
38. Porter, M. (2008). The 'Four Digital Doors'-A CEDA research perspective on digital competition. *Committee for Economic Development of Australia, 60*, 1–8.
39. Postman, J. (2009). *Social corp: Social media goes corporate*. Berkeley: New Riders.
40. Redick, T., Calvo, A., Gay, C., & Engle, R. (2011). Working memory capacity and go/no-go task performance: Selective effects of updating, maintenance, and inhibition. *Journal of Experimental Psychology. Learning, Memory, and Cognition, 37*(2), 308–324.
41. Schneckenberg, D. (2009). Web 2.0 and the empowerment of the knowledge worker. *Journal of Knowledge Management, 13*(6), 509–520.
42. Shelly, G., & Vermaat, M. (2008). *Discovering computers 2009*. Boston, Mass.: Thomson Course Technology.
43. Shipstead, Z., Hicks, K., & Engle, R. (2012). Working memory training remains a work in progress. *Journal of Applied Research in Memory and Cognition, 1*(3), 217–219.
44. Sun, X., Zhuge, H., & Li, Q. (2008). A framework for the massive knowledge Web. *Concurrency and Computation-Practice and Experience, 21*(5), 705–723.
45. Sinclair, K. (2013). Be aware of UAE privacy laws when posting Facebook content, TRA warns. *The National*. [online]. Available at: http://www.thenational.ae/uae/technology/be-aware-of-uae-privacy-laws-when-posting-facebook-content-tra-warns. Accessed January 12, 2015.
46. Sinclair, N. (2007). The KM phoenix. *The journal of information and knowledge management systems, 37*(3), 255–261.
47. Stamati, T., Papadopoulos, T., & Anagnostopoulos, D. (2015). Social media for openness and accountability in the public sector: Cases in the Greek context. *Government Information Quarterly, 32*(1), 12–29. Available at: http://linkinghub.elsevier.com/retrieve/pii/S0740624X14001592

48. The National. (2014). Sheikh Mohammed bin Rashid takes Twitter to thank 6 million social media followers. Accessible from: http://www.thenational.ae/uae/sheikh-mohammed-bin-rashid-takes-to-twitter-to-thank-6-million-social-media-followers/. Accessed January 12, 2015.
49. The National. (2014). UAE leaders harness the power of social media to deliver their message. Accessible from: http://www.thenational.ae/uae/government/uae-leaders-harness-the-power-of-social-media-to-deliver-their-message/. Accessed January 12, 2015.
50. The National. (2014). Sheikh Mohammed launched Arab Social Media Award. Accessible from: http://www.thenational.ae/uae/government/sheikh-mohammed-launches-arab-social-media-awards/. Accessed January 12, 2015.
51. The National. (2014). Social media has transformed the way people view the news and governments. Accessible from: http://www.thenational.ae/uae/technology/social-media-has-transformed-the-way-people-view-news-and-governments/. Accessed January 12, 2015.
52. The National. (2014). Dubai police seek feedback on use of social media. Accessible from: http://www.thenational.ae/uae/government/dubai-police-seek-feedback-on-use-of-social-media/. Accessed January 12, 2015.
53. Thomas, J. (2003). The new face of government: Citizen-initiated contacts in the era of E-government. *Journal of Public Administration Research and Theory, 13*(1), 83–102.
54. Tredinnick, L. (2006). Web 2.0 and business. *Business Information Review, 23*(4), 228–234.
55. Van Zyl, A. (2009). The impact of social networking 2.0 on organisations. *Electronic Library, 27*(6), 906–918.

Social Media Policy in Turkish Municipalities: Disparity Between Awareness and Implementation

Naci Karkin, Ozer Koseoglu and Mehmet Zahid Sobaci

Abstract This chapter aims to analyze the present state of social media policy implementation and evaluation in Turkish municipalities in the Marmara region. We employed a questionnaire form for this purpose. We found that only a ratio of 35.5 % have social media policy. A great majority of respondent municipalities lack a written guide in conducting social media use at institutional level. We do not observe a common policy for personnel education addressing social media use for better personal, or institutional interest, neither do we see a diffusive evaluation of social media use. Thus, we argue that there is an increasing rate of awareness in terms of benefitting from social media use but there is a clear deficiency with regard to implementing and evaluating the social media policy.

Keywords Social media · Social media policy · Municipalities · Marmara region · Turkey

1 Introduction

Social media is among online applications to communicate with citizens, improving the public services and strengthening democracy. Day by day public institutions including local governments intensively use social media tools as Facebook, Twitter, or Youtube. Today local governments employ various social media tools

N. Karkin (✉)
Pamukkale University, Denizli, Turkey
e-mail: nkirgin@pau.edu.tr; n.karkin@tudelft.nl

N. Karkin
Delft University of Technology, Delft, The Netherlands

O. Koseoglu
Sakarya University, Adapazan, Turkey

M.Z. Sobaci
Uludag University, Bursa, Turkey

© Springer International Publishing Switzerland 2015
S. Nepal et al. (eds.), *Social Media for Government Services*,
DOI 10.1007/978-3-319-27237-5_5

to implement their different functions. For instance, they may use blogs to gather opinions and proposals from different stakeholders disseminate certain documents and presentations through media sharing platforms, and broach discussions about activities pertaining to corporate social responsibility and other related initiatives. Moreover, social networks as Facebook and Twitter can be used to send local service-related messages to the public and collect citizen feedback in return [1].

Regardless of these opportunities, social media use by local governments introduces new challenges related to resources, legal issues, privacy, security, reputation management, governance, and information and content issues [2–5] which entail designating a social media policy in local governments and a relevant guide for elected members, managers, and other personnel. Additionally, as the social media tools that local governments employ diversifies and usage of Web 2.0 gets complicated, a necessity to design social media policy increases.

Due to the fact that social media policy has been a central theme only after 2009 [6], issues relevant to social media policy have been a quite new theme for both practitioners and scholars of social media. Though there are studies in the fields of libraries [7], medical schools [8], cultural heritage institutions [9], and ministries [10], there is a lack of studies that focus on the issues of designing, implementing and maintaining social media policies in local governments [3, 11, 12]. Thus, the aim of this chapter is to analyze whether municipalities in the Marmara Region in Turkey exploit from social media tools in the context of a policy. For this aim, we used a survey method. Therefore, this study aims to contribute to the knowledge regarding the social media policy for local governments and to fill in the gap in the relevant literature.

This chapter is separated into six sections. After introduction, need for social media policy in local governments is discussed in second section. In the third section an outline for designing and implementing social media policy in local governments is put forth. The fourth section explains the data and method of the empirical study and presents the findings of analysis. The fifth section discusses the findings of the empirical study. The chapter concludes with suggestions regarding social media policy in local governments.

2 Why Local Governments Need a Social Media Policy?

Social media have rapidly been disseminated among local authorities who recognize the benefits and advantages of Web 2.0 tools. Local governments popularly use specific social media sites such as Facebook and Twitter for information exchange, better-quality services, and public engagement [2] (p. 34). To one extent social media apps provide opportunities for local governments, however, social and extremely public nature of these services bring potential hazards [7]. They provide an ingenuous setting for communication between officials and audiences. They provide opportunities for public officials to interact with service users in addition to the formal flow of knowledge. Due to the implicit roles and responsibilities in the interaction process through social media confusion arises for public officials and managers [13]. This complex interaction process bring about additional pitfalls that should be avoided such as posting of inappropriate content, mixing personal social media use with professional social media use, handling public comments in an unprofessional manner, and posting of redundant or inaccurate information [12]. Due to these risks and hazards, social media policies have progressively been adopted to local governments in recent years.

Social media policy, as defined "the prescribed principle of action or practice relating to an online channel, space or environment in which people engage and converse" [9] (p. 4), is a component of government's regulatory function. In essence, designing social media policy is one of the elements of a regulatory effort that includes laws such as individuals' rights, employment law, administrative law and criminal law, as well as user norms, social norms, and affordances [3, 11]. When there is a broader government policy on the adoption and use of social media, it is mandatory for public bodies, and particularly local governments to design their own policies. For instance, in the U.S., there is a range of legal arrangements including laws, memos, and orders that are directly or indirectly related to the adoption and usage of social media by government agencies, which thus, in turn, impel local governments to design their own social media policies depending on instruments such as guidelines to clarify and reify the broader policy [2].

Local governments are increasingly documenting their need for organization-specific rules for the management of their various social media accounts in forms of social media handbooks, social media strategy, policy for the use of social media, or linking strategy as well as their counterparts at government level [14] (pp. 95–96). These kind of documents that represent official social media policy of an institutional explicit how to govern the use of social media [3] by employees in a local government, but they also often extend beyond the official use of social media to build awareness that address the responsible and professional use of social media [14] (p. 96).

3 Designing and Implementing Social Media Policy in Local Governments

In the beginning, government managers responded to social media challenge in a negative manner like their counterparts in private sector. Usage of social media in the workplace during regular work hours was banned even for employees who wanted to benefit Web 2.0 tools for service issues [15]. However, undeterred dissemination of social media not only for personal usage but for numerous governmental services, opportunities that social media offer for governmental bodies, and problems that rise in official usage of social media have led governments to regulate social media, and designate policies and strategies for more open, accountable and participative government. Because local governments are the closest tier of government to citizens, they face abovementioned challenges more fiercely. Accordingly, local governments have begun to formulate their own social media policies to ensure the proper usage for both personal and professional aims.

As the use of social media in local governments increase, the need for rules, regulations, and standardization has grown as well. Local governments, in line with their counterparts at government level, mostly adopt instruments such as handbooks, strategy documents, codes, guidelines, protocols or standards for developing social media policy.

Strategy documents are preferred to reveal social media strategies and handle the use of the social media in a professional and responsible way. A properly designated social media strategy should be based on the mission of the organization. As a first step, the strategic communication and interaction objectives should be identified, and secondly, the divergent audiences of the organization should be defined [14].

As mostly addressed social media regulation form, *guidelines*, "provide advice on how to best use social media tools to achieve a desired result, such as eliciting citizen engagement or providing suggestions for creating interesting content" [3] (p. 3). Klang and Nolin [11] have separated four types of guidelines that local governments use in regard to their empirical analysis of 26 Swedish municipalities. Homogenous guidelines are general guidelines that appropriate for YouTube, Wikipedia and Facebook, and heterogeneous guidelines are specific guidelines that refer to a number of different applications in character. Problem oriented guidelines take social media as an administrative problem that needs to be disciplined and resource oriented guidelines are used as an opportunity for engaging in new practices.

A social media policy guideline should include a body of essential policies or strategies on employee access, social media account management, acceptable use of social media sites for personal use while at work, ethical social media conduct for public officials, posting content on official social media sites, security concerns, legal issues, and code of conduct for citizens that refer to limitations such as offensive language, inciting violence, or promoting illegal activity [3].

Designing written documents to ensure the proper use of social media in local governments for personal, institutional, and professional aims do not necessarily assure a successful implementation and outcomes. Local governments can create social media training programs to show their employees how social media tools can be used for governmental activities, and even to improve performance and efficiency to improve the effectiveness of the designated social media policy in the implementation stage. Additionally, as Hrdinová et al. [3] put social media policies should be reviewed periodically to ensure that they continue to reflect local government's changing strategy and priorities. The accomplishments of the policy, that is to say, should be evaluated with qualitative and quantitative techniques.

Despite the measurement challenges, a local government probably will begin measuring social media by primarily using baseline indicators like website statistics and search engine measures, followed by more sophisticated measures like affect analysis or social network analysis [16]. However, it should be stressed that a measurement strategy should focus not just on the quantitative data such as the number of followers or shares, but also aim to measure engagement in the content that is posted by local government and whether the content is influencing the conversation. Local governments can use tools provided by firms such as

MeasureMap and *BlogBeat* to gauge many applications such as blogs. There are also firms like Web Analytics and Google Analytics that ensure measurement of direct engagement of citizens in terms of their session lengths, comments, uploads, invitations to others, and so on. Moreover, if a local government intends to evaluate effectiveness of its social media policy, it should use measures such as posting comments and interacting to the quality of decision making, citizen satisfaction with the process, increase in citizen trust and loyalty [17].

4 Empirical Analysis

4.1 Data and Methodology

For the methodology, we employed a questionnaire form through which the raw data is obtained. The sample is deducted from the members of a local government union affiliated with the Marmara region in Turkey. The questionnaire form is delivered to the municipalities by the Union. We had a great hospitality and help at the Union officials before and after the completion of the survey.

The region choice has various rationales as; (a) accessibility, (b) socio-economic indicators (c) measurability. The Marmara region and its municipalities were easily reachable due to union's location which were close enough to reach and access. This accessibility is a key factor in case of having some troubles in questionnaire filling process. Secondly, the region is the most developed region in terms of socio-economic indicators [18], including immigration [19] which were among key factors in terms of municipalities and citizens' perceptions. Technological infrastructure necessities of municipalities are related to socio-economic indicators and citizens living in the region are supposed to have necessary literacy to engage through social media tools, or are inclined to do so. Thus municipalities in the region are expected to get involved in social media use more than the rest of the country.

The questionnaire is derived from some sample questionnaires as the one as ACELG 2011 survey of social media use in Australian local governments [20], and some other studies [21, 22]. Using the sample scales adopted, we made necessary changes in the questionnaire form in order to make some adaptations to municipal structure in Turkish administrative system. After all, reliability of the scale produced is turned out to have high reliability through *Cronbach Alpha test* in SPSS with a ratio of 0.723.

We expected that officials, directly or indirectly related to information and communications management, are supposed to fill in the questionnaire form. The questionnaire forms were sent to the municipalities by and returned to the Union during June 20, 2014–September 20, 2014. Though the data was obtained from 95 municipalities but 2 of them is excluded due to excess missing information. Since the total number of union members is 224, the sample size reaches to an amount of 42.5 % in representation. We employed SPSS 15.0 evaluation version in data analysis.

4.2 Findings

Below do we present the findings obtained through frequency analysis in relevant tables. The findings start with the positions of personnel in municipalities who filled the questionnaire forms, and conclude with a table that displays a summary of the methods through which municipalities evaluate the efficiency of social media as an administrative tool (Table 1).

That the questionnaire form is filled by authorized personnel is a good sign. We attach importance to that matter and put a blank in the questionnaire form in order to reveal who filled in the form. It is explicit that there is a divided appearance on "who to fill in". The five group of personnel consisting of personnel at directorate of press, documentation and public relations (11.8 %), personnel working in management of information processing center (10.8 %), personnel in charge of social media/networking (10.8 %), director of records (9.7 %), and press advisors to mayors (7.5 %) constitute a ratio of 50.6 % among the total personnel who filled the form. The rest are divergent municipal officials such as team leaders in charge, director of culture and social affairs and personnel at directorate records with a total ratio of 43.6 %.

In Table 2, we aim to reveal whether strategic plans of municipalities include some provisions targeting to get benefitted from social media use. From the table, it is apparent that 67.7 % assert that their institutional strategic plans have provisions with regard to utilize social media for the sake of municipality's goals and policies. The ratio of saying "No" apparently describes a low level as of 26.9 %.

Table 1 Positions hold in institution

	Frequency (f)	Percent (%)
Personnel at directorate of press, documentation and public relations	11	11.8
Personnel at information processing center	10	10.8
Personnel in charge of social media or networking	10	10.8
Director of records	9	9.7
Press advisor	7	7.5
Director of press, documentation and public relations	4	4.3
Team leader in charge of social media	4	4.3
Director of information processing center	3	3.2
Clerk	3	3.2
Mayor	2	2.2
Deputy mayor	2	2.2
Personnel at directorate of records	2	2.2
Director of culture and social affairs	2	2.2
All others including missing	24	26.3
Total	93	100.0

Table 2 Does your institutional strategic plan include some provisions (aims, tools, manners etc.) aiming that your institution get benefited from social media use?

	Frequency (f)	Percent (%)
Yes	63	67.7
No	25	26.9
Total	88	94.6
Missing	5	5.4
Total	93	100.0

Whether municipalities have a written and formal social media policy, or not is crucially important for the smooth execution of duties, including engagement with citizens. As seen in Table 3, while the ratio of saying that they have an institutional social media policy is 35.5 %, the ratio of uttering that they are on to develop a formal social media policy is 26.9 %. Taken together, totally 62.4 % of participant municipalities are implying the awareness on raising a social media policy in benefitting better from the use of social media on institutional level. On the other hand, a ratio of 33.3 % (exactly 1/3) is saying that they do not have one. It is clear that the ratio of actually having one is slightly more than 1/3.

In Table 4, we present the results of the question picked by participants on what the best reflects social media policy of their municipalities. Before replying to these questions, participants were asked to pass to the next question if they did not pick the option of the previous question as "Yes, we have an institutional social media policy". In result, 63.4 % of the participants passed to next questions.

Table 3 Is your municipality has developed/developing a written (formal) social media policy?

	Frequency (f)	Percent (%)
Yes, we have an institutional social media policy	33	35.5
No, we do not have an institutional social media policy	31	33.3
Yes, we are working on to develop an institutional social media policy	25	26.9
Total	89	95.7
Missing	4	4.3
Total	93	100.0

Table 4 Which of the following does the best reflect your municipality's social media policy?

	(f)	Percent (%) in-all	Percent (%) in-group
We developed our social media policy by following our own institutional aims	17	18.3	56.7
We adopted an existing social media policy and applied to our municipality	7	7.5	23.3
We adopted an existing social media policy but adapted to our municipality to a certain extent	6	6.5	20
Total	30	32.3	100.0

For the rest, we see that 18.3 % of all participants (56.7 % of participants having an institutional social media policy) affirm that they have developed their social media policy by putting their institutional aims first. 7.5 % of all participants (23.3 % of participants having an institutional social media policy) say that they adopted an already existing social media policy and applied it to our municipality. The remaining 6.5 % of all participants but 20 % of participants having an institutional social media policy argue that they have adopted an existing social media policy but they have adapted already present social media policies to some certain extent. Actually there should be 33 participant municipalities that were supposed to reply to this very question; however we see that 3 more municipalities were passed to next question.

In Table 5, we give the ratios about the question dealing with whether municipalities have a formal and written guide in social media use at institutional level. As being clear at the Table 5, 87.1 % of the participants accept that they do not have one, while just a portion of participants (7.5 %) confirm that they have one.

Through this table we aim to give an opinion about municipalities' attitudes whether municipal personnel could reach to their own personal social media accounts during working times. From the Table 6, it is clear that 58.1 % is confirming that they allow the personnel to reach to personal social media accounts. On the other hand, 36.6 % of the participants assert that they do not allow the personnel to reach their social media accounts during office hours.

In Table 7, we focus on to reveal whether municipalities tend to regulate personal social media use since institutional affiliations might have repercussions on other parties including citizens. 34.4 % of the municipalities assert that they do not have regulations over personnel use of personal social media accounts on the agenda yet. 26.9 % of the participants argue that they are on to develop a policy regarding the regulation of personal social media use of their personnel. A ratio of 14 % state that they keep this issue hot for the time being. That means a ratio

Table 5 Has your municipality prepared a written (formal) guide for institutional social media use?

	Frequency (f)	Percent (%)
No	81	87.1
Yes	7	7.5
Total	88	94.6
Missing	5	5.4
Total	93	100.0

Table 6 Could municipality personnel reach to their own personal social media accounts (i.e. Twitter, or Facebook) during office hours?

	Frequency (f)	Percent (%)
Yes	54	58.1
No	34	36.6
Do not know	4	4.3
Total	92	98.9
Missing	1	1.1
Total	93	100.0

Table 7 Do you have a social media policy regulating personal social media use if personnel use of social media might appear institutional opinion, or if understood as such?

	Frequency (f)	Percent (%)
Not yet on the agenda	32	34.4
Yes, we are developing a policy regarding this issue	25	26.9
Keeping the issue hot for the time being	13	14.0
Do not know	9	9.7
Yes, we developed a policy for the regarding issue	6	6.5
We evaluated the issue and decided not to develop a policy regarding the issue	5	5.4
Total	90	96.8
Missing	3	3.2
Total	93	100.0

Table 8 Do you educate your personnel in social media use?

	Frequency (f)	Percent (%)
No	64	68.8
Yes	28	30.1
Total	92	98.9
Missing	1	1.1
Total	93	100.0

of 14 % of the participants say that they still discuss the issue and continuing to keep the issue on the institutional agenda but without a positive, or negative move. A ratio of 9.7 % argues that they have no information on this issue. Only a ratio of 6.5 % confirm that they have already developed such an institutional policy to regulate the issue. 5.4 % of the participant municipalities say that they previously evaluated the issue and decided not to move in that direction yet.

In Table 8, we present the frequency analysis directed to evaluate whether municipalities have an education policy conducted on personnel in order to use social media effectively. Apparently most of the municipalities do not have such a policy to educate the personnel in proper use of social media. A ratio of 68.8 % assert that they do not educate their personnel. However, we see that a ratio of 30.1 %, meaning 1 over 3, has an institutional policy directed to manage this education issue.

In Table 9, we present the frequency analysis stating whether the municipalities have an institutional education policy over members of the municipal council in order to get benefitted from social media use. A vast majority (92.5 %) accept that they have no such a policy but a ratio of 5.4 % confirming the presence of institutional education policy over elected.

In Table 10, we asked the municipalities whether they evaluate the efficiency of their institutional social media use. There is a slight difference between respondents who say "yes, we evaluate" (53.8 %), and "no, we do not evaluate" (46.2 %).

Table 9 Do you educate members of the municipal council in how to use social media?

	Frequency (f)	Percent (%)
No	86	92.5
Yes	5	5.4
Total	91	97.8
Missing	2	2.2
Total	93	100.0

Table 10 Do you evaluate the efficiency of your municipality's social media use?

	Frequency (f)	Percent (%)
No	50	53.8
Yes	43	46.2
Total	93	100.0

Table 11 exhibits the answers to the question of how they evaluate the efficiency of social media use as a complementary question to the question whose frequency analysis presented in the Table 10. The six options available to the participants through this question are as follows:

a. To be evaluated by independent companies (option 1),
b. To follow regularly the basic statistics like retweets, likes, favorites, followers, comments in social media accounts such as Facebook and Twitter and discuss them with officials in charge (option 2),
c. To conduct an end-user satisfaction questionnaire (option 3),
d. To employ some functional tools like Google alerts (option 4),
e. To meet with the basic stakeholders (option 5),
f. Other (option 6)

According to the replies for this question, we see that 53.8 % passed to next question. Out of the rest, 32.3 % picked just one option of all. The ratio of two-option picking participants is 6.5 % as the same rate with 3-option picking participants. Only one participant represented a four-option choice. Note that participants were told that they would pick options more than one. Thus the ratios for picking ups are independent of each other. When we evaluate the frequencies compared to in-group dispersions, we see that 69.7 % of the option pickings in this question

Table 11 How do you evaluate the efficiency of social media as an administrative tool used in your municipality?

	Frequency (f)	Percent in-all (%)	Percent in-group (%)
1 Option picked	30	32.3	69.7
2 Options picked	6	6.5	14
3 Options picked	6	6.5	14
4 Options picked	1	1.1	2.3
Total	43	100.0	100.0

just picked one option. The rest is divided among 2-option, 3-option and 4-option pickers with the ratios as 14, 14 and 2.3 % respectively.

To reveal the details of the abovementioned options, participant municipalities contend that they regularly follow basic statistics like retweets, likes, favorites, followers, comments in social media accounts such as Facebook and Twitter and discuss them with officials in charge (45.2 %); employ some functional tools like Google alerts (8.6 %); conduct an end-user satisfaction questionnaire (5.4 %); are evaluated by independent companies (5.4 %); meet with the basic stakeholders (2.2 %), and address to "the other" options that are not clearly defined (2.2 %) in the questionnaire but open to participants' indications as input for evaluating the efficiency of social media use.

5 Discussion

As among the part of administrative reform process that public sector institutions including municipalities have to prepare and execute, strategic plans [23] are among the very sources for institutions in order to put priorities and aims of institution [24]. As being at the interconnectedness as a result of a series of legal and administrative regulations [25], these plans foresee necessary efforts, actions and processes to meet the needs of end-users, citizens in that context, though not confined to meeting the digital needs. Therefore, any provisions in strategic plans with regard to institutional aims, tools, and manners would be great importance of social media use. In Table 2 it is clearly presented that approximately 2/3 of the municipalities have regarded provisions in their strategic plans for institutional social media use. However we did not ask any question in order to evaluate whether there are negative value loaded provisions in relevant strategic plans. For example, there are three times "social media" phrase is used in Istanbul Metropolitan municipality's strategic plan of 2015–2019 (http://www.ibb.gov.tr). In first time that the phrase used with a positive value, there seems a connection between social media use and public awareness about natural catastrophes, mostly earthquakes in this case (p. 72). In the second use of social media phrase in strategic plan, there is a clear negative connotation attached to social media since it circulates unchecked or misguided information in mass communication (p. 77). The final use of social media in strategic plan that has a neutral connotation arguing for a one-hand management of all institutional social media accounts (p. 242).

From the perspective of whether having a written/formal and binding institutional social media policy, or not, is of great importance. Martín et al. [26] recommends having an institutional policy to get better benefitted from social media, particularly in the improvement process of institutional strategies. Clearly seen from the statistical dispersion, it seems that only 1/3 of the municipalities already have one while approximately another 1/3 is currently on develop to have one. The remaining 1/3 of the municipalities do neither have one, nor in a position to develop one. When compared to Ontario's municipalities, according to Spring 2014 results by Redbrick Communications [27] stating that 28 % of municipalities have social media policy while a 7 % is on to develop, it seems that ratios obtained due to this survey are not satisfactory, but good to keep on. Purser [20] asserted that municipalities in Australia have a social media policy with a ratio of 25.5 % and a portion of 49.7 % is on to develop one, while 24.8 % has no social media policy for the time being. Besides Scott [28] asserts that it is found that 34 % of the municipalities neither do have a social media policy nor do have a link directed to institutional social media account on institutional website. Eventually, the ratios found by our research and found in the literature appear to resemble for having a formal social media policy at institutional level.

Throughout the literature analysis part we asserted the conceptual framework where we imply why municipalities should have a social media policy in addition to tools and manners that municipalities implement and designate it. However we should also keep an eye on what are the priorities while having and implementing this policy. We see through the Table 4 that municipalities put institutional objectives first while designing and implementing social media policy with a rate of 19.1 %. In total a ratio of 14.6 % is either adopted or adapted an already present social media policy to their municipalities among the participant municipalities, evident from the Table. On the other hand, when evaluated form in-group percentages, we see that municipalities with a rate of more than half (56.7 %) is confirming that contextual, or institutional conditions are the first to frame the social media policies among all. Together with the ratio of 20 % that saying they have adopted but adapted to a certain extent, we see that nearly 76.7 % of municipalities having social media policy asserting the priorities and circumstances of their own institutions as the main definer of institutional social media policy. We may argue that there is some level of harmony between institutional circumstances playing important role in defining social media policy and Fountain's conceptualization of technology enactment framework [29] where she argued for objective technologies being enacted by subjective institutional factors and organizational environment [30].

As a complementary but not necessary step to having an institutional social media policy, social media guides are quite functional to move as an allied entity, free from being unharmonious as an institution present in any social hub. Departing from that point of view, we see that 87.1 % of the participant municipalities do not have a formal and advising guide addressing both elected and appointed personnel. This is of importance since public institutions should have an awareness to have citizens' trust and interactions by employing social media tools. Zavattaro [31] argues that public institutions employ social media policies and guides to control employee use of social media tools by referencing the U.S. GSA [31] that released a social media guide including 18 rules to align both employees and contractors representing the institution. On the other hand Bonsón et al. [32] states that recent guidelines on social media use proposes to post/send tweets, or postings between 2 and 10 per day at institutional level.

Personnel loafing, misinterpretation by public and uncontrolled nature of online sources in terms of exact addressees are among the potential barriers that could be put before personal social media use during office hours. In order to propose a solution, for instance, Model Employee Handbook for South Carolina Municipalities says that municipalities must produce a solution for "employee's rights of free expression with the municipality's need to maintain an orderly work environment" [33]. Similarly, it is advised in another social media tools report prepared for Tennessee municipalities that access to social media could be banned or allowed during working hours for the municipality's best interest, but cell phones or handheld devices [34]. Thus it can be argued that access to social media accounts could be limited, prohibited or allowed by using municipality infrastructure but there should be no interferences if personal devices are used. From Table 6, it is evident that 58.1 % of the participant municipalities allow the employees to reach to their personal accounts, while a ratio of 36.6 % does not allow to do so, irrespective of using municipality's infrastructures, or through personal devices.

Complementary to employee use of social media in or out of office, personal use of employees or contractors to municipalities that represent the municipality is another important issue with regard to institutional social media use. Misinterpretation, misuse or unintended shares, or postings may lay institutions under suspicions. Uncontrolled and unconfirmed postings over social media may produce compensations to pay for municipality, or degrade the trust in the eyes of citizens. Clarifying this point in legal perspective, Bojorquez and Shores [35] (p. 46) state that "even unofficial, non-sanctioned postings by an agency employee to friends can trigger obligations under the Records Retention Act, the Public Information Act, and the Open Meetings Act" in U.S. case. Similarly, Cox and Rethman [36] (p. 17) assert that "personal use of social networking by employees—both on the job and off the clock—can cause major headaches for employers who fail to take the proper precautions".

For this dimension, we asked a question focusing on whether there is a specific set of criteria that regulate the personal use of social media in case of a potential representativeness for the municipality. Dadashzadeh [37] sees "the formalization of how agency evaluates social media use and employees' participation in it" as among the important outputs of organizational strategy pertaining to institutional social media use. A survey performed in 2011 shows that federal employees use social media at work with a rate of 74 and 19 % arguing there being a ban over social media tools, proving the federal institutions trust over employee use of social media during office hours [38]. Purser [20] found that 27.4 % of the respondent municipalities have a social media regulation policy and a rate of 19.7 % is about to develop a policy while a ratio of 31.8 % is currently evaluating the issue. In contrast, this study shows that municipalities in the Marmara region have no clear steps taken, or to be taken in regulating this issue except for a ratio of 6.5 % who have already regulated, or a ratio of 40.9 % who are on to develop a regulation in future.

Education of elected and appointed personnel for social media use is among the hot topics for local governments, including the municipalities. Lori Lein, author of the article "Social Media and Municipal Employees: Tweet Them Right" argues that completely banning social media in work places is not realistic, rather she argues for a social media policy and employee training for smooth use of social media in and out of office hours [39]. Purser [20] found that respondent municipalities in Australia have no educational providence to elected and appointed employees. Our study also shows that participants are not delivering necessary training for their elected and appointed personnel with ratios of 92.5 and 68.8 % respectively.

Evaluating the efficiency of institutional social media use proves the functionality of social media in government business at local level, among others. Majority of the respondents contend that they do not evaluate the efficiency and effectiveness of official social media accounts with a slight disparity. Additionally, municipalities state that they mostly (32.3 %) utilize only one tool for evaluation. However, as mentioned above evaluation of social media use in municipalities is important for monitoring the success of social media strategies and policies. Among the tools that are employed to gauge the efficiency of social media most of the participants (45.2 %) regularly follow basic statistics like retweets, likes, favorites, followers, comments in social media accounts such as Facebook and Twitter that all belong to the category of so-called baseline indicators. A slight number of participants resort to surveys for measuring citizen satisfaction with the official social media management and policy, and meeting with stakeholders is the sole qualitative technique that municipalities use for evaluating social media performance.

6 Conclusion

In this study we aimed to examine the potential expectations and present attitudes of municipalities in the Marmara region in Turkey, towards designing, implementing and measuring social media policy. We contend that there is a high level of awareness with regard to having a social media policy. Nonetheless, it is arguable that this level of awareness has no practical return if we take the present ratios that just 35.5 % of participant municipalities have a policy and 87.1 % has no formal guide in conducting social media use at institutional level. In addition to that, due to the fact that delivering education and training on how to use social media accounts properly for council members and administrative personnel are not a common approach for the participant municipalities, it seems there is a clear deficiency in terms of social media policy implementation.

This study has some limitations as; having a limited focus in terms of sample selection (one geographical region, the most developed, out of seven regions). We propose the next studies to focus on all the geographical regions, or to focus on sample gathered from all the regions. Besides, scholars may incline to make researches on countries from comparative perspective.

We argue that at least three conclusions could be drawn from this study: (a) social media use has become globally pervade and developing a social media policy is also becoming a common necessity for all local governments in both developed and developing countries, (b) though it seems there is no governmental policy on regulating social media use in public institutions in Turkey, local governments, depending on their dynamic, entrepreneur, and innovative characteristics, have recently begun to develop their own social media policy, (c) not compliant with the conclusion (b), there is a lack of implementation and evaluation of the designated social media policy which entails an institutional capacity improvement for municipalities that intend to maintain their social media policy.

References

1. Bonsón, E., Torres, L., Royo, S., & Flores, F. (2012). Local e-government 2.0: Social media and corporate transparency in municipalities. *Government Information Quarterly, 29*(2), 123–132.
2. Bertot, J. C., Jaeger, P. T., & Hansen, D. (2012). The impact of policies on government social media usage: Issues, challenges, and recommendations. *Government Information Quarterly, 29*, 30–40.
3. Hrdinová, J., Helbig, N., & Stollar Peters, C. (2010). *Designing social media policy for government: Eight essential elements. Center for Technology in Government*, New York, USA. http://www.ibb.gov.tr/tr-TR/kurumsal/Birimler/StratejikPlanlamaMd/Documents/2010_2014/stratejikplan15_19.pdf. Accessed March 26, 2015.
4. Center for Technology in Government (2009). *Exploratory Social Media Project: Phase I-Identifying benefits and concerns surrounding use of social media in government.* http://www.ctg.albany.edu/publications/reports/social_media/social_media.pdf. Accessed March 4, 2015.
5. Sobaci, M. Z. (forthcoming). Social media and local governments: An overview. In M. Zahid Sobaci (Ed.), *Social Media and Local Governments: Theory and Practice.* New York: Springer.
6. Magro, M. J. (2012). A review of social media use in e-government. *Administrative Sciences, 2*, 148–161.
7. Kroski, E. (2009). Should your library have a social media policy? *School Library Journal, 55*(10), 44–46.
8. Kind, T., Genrich, G., Sodhi, A., & Chretien, K. C. (2010). Social media policies at US medical schools. *Medical Education Online, 15*, 1–8.
9. Cadell, L. (2013). Socially practical or practically unsociable? A study into social media policy experiences in Queensland cultural heritage institutions. *Australian Academic & Research Libraries, 44*(1), 3–13.
10. Kenawy, G. S. S. (2014). Social Media Policy in Egypt: Case Studies of three ministries. *Unpublished M. A. Thesis.* Cairo, Egypt: The American University in Cairo, School of Global Affairs and Public Policy.
11. Klang, M., & Nolin, J. (2011). Disciplining social media: An analysis of social media policies in 26 Swedish municipalities. *First Monday, 16*(8), http://journals.uic.edu/ojs/index.php/fm/article/view/3490/3027. Accessed March 19, 2015.
12. Hansen-Flaschen, L., & P. Parker, K. (2012). The rise of social government. An advanced guide and review of social media's role in local government operations. *Fels Institute of Government*, http://www.fels.upenn.edu/sites/www.fels.upenn.edu/files/fels_promising_practices_the_rise_of_social_media_website_final.pdf. Accessed February 20, 2015.
13. Hellman, R. (2014). *The cloverleaves of social media challenges for e-governments.* http://medialt.no/the-cloverleaves-of-social-media-challenges-for-e-governments/1127.aspx. Accessed February 16, 2015.

14. Mergel, I., & Greeves, B. (2013). *Social media in the public sector field guide*. San Francisco, CA: Jossey-Bass.
15. Staab, A. E. (2014). 6 tips for creating a social media policy. *Benefits Magazine, 51*(5), 14–20.
16. Deschamps, R. (2012). Evaluating social media. In: McNutt, K. (Ed.), *Social media & Government 2.0*. University of Regina, Graduate School of Public Policy. http://www.scho olofpublicpolicy.sk.ca/resources/Government/Environmental%20Scan%20on%20Social%20 Media%20in%20the%20Public%20Sector/Social%20Media%20and%20Government%20 Final_2012.pdf. Accessed February 20, 2015.
17. Chang, A., & Kannan, P. K. (2008). Leveraging web 2.0 in government. *IBM Center for Business of Government*, E-Government/Technology Series.
18. Dulupcu, M. Ali, Karaoz, M., Sungur, O., & Unlu, H. (2015). Cluster(ing) policies in Turkey: The impact of internationalization or the imitation of internationals. In Rui Baptista & João Leitão (Eds.), *Entrepreneurship, Human Capital, and Regional Development, International Studies in Entrepreneurship* (Vol. 31, pp. 239–262). Switzerland: Springer International Publishing.
19. Akın, D., & Dökmeci, V. (2015). Cluster analysis of interregional migration in Turkey, *Journal of Urban Planning and Development, 141*(3), CID: 05014016, http://dx.doi.org/10.1061/(ASCE)UP.1943-5444.0000223
20. Purser, K. (2012). Using social media in local government: 2011 survey report. *Australian Centre of Excellence for Local Government*. Sydney, Australia: University of Technology.
21. NASCIO. (2010). *Friends, Followers and Feeds: A National Survey of Social Media Use in State Government*. http://www.nascio.org/publications/documents/NASCIO-SocialMedia.pdf. Accessed March 23, 2015.
22. Wakeman, S. (2008). *What is the Role of Social Media in UK Local Government Communications?* http://www.simonwakeman.com/wp-content/uploads/2008/11/sw-cipr-project-final-version-public.pdf. Accessed March 23, 2015.
23. Velibeyoglu, K. (2008). Urban ICT policies for Turkish local governments: The case of Yalova IT City. In U. Bucher & M. Finka (Eds.), *The Electronic City*. Germany: Berliner Wissenschaftsverlag BWV.
24. Arslan, A. (2009). A strategic orientation model for the Turkish local E-governments. *1st International Conference on eGovernment and eGovernance of TURKSAT* (Turksat Satellite Communication Cable TV and Operation Inc.). Ankara, Turkey: Social Sciences Research Society (SoSReS).
25. Yildiz, M. (2009). An overview of local E-government adoption and implementation in Turkey. In C. Reddick (Ed.), *Handbook of Research on Strategies for Local E-Government Adoption and Implementation: Comparative Studies* (pp. 419–436). Hershey, PA, USA: Information Science Reference. doi:10.4018/978-1-60566-282-4.ch022.
26. Martín, A. S., de Rosario, A. H., & Pérez, M. D. C. C. (2015). Using twitter for dialogic communication: Local government strategies in the European Union. *Local Government Studies*. doi:10.1080/03003930.2014.991866.
27. Redbrick Communications. (2014). *Municipal Social Media Survey*. http://www.redbrick.ca/assets/file/resource/Redbrick-2014-Ontario-Municipal-Social-Media-Survey-Final.pdf. Accessed March 11, 2015.
28. Scott, J. (2013). Facing the future: local governments adapt to social media trends. In P. Kamnuansilpa & C. L. Sampson (Eds.), *Public Management and the Blue Economy* (pp. 35–54). Khon Kaen University: College of Local Administration.
29. Fountain, J. E. (2001). *Building the Virtual State: Information Technology and Institutional Change*. Washington, DC: Brookings Institution Press.
30. Gil-Garcia, J. R., & Luna-Reyes, L. F. (2009). Fostering the information society through collaborative E-government: digital community centers and the E-learning program in Mexico, In A. Meijer, K. Boersma & P. Wagenaar (eds.), *ICTs, Citizens & Governance: After the Hype!*, (pp. 99–118). The Netherlands: IOS Press.

31. U.S. General Services Administration (2012). GSA social media navigator, retrieved from http://www.gsa.gov/graphics/staffoffices/socialmedianavigator.pdf
32. Bonsón, E., Royo, S., & Ratkai, M. (2014). Facebook practices in Western European municipalities: An empirical analysis of activity and citizens' engagement. *Administration & Society*. doi:10.1177/0095399714544945.
33. Municipal Association of South California. (2013). *Model Employee Handbook for South Carolina Municipalities*. https://www.masc.sc/SiteCollectionDocuments/Human%20 Resources/Model_employee_handbook.pdf. Accessed March 25, 2015.
34. Jones, B., & Jones, J. (2010). Social media as a tool for tennessee municipalities. *MTAS Publications: Full Publications*, http://trace.tennessee.edu/utk_mtaspubs/151. Accessed March 14, 2015.
35. Bojorquez, A. J., & Shores, D. (2009). Open government and the net: Bringing social media into the light. *Texas Tech Administrative Law Journal, 11*(1), 45–67.
36. Cox, J. T., & Rethman, K. M. (2011). Personal use of social networking by employees—Both on the job and off the clock—Can cause major headaches for employers who fail to take the proper precautions. *Ohio Lawyer*. http://www.ficlaw.com/links/cline/socialmedia3.pdf. Accessed March 15, 2015.
37. Dadashzadeh, M. (2010). Social media in government: From e-government to e-governance. *Journal of Business and Economics Research, 8*(11), 81–86.
38. Kash, W. (2011). Social media use jumps dramatically among federal employees. http://br eakinggov.com/2011/10/18/social-media-use-jumps-dramatically-among-federal-employees. Accessed March 25, 2015.
39. Lein, L. (2013). Social media and municipal employees: Tweet them right. *The Missouri Municipal Review*. http://c.ymcdn.com/sites/www.mocities.com/resource/resmgr/review_ sept_articles/socialmediaandmunicipalemplo.pdf. Accessed March 22, 2015.

From Social Media to GeoSocial Intelligence: Crowdsourcing Civic Co-management for Flood Response in Jakarta, Indonesia

Tomas Holderness and Etienne Turpin

> *From now on there is an interconnection, an intertwining, even a symbiosis of technologies, exchanges, movements, which makes it so that a flood—for instance—wherever it may occur, must necessarily involve relationships with any number of technical, social, economic, political intricacies that keep us from regarding it simply as a misadventure or a misfortune whose consequences can be more or less easily circumscribed.*
> —Jean-Luc Nancy [17, pp. 3–4].

Abstract Here we present a review of PetaJakarta.org, a system designed to harness social media use in Jakarta for the purpose of relaying information about flood locations from citizen to citizen and from citizens and the city's emergency management agency. The project aimed to produce an open, real-time situational overview of flood conditions and provide decision support for the management agency, as well as offering the government a data source for post-event analysis. As such, the platform was designed as a socio-technological system and developed as a civic co-management tool to enable climate adaptation and community resilience in Jakarta, a delta megacity suffering enormous infrastructural instability due to a troubled confluence of environmental factors—the city's rapid urbanization, its unique geographic limitations, and increasing sea-levels and monsoon rainfalls resulting from climate change. The chapter concludes with a discussion of future research in open source platform and their role in infrastructure and disaster management.

Keywords Civic co-management · Geosocial intelligence · Social media · Climate adaptation · Infrastructure management · Socio-technological systems · Digital ecosystems · Disaster risk management · Crowdsourcing

T. Holderness · E. Turpin (✉)
SMART Infrastructure Facility, University of Wollongong, Wollongong, Australia
e-mail: etienne@petajakarta.org

T. Holderness
e-mail: tomas@uow.edu.au

© Springer International Publishing Switzerland 2015
S. Nepal et al. (eds.), *Social Media for Government Services*,
DOI 10.1007/978-3-319-27237-5_6

1 Introduction

Social media has a powerful role to play in infrastructure management in the twenty-first century, particularly where infrastructural systems are strained by complex and unpredictable events (e.g. erratic weather or power disruptions), and where quick response times are of the essence. Information gathered from social media users and networks can yield a real-time picture of rapidly changing conditions that affect—and often threaten—the well-being of infrastructural systems and, more importantly, their users. However, the great technical challenge for systems designers and administrators is to elicit or invite social media users to provide this valuable information *and* to make this information valuable in high-pressure situations—i.e. to filter and visualize this information quickly and reliably.

In this chapter, we present an overview of PetaJakarta.org (*peta*: map), a platform designed to harness social media use for the purpose of relaying information about flood locations amongst Jakarta's citizens and between citizens and the primary government stakeholder, the emergency management agency of Jakarta (BPBD DKI Jakarta). We saw that the remarkably high level of mobile device and social media use amongst Jakartans, particularly their use of Twitter,[1] afforded the city an incredible information resource. The aim of the project was thus to elicit and process relevant information in order to produce an open, real-time situational overview of flooding conditions and to provide decision support for the management agency, as well as offering the government a data source for post-event analysis. As such, the platform was designed as a socio-technological system and developed as a civic co-management strategy to enable climate adaptation and community resilience in Jakarta, a delta megacity suffering enormous infrastructural instability due to a troubled confluence of environmental factors—the city's rapid urbanization, its unique geographic limitations, and increasing sea-levels and monsoon rainfalls resulting from climate change.

Before detailing the technical aspects and outcomes of PetaJakarta.org, however, it is important to first survey the environmental context from which the project emerged and in which it was intended to serve the residents of the city of Jakarta.

2 Jakarta: A Delta Megacity

Jakarta, and the surrounding conurbation known as Jabodetabek, is the world's second largest contiguous conurbation (after the metropolitan area of Tokyo), and one of the fastest urbanising environments on the planet. Figure 1 shows the

---

[1]Jakarta has one of the highest numbers of Twitter users of any city on the planet, contributing to approximately 2.4 % of the world's total tweets in 2012 [24].

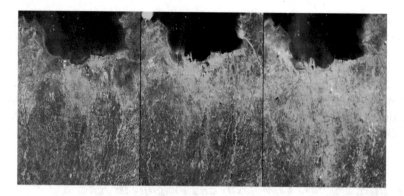

Fig. 1 False-colour images of Jakarta from the Landsat and ASTER earth observation satellite sensors showing the growth of urban hardscape (*green*) and reduction in vegetation (*red*). From *left* to *right*: 1972 (population 11 million), 1994 (population 19 million), 2006 (population 25 million). Image credit: NASA/GSFC/METI/Japan Space Systems and U.S./Japan ASTER Science Team

simultaneous urban sprawl and densification of the city since the early 1970s; the region's population has exploded from approximately 11 million in 1972 to almost 28 million by 2014 estimates. In Jakarta, change is simply a fact of life [28].

Situated in a low-lying delta region, the city is fed by 13 rivers that flow north-ward from the mountains south of the city out to the Java Sea. To understand the context of flooding in Jakarta, three of its defining geographical features must be considered. First, drinking water for its millions of inhabitants is extracted from ground aquifers, which causes subsidence of more than 180 mm per year in some districts of the city. Second, the majority of water from the 13 rivers must be pumped up from the city, 40 % of which is below sea level, over the sea wall in North Jakarta. Third, to support its rate of growth and combat these environ-mental conditions, the city has an extremely high density of interconnected infra-structure. The overlay of these three geographical features results in a series of critical infrastructure interdependencies that bear heavily on flood management in Jakarta. The collapse of one infrastructure component can trigger cascading fail-ures across urban systems, dramatically worsening the situation. If the power to the pumps fails or is disrupted, the pumps will not operate, causing further flood-ing, as was the case in 2015 [12]. Notably, in this instance, the power grid of the flooded neighbourhood was shut down to reduce the risk of electrocution, one of the leading causes of mortality during flooding [20]. However, this inadvertently cut power to the pump, which in turn increased the severity of the flooding. This example, and the many others like it, demonstrate how, in the context of flood management in Jakarta, the assessment of infrastructure cannot simply attend to physical assets, such as power stations and pumps, but must use a more holistic methodology in order to comprehend the complete socio-technological system and its interconnected character.

Indeed, by conventional standards, Jakarta is a data-scarce environment [1]. The urban environment changes so rapidly that traditional empirical observations meant to aid in governmental decision-making cannot keep pace. In this rapidly changing environment, where urban infrastructure is in direct conflict with water flowing in and through the city, existing data are often unsuitable, unavailable, or not properly coordinated between organisations charged with understanding the situation in real-time or conducting thorough post-event analyses [1]. As a result, it has not been possible to develop measures of resilience to quantify the risk of flooding across the city, nor to develop methods of adaptation or mitigation to the monsoon—a phenomenon worsening with climate change [19].

2.1 Infrastructure Complexity and Fragility in Jakarta

Jakarta is dependent on a complex system of interconnected hydraulic and hydro-logical infrastructure that moves water from the mountains of west Java into the Java Sea. Increased runoff coupled with the growing amount of impermeable sur-face ([14]; see also Fig. 1) and ground subsidence mean that over 40 % of the city is now below sea level and requires active intervention from pump stations to move water from ground to sea level. Failures in pump infrastructure during the annual monsoon season regularly lead to severe flooding events causing loss of life, property damage, and economic loss [8, 9].

In this context, flooding in Jakarta is largely a function of fragile infrastructure, whose breaking points cannot be adequately predicted with traditional modelling approaches. Given the increase in severe weather events and sea level rise under global climate change [29], if one wanted to understand Jakarta's potential for resilience in the face of future flood events, one would need to consider the city's infrastructure as a complex system of interconnected infrastructures and people. However, there is currently very little data in Jakarta detailing the city's responses to flooding, without which the government is unable to make informed evidence-based decisions concerning flood response [1, 18, 28].

Seasonal flooding has been recorded in Jakarta since the 1600s, and a formal system of hydraulic infrastructure was established and maintained by the Dutch in the colonial city of Batavia from 1850 to 1918. Despite a series of ongoing infrastructure investments by the Indonesian government following Independence in 1945, the city has been plagued by severe flooding more than six times since 1979. The floods of 1996–1997 were particularly disastrous, where over 30,000 people were forced to evacuate their homes. A decade later, the situation wors-ened: the floods of 2007 inundated 320,000 residences and claimed the lives of 80 people [25]. At present, 72.7 % of Jakarta is prone to flooding [23], threatening the lives of over nearly 1,000,000 residents (nearly 10 % of the population of Jakarta proper), with residents in North Jakarta facing the highest risk [23].

The situation in Jakarta is further worsened by changes in upstream catchment management outside of the city. The majority of the rivers flowing through Jakarta originate in the mountainous area around the city of Bogor, 60 km to the south of Jakarta. Undeveloped land around Bogor (which is the head of the catchment area) provides natural surface absorption and infiltration during rainfall events. Despite being covered by designated conservation areas, this land is under increasing pressure from development [21], decreasing natural infiltration and increasing surface runoff into the river system, putting a serious strain on the downstream hydrological system in Jakarta during the annual monsoon rains.

2.2 Jakarta's Flood Mitigation Infrastructure

Jakarta relies on hydrological and hydraulic infrastructure to manage the movement of water through the city and mitigate intense periods of rainfall that occur during the annual monsoon season (November to March). Despite previous administrations having focused investment on construction of new physical infrastructure assets, in 2012 only 414 of Jakarta's 555 pumps were operational for the monsoon season [13]. Evidence-based decision making on new infrastructure investment as well as targeted and prioritised infrastructure maintenance is currently restricted by a lack of data and understanding of Jakarta's critical interdependencies, energy demands, and integrated infrastructure assessment. Development of new infrastructure to alleviate infrastructure stress and increase resilience adds layers of complexity, uncertainty, and risk to urban planning and design [26]—complexity and risk that cannot currently be quantified using Jakarta's existing datasets on flooding. Furthermore, because infrastructure facilities are not independent but are highly interconnected [7, 26], functional failures in one flood management facility can make any attempt to add new components to the system difficult to plan [11, 28].

Related to Jakarta's data scarcity problem [1], information and communication technologies (ICT) are not currently prevalent within the city's flood management infrastructure. And yet, given the high penetration of mobile devices and social media use in the region, the Jakarta government is well positioned to collaborate with its citizens to gather data via public participation to monitor and respond to flood events across the city during the monsoon season. Such a process of civic co-management would help tackle the problem of limited data and provide an evidence base for both situational management of infrastructure as well as future planning efforts. Critically, though, such an integration of public ICT infrastructure into flood response and planning should be complemented by an open data approach, preferably using open source software, to help support and foster the disaster risk management and infrastructure planning within the megacity's digital ecosystems [11].

3 Social Media as a Platform for Civic Co-management

Jakarta has one of the highest numbers of Twitter users of any city on the planet, contributing to approximately 2.4 % of the world's total tweets in 2012 [24]. The twenty-first century rise in social media usage, particularly in Asia, has been supported by the growth of ubiquitous computing in the form of internet-connected mobile devices [6, 10]. The creation of global-scale, two-way communication networks via internet devices and social media provides unprecedented volumes of data relevant for analysis of urban systems [10, 27]. In a disaster risk management (DRM) context, data captured by mobile devices (text, images, etc.) and distributed via social media along with geospatial location metadata are an invaluable source of real-time situational information, particularly in dense urban environments with a high proportion of networked users [16].

Making sense of this flood of real-time information during emergency situations is a key challenge for governmental actors responding to extreme weather events [16]. The PetaJakarta.org project was developed as a GeoSocial Intelligence Joint Pilot Study (of the SMART Infrastructure Facility, BPBD DKI Jakarta, and Twitter Inc.) to investigate the utility of social media networks as a tool to promote intra-urban resilience during extreme weather events, and as a data source for studying the longer-term effects of climate change in Southeast Asian megacities. The key concept behind GeoSocial Intelligence is a "people-as-sensors" paradigm, where confirmed situational reports are collected directly from the street in a manner that removes the need for computationally expensive filtering and data processing undertaken either by machines or humans [16]. In the latter case, previous projects have successfully crowdsourced analysis of incoming data, creating communities of "digital humanitarians" [16], however, the disadvantage of this approach is the time lag between data received and its processing, i.e. it's availability for decision support. Extending these lessons, the PetaJakarta.org project was developed as an experimental research and design project to prototype a system for the creation of a real-time, crowd-sourced map of flood conditions in Jakarta, enabled by the submission of confirmed reports directly from the users on the ground. Based on prior research [5, 28], it was envisaged that such a map would be of direct benefit to both the public and to government decision makers tasked with responding to the flooding. The remainder of this section describes the methodology and evidence-based design practice that led to the parameterization and development of the system. Following this, Sect. 3 describes the process of system operation and use by the government stakeholder, the Jakarta emergency management agency (BPBD DKI Jakarta).

3.1 Spatio-temporal Perspectives on Flood-Related Tweets in Social Media

Jakarta was chosen as the study area for this joint pilot study because of the severity of annual flooding there, coupled with the density of social media users. Prior to the development of the operational system, analysis of flood-related social media activity was conducted using two data sets. Twitter was selected as the social media network for use in this study due to the speed of response observed on the platform in the context of previous natural hazards [2, 4] and because of the purported high density of users in Jakarta [24].

To quantify Twitter activity in Jakarta related to flooding, an initial system test was conducted by connecting to the public Twitter API and recording tweets with selected keywords related to flooding including *banjir* (flood), *tinggi* (high), *genangan* (pool), and *terendam* (submerged) within the bounding box of Jakarta. The test took place over a 24-h period spanning February 5 and 6, 2014, during which time heavy rains caused a number of significant flood events across the city. The system test captured over 150,000 tweets matching one of the aforementioned keywords within the specified period, of which 5000 tweets contained precise geolocation information.

The level of Twitter activity related to flooding captured by the system testing was corroborated using a second data set: the Twitter #DataGrant program provided an archive of eight million tweets related to flooding for the 2012–2013 and 2013–2014 monsoon seasons. Figure 2 shows the geolocated tweets across the city during the latter period. Strikingly, these data (see Fig. 2) show a high spatial coverage of relevant tweets across the city, wherein the road network is discernable.

Fig. 2 Map of tweets related to flooding during the 2013–2014 monsoon season. *Data source* Twitter #DataGrant; [11]

These results indicated confirmed that Twitter was a valuable source of real-time situational information during flood events in Jakarta.

3.2 Big Crowdsourcing

Social media provides a ready-made communication network that can be used to capture and transmit the experience of citizens during extreme weather events, which, in a DRM context, can provide actionable information for decision support in government agencies. Still, it is important to stress that social media is not a replacement for traditional forms of communication, existing data sources, community outreach, or preparedness planning during disasters. The PetaJakarta.org project was grounded in this hypothesis: leveraging social media data to transform data into information, using a geosocial intelligence methodology, would enable the creation of a real-time knowledge network of unprecedented spatial and temporal resolution.

The challenge facing decision makers seeking to use social media as a source of data for situational overview is two-fold: first, data volume and selection of appropriate filtering methodologies is critical. Second, verification of information is imperative, even after filtering. In particular, where social media data is harvested in a passive manner based on a specific keyword or hashtag, there is no indication as to whether the information received relates specifically to the situation at the user's reported location, and in many cases could simply be conversational in nature. Furthermore, the potential volume of relevant tweets in Jakarta as recorded in the system testing and Twitter #DataGrant data sets indicated that, in the case of Jakarta, a robust filtering methodology was required to transform the "noise" of Twitter activity into actionable knowledge. While approaches to removing outlying or non-relevant data have been successfully used for decision-making (see e.g. [15], 22), to conduct this kind of filtering in a real-time DRM context is challenging both from a programming and a computational perspective [16].

As part of its GeoSocial Intelligence approach, PetaJakarta.org developed a new methodology, "big crowdsourcing," to collect verified reports of flooding from residents in Jakarta, without the need for further data processing. By "listening" to the Twitter stream in a manner similar to the system testing, PetaJakarta.org was able to detect conversations featuring specific keywords. Tweets containing these words were subsequently recorded as "unconfirmed reports," and the relevant users were then invited to confirm whether flooding was taking place at their location. Based on an evaluation of the system testing and the Twitter #DataGrant, a number of keywords such as tinggi (high) generated high numbers of false-positives (i.e. tweets not related to flooding), thus for the operational system only the keywords "flood" and "banjir" were selected.

A unique aspect of the PetaJakarta.org pilot project was its attempt to harness the power of the social media network by automating the distribution of invitation tweets from the PetaJakarta.org Twitter account, @petajkt, calling on citizens to submit their flood reports. Invitation tweets also used the Twitter Card technology to feature an embedded sixty second video explaining the project. To submit a confirmed report of the situation on the ground, users were simply requested to send a geo-located tweet from their mobile device to @petajkt with the keywords "flood" or "banjir." Once received, these reports were classed as "Confirmed," and contributors were able to see their tweets appear on the publicly-available map at PetaJakarta.org in real-time. This map also acted as the government interface to the reports (see Sect. 3.4), helping to maintain transparency of data access between citizens and the government.

Similar to crowdsourcing of Earthquake reports in the late nineteenth and early twentieth centuries, PetaJakarta.org afforded users the opportunity to report the flood situation in an unrestricted manner, including text and media, to generate an effective and reliable situational data set from non-specialist observers [3]. Using this approach, PetaJakarta.org was the first project in the world to *programmatically* send invitations to Twitter users to participate in a crowdsourcing effort to map a natural hazard in order to collect confirmed situational reports from the ground.

To support the sending of programmatic invitations and the collection of data, Twitter provided access to its PowerTrack service, which provides real-time filtering of all available tweets at the specified location. Over the course of the 2014–2015 monsoon season, PetaJakarta.org sent 89,000 programmatic tweet invitations, which were seen by over 2.2 million users. This outreach generated 1000 confirmed reports of flooding during five major flood events. Figure 3 shows the relationship between Twitter impressions and the flood events, highlighting the relationship between flooding and "tweet engagement" from PetaJakarta.org on

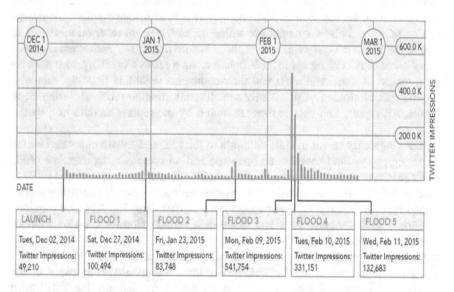

Fig. 3 Timeseries of Twitter impressions from the *@petajkt* account during five flood events of the 2014–2015 monsoon season. *Data source* Twitter Analytics; [11]

the Twitter platform. Engagement is measured by the Twitter metric "impressions," defined as the number of times a user views a specific tweet in their timeline or from a search request. This relationship occurs because programmatic invitations are sent in response to conversations about flooding, "unconfirmed reports." As more users are tweeting the word "banjir" during flood events, more invitations are sent and viewed by more users, thus generating more impressions. In this manner, the system highlights the potential for this methodology of programmatic invitation to reach a high number of users in order to generate a self-selecting filtered set of data of confirmed situational reports in real-time. The results and an evaluation of this process are discussed below in Sect. 4.

3.3 CogniCity: An Open Source GeoSocial Intelligence Framework

To facilitate the collection and mapping of citizen flood reports via Twitter, a suite of open source software (OSS) termed "CogniCity" was created. CogniCity is a GeoSocial Intelligence Framework OSS, for which PetaJakarta.org was the pilot project. The framework is divided into three components. The reports module manages the connection to the Twitter PowerTrack data stream and the sending of programmatic invitations to users in Jakarta. When a tweet is received, the module classifies the report as Unconfirmed or Confirmed, and if required sends the user an invitation to participate. To avoid repeated invitation messages being sent to the same user, the reports module keeps a record of users who have previously been contacted by the system. User privacy is a central theme within the design of CogniCity and all user names are stored separately from received messages to ensure the anonymity of submitted reports. Furthermore, user names are recorded using a one-way cryptographic hash function. As a result CogniCity does not create a record of individual users and their comments regarding flooding, minimising the risk of storage of potentially sensitive information received during flood events. All reports and user hashes are stored by the reports module in a spatial database.

The CogniCity server module connects to the spatial database populated by the incoming reports and provides an open application programming interface (API) to access the recorded data. APIs enable machine-to-machine requests and transactions of information and, in this case, provide geospatial data representing unconfirmed and confirmed reports generated from Twitter data. The API also provided additional ancillary geospatial data to aid data visualisation for decision support. The data included municipal boundaries in the city at different spatial scales, and a representation of Jakarta's hydrological infrastructure network. In addition to providing the data used by the PetaJakarta.org map, the open API, by using industry-standard geospatial data formats and protocols, enabled any interested third party to connect to the API and request data in real-time. For example, BPBD DKI

Jakarta were able to connect their existing geographical information system (GIS) directly to the PetaJakarta.org API to gather data for off-line analysis and to support scenario planning.

The server module also encompassed the third and final component of CogniCity, the PetaJakarta.org website and real-time map. The website was available in both Bahasa Indonesian and English and included instructions on how to submit reports using Twitter and the same instructional video used by the Twitter Card in the programmatic invitation. The real-time map worked by connecting the client's device to the open data API to gather the data for the required map layer. Once the data was received by the user's device, it was then able to render the data on the map. Users connecting to the website using a touch screen mobile device were presented with a point-based visualisation of confirmed and unconfirmed reports near their current location. The interface for users connecting from a non-mobile device (e.g. a personal computer) consisted of the aggregate overview of reports across the entire city, designed to match BPBD DKI Jakarta's existing reporting systems (as described in the next section).

Both the reports and server modules were developed using the NodeJS software platform to maximise scalability and were deployed in a cloud environment that automatically adjusted the computing resources required, depending on the number of incoming reports and connected users.

3.4 Cartographic Interface for Government Decision-Support

The design of PetaJakarta.org and its underlying open source software CogniCity was based on an integrated co-research methodology, and developed in partnership with the Jakarta government. To optimise the system's utility and integration within the government emergency management informatics division, it was necessary to understand the agency's existing operational procedures and protocols in response to flooding. This institutional ethnography required many formal meetings, interviews, and group discussions. Building on the existing knowledge base, CogniCity was developed to be highly transferable, not only to other regions within Indonesia but also to other domains of application, geographies, and languages. These two objectives—building a system suitable to the needs of the Jakarta government and maintaining application transferability—helped parameterize the design requirements of the PetaJakarta.org interface and its underlying software.

The Jakarta Emergency Management Agency (BPBD DKI Jakarta) is responsible for coordinating the government response to flood events in Jakarta. BPBD DKI Jakarta was the key stakeholder and government user of the information gathered by PetaJakarta.org. In October 2012, eight members of BPBD DKI Jakarta travelled to Wollongong, Australia, to participate in a research workshop hosted by the SMART Infrastructure Facility at the University of Wollongong. The objective of this workshop was to detail the institutional ethnography of BPBD DKI Jakarta's operational structure, decision-making process, and the information pathways within the existing disaster information management system (DIMS). The workshop allowed the PetaJakarta.org research team to understand how existing streams of data were consumed and used for decision support during flood events in BPBD, and enabled both organisations to agree on the design and development requirements for the interface to the PetaJakarta.org system. One of the important outcomes of the workshop was a defined perspective on the role of social media within the organisation during flood events; the purpose of PetaJakarta.org, it was agreed, was to complement existing, traditional data sources, and feed into existing decision making structures within BPBD, so as to maximise utility of the collected data. In this regard, the technical specifications of the system were developed in conjunction with an understanding of the operational concerns and existing logic of the agency. Without such an intensive institutional ethnography that included technical, social, and ethical dimensions, it is evident that the project could not have succeeded.

Building on its unique method of outreach, PetaJakarta.org is capable of transforming tweets into actionable knowledge for decision-support. As a result, reports were mapped in real-time so that users could see the location, time, and content of reports in a spatial format, highlighting areas of the city currently experiencing flooding. To match existing spatial and temporal representation of flood reports from BPBD's formal data sources, the PetaJakarta.org map aggregated counts of reports by municipal area over 1, 3 or 6 h periods (Fig. 4). This aggregation was conducted across the entire city in an interactive manner so that the user could see the situation at the city-scale and identify hot-spots of activity. The user was then able to "drill down" through the map, in a manner consistent with existing geospatial business intelligence platforms [30], to interrogate data at the street-level, including viewing individual reports. The interface was further enhanced by the inclusion of optional geospatial layers showing Jakarta's hydrological network. It is anticipated that future implementations of the system could enhance this feature by linking flood reports to failures of specific infrastructure assets, furthering the utility of information available for decision makers.

4 Functional Evaluation

The PetaJakarta.org project was officially launched in December, 2014, by the governor of Jakarta, Basuki Tjahaja Purnama. The first tweet, sent by the governor, called on the president of Indonesia, Joko Widowo (known colloquially as Jokowi), to submit his reports of flooding in Jakarta to PetaJakarta.org. The acceptance, promotion, and championing of the project by the governor helped to promote and legitimise the project for the Jakarta government and the general public. During the monsoon period, following the launch, PetaJakarta.org received

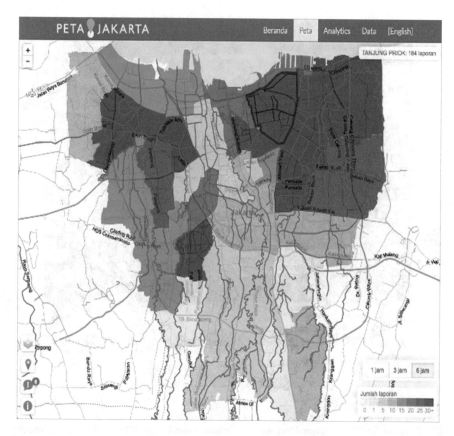

Fig. 4 Screencapture of PetaJakarta.org Map showing aggregate display of "Banjir" Tweets on 23 January, 2015

over one thousand confirmed reports of flooding. The website was visited more than 97,000 times and during the most severe flood events during more than 3000 users per hour. This section describes the reports received, and evaluates the system's use and uptake within the Jakarta government.

4.1 Tweet Typologies

Of the 1000 confirmed flood reports received over the 2014–2015 monsoon season, there were three distinct typologies of message. The first consisted of flood reports detailing the current situation at the user's current location (Fig. 5). These reports contained detailed information on flood conditions, often including the height of the water either in empirical units or by reference to the human body (e.g. knee-high, etc.). Many of these reports also included photos of the flood conditions,

Fig. 5 A confirmed flood report containing estimated water height, user location by government area, and photograph of the situation

which were frequently used by BPBD DKI Jakarta in conjunction with user text as a means of verifying and classifying the severity of the situation (see Sect. 3.2).

The second report typology was made up of requests for help and evacuation. These reports involved two-way communication between citizens and the government, facilitated by PetaJakarta.org. In instances where tweets corresponded directly to individual requests for assistance, reports were sent directly to BPBD DKI Jakarta, to ensure appropriate response was coordinated. The project's strong working relationship with BPBD DKI Jakarta was critical to ensuring citizen safety. In addition to direct requests for help, PetaJakarta.org also acted as a conduit for information dissemination on government response to flooding (Fig. 6), and as a peer-to-peer re-broadcasting platform for confirmed information relating to government and community response, such as confirming the location or contact details of evacuation shelters.

The last type of tweet typology was comprised of reviews and feedback regarding the project, including thanks and votes of confidence. In some cases, these reports also contained information about pre-existing reports, either confirming their validity or reporting that the situation had changed (e.g. flood waters had

Fig. 6 Tweet from Jakarta Government Department for Social Services reporting emergency aid supplies being delivered to a flood evacuation centre

receded). Although the real-time map only displayed reports for the hour after they were received, one of the criticisms of the platform was that there was no procedure for citizen users or BPBD DKI Jakarta to remove reports which were no longer deemed relevant. Instead, many users sent PetaJakarta.org screenshots of existing reports on the map, using their mobile device, to show which reports where incorrect or no longer relevant.

4.2 BPBD DKI Jakarta Operational Usage

Using the confirmed reports received by PetaJakarta.org as described above, the project helped BPBD DKI Jakarta gain a real-time situational overview of the flood conditions in the city. In addition to the collection and aggregation of confirmed flood reports, the project also helped form a two-way communication channel between BPBD and citizens, helping to disseminate key messages back to citizen users by re-tweeting information including water levels and rainfall forecasts. Further, the @petajkt Twitter account retweeted information about response and relief efforts carried out by the Jakarta government, such as operating emergency pumps and delivering food, aid, and medical supplies to evacuation shelters. It is worth noting that this dissemination function was performed manually, based on collaborative efforts between the PetaJakarta.org social media coordinator and BPBD DKI Jakarta. In contrast to the process of soliciting, collecting, and aggregating reports for decision support, which was an automated process, the manual collaboration and sharing of information between the two organisations highlighted the value of human oversight and management as an integrated component of the system's operation.

Ultimately, BPBD found the use of the maps of aggregated Twitter activity for situational overview inadequate. Despite being designed to match the existing spatial and temporal scales of reporting used by the agency, these processes did not hold for social media because of the volume of incoming information and the potential to overlook critical reports in areas of low Twitter activity. From an operational perspective, the veracity and quality of the reports was significantly more important to BPBD DKI Jakarta than the overall volume of reports; the agency recognised that a point-based representation of reports would be more useful, especially if in future interfaces this could include a representation of change over time to enable identification and verification of incoming reports.

4.3 SmartCity Jakarta Usage

In addition to BPBD DKI Jakarta using the system as a data source for operational response to flooding, the SmartCity Jakarta project used the PetaJakarta.org open API to access reports of flooding. The Smart City project was developed by the Jakarta government's Office of Communication and Information Services (Dinas Komunikasi dan Informatika Provinsi, DKI Jakarta) as a data hub for the government and citizens alike; it is a government initiative to provide better service delivery by enabling the sharing and access of data in an open manner. Data from PetaJakarta.org was added to the project to show citizen reports of flooding alongside existing relevant data feeds from other government sectors, such as a traffic disruption as a result of flooding. The use of PetaJakarta.org by SmartCity Jakarta highlights the value in providing data beyond the interface developed for BPBD DKI Jakarta, through an open API, so that other government agencies can make use of the data for a variety of purposes.

5 Conclusion and Discussion

The PetaJakarta.org project has demonstrated the utility of using a GeoSocial Intelligence approach to derive actionable information from social media for disaster risk management. The project created a two-way communication channel between Jakarta's citizens and BPBD DKI Jakarta to coordinate the creation of a crowdsourced flood map and relay information about government responses to the flooding, both in real-time. As a result, the project was able to initiate a process of civic co-management as a methodology for promoting resilience to flooding in the flood-prone, coastal megacity of Jakarta.

PetaJakarta.org and the underlying open source software CogniCity harnessed the power of the Twitter social media network to reach a large number of Jakarta's citizens and request relevant information. Despite the potential for an overwhelming volume of non-relevant and trivial information, based on the number of conversations detected with the keywords "flood" or "banjir," citizen reports were of a high quality and veracity. This suggests that the automated programmatic invitation process used is effective in reaching a high number of users and, through the invitation text and embedded video, fostering a process of self-selection by citizens, effectively creating a real-time filter for information gathering. In this context, it is important to understand the system as a socio-technical process, wherein the human interaction by citizens, PetaJakarta.org team, and BPBD was as important, if not more so, than the computational elements. This was especially the case when classifying requests for assistance and ensuring that these were forwarded to BPBD DKI, and when using the @petajkt account to manually disseminate relevant messages from government agencies and communities. This approach is in contrast to previous studies focusing on social media for flood response, which often advocated using a technology-centric approach to disaster risk management (e.g. [11]). Such approaches undervalue existing work by government agencies who use social media as a method of two-way communication. In our view, future research in this area should focus on new, holistic approaches to flood detection, management, and response and leverage new sources of information such as social media.

PetaJakarta.org was developed in conjunction with BPBD DKI Jakarta as the key government stakeholder. Through this collaboration, it was possible to ensure that the system was compatible with existing technologies and processes at BPBD and thereby ensure its utility for decision-support during the flood season. The launch of the system by Jakarta's Governor added to the legitimacy of the system and acceptance of the potential for social media to be a useful addition to the government's existing information stack.

The use of data collected by PetaJakarta.org by the Jakarta SmartCity project, as well as BPBD, highlights the importance and value of developing systems with open data APIs to enable such collaborative data sharing between government departments. It is envisaged that the continuation and extension of this approach would also help foster the disaster risk management ecosystem, not only within government but also across public, education and private sectors as well.

BPBD used the system throughout the monsoon season in parallel with existing formal information systems and decision-making processes. As a result BPBD recognised the utility and role of social media to support real-time situational overview of flood conditions. The use of PetaJakarta.org prompted an evaluation of the existing reporting structure with regards to its suitability for social media. The Agency recognized the need for new formats of reporting from social media, focusing not on aggregate counts of activity but access and visualisation of individual reports so that they can be appropriately classified and actioned for response.

BPBD primarily used the @petajkt Twitter stream to direct their use of the PetaJakarta.org map, and to verify and cross-check information about flood affected areas in real-time. The real-time nature of the tweets often meant that they provided the most up-to-date description of the situation on the ground across the entire city. As a result of the findings from this project, future research should examine the development of an open source platform to integrate multiple sources of data, consolidating existing formal government sources with newer informal sources such as social media [11]. Such a system would further enable emergency agencies to perform real-time evaluations of flood risk; the inclusion of multiple and disparate data sources would continue to enhance decision-support during flood events, while maintaining resilience within the information ecosystem through multiple applications and media for relaying reports from citizens to one another and to the emergency agencies.

Acknowledgements   The authors would like to acknowledge the University of Wollongong Global Challenges Programme, as well as colleagues at BPBD DKI Jakarta and Twitter Inc., for supporting this research.

References

1. Baker, J. L. (2012). *Climate change, disaster risk, and the urban poor: Cities building resilience for a changing world.* World Bank Publications.
2. Bruns, A., Burgess, J. E., Crawford, K., & Shaw, F. (2012). *#qldfloods and @QPSMedia: Crisis communication on Twitter in the 2011 South East Queensland floods.* ARC Centre of Excellence for Creative Industries and Innovation: Queensland University of Technology.
3. Coen, D. R. (2012). *The earthquake observers: Disaster science from Lisbon to Richter.* Chicago: University of Chicago Press.
4. Crooks, A., Croitoru, A., Stefanidis, A., & Radzikowski, J. (2102). Earthquake: Twitter as a distributed sensor system. *Transactions in GIS*, Wiley Online Library.
5. Douglas, M. (1986). *How institutions think.* Syracuse: Syracuse University Press.
6. Easterling, K. (2014). *Extrastatecraft: The Power of infrastructure space.* London and New York: Verso.
7. Ebrahimy, R. (2014). *Investigating SCADA failures in interdependent critical infrastructure systems.* Newcastle, UK: School of Computing Science, Newcastle University.
8. Hartono, D. M., Novita, E., Gusniani, I., & Oriza, I. I. D. (2010). The role of water supply and sanitation during floods: Case study of flood disaster in five regions of jakarta. *International Journal of Technology, 1*, 29–37.
9. Hallegatte, S., Green, C., Nicholls, R. J., & Corfee-Morlot, J. (2013). Future losses in major coastal cities. *Nature Climate Change, 3*, 802–806.
10. Holderness, T. (2014). Geosocial intelligence. *IEEE Technology and Society Magazine, 33*(1), 17–18.
11. Holderness, T., & Turpin, E. (2015). *White paper—PetaJakarta.org: Assessing the role of social media for civic co-management during monsoon flooding in Jakarta, Indonesia.* University of Wollongong, Wollongong.
12. Jego, L. (2015). [Jakarta Banjir] Ahok Meets President Jokowi on power supply to flood pumps. *Global Indonesian Voices*, February 11, 2015. http://www.globalindonesianvoices.com/19078/jakarta-banjir-ahok-meets-president-jokowi-discussed-power-supply-to-flood-pumps. Accessed June 1, 2015.

13. Kompas. (2014). Jakarta Siap Antisipasi Banjir, tetapi 141 Pompa Air Rusak, 24 November. http://megapolitan.kompas.com/read/2014/11/24/11190751/Jakarta.Siap.Antisipasi.Banjir.tet api.141.Pompa.Air.Rusak. Accessed 29th May 2015.
14. Li, H. (2003). Management of coastal mega-cities—A new challenge in the 21st century. *Marine Policy, 27*, 333–337.
15. Medina, E. (2011). *Cybernetic revolutionaries: Technology and politics in Allende's Chile.* Cambridge MA: MIT Press.
16. Meier, P. (2014). *Digital humanitarians: How big data is changing the face of humanitarian response.* Boca Raton: CRC Press.
17. Nancy, J.-L. (2015). *After Fukushima: The equivalence of catastrophes* (C. Mandell, Trans.). New York: Fordham University Press.
18. Paar, P., & Rekittke, J. (2011). Low-cost mapping and publishing methods for landscape architectural analysis and design in slum-upgrading projects. *Future Internet, 3*, 228–247.
19. Pachauri, R. K., & Meyer, L. A. (2014). *Climate change 2014: Synthesis report.* Contribution of Working Groups I, II and III to the Fifth Assessment Report of the Intergovernmental Panel on Climate Change. IPCC, Geneva.
20. Peters, G., Butsch, C., Krachten, F., Kraas, F., Namperumal, S., & Marfai, M. A. (2015). *Analyzing risk and disaster in Megaurban systems—Experiences from Mumbai and Jakarta.*
21. Rahmawati, L. (2015). *Vila-vila bekas bongkar di Puncak dibangun kembali.* Antara News, 23 April. http://www.antaranews.com/berita/492388/vila-vila-bekas-bongkar-di-puncak-dibangun-kembali. Accessed 2 June 2015.
22. Reeves, J. (2015). *Crowdsourcing tools for flood reporting in Jakarta.* Humanitarian OpenStreetMap Team. Indonesia-Australia Facility for Disaster Reduction
23. Rostanti, Q. (2012). *13 Sungai di Jakarta Berpotensi Banjir,* Republika Online 19 November. http://www.republika.co.id/berita/nasional/jabodetabek-nasional/12/11/19/mdq562-13-sungai-di-jakarta-berpotensi-banjir. Accessed May 22, 2015.
24. Semiocast. (2012). *Twitter reaches half a billion accounts.* http://semiocast.com/en/publications/2012_07_30_Twitter_reaches_half_a_billion_accounts_140m_in_the_US. Accessed 20 April June 2015.
25. Taufik, M. (2014). *Ini 5 banjir besar yang pernah melumpuhkan Jakarta.* Merdeka, 16 January. http://www.merdeka.com/peristiwa/ini-5-banjir-besar-yang-pernah-melumpuhkan-jakarta. Accessed May 22, 2015.
26. Tran, M., Hall, J., Hickford, A., Nicholls, R., et al. (2014). *National infrastructure assessment: Analysis of options for infrastructure provision in Great Britain, Interim results.* UK Infrastructure Transitions Research Consortium, Environmental Change Institute. University of Oxford.
27. Townsend, A. M. (2013). *Smart cities: Big data, civic hackers, and the quest for a New Utopia.* New York: W.W. Norton and Co.
28. Turpin, E., Bobbette, A., & Miller, M. (Eds.). (2013). *Jakarta: Architecture + adaptation.* Jakarta: Universitas Indonesia Press.
29. Walsh, C. L., Dawson, R. J., Hall, J. W., Barr, S. L., Batty, M., Bristow, A. L., et al. (2011). Assessment of climate change mitigation and adaptation in cities. *Proceedings of the ICE—Urban Design and Planning, 164*(9), 75–84.
30. Wickramasuriya, R., Ma, J., Berryman, M., & Perez, P. (2013). Using geospatial business intelligence to support regional infrastructure governance. *Knowledge-Based Systems, 53*, 80–89.

Detecting Bursty Topics of Correlated News and Twitter for Government Services

Takehito Utsuro, Yusuke Inoue, Takakazu Imada, Masaharu Yoshioka and Noriko Kando

Abstract This chapter presents a framework of detecting bursty topics of correlated news and twitter, and discusses how to integrate the framework into government services. Especially, as a specific application of the proposed framework of detecting bursty topics of correlated news and twitter, this chapter gives an example of collecting news and twitter that are related to "the 2012 London Olympic game" and applying the proposed framework.

Keywords Time series news and twitter · Topic model · Kleinberg's burst model

1 Introduction

This chapter presents a framework of detecting bursty topics of correlated news and twitter, and discusses how to integrate the framework into government services. This framework is quite applicable to various situations that are concerned with formulation of governmental policies on government services including education, economy, diplomacy, technology, welfare, finance, etc. Among those issues, this chapter concentrates on issues regarding government services for sports event. Especially, as a more specific application of the proposed framework of detecting bursty topics of correlated news and twitter, this chapter gives an example of collecting news and twitter that are related to "the 2012 London Olympic game" and applying the proposed framework.

T. Utsuro (✉) · Y. Inoue · T. Imada
University of Tsukuba, Tsukuba 305-8573, Japan
e-mail: utsuro@iit.tsukuba.ac.jp

M. Yoshioka
Hokkaido University, Sapporo 060-0808, Japan

N. Kando
National Institute of Informatics, Tokyo 101-8430, Japan

© Springer International Publishing Switzerland 2015
S. Nepal et al. (eds.), *Social Media for Government Services*,
DOI 10.1007/978-3-319-27237-5_7

Olympic games are known as one of the most important international and national sports event, where governments of many countries in the world are involved in various processes regarding the events. In the case of Japan, the Ministry of Education, Culture, Sports, Science and Technology which is responsible for the events of the Olympic games has budgets on the Olympic games and works on promoting the events. When the ministry formulates its policy on how to promote the Olympic games, it is quite desirable that it carefully watches how the news and the TV report the events and how people feel and have opinion on the policies of the ministry regarding the Olympic games. Especially, it quite often happens that the situation all over the world as well as in one's own country suddenly changes and the news and the TV report the sudden changes and people occasionally react to the changes through various social media including twitter. For example, in the case of sports events such as the Olympic games, a large number of people have concerns as well as opinions on matters such as who takes over as the coach of a national team, who are to be selected as members of the national teams, whether the national teams of one's own country are to have berths in the next Olympic game, as well as whether the national teams of one's own country win or lose in the Olympic game. An example of one typical situation is that, if people might have concerns on how to spend the budget for the 2020 Olympic game to be held in Tokyo, and the concerns might grown into a burst, then the local Olympic Organizing Committee has to carefully watch people's concerns and opinions.

Considering such a motivation, this chapter presents the framework of detecting bursty topics of correlated news and twitter, and shows how to apply the framework to news and twitter that are related to "the 2012 London Olympic game".

2 Overview of the Framework of Detecting Bursty Topics of Correlated News and Twitter

The background of our framework is in two types of modeling of information flow in news stream, namely, burst analysis and topic modeling. Both types of modeling, to some extent, aim at aggregating information and reducing redundancy within the information flow in news stream.

First, when one wants to detect a kind of topics that are paid much more attention than usual, it is usually necessary for him/her to carefully watch every article in news stream at every moment. In such a situation, it is well known in the field of time series analysis that Kleinberg's modeling of bursts [1] is quite effective in detecting burst of keywords.

Second, topic models such as LDA (latent Dirichlet allocation) [2] and DTM (dynamic topic model) [3] are also quite effective in estimating distribution of topics over a document collection such as articles in news stream. Unlike LDA, in DTM, we suppose that the data is divided by time slice, for example by date. DTM models the documents (such as articles of news stream) of each slice with a K-component topic model, where the kth topic at slice t smoothly evolves from the kth topic at slice $t - 1$.

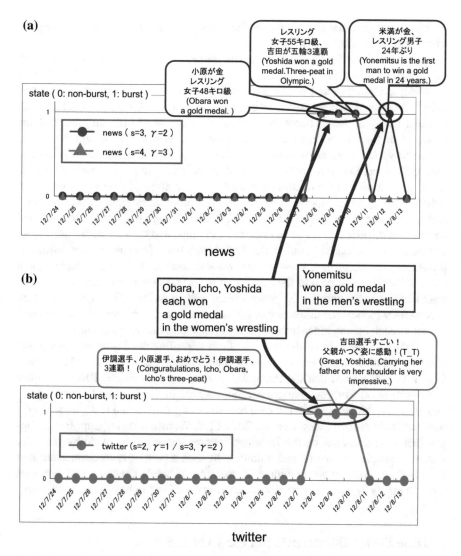

Fig. 1 Optimal state sequence for the topic "wrestling". **a** News. **b** Twitter

Based on those arguments above, Takahashi et al. [4] proposed how to integrate the two types of modeling of information flow in news stream. Here, it is important to note that Kleinberg's modeling of bursts is usually applied only to bursts of keywords but not to those of topics. Thus, Takahashi et al. [4] proposed how to apply Kleinberg's modeling of bursts to topics estimated by a topic model such as DTM. Typical results of applying the technique to time series news stream can be illustrated as in Fig. 1a. In this example, we first estimate time series topics through DTM, among which is the one "wrestling" as shown in this figure. Then, we can detect the burst of the topic on the dates when those two Japanese wrestlers won the gold medals.

In order to show the applicability of the framework proposed in Takahashi et al. [4] as well as how general the framework is, we study another issue, which is time series topic modeling and bursty topic detection of possibly correlated news and twitter. News and twitter are sometimes closely correlated, while sometimes each of them has quite independent flow of information, due to the difference of the concerns of their information sources. In order to effectively capture the nature of those two text streams, it is very important to model both their correlation and their difference. Our framework first models their correlation by applying a time series topic model to the document stream of the mixture of time series news and twitter. This approach successfully models the time series topic models of news and twitter as closely correlated to each other. Next, we divide news streams and twitter into distinct two series of document streams, and then we apply our model of bursty topic detection based on the Kleinberg's burst detection model. With this procedure, we show that, even though we estimate the time series topic model with the document stream of the mixture of news and twitter, we can detect bursty topics individually both in the news stream and in twitter. This approach again successfully models the difference of the two time series topic models of news and twitter as each having independent information source and its own concern.

Actually, in the case of the real situations regarding the Japanese government and international sports events such as the Olympic game and the FIFA World Cup, it is well known that the Prime Minister of Japan bestowed People's Honor Awards to Saori Yoshida, who won a gold medal in the London Olympic game and achieved thirteen-peat in international wrestling games, and to Japan women's national football team, who won the 2011 FIFA Women's World Cup. It can happen that such decisions by the Japanese government are to be made by carefully watching people's concerns and opinions. In such a case, it is recommended that the Japanese government continues to examine people's concerns and opinions through bursty topics in twitter that are closely correlated to bursty topics in news.

3 Time Series Documents Set for Evaluation

In this chapter, we collect time series news articles of a certain period as well as tweets texts of the same period that are closely related to the news articles. Then, as shown in Table 1, we construct a time series document set consisting of the mixture of the news articles and tweets texts and use it for evaluation.

Table 1 Time series documents set for evaluation

News	Twitter	Total # of document
2,308 articles relevant to "the London Olympic Games" (2012/07/24–2012/08/13)	57,414 tweets relevant to "the London Olympic Games" (2012/07/24–2012/08/13)	59,722

3.1 News

As the news stream documents set for evaluation, during the period from July 24 to August 13, 2012, we collected 3,157 Yomiuri newspaper articles,[1] 4,587 Nikkei newspaper articles,[2] and 3,458 Asahi newspaper articles[3] which amount to 11,202 newspaper articles in total. Then, we select a subset of the whole 11,202 newspaper articles which are related to "the London Olympic game", where we collect 2,308 articles that contain at least one of 8 keywords[4] into the subset. The subset consists of 659 Yomiuri newspaper articles, 679 Nikkei newspaper articles, and 970 Asahi newspaper articles.

3.2 Twitter

As the tweet text data set for evaluation, during the period from July 24 to August 13, 2012, we collected 9,509,774 tweets from the Twitter[5] with the Streaming API. Then, we removed tweets with official retweets and those including URLs, and 7,752,129 tweets remained. Finally, we select a subset which are related to "the London Olympic game". Here, we collect 57,414 tweets that contain at least one of the 8 keywords listed above, which are closely related to "the London Olympic game", into the subset. Since each of the collected 57,414 tweets contain at least one of the 8 keywords, most of them have certain contents regarding "the London Olympic game".

4 Kleinberg's Bursts Modeling

Kleinberg [1] proposed two types of frameworks for modeling bursts. The first type of modeling is based on considering a sequence of message arrival times, where a sequence of messages is regarded as bursty if their inter-arrival gaps are too small than usual. The second type of modeling is, on the other hand, based on the case where documents arrive in discrete *batches* and in each batch of documents, some are *relevant* (e.g., news text contains a particular word) and some are

---

[1]http://www.yomiuri.co.jp/.

[2]http://www.nikkei.com/.

[3]http://www.asahi.com/.

[4]*Gorin* ("Olympic" in Chinese characters), *rondon* ("London" in katakana characters), *orinpikku* ("Olympic" in katakana characters), *kin medaru* ("gold medal"), *gin medaru* ("silver medal") *dou medaru* ("bronze medal"), *senshu* ("athlete"), and *nihon daihyo* ("Japanese national team").

[5]https://twitter.com/.

irrelevant. In this second type of bursts modeling, a sequence of batched arrivals could be considered bursty if the fraction of relevant documents alternates between reasonably long periods in which the fraction is small and other periods in which it is large. Out of the two modelings, this chapter employs the latter, which is named as *enumerating bursts* in Kleinberg [1].

Enumerating Bursts Suppose that there are m batches of documents; the tth batch B_t in the sequence $\mathbf{B} = (B_1, \ldots, B_m)$ of m batches contains r_t relevant documents out of a total of d_t. Let $R = \sum_{t=1}^{m} r_t$ and $D = \sum_{t=1}^{m} d_t$. Now, we define a 2-state automaton $\mathcal{A}^2$, where the state q_0 denotes the non-burst state, while the state q_1 denotes the burst state. For each q_i of the two states q_0 and q_1, there is an expected fraction p_i of relevant documents. Set $p_0 = R/D$, and $p_1 = p_0 s$, where $s > 1$ is a scaling parameter, while $p_1 \leq 1$ holds for p_1.

Viewed in a generative fashion, state q_i produces a mixture of relevant and irrelevant documents according to a binomial distribution with probability p_i. The cost of a state sequence $q = (q_{i_1}, \ldots, q_{i_m})$ in $\mathcal{A}^2$ is defined as follows. If the automaton is in state q_i when the tth batch B_t arrives, a cost of

$$\sigma(i, r_t, d_t) = -\ln\left[\binom{d_t}{r_t} p_i^{r_t}(1 - p_i)^{d_t - r_t}\right]$$

is incurred, since this is the negative logarithm of the probability that r_t relevant documents would be generated using a binomial distribution with probability p_i. There is also a cost of $\tau(i_t, i_{t+1})$ associated with the state transition from q_{i_t} to $q_{i_{t+1}}$. $\tau(i_t, i_{t+1})$ is defined so that the cost of moving from the non-burst state to the burst state is non-zero, but there is no cost for the automaton to end a burst and drop down to a non-burst. Specifically, when $j > i$, moving from q_i to q_j incurs a cost of $(j - i)\gamma$, where $\gamma > 0$ is a parameter[6]; and when $j \leq i$, the cost is 0.

$$\tau(i, j) = \begin{cases} (j - i)\gamma & (j > i) \\ 0 & (j \leq i) \end{cases}$$

Then, given a sequence of batches $\mathbf{B} = (B_1, \ldots, B_m)$, the goal is to find a state sequence $\mathbf{q} = (q_{i_1}, \ldots, q_{i_m})$ that minimizes the cost function:

$$c(\mathbf{q}|\mathbf{B}) = \left(\sum_{t=0}^{m-1} \tau(i_t, i_{t+1})\right) + \left(\sum_{t=1}^{m} \sigma(i_t, r_t, d_t)\right)$$

---

[6]In Kleinberg [1], $\tau(i, j)$ is defined not as $(j - i)\gamma$, but as $(j - i)\gamma \ln m$, where m is the number of batches in the sequence $\mathbf{B} = (B_1, \ldots, B_m)$. In this chapter, we omit the term $\ln m$ in this definition for simplicity.

5 Applying Time Series Topic Model

5.1 Topic Model

As a time series topic model, this chapter employs DTM (dynamic topic model) [3]. Unlike LDA (Latent Dirichlet Allocation) [2], in DTM, we suppose that the data is divided by time slice, for example by date. DTM models the documents (such as articles of news stream) of each slice with a K-component topic model, where the kth topic at slice t smoothly evolves from the kth topic at slice $t − 1$.

In this chapter, in order to model time series news stream in terms of a time series topic model, we consider date as the time slice t. Given the number of topics K as well as time series sequence of batches each of which consists of documents represented by a sequence of words w, on each date t (i.e., time slice t), DTM estimated the distribution $p(w|z_n)(w \in V$, the vocabulary set) of a word w given a topic $z_n(n = 1, ..., K)$ as well as that $p(z_n|b)(n = 1, ..., K)$ of a topic z_n given a document b, where V is the set of words appearing in the whole document set. In this chapter, we estimate the distributions $p(w|z_n)(w \in V)$ and $p(z_n|b)(n = 1, ..., K)$ by a Blei's toolkit,[7] where the parameters are tuned through a preliminary evaluation as the number of topics $K = 50$ as well as $\alpha = 0.01$.

5.2 The Procedure of Applying a Topic Model to the Mixture of News and Twitter

The DTM topic modeling toolkit is applied to the time series document set shown in Table 1, which consists of the mixture of the news articles and tweets texts. Here, as a word w ($w \in V$) constituting each document, we extract Japanese Wikipedia[8] entry titles as well as their redirects.

6 Modeling Bursty Topics in a Topic Model

Based on the formalization of Kleinberg's bursts modeling, this section proposes how to model bursty topics [4] among those estimated through the topic modeling framework of the previous section.

In the modeling of keyword bursts, Kleinberg [1] simply regarded a document as *relevant* when containing a particular keyword, and then count the number r_t of relevant documents out of a total of d_t. In the modeling of topic bursts [4], on the

---

[7]http://www.cs.princeton.edu/~blei/topicmodeling.html.

[8]http://ja.wikipedia.org/.

other hand, a document b is first regarded as *relevant* to a certain topic z_n that are estimated through the DTM topic modeling procedure, to the degree of the amount of the probability $p(z_n|b)$. The number r_t of relevant documents out of a total of d_t is then estimated simply by summing up the probability $p(z_n|b)$ over the whole document set:

$$r_t = \sum_b p(z_n|b)$$

Once having the number r_t, then the total number of relevant documents through-out the whole batch sequence $\mathbf{B} = (B_1, \ldots, B_m)$ as $R = \sum_{t=1}^{m} r_t$ can be estimated. Having the total number of documents throughout the whole batch sequence as $D = \sum_{t=1}^{m} d_t$, the expected fraction of relevant documents can be estimated as $p_0 = R/D$. Then, by simply following the formalization of keyword bursts presented in the previous section, it is quite straightforward to model bursty topics in a topic model.

7 Modeling Bursty Topics Independently from News and Twitter

The previous section describes how to model bursty topics given the result of esti-mating the time series topic model with DTM. It is assumed in the bursty topic modeling of the previous section that the time series documents originate from a single source.

In this section, on the other hand, we are given a time series document set which consists of the mixture of two types of documents originating from two dis-tinct sources, e.g., news and tweets. In this situation, we assume that a time series topic model is estimated with the mixture of two types of time series documents, where the distinction of the two sources is ignored at the step of time series topic model estimation. Then, the following procedure presents how to model bursty topics for each of the two types of time series documents independently. This means, in the case of news and twitter, that, although the time series topic model is estimated with the mixture of time series news articles and tweets texts, bursty topics are detected independently from news and twitter.

In this bursty topic modeling, first, we suppose that, on the date t (i.e., time slice t), we have two types of documents b_x and b_y each of which originates from the source x and y, respectively. Then, for the source x, we regard a document b_x as *relevant* to a certain topic z_n that are estimated through the DTM topic modeling procedure, to the degree of the amount of the probability $p(z_n|b_x)$. Similarly for the source y, we regard a document b_y as *relevant* to a certain topic z_n, to the degree of the amount of the probability $p(z_n|b_y)$. Next, for the source x, we estimate the number $r_{t,x}$ of relevant documents out of a total of $d_{t,x}$ simply by summing up the probability $p(z_n|b_x)$ over the whole document set (similarly for the source y):

$$r_{t,x} = \sum_{b_x} p(z_n|b_x) \quad r_{t,y} = \sum_{b_y} p(z_n|b_y)$$

Once we have the number $r_{t,x}$ and $r_{t,y}$ for the sources x and y, then we can estimate the total number of relevant documents throughout the whole batch sequence
$\mathbf{B} = (B_1, \ldots, B_m)$ as $R_x = \sum_{t=1}^{m} r_{t,x}$ and $R_y = \sum_{t=1}^{m} r_{t,y}$. Denoting the total numbers
of documents on the date t for the sources x and y as $d_{t,x}$ and $d_{t,y}$, respectively,
we have the total numbers of documents throughout the whole batch sequence
as $D_x = \sum_{t=1}^{m} d_{t,x}$ and $D_y = \sum_{t=1}^{m} d_{t,y}$, respectively. Finally, we can estimate the
expected fraction of relevant documents as $p_{0,x} = R_x/D_x$ and $p_{0,y} = R_y/D_y$, respectively. Then, by simply following the formalization of bursty topics presented in
the previous section, it is quite straightforward to model bursty topics independently for each of the two sources x and y. In the following evaluation, we consider the sources x and y as time series news articles and tweet texts shown in
Table 1. As the two parameters s and γ for bursty topic detection, for time series
news articles, we compare two pairs $s = 4$, $\gamma = 3$ and $s = 3$, $\gamma = 2$, and for tweets
text, we compare two pairs $s = 3$, $\gamma = 2$ and $s = 2$, $\gamma = 1$.

8 Evaluation

8.1 The Procedure

As the evaluation of the proposed technique, we examine the correctness of the
detected bursty topics, where we judge the detected bursty topics as appropriate
when the following two requirements are satisfied:

(i) For each topic z_n, collect the documents b which satisfies $z_n = \underset{z'}{\operatorname{argmax}}\, p(z'|b)$
     into the set $B_{1st}(z_n)$.

$$B_{1st}(z_n) = \{b | z_n = \underset{z'}{\operatorname{argmax}}\, p(z'|b)\}$$

Then, judge whether most of the collected documents (both news articles and
tweets texts) $b \in B_{1st}(z_n)$ have relatively similar contents.

(ii) Examine the dates when bursty topics are detected, and also examine news
      articles or tweets texts on the dates of the bursty topics, then judge whether
      contents of news articles and/or tweets texts of the bursty topics can be
      regarded as a certain kind of bursts.

More specifically, we evaluate the detected bursty topics per day or per topic.
As for "per day evaluation", we examine whether, on each day of the burst, the
detected burst is appropriate or not. As for "per topic evaluation", we examine
whether, for each topic, all of the detected bursts are appropriate or not.

Table 2 Evaluation results: detecting bursty topics (for 34 Topics relevant to "the London Olympic Games" out of the whole 50 topics)

	Precision of bursts detected in both news and twitter on the same date/topic (# of correctly detected bursts/# of detected bursts)	Precision of bursts detected only in one of news and twitter (# of correctly detected bursts/# of detected bursts)
News	Per day: 87.5 % (14/16)	Per day: 100 % (2/2), per topic: 100 % (1/1)
Twitter	Per topic: 87.5 % (7/8)	Per day: 100 % (32/32), per topic: 100 % (13/13)

Out of the whole 50 topics, we manually select 34 that are relevant to "the London Olympic games", and show the evaluation results of detecting bursty topics in Table 2. Here, as the two parameters s and γ for bursty topic detection, we show those with $s = 4$ and $\gamma = 3$ for news and $s = 3$ and $\gamma = 2$ for tweets, for which we have the highest precision in bursty topic detection.[9] We also classify the detected bursts per day and detected bursty topics (i.e., *per topic*) into the following two types:

(a) If, on a day, a topic is detected as bursty for both news articles side and tweets texts side, then we judge that *the bursty topic is shared between news and twitter* on the specific day of the burst. We also count the number of distinct topics for all of the detected dates of bursts.

(b) Otherwise, we judge that *the bursty topic is detected only in one of news and twitter* on the specific day of the burst. Also, separately for news and for twitter, we count the number of distinct topics for all of the detected dates of bursts.

In Table 2, precisions of the bursts of type (a) are shown in the column "precision of bursts detected in both news and twitter on the same date/topic", while those of the bursts of type (b) are shown in the column "precision of bursts detected only in one of news and twitter", separately for news and for twitter.

8.2 Evaluation Results

As shown in Table 2, for the bursty topic of type (b) that is *detected only in one of news and twitter*, precisions for both "per day" and "per topic" evaluation are

---

[9]Those evaluation results are still based on inside evaluation, which means that the two parameters s and γ are optimized with the news and tweets for evaluation we show in this chapter. However, we tune the two parameters across the 34 topics for evaluation, where we observed that the optimal values of the two parameters are mostly consistent across 34 topics for evaluation. Parameter optimization with held-out training data is one of our future work.

100 % (both for news and twitter).[10] This result clearly shows that the proposed technique is quite effective in detecting many bursty topics that are observed only in twitter.

For the bursty topic of type (a) that is *shared between news and twitter*, over detection of bursty topics is only for one topic, which is about *"politics"*. The reason why this over detection occurred is mainly because we observed fewer numbers of news articles and tweets on politics during the period of "the London Olympic games", and then, the periods other than "the London Olympic games" are detected as bursty.

Also for the bursty topic of type (a), reasons of bursts in news articles and tweets texts are almost the same as each other. This result clearly supports our claim that the proposed technique is quite effective in detecting closely related bursty topics in news and twitter.

8.3 Examples

Figures 1 and 2 plot the optimal state sequence for the topic "wrestling" and "soccer" for both news and twitter. For those two topics, some of the bursts are shared between news and twitter, so we also show the results of aligning bursts between news and twitter. Figure 3 also plots the optimal state sequence for the topic "good looking athletes", where for this topic, all the documents are from the source twitter and bursts are detected only for twitter. In Figs. 1, 2 and 3, we compare performance for two pairs of the values of the parameters s and γ, i.e., $s = 4$, $\gamma = 3$ and $s = 3$, $\gamma = 2$ for news articles, while $s = 3$, $\gamma = 2$ and $s = 2$, $\gamma = 1$ for tweets texts.

First, as shown in Fig. 1, in the case of the topic "wrestling", in both news and tweets, bursts are detected when each of three wrestling athletes won a gold medal in the women's wrestling. Also as shown in Fig. 1a, in the case of news articles, when detecting bursty topics with values of parameters as $s = 3$, $\gamma = 2$, we observe an additional burst focusing on the fact "Yonemitsu won a gold medal in the men's wrestling". By carefully examining the news articles of the topic "wrestling" on that day, we found that they reported that another wrestling athlete won a bronze medal, and they also had articles on reporting the fact that Japan won a gold medal in the men's wrestling for the first time in 24 years. Also by carefully examining tweets texts of the topic "wrestling" on that day, we found that people did not pay so much attention to the event, compared with the days when each of the three wrestling athletes won a gold medal in the women's wrestling.

---

[10]Although Table 2 only shows the evaluation results for 34 topics that are relevant to "the London Olympic games", even for the whole 50 topics, precision of the detected bursty topics is about 90 % per day/topic for both news articles and tweet texts.

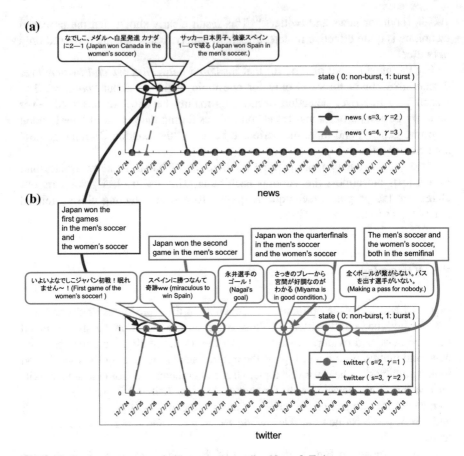

Fig. 2 Optimal state sequence for the topic "soccer". **a** News. **b** Twitter

Next, as shown in Fig. 2, in the case of the topic "soccer", in both news and tweets, bursts are detected when Japan won the first games in the men's soccer and the women's soccer. However, after that event, we observed bursts only in tweets. Throughout the whole period of "the London Olympic games", both Japan's men's and women's soccer national teams continued to win the games until they had the semifinals. This is why people kept paying attention to soccer in "the London Olympic games". It is also true that they reported the results of the games of Japan's men's and women's soccer national teams in news articles. However, throughout the whole period of "the London Olympic games", the number of news articles reporting the results of the Olympics soccer games were constantly large and it is rather difficult to be judged as bursty in time series news.

Finally, Fig. 3 shows the case of the topic "good looking athletes", where bursts are detected only for twitter. It is surprising that tweets that mentioned good looking athletes are collected altogether in this topic. Many tweets collected in this topic on the non-bursty days said that one who posted the tweet likes a certain

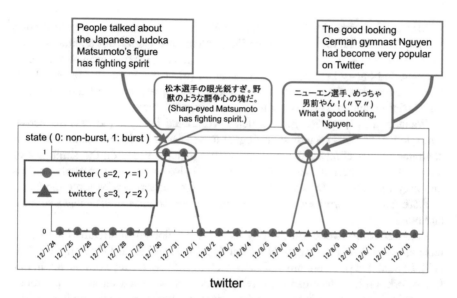

Fig. 3 Optimal state sequence for the topic "good looking athletes" (observed only in twitter)

athlete. And, those tweets share the terms *senshu* (athlete) and *suki* (like). This means that, throughout the whole period of "the London Olympic games", many people posted that they liked certain athletes. But, especially on the days when the bursts were observed, much more people posted that the Japanese judoka Matsumoto and the German gymnast Nguyen were so impressive because of their looking. This is why we observed bursts on those days. These bursts are typical cases of source specific bursts that are observed only for twitter. Obviously, specific benefit of detecting such source specific bursts observed only for twitter is that the proposed model is sensitive to people's concerns and opinions that are not directly concerned with events reported in news. This is actually beneficial for governments that carefully watch people's concerns and opinions, especially when they are regarding issues other than those reported in news such as subcultures like comics and cartoon films.

9 Related Work

Compared with related works, the proposed method has its own significance in that it applies the Kleinberg's burst modeling to statistical time series topic models such as DTM [3]. This chapter shows that the Kleinberg's burst modeling can be easily applied to statistically estimated time series topic models in a quite straightforward fashion. Furthermore, this chapter shows that, even though we estimate the time series topic model with the document stream of the mixture of news and twitter, we can detect bursty topics independently both in the news stream and in twitter.

Mane and Borner [5] also employs the Kleinberg's modeling of keyword burst and applies it to the time series scientific publications. Unlike our approach, however, Mane and Borner [5] represent topics in terms of co-occurrence matrix of frequent and bursty keywords. AlSumait et al. [6] also studied how to rank LDA topics in terms of their significance, although AlSumait et al. [6] did not study time series document streams nor the issue of bursty topics.

Wang et al. [7] studied how to detect correlated bursty topic patterns across multiple text streams such as multilingual news streams, where their method concentrated on detecting correlated bursty topic patterns based on the similarity of temporal distribution of tokens. Zhang et al. [8] also studied how to apply an evolutionary hierarchical Dirichlet process to the task of time series topic modeling of more than one correlated time series information sources such as news streams and blogs.

Some of recent works on event detection from document streams focused on techniques of detecting events in twitter (e.g., Petrović et al. [9], Weng and Lee [10], Li et al. [11]), where most of those techniques rely on keyword bursts. In our framework, on the other hand, we reply on topics estimated through topic modeling techniques, which is the most important difference between previous works and the technique proposed in this chapter. Unlike those works above, Diao et al. [12] proposed a topic model for detecting bursty topics from microblogs, where we are planning to comparatively evaluate our DTM based bursty topic detection technique with that of Diao et al. [12]. One of the major differences between our proposal in this chapter and that in Diao et al. [12] is in that we mainly focus on the modeling of correlation and difference between news and twitter.

10 Conclusion

This chapter presented a framework of detecting bursty topics of correlated news and twitter, and discusses how to integrate the framework into government services. Especially, as a specific application of the proposed framework of detecting bursty topics of correlated news and twitter, this chapter gave an example of collecting news and twitter that are related to "the 2012 London Olympic game" and applying the proposed framework.

From a technical viewpoint, this chapter studied an issue of time series topic modeling and bursty topic detection of possibly correlated news and twitter. This chapter first modeled the correlation of time series news and twitter by applying a time series topic model to the document stream of the mixture of time series news and twitter. This approach successfully modeled the time series topic models of news and twitter as closely correlated to each other. We actually observed that, although the length and term distribution of news and twitter texts have quite different nature, the approach of having the mixture of time series news and twitter is quite beneficial in terms of ignoring the noise in twitter. Quantitative evaluation on the advantage of this approach is one of our future works. Next, we divide news streams and twitter into distinct two series of document streams, and then we apply our model of bursty topic detection based on the Kleinberg's burst detection model. This approach again successfully modeled the difference of the two time series topic models of news and twitter as each having independent information source and its own concern.

Future plans include improving the proposed framework through a larger scale evaluation from various perspectives. Evaluation of recall should be introduced within the overall evaluation procedure. Parameters of topic models such as the number of topics should be examined through further evaluation. Other topic models such as hierarchical ones should be also examined. More theoretical formalization where topic estimation and bursty topic detection are integrated within a single model is also along the direction of future plans. Another issue is how to incorporate online features in the process of detecting bursty topics, where bursty topics should be detected exactly on their early dates when their bursts start without any future time series stream data. Toward this direction, online topic models such as on-line LDA [13] should be examined.

References

1. Kleinberg, J. (2002). Bursty and hierarchical structure in streams. In *Proceedings of 8th SIGKDD* (pp. 91–101).
2. Blei, D. M., Ng, A. Y., & Jordan, M. I. (2003). Latent Dirichlet allocation. *Journal of Machine Learning Research, 3*, 993–1022.
3. Blei, D. M., & Lafferty, J. D. (2006). Dynamic topic models. In *Proceedings of 23rd ICML* (pp. 113–120).
4. Takahashi, Y., Utsuro, T., Yoshioka, M., Kando, N., Fukuhara, T., Nakagawa, H., & Kiyota, Y. (2012). Applying a burst model to detect bursty topics in a topic model. In *JapTAL 2012* (Vol. 7614 of LNCS, pp. 239–249) Berlin: Springer.
5. Mane, K., & Borner, K. (2004). Mapping topics and topic bursts in PNAS. In: *Proceedings of PNAS* (Vol. 101, Suppl 1, pp. 5287–5290).
6. AlSumait, L., Bardara, D., Gentle, J., & Domeniconi, C. (2009). Topic significance ranking of LDA generative models. In *Proceedings of ECML/PKDD* (pp. 67–82).
7. Wang, X., Zhai, C. X., & Hu, R. S. (2007). Mining correlated bursty topic patterns from coordinated text streams. In *Proceedings of 13th SIGKDD* (pp. 784–793).
8. Zhang, J., Song, Y., Zhang, C., & Liu, S. (2010). Evolutionary hierarchical Dirichlet processes for multiple correlated time-varying corpora. In *Proceedings of 16th SIGKDD* (pp. 1079–10881).
9. Petrović, S., Osborne, M., & Lavrenko, V. (2010). Streaming first story detection with application to twitter. In *HLT-NAACL* (pp. 181–189).
10. Weng, J., & Lee, B. S. (2011). LDA-Based document models for ad-hoc retrieval. In *Proceedings of Fifth ICWSM* (pp. 401–408).
11. Li, C., Sun, A., & Datta, A. (2012). Twevent: Segment-based event detection from tweets. In *Proceedings of 21st CIKM* (pp. 155–164).
12. Diao, Q., Jiang, J., Zhu, F., & Lim, E. P. (2012). Finding bursty topics from microblogs. In *Proceedings of 50th ACL* (pp. 536–544).
13. AlSumait, L., Bardara, D., & Domeniconi, C. (2008). On-Line LDA: Adaptive topic models for mining text streams with applications to topic detection and tracking. In *Proceedings of 8th ICDM* (pp. 3–12).

Webcare in Public Services: Deliver Better with Less?

Arthur Edwards and Dennis de Kool

Abstract Social media monitoring and webcare are gradually becoming common practice in public organizations in the Netherlands. This chapter focuses on webcare, i.e. the act of engaging in online communication with citizens to address client feedback. We investigate four cases of webcare by Dutch public organizations. The main goal of webcare is to gain a better insight into relevant sentiments within target groups. Reputation management and anticipation of clients' questions and needs prevail in this endeavour. Improvement of information provision and service delivery on the basis of citizens' feedback are other important motives. In some of our cases, signs of co-production are visible. However, in none of the cases are the impacts of webcare systematically monitored.

Keywords Social media · Social media monitoring · Webcare · Public service delivery

1 Introduction

Social media are becoming important instruments for interactions between governments and citizens [13]. Social media technologies enable citizens to be "active participants in creating, organizing, sharing, commenting, and rating Web content as well as forming a social network through interacting and linking to each other" [7, p. 2]. Clearly, the public sector could benefit from the capabilities of social

A. Edwards · D. de Kool (✉)
Department of Public Administration, Center for Public Innovation,
Erasmus University Rotterdam, P.O. Box 1738, 3000 DR Rotterdam, The Netherlands
e-mail: dekool@risbo.eur.nl

A. Edwards
e-mail: edwards@fsw.eur.nl

media tools, which include, but are not limited to, micro-blogs, content communities, social network sites, multimedia sharing, and internet-based platforms [8, 21]. At the same time, the organizing and sharing potential of social media poses several challenges for public organizations. Social media facilitate a scale shift that makes the organization of collective action, with large numbers of participants, more efficient [6]. Strategic surprises may occur through the number and content of virtual complaints about the quality of public services. The revolt of Dutch secondary school students in 2007 is one such example. The rapid expansion of issues regarding the quality of education and the ad hoc synchronization of messages in web-based protest politics produced a strategic surprise for the Ministry of Education [3]; see also [27].

Public organizations may perceive a need for strategies to cope with these surprises. These strategies include social media monitoring and webcare. This chapter addresses the practice of webcare by public organizations in the context of service delivery. In this context, webcare can be defined as the act of engaging in online communication with citizens (in their role of clients of public services) by actively searching the web to address client feedback (e.g. questions, concerns, and complaints), with the aim of improving the quality of public service delivery.[1] Social media monitoring means actively searching the web to retrieve online communication between clients *without* engaging in online interactions with them. Various software tools are available to perform this activity. In many cases, agencies need first to monitor the online platforms on which their services are likely to be discussed. In other words, social media monitoring can be followed up by webcare.

In terms of public values, social media monitoring and webcare entail some tensions. On the one hand, they can facilitate the tuning of policies to citizens' needs and demands, and this may result in more responsiveness. On the other hand, webcare involves communication with ordinary citizens in virtual domains that they may perceive as private. This poses ethical questions, especially when the public agency is not transparent regarding its activities vis-à-vis social media users. Our central research question is how public organizations use webcare, for what purposes, and how they deal with aspects regarding privacy and transparency. The empirical part of the chapter addresses emerging practices of webcare in four public organizations in the Netherlands. Section 2 introduces webcare, indicating the origins of these practices in the private sector. Section 3 presents our theoretical framework and discusses a number of dilemmas. Section 4 presents the research strategy and the analytical framework. Section 5 analyses the four selected cases. Section 6 concludes and provides further reflections on this new phenomenon of webcare by public organizations.

---

[1]This definition is based on van Noort and Willemsen [33], who refer to webcare by companies in support of customer relationship, reputation, and brand management.

2 Webcare: A First Exploration

The rapid increase in citizens' usage of internet and social media, the possibility of strategic surprises, and security threats have induced governments to develop various online strategies and tools. The use of tools to access and follow relevant communications on social media, as well as to engage in online communication with citizens and clients, is a new development. Social media monitoring and webcare have their origins in the private sector. Dutch examples of companies deploying webcare teams are ING Bank, Rabobank, KLM Royal Dutch Airlines, and the Dutch Railways (NS).

Broadly speaking, these practices are aimed at customer relationships and reputation management. Most publications about these practices and tools are handbooks for companies (e.g. [9, 26, 29]). Building on van Noort and Willemsen's [33, p. 133] definition of webcare in the private sector, we define webcare as the act of engaging in online transactions with citizens to provide information and to address questions, concerns, and complaints. Two forms of webcare can be distinguished. In reactive webcare, messages are sent in a situation of two-way or dialogical communication, in which participating citizens may expect the organization to react to their individual comments. In proactive webcare, messages are sent unsolicitedly [33]. In many cases, webcare will be preceded by social media monitoring, which involves "the continuous systematic observation and analysis of social media networks and social communities" [12].

3 Theoretical Framework

3.1 Theoretical Approaches to Social Media Monitoring and Webcare

Bekkers et al. [4] distinguished three approaches to social media monitoring and webcare, namely, a rational-instrumental, a political-strategic, and a communicative approach. The three approaches start from different premises about the relationship between the monitoring organization and the monitored subjects.

In the rational-instrumental approach, social media monitoring and webcare are primarily conceived of as a means to find out what is going on in the virtual world in order to intervene in this environment with communication that can be expected to be successful in accomplishing certain policy goals. The main advantage of social media monitoring in this approach is that it can be a useful tool to identify relevant trends in society, citizens' opinions about specific policy issues, and target groups' needs. Furthermore, social media monitoring, if embedded in webcare, can be used to correct false, incomplete, or misperceived statements by citizens on social media. Webcare is primarily aimed at fine-tuning policies within the existing policy frameworks.

In the rational-instrumental approach, social media monitoring faces several risks. First, the reliability and quality of information shared in social media can be doubtful [2]. There is a strong perception that an overwhelming amount of irrelevant 'noise' and 'chatter' flows through social media outlets [5, 31]. Furthermore, social media can distribute and enlarge news very quickly, potentially leading to lots of attention on incidents and misconceptions of the day. Third, it is often unclear whether the participants in social media are representative of a larger group. It is a real challenge to select and interpret the relevant and representative signals from the mass of online interactions. An important risk of social media monitoring is that it can result in information overload, which can result in a 'paradox of choices,' in which one cannot see the wood for the trees [25]. For all these reasons, social media monitoring can entail an overestimation of the signalizing power of public sector organizations, i.e. their ability to detect and select relevant signals from citizens.

In the political-strategic approach, the public agency acknowledges the presence of other actors in the environment who have their own orientations, goals, and action plans. Information is seen as a source and an object of power [23]. In this approach, agencies perceive their clients not as passive recipients of communicative interventions, but as active players and opposite numbers. Information generated by social media monitoring can be used by government agencies to serve their organizational interests, for example to find out what is being said about the agency and its policies. In this way, social media monitoring and webcare can contribute to online reputation management. Through webcare, government agencies can try to mitigate (potential) resistance to a policy measure by influencing citizens' points of view in certain directions. In this context, one can speak about 'strategic communication'.

However, online interactions with citizens and clients are politically risky. Statements or messages on social media sent by public organizations can be misperceived or unwelcomed by citizens, thereby (further) harming the public organizations' reputation. Furthermore, information that a public service agency puts on social media can be wrong or incomplete, a mistake, or a result of insufficient internal coordination. Information can also be political, although public service agencies are expected not to make political statements. An example is a police chief who made a political statement about a Dutch political party. This was a clear case of misjudgement. Specific conditions pertaining to the character of public organizations also constrain the use of webcare for strategic communication. Government organizations face some formal restrictions and regulations in their interactions with citizens because in representative democracies they have to consider the primacy of politics. Political decision makers function within a highly politicized environment. Public servants always have to ensure that their statements are consistent with the policies endorsed by the political decision makers.

In the communicative approach, social media monitoring and webcare are aimed at a co-production of policies [15] on the basis of a shared problem definition. The first stage involves gathering information about citizens' perceptions, needs, grievances, and demands, and getting feedback about policies that are being developed or implemented. In the second stage, government organizations react to, and interact by organizing 'collective intelligence' [30]. This can result in new ideas and lead to policies that are better attuned to the problems experienced on the 'work floor' of public policies and in the life world of citizens.

An important risk in this communicative approach is that monitoring can be perceived as an unwelcome interference in peer-to-peer interactions or even a violation of privacy in the social media domain. Furthermore, webcare raises certain expectations among the participants. In a communicative approach, a government agency has to be sincere and consistent in its behaviour, in terms of giving serious attention to citizens' wishes and grievances, and providing room for real cooperation in designing policies. The risks concerning the primacy of politics in representative democracy also apply.

3.2 The Main Challenges of Social Media Monitoring and Webcare

The three approaches indicate the most important goals or driving principles [24] of social media monitoring and webcare. First of all, social media monitoring and webcare can be used to strengthen the effectiveness and efficiency of public service delivery, by fine-tuning and adapting public services, and by serving a variety of customers together ('one to many' principle). However, ethical questions regarding privacy and transparency are at stake, especially when agencies enter online communities which the participants regard as private [1]. 'Perceived privacy' denotes "the degree to which group members perceive their messages to be private to that group" [14, p. 126]. If citizens' online activities take place in networks that are (perceived by them as) public, social media monitoring can be seen as an extension of traditional media monitoring directed at gauging public opinion on political issues. Few ethical considerations seem to apply when these communications are used for social media monitoring and webcare. When citizens communicate on networks that they perceive as private, social media monitoring and webcare can be seen as an unwelcome intrusion into their private sphere [2, 11]. If the perceived privacy of a social network is higher, there is a greater need to approach the network as protected [10]. Public organizations can make different ethical decisions based on their organizational goals and the role of citizens. Webcare by the police and the tax agency, where the citizen has the position of a subject of the state, has a different function than social media monitoring by public agencies with a service function, such as in the domains of education and welfare [4]. The position of a subject of the state implies that the notion of compliance with rules and regulation takes precedence over considerations regarding reputation.

Secondly, public organizations can engage in webcare activities to increase their reputation or to avoid reputational damage. Webcare activities provide various opportunities for approachable interactions with citizens, or to react to questions or complaints from citizens. However, wrong information or political statements by civil servants can harm the reputation of public organizations.

Webcare can also facilitate more responsiveness. This can be accomplished in a top-down manner by fine-tuning communicative messages and policy content to citizens' wishes. However, it can also be used to facilitate governance processes in which citizens participate on a more or less equal footing with public officials, and in which public organizations take into account the ideas and suggestions expressed by citizens. The emergence of the governance paradigm since the 1990s reflects the attention that should be paid to the network interactions through which actors with different interests, beliefs, and resources co-produce policies (e.g. [28]). Social media constitute a new challenge to the classic government paradigm, because they can facilitate bottom-up participation and self-organization. It is interesting to investigate how webcare can support co-production with citizens and responsiveness.

3.3 Conceptual Framework

The use of social media monitoring and webcare can be placed in a broader framework of involving citizens through social media interactions in public service delivery. Figure 1 presents this broader overview.

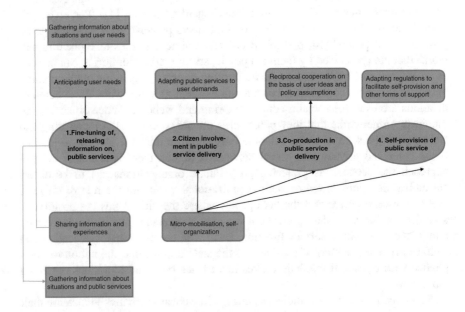

Fig. 1 Involving citizens through social media interactions in public service delivery

The upper part of the figure represents the agency's online activities, the lower part the online activities of citizens. These activities are ordered along a 'ladder of participatory social service delivery'. Building upon Mergel's [17] conceptualization of three objectives of social media uses by governments (transparency, participation, and collaboration), we distinguish four models of public service delivery. In the first model, a government agency uses social media monitoring and webcare for gathering information about user needs. This information can be tapped from social media platforms, where users share information and experiences about public services and their life circumstances. This enables the agency to better anticipate user needs and to fine-tune their service delivery. In this model, there is no direct citizen involvement in the design of service delivery. Government information about public services is broadcast via social media sites. The second model provides for citizen engagement in public service delivery. Citizens are invited to provide opinions and give their feedback. Alternatively, users can organize themselves through social media ('micro-mobilization': [3]), thereby expressing their demands unsolicitedly. Depending on the openness and responsiveness of agencies, this will lead to public services being adapted to user demands. Webcare involves dialogical communication, in which participating citizens may expect the agency to react to their comments ('reactive webcare': [33]). The third model (co-production) indicates a higher level of citizen engagement. In this case, social media are used for reciprocal conversations that might lead to innovative insights and ideas on how existing services can be improved or new services can be conceptualized. Community building can be an outcome of collaboration [17]. In collaborative practices, user ideas are treated on an equal footing with policymakers' assumptions ('reciprocal cooperation'). Under certain conditions, citizens may attempt to satisfy their needs by self-provision of services. These conditions may include situations of combined market and government failures [22], but in some countries (the United Kingdom and the Netherlands are prominent examples: [34]) governments are deliberately and explicitly encouraging citizens to create self-production arrangements, especially in the domains of care and neighbourhood and community services. Social media and online collaboration platforms enable citizen groups and communities to self-organize and engage in self-service [15].

4 Research Design

4.1 Research Strategy

The strategy adopted in this research is a multiple case study approach. A case study recognizes the complex nature of social phenomena in a coherent and integrated way, thereby acknowledging the complex and meaningful interaction between relevant social processes and actors instead of limiting the study of social phenomena to a very specific set of variables and the relations between them [35]. We sought cases of (semi-) public organizations that fulfil or deliver different types of tasks and public services, from which we selected four. The first case is the Dutch Tax and Customs Administration. This agency fulfils a traditional government function, in which the citizen has the role of a subject rather than a client. However, because the effective implementation of taxation laws depends on compliance, the agency's reputation among the taxpayers is an important concern. This organization started social media monitoring activities in 2009. Two years later, the webcare domain was explored by a Twitter experiment around citizens' questions about tax returns. More webcare pilots followed. The second case is the Employee Insurances Implementing Agency. The tasks of this agency are comprised of government functions that are typical for the welfare state. The role of the citizen is that of both a subject and a client. To a certain extent, this agency can adapt its services to the specific needs of (individual or categories of) clients. This agency formed a webcare team in 2009 with the idea of increasing customer satisfaction. The third case is the Dutch Police. The maintenance of domestic order and security is a traditional government function, and in this respect is of the same type as taxation. However, effective policing, especially at local level, entails close relationships between the police and local residents. Local policing is a public service, the implementation of which can be adapted to the needs and wishes of the public. Moreover, (local) policing is dependent on information from the public. The fourth case is an institution for secondary education ('*ROC Mondriaan*'), comprised of five campuses in the western part of the Netherlands. The system of secondary education in the Netherlands is characterized by public funding of privately governed (including privately founded) schools. In the 1990s, the system underwent a process of deregulation and autonomization. Moreover, the government has encouraged larger schools and school mergers. As a result, the Dutch system approaches a market-like situation relatively closely [32].

We used different research techniques to collect the empirical data, namely, a combination of desk research and semi-structured interviews. The interviews were conducted in two time periods. In 2012 and 2013, we conducted interviews with five public servants responsible for social media monitoring and webcare within the tax agency and the employees' insurance agency. Some additional questions to the two agencies were answered by e-mail. In 2014, we conducted additional enquiries by e-mail with our contact persons within these two agencies. In 2012, we conducted five interviews with police officers and communication staff in the Rotterdam-Rijnmond police region. The data collection for the Dutch Police case is also based to a great extent on secondary sources (research reports and articles). We conducted two interviews with communication staff in the ROC Mondriaan in 2014.

4.2 Analytical Framework

Our analytical framework, presented in Table 1, consists of a framework of topics and items for the description of cases, combined with key characteristics of the

Table 1 Analytical framework

Primary topics	Research items/characteristics
Goals	– Goals of webcare Effectiveness, efficiency Reputation management Dialogue, co-production
Way of operating, Surveillance	– Selection of medium, relevant online forums and communities – Selection of relevant content – Performers of webcare within the organization – Analysis of communication – Position of webcare in communication package of the organization – Openness towards social media users
Usage	– Usage of results of webcare, e.g. Anticipating user needs, fine-tuning Adapting services to user demands Co-production of services
Effects	– Effectiveness, strategic control, responsiveness – Costs and benefits (efficiency)

three theoretical approaches referring to the goals of webcare, and its usage. This framework also covers the topics discussed in the second round of interviews.

5 Analysis

5.1 The Dutch Tax and Customs Administration

The interest in social media monitoring and webcare that had been gradually taking hold in the Dutch Tax and Customs Administration (*Belastingdienst*) was given concrete form in 2009. This interest was not triggered by a strategic surprise but was rather driven by an innovative quest for more organizational openness. Because the implementation of taxation laws strongly depends on taxpayers' compliance, the agency's reputation among the taxpayers is an important concern. Furthermore, efficiency considerations were important because the facilities for telephone communication with taxpayers were becoming more and more overburdened.

Goals—The tax agency's primary goal in social media monitoring is to gain insight into taxpayers' sentiments about taxes and their images of the organization. Many sentiments on the internet are fuelled by the traditional press: "Popular moods in the traditional media often result in a snowball effect on social media" (interview). A second goal is to gain a better insight into the questions and problems that clients have with their tax return forms. This can result in a fine-tuning of the information provided to taxpayers as well as in more client-friendly implementation procedures.

Way of operating—The agency focuses more or less permanently on a small set of online communities where members of important target groups communicate about tax issues. Until now, the number of personnel engaged in social media monitoring and webcare has been very limited, but the agency's ambition is to enlarge this capacity. In 2014, the webcare team became a line department, so webcare activities are strongly embedded in the organization. Furthermore, the professionalization of the webcare team has been strengthened through training, including social and language skills. Process indicators have been developed to steer the webcare process.

Since 2011, the agency has launched various experiments with webcare, including a Twitter experiment to help people with filling in their tax return forms. This experiment is celebrated as a success within the organization. Since 2012, the webcare team has been present with reactive webcare (direct interaction) on some online forums—including *higherlevel.nl*, a platform for entrepreneurs with innovative ideas. When necessary, the webcare team participates in discussions and answers questions. Only small steps are being taken in webcare because of the (potential and perceived) risks of interaction with citizens, for example by making errors that could damage the reputation of the organization.[2]

Surveillance—The agency is transparent about its involvement when giving answers to taxpayers' que stions. Because of the agency's reactive webcare presence on some online forums, participants can be aware of the agency's presence in terms of monitoring as well. On the *higherlevel.nl* website, the tax agency is named as one of the partners.

Usage—Insights yielded by social media monitoring into the sentiments of taxpayers can lead to concrete interventions in the context of reputation management. Various managerial issues are addressed in the webcare team so that the organization is less vulnerable as well as more client-friendly. For instance, signals from clients about weaknesses in the information provided result in improvements in website content.

Effects—Analysis of the Twitter experiments showed that the community appreciated this initiative and that many questions were answered [16]. According to our interviewee, it is very difficult to measure the effects of webcare, specifically to ascertain whether it leads to adjusted images of the organization and gains in terms of efficiency and quality of service delivery.

5.2 Employee Insurances Implementing Agency

The Employee Insurances Implementing Agency (UWV) is an autonomous agency that implements the laws and regulations on unemployment benefits and

---

[2]One such example is a Tweet from a civil servant working at the Dutch Department of Security and Justice. She characterized Islamic State as a Zionist plan to cast Islam in a bad light. After this Tweet, she was suspended.

employment reintegration. Against the background of a thorough reorganization process aimed at more efficiency and client satisfaction, the UWV decided to use the internet as its primary communication channel. In 2009, the organization started a pilot with social media monitoring, followed one year later by webcare.

Goal—The UWV's primary webcare goal is to help clients with their questions in their own virtual environment. The social media monitoring pilot revealed that clients often pose questions to one another about benefits and regulations. In quite a few cases however, they get wrong answers from other people. Another goal concerns the conversion from individual answers by telephone to answers within an online community, which is more efficient for the organization. Reputation management is not a primary goal of social media monitoring and webcare in this case; rather, it is seen as a by-product of better service and more client satisfaction.

Way of operating—The webcare team consists of about five experienced employees of the Client Contact Centre. Special attention is given to complaints. In most cases, questions are dealt with by placing links in communities to information on the UWV's website. In this way, the UWV maintains unity in information provision and tries to strengthen clients' self-reliance. Clients with complicated questions are contacted by telephone.

Surveillance—At the beginning, when the webcare started, negative reactions were encountered from clients who wondered why the UWV was penetrating 'their' communities. Since then, webmasters and moderators of communities and web forums have been informed beforehand about the UWV's virtual presence and the goals behind it. They then inform their forums and in this way often serve as ambassadors for the UWV. In November 2012, the webmaster's team of the 'partners-in-misfortune-forum' (*lotgenotenforum.nl*) congratulated the UWV's webcare team on winning the public's Accenture Innovation Award.

Usage—The organization is trying to develop a more proactive approach to information provision. As noted above, one important aim of webcare is to strengthen clients' autonomy and self-reliance in solving their problems. A further usage of the webcare results would consist of offering products and services that make this possible. This can be seen as a specific way to enhance responsiveness.

Effects—According to our interviewee, the return on investment in webcare is difficult to establish. Gaining a better insight into the impact of webcare on efficiency and quality of service delivery is currently one of the UWV's priorities.

5.3 The Dutch Police Force

The Dutch Police Force is increasingly using social media to send information to citizens and to receive information from citizens. The number of Twitter accounts within the police organization is growing rapidly, especially among community police officers. New media, such as Twitter, are supposed not only to help the police to communicate effectively and fast with large groups of citizens, but also to facilitate citizen input in police work. The use of Twitter can also contribute to police effectiveness and public trust in the police [20].

Goals—The Dutch police use Twitter to strengthen their contacts with citizens, to boost feelings of safety, to urge citizens to take preventive action, to improve the knowledge, and the image, of the police (reputation management), and to obtain information from citizens about criminal investigations [19]. A distinction can be made between two levels. At the local level, community police officers use social media in order to improve safety in neighbourhoods. At the regional level, social media are primarily used by the police with the intention of strengthening the detection of crime.

Way of operating—Twitter is used by police officers at various levels in the organization. Most Twitter communication takes place through decentralized channels. The number of centrally controlled Twitter accounts is lower, but these accounts are used more intensively and have a much bigger audience than the decentralized Twitter accounts. The message content of Tweets is quite diverse. Police officers tweet messages about criminals that have been apprehended, they tweet informative messages about traffic situations and warnings about specific crime scams, they ask citizens for information about crime and inform them about safety in the neighbourhood, and they urge citizens to stay alert to certain types of crime. A rather successful system implemented nationwide in 2012 (after two pilots between 2004 and 2006) is *Burgernet* ('Civil network'), a cooperation between citizens, municipalities, and the police, aimed at enhancing safety in the local environment [18]. Citizens who are willing to participate register on the *Burgernet* website by providing their name and address. They receive messages from the police and the municipality via SMS, e-mail, Twitter, or a special *Burgernet* app. These messages are aimed at engaging citizens by alarming them, tracing suspect or missing persons, and the less time-critical activities of informing and involving. Citizens are viewed as partners in the domain of safety, a focus which constitutes a dimension of co-production. However, the use of *Burgernet* in specific situations can be initiated only by the police, not by citizens.

The police officers tweet thousands of messages every day which are received by more than one million (non-unique) followers [20]. Most police departments have strict guidelines for Twitter use that prescribe how the medium should be used. Policy officers are generally instructed to ensure that their messages are in line with department policies and the general 'Code Blue'. Nevertheless, errors can be made. An example is a police chief who compared the Dutch Party for Freedom (*Partij voor de Vrijheid*) to a fascist organization. After this political statement, the police chief was put on non-active duty. These incidents can damage the reputation of the police. Improper use of Twitter can also have a negative effect on police investigations when sensitive information leaks out. The management of communicative risks is an important challenge for the Dutch police [20].

Effects—The perceived benefits of social media in this context are the realization of a better network in the neighbourhood, the police sharing better information, and better informed citizens. This can improve the detection of crimes and co-production in the security domain. However, it is too early to detect 'hard' effects, because the use of social media by the police is still in an experimental phase.

5.4 ROC Mondriaan

ROC Mondriaan is an institution for intermediate vocational education. It offers education to 18,000 vocational students and 4000 adult students. It employs about 1900 teachers and staff. The interest of this school in crisis management, including social media monitoring and webcare activities, was triggered by a strategic surprise in September 2011, namely, a weapon incident at one ROC Mondriaan location in Delft. In January 2015, another incident occurred at the same location.

Goals—The primary goal of social media monitoring in this case is to find out what is being said about the school (reputation management) and to anticipate possible calamities (strategic issue management). An important goal of webcare is to inform (potential) students and other relevant stakeholders and to answer their questions.

Way of operating—On the central level of ROC Mondriaan, two employees within the communication department are involved in monitoring social media and webcare, in addition to their other (offline) activities. Social media activities are not part of a specific online strategy. ROC Mondriaan does not have specific social media guidelines for their employees, because the school relies on the professionalism of its staff. The practical advice of the communication department is to 'use common sense'.

A challenge is that social media are fast, but in an organization of 28 schools a quick response is not always possible. At specific times, especially during holidays, schools are closed and cannot answer (online) questions from (potential) students. "Because of the costs, it is unthinkable for schools to be online 24/7" (interview).

Surveillance—Searching activities online are based on a combination of general search terms (for example 'ROC Mondriaan') and customized search terms, based on specific incidents (for example fraud and violence at schools). One problem with social media software is the high level of irrelevant data. "For ROC Mondriaan in The Hague it is less relevant to identify online what is going on at another ROC" (interview). Another problem is that a growing number of young people, including students, use mobile social media like WhatsApp instead of Twitter and Facebook.

Usage—Within ROC Mondriaan, around 50 Twitter accounts are in use. The utilization of these bottom-up-activated accounts varies. Some Twitter accounts are hardly ever used, whereas others are used actively. The perception exists that many accounts are opened without the intention to interact. "Some accounts are opened because people feel the 'need' to do something with social media (supply-driven focus) instead of solving specific problems" (interview). Another factor is that the number of questions on Twitter is relatively too low to justify major investments in social media tools. Finally, many followers on the ROC Mondriaan Twitter accounts are not (potential) students, but professionals. In terms of information provision and service delivery, social media fulfil as yet a supplementary role alongside surveys, the website, face-to-face contacts (e.g. information days) and surveys (feedback).

Effects—The effects of social media monitoring and webcare are not system-atically investigated, because the interactions with the outside world are rather limited. "The volume of our webcare activities is too modest to make founded statements about it" (interview). Feedback on issues such as class schedules is mainly collected in other ways, for example by surveys among students. A current challenge is linking the website, social media, and face-to-face communication in the front office of the Study and Career Centre. An encompassing communication strategy is still lacking.

Lessons and experiences with social media are shared within the network of communication professionals in secondary Vocational Education and Training (VET: MBO 'MBO' in Dutch) in the Netherlands.

6 Conclusions and Discussion

The three theoretical approaches enable us to distinguish typical practices in pub-lic organizations' use of social media monitoring and webcare in policymaking and external communication. This involves analytical generalization, in which a case study seeks to generalize a particular set of results to some broader theory [35]. The rational-instrumental approach is clearly present in the Dutch Police Force, because webcare is assumed to strengthen the effectiveness and efficiency of police work. Efficiency was, initially, also a main driver of the UWV's and tax agency's webcare activities, because it allowed a conversion from individual com-munication by telephone to communication within an online community.

The strategic approach can be recognized in the tax agency's orientation towards gauging taxpayers' sentiments for purposes of reputation management, as well as in the orientation of ROC Mondriaan. Educational institutions have a very strong interest in having a good reputation to attract students, because they operate in a market-like environment.

The communicative approach is visible in the case of the UWV. This agency integrates social media monitoring into webcare, with the aim of strengthening cli-ents' autonomy and self-reliance in solving their problems. Whether this can be seen as a communicative approach, however, depends on whether the agency also integrates its clients' problem definitions into the design of services. In that case, a quest for responsiveness comes somewhat closer to real co-production between the agency and its clients. In the *Burgernet* system also, the Dutch police exhibit a communicative approach towards citizens. A communicative approach is also discernible in the tax agency's endeavour to improve its information services on the basis of online feedback from specific target groups. The UWV stands out for its transparency about its presence in virtual communities. This transparency was more or less enforced by the participants when they challenged the agency's covert presence in 'their' community. This can also be taken as a sign of a communica-tive approach to social media monitoring and webcare. On our ladder of participa-tory citizen delivery (Fig. 1), the Mondriaan school hardly reaches stage 1, the tax agency reaches stage 2 (if we see information provision as a specific service in this case), whereas the police and the UWV are approaching stage 3.

The cases suggest that among public organizations in the Netherlands webcare is gaining a fully-fledged position alongside the more traditional ways of interacting with citizens. The main goal of social media monitoring and webcare is to gain a better insight into the relevant sentiments within each organization's target groups. Reputation management and anticipation of clients' questions and needs prevail in this endeavour. Improvement of information provision and service delivery on the basis of citizens' feedback are other important motives. In some of our cases, signs of co-production are visible. Real co-production would involve the direct participation of clients in product development on the basis of their problem definitions.

Webcare is not only a communicative task, it requires various organizational efforts, including front- and back-office attunement, and the integration of different information streams from social media as well as from traditional media. The challenge is to translate webcare into an overall communication strategy. We concur with Mickoleit's [21] observation that there is little guidance on how government agencies can appraise the impact of social media monitoring and webcare on people's satisfaction with public services, on the effectiveness and efficiency of public service delivery, and on greater openness overall. In none of the cases are the impacts of social media monitoring and webcare systematically monitored. The question of how citizens' perceptions match those of the public organizations also needs to be explored.

References

1. Bannister, F. (2005). The panoptic state: Privacy, surveillance and the balance of risk. *Information Polity, 10*, 65–78.
2. Beer, D., & Burrows, R. (2007). *Sociology and, of and in Web 2.0: Some initial considerations*. Retrieved from http://www.socresonline.org.uk/12/5/17.html
3. Bekkers, V. J. J. M., Edwards, A. R., Moody, R., & Beunders, H. (2011). Caught by surprise? Micro-mobilization, new media and the management of strategic surprises. *Public Management Review, 13*, 1003–1021.
4. Bekkers, V., Edwards, A., & de Kool, D. (2013). Social media monitoring: Responsive governance in the shadow of surveillance. *Government Information Quarterly, 30*, 335–342.
5. Carr, N. (2005). *The amorality of Web 2.0, Nicolas Carr's blog*. Retrieved from http://www.roughtype.com/archives/2005/10/the_amorality_o.php
6. Chadwick, A. (2009). Web 2.0. New challenges for the study of e-democracy in an era of informational exuberance. *I/S: A Journal of Law and Policy for the Information Society, 5*, 9–41.
7. Chun, S. A., Shulman, S., Sandoval, R., & Hovy, E. (2010). Government 2.0. Making connections between citizens, data and government. *Information Polity, 15*, 1–9.
8. Criado, J. I., Sandoval-Almazan, R., & Gil-Garcia, J. R. (2013). Government innovation through social media. *Government Information Quarterly, 30*, 319–326.
9. Croll, A., & Power, S. (2009). *Complete web monitoring*. Sebastopol: O'Reilly.
10. de Koster, W. (2010). *'Nowhere I could talk like that': Togetherness and identity on online forums*. PhD dissertation, Erasmus University, Rotterdam.

11. Eggers, W. D. (2007). *Government 2.0: Using technology to improve education, cut red tape, reduce gridlock, and enhance democracy*. Lanham, MD: Rowman & Littlefield.
12. Fensel, D., Leiter, B. & Stavrakantonakis, I. (2012). *Social media monitoring*. Innsbruck: Semantic Technology Institute. Retrieved from http://oc.sti2.at/sites/default/files/SMM%20 Handouts.pdf
13. Khan, G. F., Swar, B., & Lee, S. K. (2014). Social media risks and benefits: A public sector perspective. *Social Science Computer Review, 32*, 606–627.
14. King, S. A. (1996). Researching internet communities: Proposed ethical guidelines for the reporting of results. *The Information Society: An International Journal, 12*, 119–127.
15. Linders, D. (2012). From e-government to we-government: Defining a typology for citizen coproduction in the age of social media. *Government Information Quarterly, 29*, 446–454.
16. Intelligence, Media. (2012). *Twitter Analyse Belastingdienst*. Leiden: Media Intelligence.
17. Mergel, I. (2013). A framework for interpreting social media interactions in the public sector. *Government Information Quarterly, 30*, 327–334.
18. Meijer, A. J., Grimmelikhuijsen, S. G., Bos, A., & Fictorie, D. (2011). *Burgernet via Twitter: onderzoek naar de waarde van dit nieuwe medium*. Utrecht: USBO, Universiteit van Utrecht. Retrieved from http://socialmediadna.nl/burgernet-via-twitter/
19. Meijer, A. J., et al. (2013). *Politie & sociale media*. Utrecht, Rotterdam: Universiteit Utrecht, Center for Public Innovation.
20. Meijer, A. J., & Torenvlied R. (2014). Social media and the new organization of government communications: An empirical analysis of twitter usage by the Dutch police. *American Review of Public Administration*, 1–19. doi:10.1177/0275074014551381
21. Mickoleit, A. (2014). Social media use by governments: A policy primer to discuss trends, identify policy opportunities and guide decision makers. *OECD Working Papers on Public Governance*, No. 26. Paris: OECD Publishing
22. Mizrahi, S. (2011). Self-provision of public services: Its evolution and impact. *Public Administration Review, 72*, 285–291.
23. Pfeffer, J. (1992). *Managing with power: Politics and influence in organizations*. Boston, MA: Harvard Business School Press.
24. Prins, C., Broeder, D., Griffioen, H., Keizer, H. G., & Keymolen, E. (2011). *iGovernment*. Amsterdam: Amsterdam University Press.
25. Schwartz, B. (2004). *Paradox of choices: Why more is less*. New York: Reed.
26. Sen, E. (2011). *Social media monitoring für Unternehmen*. Cologne: Social Media Verlag.
27. Shirky, C. (2011). The political power of social media. *Foreign Affairs, 90*, 28–41.
28. Sørensen, E., & Torfing, J. (2007). *Theories of democratic network governance*. Houndsmills, UK: Palgrave MacMillan.
29. Steimel, B., Halemba, Chr, & Dimitrova, T. (2010). *Social media monitoring: Erst zuhören, dann mitreden in den Mitmachmedien!*. Meerbusch, Germany: MIND.
30. Surowiecki, J. (2004). *The wisdom of crowds: Why the many are smarter than the few and how collective wisdom shapes business, economies, societies, and nations*. New York: Doubleday.
31. Sutton, J. N. (2009). Social media monitoring and the democratic national convention: New tasks and emergent processes. *Journal of Homeland Security and Emergency Management, 6*, 1–20.
32. Teelken, Chr. (1999). Market mechanisms in education: School choice in the Netherlands, England and Scotland in a comparative perspective. *Comparative Education, 35*, 283–302.
33. van Noort, G., & Willemsen, L. M. (2011). Online damage control: The effects of proactive versus reactive webcare interventions in consumer-generated and brand-generated platforms. Online first. *Journal of Interactive Marketing, 26*, 131–140.
34. Verhoeven, I., & Tonkens, E. (2013). Talking active citizenship: Framing welfare state reform in England and the Netherlands. *Social Policy and Society, 12*, 415–426.
35. Yin, R. (2003). *Case study research: Design and methods* (3rd ed.). Thousand Oaks, CA: Sage.

Part II
Systems and Applications

Next Step: An Online Community for Delivering Human Services

Cécile Paris and Surya Nepal

Abstract With the expansion of the Internet, the number of online support groups has grown rapidly, and they have become a serious alternative to face-to-face meetings. Online support groups or communities allow their members to connect and share with others and get the support they need. In our work, in collaboration with a Government Department, we wanted to investigate whether these benefits could also occur in the public administration domain, in particular to support people in receipt of welfare payments. We designed and deployed an online community to support a specific group of welfare recipients. Our intent was to provide them with both informational and emotional support. In this paper, we present the design of the community, with a specific focus on the support it provided its members, together with a qualitative analysis of what happened during our trial. We observed that people found the targeted information and the emotional support they received in the online community useful and that they welcomed it. We also found that the community provided a way for participants to feel heard by the government.

Keywords Social networks · Online community · Human services · Gamification · Content analysis

1 Introduction

Social media has become a crucial way in which people engage with each other, with businesses and governments. According to a 2015 Sensis report, close to 50 % of consumers access social media every day, and even more for young

C. Paris (✉) · S. Nepal
CSIRO Data61, Sydney, Australia
e-mail: cecile.paris@csiro.au

S. Nepal
e-mail: Surya.Nepal@csiro.au

© Springer International Publishing Switzerland 2015
S. Nepal et al. (eds.), *Social Media for Government Services*,
DOI 10.1007/978-3-319-27237-5_9

people (18–29 age group) [1]; 93 % of internet users have a Facebook account. Government agencies have started to recognise the power of social media and to make use of it to disseminate information, listen to citizens and engage with the public (e.g. [2–4]; Chaps. 2 and 10 in this book).

In this chapter, we report on our investigation on the use of online communities by governments to provide support to specific groups of citizens. Such online communities are now common in a number of domains: e.g., health (see, for example, patientslikeme,[1] or Daily Strength[2]), parenting, e.g., Community baby centre,[3] or sports.[4] These communities typically provide information deemed relevant to their members. Equally important, by enabling people to meet others with similar circumstances, they offer social and moral support to their members, which in turn leads to positive outcomes [5–7]. For example, [7] found that an online support forum on smoking cessation had a significant positive impact for its participants.

To our knowledge, there has not been any research on the use of online communities by government to support specific group of citizens. Governments have recognised the potential of the social web, and they have begun to actively increase their online presence, both to disseminate information and to engage citizens (e.g., [4]). Politicians and public servants now use Twitter and Facebook extensively to keep the public informed (e.g., tweetMP to follow Australian Members of Parliament on Twitter, the Facebook page of the Bedfordshire Police in the UK, the Facebook pages[5] of Centrelink in Australia, etc.). They also use social media for campaigning purposes, e.g., [8–12]).

Many governments (at all levels: local, state or national) capitalise on social media to engage citizens. For example, Public Sphere[6] was a platform to involve people in public policy development; the city of Wellington (New Zealand) introduced E-petitions to improve citizen participation [13]. In these initiatives, citizens are encouraged to contribute to the design of government policies and have a voice.

In other initiatives, the government is crowdsourcing information. For example, the Victorian State Road Authority uses social media to obtain information about road hazards. In our work, we are exploring the use of social media not as a way to engage citizens in policy making, but to support specific groups of citizens through the creation and mediation of online communities.

---

[1]www.patientslikeme.com/.

[2]www.dailystrength.org/support-groups.

[3]www.babycenter.com.au/community.

[4]http://www.athletenetwork.com/.

[5]For example, the page for students, accessed May 7th, 2013. https://www.facebook.com/Student Update.

[6]While the original site www.katelundy.com.au/category/campaigns/publicsphere/ is no longer available, a full archive of the original website from when Kate Lundy was Senator for the ACT has been retained by The National Library of Australia through Pandora and is accessible at: pandora.nla.gov.au/pan/38983/20140908-1403/www.katelundy.com.au/index.html—Accessed September 19th, 2015.

Online communities (and social networks in general) have been shown to have the potential to provide social and emotional peer-support—e.g., [14–18]. For some groups of citizens, such support would be important. Some researchers have looked into the use of new media to empower disadvantaged groups of citizens, e.g., [19], but these initiatives were organised by Non-Government Organisations, not governments. To the best of our knowledge, none of the previous work has looked at providing emotional and information support to disadvantage citizens through a government-run online community. This is what our research addresses.

Together with the Australian Government Department of Human Services (herein after referred to as Human Services), we trialled an online community for a specific group of welfare recipients, to provide them with informational and emotional support. The specific cohort we worked with were transitioning from one type of welfare payment to another, as a result of new legislation introduced to encourage welfare recipients to increase their amount of paid employment. The new payment type resulted in less income and came with a requirement to look for a job. Understandably, the transition was a difficult one for many people, causing them a large amount of stress. Our trial aimed to see if an online community, with the support it can bring its members, could be useful to ease the transition process. This chapter reports on the design, implementation, deployment and analysis results of this community.

The chapter is structured as follows. Section 2 provides some background on our research project. Section 3 describes the design and implementation of the online community we developed, while Sect. 4 describes the result of our analysis of the interactions in the community. We provide a discussion and some perspectives on the work in Sect. 5, and, finally, we conclude in Sect. 6.

2 Background

In many countries, including Australia, governments play a social role. Welfare systems provide a safety net for disadvantaged citizens, such as parents with low or no income, the disabled and the elderly, ensuring they have a minimum standard of living. Recent past has seen some of the systems change, with increasing restrictions on the financial assistance provided, or the assistance provided in exchange for work. Examples of such changes include TANF legislation in the US[7] introduced in 1996 or the Work for the Dole Legislation introduced in 1997 in Australia.[8]

Early studies on the impact of these reforms have found that the new requirements (and transitioning to them) could be very difficult and stressful for some, and thus people need help—e.g., [20–22]. A lot of research has looked at the role

---

[7]TANF: Temporary Assistance for Needy Families: http://www.tanf.us/ (retrieved September 15th, 2015).

[8]Work for the Dole (Legislation introduced to Parliament 1997) https://employment.gov.au/work-dole (retrieved September 15th, 2015).

of social support in handling stress (e.g., [23–26]). We hypothesised that social and emotional support, provided through a social network, could therefore be beneficial. This was supported by the results of a requirements gathering activity performed through focus groups and a questionnaire [27–29].

We thus set out to design, develop and deploy an online community in collaboration with Human Services to help deliver this support to a specific group of welfare recipients in a transition phase. These citizens were required as a result of a new legislation to move from a parental payment to a new payment type, Newstart, typically paid at a lower rate than the parental payment and with the requirement to find a job. Our aim was to provide a community which would bring people in similar circumstances together, so that they could share experiences, information, tips, etc., thus providing social, emotional and moral support to each other. The community would also enable the government to target its information and services to this specific cohort. Finally, the online community was intended to provide a platform for its members to go on a reflection journey, through a set of weekly activities, in order to better prepare them for the transition and their return to work [30].

Our design was based on the results of our requirements gathering activity [27–29] and many discussions with relevant staff at Human Services. The community, *Next Step*, was launched in March 2012 and lasted one year. Our participants were invited directly by Human Services, using a double blind process, as follows. We provided a set of tokens to Human Services, who, in turn, invited parents from their customer data base and gave them a unique token. Parents used their token to register in the community and choose a screen name and a password. They could also set a security question to retrieve their forgotten password.

With this process, Human Services knew who had which token, but did not know who had actually used their token to register and what their screen name was. In contrast, we knew which screen name corresponded to which token, but had no information about the real identity of the participants. The letter of invitation made it clear that this was an experiment with a fixed duration, and that we (the authors) were present as researchers who would be collecting and analysing data during the trial. This process was put in place to address ethical issues, which are particularly important when the research involves Government and citizens who receive payments from the Government [31].

Once the registration was completed, a user became a member of the community and could log in the community portal at any time with their screen name and password.

3 *Next Step* Design and Implementation

Next Step was designed as a portal with a set of pages, and it included both individual and community spaces. Its main components and features, and how they appear on the community home page, are shown in Fig. 1.

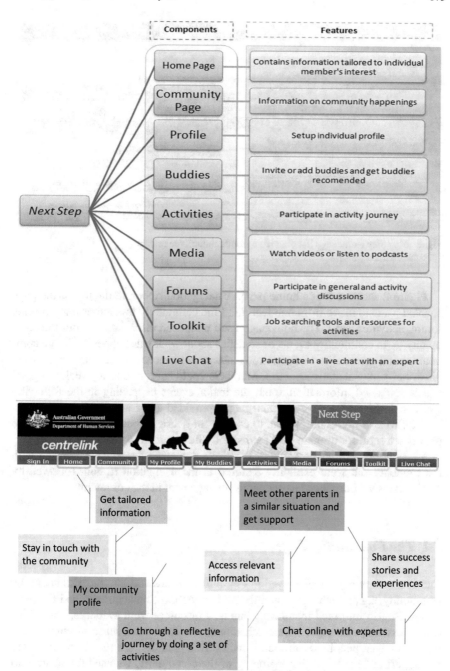

Fig. 1 *Next Step* components and features

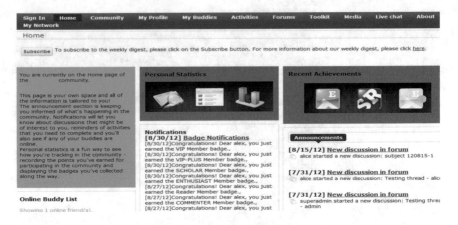

Fig. 2 *Next Step* HomePage (landing page) for community members

Figure 2 shows a user's home page. A navigation ribbon at the top of the page enabled users to move from one feature of the community to another (e.g., profile, forum, activities, etc.). The homepage itself contained information about the community (e.g., community events or statistics about what was happening in the community) and personalised information (such as announcements relevant to the user, his or her personal statistics, etc.). Members could subscribe to a "weekly digest" which contained information about the major events happening in the following week (e.g., Live Chats). An "*About page*" provided explanations about the community: what it was about, whom to contact for queries, concerns and help. It also provided a form for users to give feedback to the community providers.

We now briefly explain some of the main elements of *Next Step*, starting with the elements that were explicitly featured in the navigation ribbon, followed by mechanisms we introduced to encourage engagement in the community.

3.1 The Community Page

The community page is displayed in Fig. 3. It provides various statistics about the community, e.g., which discussion thread had the most readers, who had the most ratings. It also informed members when new resources were available, when Live Chats sessions with experts were scheduled, etc. To foster a sense of community, we encouraged people to introduced themselves publicly (see the "Meet me" box on the left of Fig. 3). At the beginning of the community, we used this feature to introduce ourselves (both the CSIRO staff and the Human Services moderators) and start a trust relationship with the members. We encouraged new comers to the community to fill in such a "meet me" template, and sometimes invited specific members based on their interactions in the community. Figure 4 shows a profile

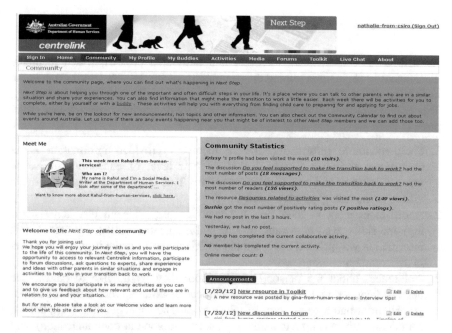

Fig. 3 The community page

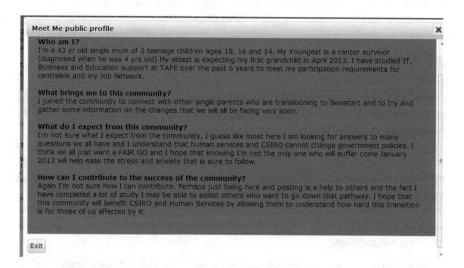

Fig. 4 A meet me profile from a community member

filled in by a community member. We note that it indicates the desire to connect with others in this situation, get social, emotional and informational support, and share one's own knowledge with others to support them.

3.2 Individual Profiles

As with other communities, members had individual profiles, which members were meant to fill in upon joining the community, using the "My Profile" tab in the navigation ribbon. This was in fact done as the first activity in our activity journey. This profile included information that was used for recommendations. It was structured in three parts:

1. Socio-economic information, where members provided information about themselves and their family, including their level of education, source of income, housing and transport arrangements. This information was never made visible to the rest of the community.
2. A self-assessment of their personal qualities (e.g., dependable, honest, caring) and skills (e.g., numeracy, people, communication skills). By default, this information was private, but members could choose to make it public to others in the community.
3. Preferences about the person(s) with whom they would like to buddy (see below). People could choose from a number of criteria, with a mix of demographic information (e.g., someone close to me), personal qualities (e.g., honest, confident, enthusiastic) and skills (e.g., someone good at communication), and give a weight to each of them from 0 (not important at all) to 5 (very important).

Members were free to complete as much of the profile as they wished.

3.3 A Buddy Programme

One of the aims of the *Next Step* community was to provide emotional and social support to its members. We hypothesised that one way this would happen was for participants to find a "buddy", someone who could support them through the journey, in a more personal way than the community as a whole. As participants were strangers to each other, the buddy programme aimed to help find such a buddy, by recommending community members to each other. This followed the social matching model proposed in [32]—profile, match and introduce users, and enable their interactions. We designed and implemented two types of profiling and matching processes: one based on the individual profiles members filled in, and the other based on interactions.

1. **Exploiting the profiles members provided** [33]. This implementation of the buddy programme relied on the explicit profile information (social-economic, qualities and skills, preferences) that the community members provided upon joining the community. Three social matching algorithms exploited these profiles. One matched people based on demographic similarities, as people typically like others who are similar to themselves, and demographic attributes are shown to correlate with interpersonal attraction [34]. The second one used the members' stated skills, based on how well members would complement

Fig. 5 "My Buddies" page—from *left* to *right*: the list of buddies; the list of invitations received and sent; the list of all members with at the top the buddy recommendations

each other's skills and personal qualities. The third one exploited the preferences people selected about the characteristics of their buddy. With all three algorithms, we ensured that the same person was not recommended to several people, to increase the likelyhood that everyone would be recommended as a buddy to someone else.

2. **Exploiting social interactions**. In this implementation of the buddy programme, the system exploited user behaviour and observed interactions [35]. The idea behind this implementation is as follows: if two users interact (whether passively, e.g., a user reading the other user's posts, or actively, e.g., a user rating the other user), they are similar in some way and might enjoy being buddies. While the recommender based on profiles could be used immediately, this implementation of the buddy programme was used once there were enough interactions and behaviours in the community.

On their "My Buddies" page, a community member could invite someone to become their buddy. They could invite anyone in the community or select a person from the recommended list. The "My Buddies" page displayed the list of current buddies, the invitations this member had received and the ones he or she sent out, the list of people recommended by the system, and the list of all community members (see Fig. 5).

3.4 Journey of Reflection Through Activities

Finally, to support people going through the required transition process, we developed a *journey of reflection* through a set of reflective activities, released to community members one at a time, in a structured format. The activities were designed with the help of social workers from our government collaborators. They aimed to help parents face obstacles, regain confidence, plan their return to work, and enable a critical self-review (with respect to attitudes, beliefs, skills and aspirations), self-development and empowerment. There were two main types of activities:

- Activities to help people be better equipped to look for a job—e.g., exploring the type of jobs one desires, or writing a CV.
- Activities to encourage people to develop a support network.

Some activities were to be done individually, others in collaborations with others (e.g., a buddy). Activities were typically accompanied by resources. The interested reader is referred to [36] for additional details.

3.5 The Discussion Forum

To enable participants to communicate with each other—e.g., ask questions, get advice, share their knowledge and experiences, or simply chat with each other, *Next Step* included a discussion forum. One concern that was raised during our requirements analysis was the veracity of the information that would be disseminated through the community. To address this concern, staff from Human Services moderated the discussion forum. They also were active participants in it, responding to questions as the need arose, providing support (for example for people in distress), actively helping participants getting access to the appropriate help when required, giving relevant information, and, especially at the beginning, trying to encourage members' participation by initiating discussions. They also ensured that the forum remained as positive as possible under the circumstances and did not focus solely on people's frustration and negative feelings (another concern that had emerged from our initial analysis).

3.6 Providing Useful Resources: Media, Toolkit and Live Chats

As is common in many online communities, *Next Step* also provided a variety of resources that were deemed to be relevant and useful for this cohort ("Media" and "Toolkit"). This enabled staff from Human Services to provide specific information to members, for example fact sheets about the transition process, list of useful websites, etc. These resources were provided in text, videos or audio materials (with transcripts), as appropriate.

Another way in which *Next Step* participants received relevant information was through Live Chat sessions, which provided opportunities to chat online on specific topics with experts during designated times. These Live Chat sessions usually lasted 1 or 2 h, and anybody was free to join the session and participate in the discussion. A transcript was later made available, so that those who had missed the sessions could still read the questions and their answers.

3.7 Gamification

Gamification is often used in online communities to enhance engagement and foster collaboration [37–39]. We applied some gamification techniques for this purpose in *Next Step*. We briefly describe them here. Chapter 10 provides further details about gamification in general, its origin, its elements and its application in our online community.

The main gamification element we used in *Next Step* was in the form of badges that were awarded to participants based on their activities in the community—see Fig. 6. These badges were displayed in the individual member's landing page (i.e., their home page), so that members could reflect on their achievement—see Fig. 2. There were two types of badges: permanent and temporary. Each of the temporary badges was refreshed fortnightly, and, to keep them, members had to sustain a particular behaviour or being ranked among the top ten performers. In contrast, permanent badges were retained by members throughout their time in the community.

3.8 Content Recommendation

We mentioned above that we implemented a people's recommender (recommending a buddy) based on the social interactions that were taking place in the community. We also used the social interactions to recommend content to members. This was another mechanism to further engage members, encouraging them to read someone's post, a new discussion or a new resource.

Fig. 6 Member activities and badge allocation

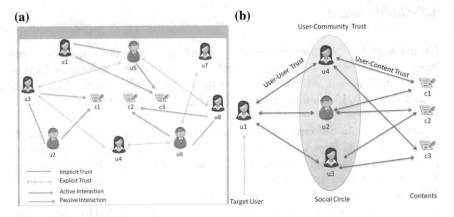

Fig. 7 The different variables contributing to content score

Given individual users, this recommender identified and ranked a set of content items with which others in their network had interacted. Several variables contribute to the content items relevance score (1) the network graph, (2) the user to user trust, (3) the user to content trust, (4) the user to community trust. These variables are illustrated in Fig. 7. The reader is referred to [35] for details.

3.9 Next Step Implementation

Next Step is implemented by customising Liferay[9] core functionalities through the Hooks Plug-in.[10] New services and portlets have been added using the Service Builder and portlet Plug-ins.[11] We developed Model View Controller (MVC) portlets[12], and the connection between presentation layer and core was through JSP/Tags/Http and Ajax calls. Sending emails was done using Java Mail embedded system. Custom SQL have been executed using embedded JDBC connection. The platform was instrumented so that we could record all interactions both to monitor the community and for future analysis.

A lot of preparation occurred prior to the community's launch, alongside the design. The project underwent a careful ethics process, approval was obtained, and we liaised with privacy, security and legal experts at Human Services. Together with our collaborators in Human Services, we planned the whole activity journey

---

[9]http://www.liferay.com/.

[10]http://www.liferay.com/community/wiki/-/wiki/Main/Portal+Hook+Plugins.

[11]http://www.liferay.com/documentation/liferay-portal/6.2/development/-/ai/leveraging-the-plugins-sdk-liferay-portal-6-2-dev-guide-02-en.

[12]https://dev.liferay.com/develop/tutorials/-/knowledge_base/6-2/developing-jsp-portlets-using-liferay-mvc.

and had a schedule for the release of each activity. Staff from the Human Services compiled a set of resources to be made available. Together, we thought of discussion topics to bootstrap the discussion forum, to mitigate the risk of the community never taking off because of the "cold start" problem [40].

Human Services call centre staff were briefed when the invitation letters were sent to potential members to ensure that they could answer any questions recipients might have about the community. Finally, throughout the community, the discussion forum was constantly monitored for expressions of distress on the part of participants, which would have necessitated direct intervention from a Human Services staff or a social worker. As per our ethics approval, it was only when such intervention was required that Human Services would be able to obtain the identity of a participant, by requesting from CSIRO the token corresponding to the screen name. A process was put in place to decide whether an intervention was required and how to proceed. Human Services established a roster to ensure the forum was monitored at all times, and CSIRO staff also had a roster to ensure someone would be available at any time to provide the token information if required. We are pleased to note that no such direct intervention was required throughout the trial.

4 *Next Step*: The Trial

The community was launched in March 2012 and remained open for 12 months. The community portal was hosted by our organisation, whereas staff from Human Services were responsible for producing resources and moderating the interactions in the forum.

During the trial, four groups of parents were successively invited to join the community. All were parents on the appropriate payment schemes (e.g., either on parental payment, about to transition, or on the new payment, having just transitioned). In addition, they had to have an online account with Human Services and have agreed to participate in research activities.

A small subset of invited people actually registered, and yet a smaller number accepted the Terms of Use. While this was disappointing, this is a typical pattern of participation in online communities, and a good result given that the community was a closed one (i.e., by invitation only), so that not everyone could join at will. (We had in fact a number of examples of community participants wanting to invite their friends but unable to do so as the latter were not eligible—this is illustrated in the following post: "*I know of some single parents that would probably come and maybe even find the forum useful. Am i able to give them the link or do they have to be specifically invited?*".) In total, 263 people registered, from which 181 actually visited the community.

Table 1 The community at a glance

Viewing of forum	6075
Commenting	734
Ratings	491
Viewing of resources	666
Media views	38
Activities	280
Live Chat	7
Profile updates	512
Buddies invited/accepted	53/15

We now turn to the number of active participants. Not all community participants were active in the community. Again, this follows a known pattern of participation in online community, the so-called "90-9-1 Jacob Nielson rule",[13] which states that although only 1 % of people might be highly active, 9 % are active and 90 % "lurk", meaning that *Next Step* was no different than other communities. We note that the word "lurk" is a negative word which we do not believe is appropriate—we refer to these people as "passive" participants, or people who absorb information even if they do not produce any. These people were members who came to the community to read the forum, the resources and take advantage of what was on offer in the community, but did not necessarily make themselves heard by writing comments in the forum. We should not expect all members of a community to be active participants. (After all, in non virtual communities, not everyone talks—some people choose to listen. Virtual communities are no different in this respect.) We observed from the statistics we collected during the trial that a reasonable number of participants logged in, viewed the forum and the resources, did some activities and then logged out. They were not visible in the community through the forum, but they benefited from the community (reading the discussions and resources). Some people logged in consistently every week, sometimes several times a week (up to 39 times a week). We had a total of 2268 logins, and 696 posts by members. This clearly indicates that many people entered the community but did not submit a post to the forum. If people came consistently several times a week, we presume they saw benefits in coming to the community.

Table 1 shows various statistics about the community. The resources were heavily consulted, and many participants worked on the activities. People did not take much advantage of the buddy programme, and few members attended the Live Chat Sessions, potentially as it turned out to be very hard to find a time for these sessions that would be good for many people.

We now focus on the forum, as it was by far the most popular feature of the community. In total, 180 threads were initiated, generating 1233 posts. The forum was organised into two sections: one for general discussion, and one for

---

[13]Nielsen Norman Group. http://www.nngroup.com/articles/participation-inequality/—Accessed September 14th, 2015.

discussions specifically related to the activities. The general discussion section was the most active (1139 posts). The in-depth analysis that follows was performed on this section.

In the first 6 months of the community, the moderators initiated twice as many threads as members, as they attempted to bootstrap discussions—see Table 2. This reflects a normal "cold start" problem. In the second half of the trial, however, the community started having "a life of its own", with the moderators initiating much fewer threads than members, and members generating many more replies than moderators. This is illustrated graphically in Fig. 8, which shows the cumulative counts of posts by both members and moderators. Week 34, when Group 4 joined the community, saw a surge in activity. This is likely due to two factors: (1) Group 4 was generally the most active and vocal, and (2) there were already many posts and resources in the community at that point, so that it was also easier to engage immediately. In general, we found that people talked about a variety of topics and expressed a number of emotions.

We performed a number of qualitative analysis on the data collected, including:

1. A three-prong language analysis of the forum posts to get an understanding of (1) the types of communications that occurred (a speech-act analysis); (2) what people talked about (a topic analysis) and (3) how people felt (a sentiment analysis). This was done through a manual annotation task.
2. An analysis of the role the moderators played throughout the project, from the planning of the community to the trial itself. We examined the tasks that had to be fulfilled and the skills they required. We also looked at the impact the moderators had in the community.

Table 2 Discussion threads

	Initiated by moderators	Initiated by members	Replies from moderators	Replies from members
First 6 months	20	10	74	83
Last 6 months	13	95	231	613

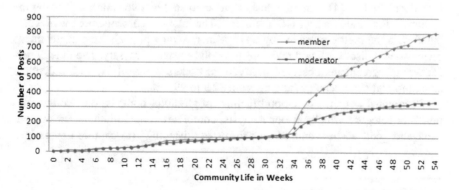

Fig. 8 Cumulative counts of posts by members and moderators, per week during the trial

3. An analysis of the content of the forum with the explicit aim of identifying the "barriers to work" presented, as it provides some valuable insights into this specific user group and their challenges.

We now briefly describe our results below, focusing on what actually happened in the forum in terms of support. As we had hoped, we saw members supporting each other through their posts, listening and acknowledging each other's posts, agreeing and empathising with each other, providing encouragement and advice, and also sharing tips and information.

4.1 Communications Amongst Community Members

We observed that many members shared their stories, as a way to introduce themselves to the community, to take part in the conversation, to acknowledge each other and to empathise with others. We note that acknowledging someone and empathising with someone is a form of emotional support.

Members also often expressed some negative feeling (e.g., frustration) about the situation, the transition and the process, to which others agreed and sometimes reinforced. This was reflected in the use of language, with expressions such as "the majority of us", "our plight", and "how we feel", suggesting that people were thinking of themselves as a united group. A sense of cohesiveness is also a form of emotional support, as individuals no longer felt alone in their situation, and they could share their stories and feel understood. Finally, participants started sharing ideas and tips, and asking information of each other.

Beyond simple acknowledgements or sharing life stories and information, interactions also showed evidence of explicit support between members, with people offering help, advice or posting caring comments. Examples of posts from members to members are provided in Table 3.[14]

We analysed the marks of support conveyed between members, looking at the expressions of positive and neutral feelings. We employed a subset of the taxonomy developed by [41], and the posts were annotated by two annotators, using the commercial annotation tool QDA Miner.[15] The inter-coders agreement were computed with the metric provided by QDA Miner, Scott's pi [42], the disagreements reviewed and discussed, and revisions took place when necessary. The overall percentage of agreements observed between the coders was 94.1 %, with individual annotation label percentage ranging from 82.9 to 99.7 %.

We counted as marks of support feelings of gratitude, compassion, "congratulations" (a category which, in our analysis, comprises congratulations, encouragement and good wishes) and various forms of "listening" (to capture expressions

---

[14]All posts are reported verbatim.

[15]http://provalisresearch.com/products/qualitative-data-analysis-software/.

Table 3 Examples of posts, showing relationship building amongst community members

Communicative act	Example
Introducing oneself by sharing one's life story and providing personal information	*"Hi there, I am a new forum member, received my letter on Friday. I became a single parent in 2003 with a 6 month old. I Started uni in 2007, completed a cert 3 in aged care this year and. [...]"*
Agreeing with a previously expressed negative sentiment	*"Hi bewildered, can I just say that I think your posts high-light our plight very well.[...]"*
Responding to tips	*"Emm, I like your idea of paying the advance on your credit card, I might use some of mine to do that too and then work on my low interest loan."*
Providing explicit support	*"hi Kayte, would you like to have a chat, I understand your frustration, I know a little about the changes, maybe two heads could work on your situation with your health card. Call me [phone number removed for privacy reasons] and I will give you my home number. My real name is Maree."*
Providing emotional support	*Hugs to you Tox* *Wishing you and your son the best outcome for his health. The rest just sucks! Hang in there!*

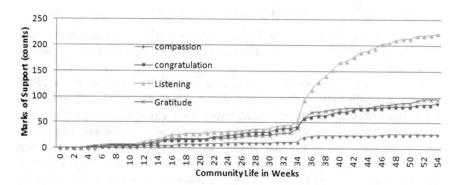

Fig. 9 Cumulative counts of marks of support offered from members to members

of interests, use of language showing that people paid attention, listened and acknowledged what was being said).

Figure 9 reports the cumulative counts over the trial of all these expressions of support. We observe that members started to acknowledge each other (labeled "listening") quite early in the trial, and, later, showed marks of gratitude, compassion and encouragement.[16] We conclude that our participants did obtain emotional support and, to a lesser extent, informational support from each other.

---

[16]We also observed 341 positive ratings, another form of support from members to each other.

4.2 Communications Between Community Members and the Moderators

Members quickly used the forum as a channel to get accurate and timely information. The moderators became an interface to Human Services, and the community a privileged way to source information that was sometimes difficult to obtain.

Some examples of questions asked are shown in Table 4. ("Gigi", mentioned in post 2, was a moderator.) Some were of a general nature (e.g., 1 and 3 in Table 4), others very specific to the member's circumstances (e.g., 2 in Table 4).

Throughout the trial, the moderators provided relevant and up-to-date information to members in the forum (and by publishing resources). They did so in a number of ways:

- By responding to explicit requests or demands for clarifications. Typically, moderators included explanations in their responses so that people could understand the information given and put it in the appropriate context;
- By spontaneously offering information on a topic, when that topic was raised by members;
- By taking advantage of responding to a specific question to add more information about the topic more generally, to ensure the post was relevant to more than one person; and
- By providing links and additional pointers for people to investigate further.

Because of the information the moderators were providing, some members started to come quite regularly to get updates; some several times a week, others several times a day.

The moderators also provided emotional support by listening to members' concerns and collecting feedback about the transition and social welfare policies in general. Listening to people's experiences, their struggles in coping with the changes, and their frustrations towards Human Services or the government in general was an important part of the moderators' role. It also became an important aspect of the community. People wanted to be heard and understood. The moderators responded to this need by letting members know that they were listening to them, and by showing understanding, concern and compassion. Table 5 shows some sample posts from the moderators displaying compassion and understanding. As we will see below, this support was greatly appreciated by community members.

Table 4 Examples of questions to moderators

1	*"I live in a regional area that seems to be limiting my ability to gain employment. Is there any help in relocating to a city to increase chances of employment?"*
2	*"Hi Gigi, I know u r busy, do u have time to see how my Education Entry Payment query is going. Because it was showing online as being paid, I have actually spent this money and need to repay it. Thanks!"*
3	*"can we earn $400 a fortnight or $62"*

Table 5 Examples of posts by moderators, explicitly acknowledging members

"Hi Angbrennil. Thanks for coming back to the forums and giving us an update on what's been happening. I really hope you get the support and advice you need to help you through. Let us know if there are any resources, activities or live chat sessions we can organise to help you be as prepared as possible to 'hit the pavement'".
"I wish you all the best in this tough time - keep us posted :-)"
"Hi bunniesmum A few people have reported similar issues. We have asked these people to email our boss so we can investigate on 2 Jan. If you would like us to do this for you too, [...]"

Finally, the moderators collected feedback, whether it was in the form of complaints, reports of communication breakdown, system malfunctions, concerns, frustration or angst, and passed on the information to the relevant entities (i.e., business units, policy makers, government departments, etc.).

4.3 Usefulness of the Support Provided

We now examine the impact of the support provided in the community and whether it was considered useful and welcome by the community members. We asked for explicit feedback, but very few people provided it. Instead, we take the ongoing feedback we obtained throughout the trial, via the posts (e.g., thanking the moderators for "useful links", or for their support) to be a good reflection of people's feelings about the community and the support they received.

We looked at the expressions of gratitude. This is shown in Fig. 10. We note that members expressed gratitude towards the moderators from the beginning of the community (essentially because moderators answered their questions and listened to their concerns). We see the expressions of gratitude from members (to both members and moderators) increasing steadily during the trial, with a sharper increase starting week 34 (when Group 4 joined).

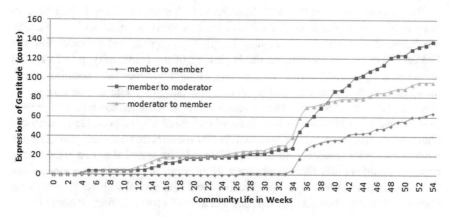

Fig. 10 Cumulative count of expressions of gratitude expressed in the community

Table 6 Sample posts showing gratitude from members to moderators

"Thank you for the quick answer and the Link Gigi. :D."
"Hi Gigi, Thanks for the prompt response and the welcome."
"Thanks Gigi, your support is great. I'd also like to thank you for your promptness in answering our queries and for looking into more serious issues - normally we just wait on hold with the call centre. It's great that you are really involved in this project and your sincerity is very welcome."
"Thanks Marian [another moderator]. It's good to get some positive reinforcement and encouragement."

Table 6 shows some expressions of gratitude towards the moderators. We see that this gratitude is in response both to information that the moderators provided (and the speed with which they provided it) and their emotional support. We conclude that community members appreciated the support the moderators gave them.

Next Step became a hub for information, and members visited the site regularly for information and updates. The information was relayed to others sites, other single parents and friends. Some wanted to invite their friends to join. We believe this shows that the community was useful to its members, and that they thought it could be helpful for others. We have already mentioned how members appreciated the support they received from the moderators. They also appreciated the support they received from each other, as illustrated by the following post: *"It has also been a pleasure to interact with other members of the community, I wish you all the best of Luck, good health and understanding from all you come in contact with."* It is also worth noting that, although the *Next Step* community was closing, the community formed was not to be completely dissolved as active members were organising themselves to continue staying in touch with each other as illustrated by these comments (*"Hi everyone, Just wanted to invite anyone who is interested to come and join the forum I have set up so we can continue to keep in contact and up to date with what's going on."*). We thus conclude that, all and all, the participants did find the support useful.

We also observed that the moderators had another impact through their interactions in *Next Step*. Because of their prompt, courteous, accurate and sympathetic responses, they were able to change people's perception and attitudes towards Human Services and its staff. At the beginning of the community, people tended to bundle the government (and its policies), Human Services (as a specific department) and its staff into one "nasty" entity, and one that could not be trusted. As time passed, members established a relationship with the moderators, and started to understand that Human Services (as a whole) were only responsible to carry out policies (not make them), and that staff in Human Services (as exemplified by the moderators) were really trying to help. This shift increased the trust relationship between members and Human Services. In general, we saw that the moderators played an important role both in increasing the social capital and social trust in the community and in changing perceptions and attitudes towards Human Services.

4.4 Barriers to Work Analysis

Our aim in building *Next Step* was to provide informational and emotional support to a specific cohort of citizens. Through our analysis of the posts, we also noticed that they contained a lot of information that could be useful to Human Services to understand the difficulties these citizens were facing with respect to re-entering the workforce, what we termed "Barriers to work". We thus performed another annotation task to identify these barriers, as expressed in the forum. We first identified all topics related to barriers to work mentioned in discussions, by going through all members' posts. We then grouped all the topics into categories, and all member posts were annotated by two researchers into these categories.[17] Finally, we examined the annotated content to identify more precisely the major topics related to barriers to work discussed in the forum.

We used the following high-level categories:

1. Job market. This referred to the current economic situations, potentially for a specific (regional) area.
2. Processes and policies. Participants found many of the government policies and processes becoming difficulties to overcome to find a job. This category included communication issues, issues with the specific agencies that customers were meant to work with, and clarity in the required processes. Some of these topics may not have been clearly identified as a barrier to work, but they were discussed in the forum in the context of looking for jobs.
3. Cultural. Cultural issues included flexibility, ageism, exploitation, incentives, etc. Some of these issues were related to members, whereas some belonged to employers. We also noted that, in many discussions, parents showed their frustration at not being able to be flexible to fit in employers' environments. Parents considered this as a burden to the employer.
4. Life situation. Many parents expressed the fact that their own life situations prevented them from transitioning to work. Some parents felt that they were not even in a position to look for a job, whereas others could not find a job that fitted their life situation. Examples of life situations included children with special medical conditions, lack of recent work experience, etc.
5. Logistics. This included caring of children while at work, transport to and from work, etc. These topics were discussed in terms of their affordability and availability. Affordability is related to finance and policies, but we chose to label such posts as logistics, as we identified logistics as a primary issue in these cases.
6. Financial. This topic included the need for financial support to prepare and appear for job interviews, cost related to further education and retraining, etc.

We also identified an additional orthogonal dimension on which we could place the topics above: intrinsic versus extrinsic. We defined intrinsic factors as those

---

[17]We had a high level of inter-annotator agreement, ranging from 87 % to 100 % depending on the categories.

factors that are inherently associated with parents' own conditions and environment (e.g., having a sick child, the lack of recent work experience). In contrast, extrinsic factors were factors outside the parents' control (e.g., non-availability of childcare or the lack of jobs in their area).

All posts were annotated along these dimensions. Figure 11 summarises our findings: the occurrences of various categories over all the members' posts. We first look at barriers using high-level categories. The dimensions of Intrinsic/Extrinsic are represented by the two left-most columns in Fig. 11, and the remaining columns are the high-level categories mentioned above. We see that the Intrinsic category is the largest. This means that members expressed their own situations and environments as major barriers to work. This is also seen through the fact that the *"life situation"* and *"financial"* categories (both intrinsic factors) are the top two high-level categories for the topics. We examine these categories and identify specifically what contributes to their high number of occurrences.

Within the *"life situation"* category, all low-level categories (i.e., "Children with special needs", "No social/family support", "Education" (other than cost), "Medical/disability" and "No recent experience") were discussed about the same number of times. Many people explained why they found themselves having "No social/family support": very often, they had moved away from their family while in a stable relationship with their partners. When the relationship had broken up, they had found themselves away from their own family, and often unable to move for many reasons.

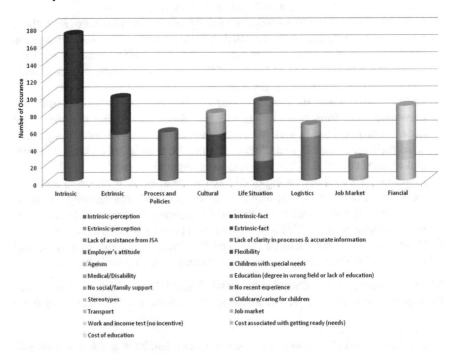

Fig. 11 Topics mentioned as barriers to work

In the *"financial"* category, the "cost of education" was the major topic discussed, followed by "work and income" test. With respect to education costs, parents were very willing to take further education to improve their chances of getting back into the workforce. However, parents who did not have savings and were left with no or very low discretionary money after meeting their basic needs found the cost of education to train themselves to enter the workforce to be a real barrier. We also found a number of occurrences of the lack of clarity on various processes and policies (e.g., "the Pensioner Education Supplement" and the "Job Education and Training child care fee assistance"). As for the issues with "work and income test", it was clear that members found no incentive to join the workforce, as there was no financial incentive: the amount of money they would receive after tax was low compared to the other costs (cost of childcare, transport, etc.). As a result, our members did not see the advantage of working as making up the disadvantages (e.g., working long hours, being away from children, etc.).

In the *"logistics"* category, "childcare" occurred more often than "transport". Parents found it hard to find good arrangements for their children while they were at work. We found that this was, in fact, the biggest barrier faced by our participants, as expressed through their posts. We had indeed observed during the topic identification process that a large number of discussions in the forum were about childcare availability, affordability, quality, cost, and flexibility. We note that this is consistent with other studies on barriers to work [43–45].

A significant number of parents talked about jobs availability (the *"job market"* category). Two major factors were mentioned here: the global financial crisis and the local job market in rural and regional areas. Well educated parents in rural and regional areas found it difficult to find jobs suited to their skills. Finally, the *"processes and policies"* category is fairly evenly split between the "lack of support from government hired providers" and the "lack of clarity in processes and accurate information".

A close observation of discussions in the forum also revealed that there was hardly a single category responsible for creating hurdles for parents to enter the workforce. Most parents expressed a number of categories within a single post. We conducted a co-occurrence analysis to identify which set of barriers were mentioned together, and observed the following:

- "Ageism" appeared together with "job market" and "no recent experience". We observed that many parents felt that there were no jobs for them. Members explicitly mentioned the age 45+ when they discussed ageism. As for work experience, members felt that they were discriminated in situations where jobs meeting their skills were advertised at a junior level; members felt that, in these situations, employers would not offer them the jobs, despite them having the right skills, because of their age—even though parents clearly indicated that they would be willing to take up the positions with a pay at the junior level.
- "Childcare/caring for children" occurred most times with "flexibility" and "no social/family support". Members felt (or had the experience) that employers were not willing to offer flexible working hours to enable parents to provide

quality care to their children while working. They also mentioned that they would feel comfortable leaving their children under the supervision of family members while at work, but that they were away from their immediate family for a variety of reasons, and hence this option was not available to them.

- "Children with special needs" occurred more frequently with "education" and "no social/family support". Some members told us that they had children with medical conditions, such as autism. These members expressed the hurdle of obtaining further education and training while looking after autistic children with no family support available.

5 Discussion

The goal of our community was to trial a new way of providing services and support to customers. We found that community members became actively involved—logging in regularly, commenting, asking questions and providing peer support. As with other communities, some members were very vocal (i.e., posting heavily on the forum), while others were more passively engaged (e.g., logging in frequently and reading the forum, thus indicating that what they were reading was useful to them, but not posting any messages).

Even if it was not explicitly acknowledged, the community became a hub for information. Often members would post their questions in the community before calling Human Services in the hope they could avoid the need to call. Some people mentioned they only had mobile phones and could not afford to call, others wanted to avoid the waiting times experienced at Human Services call centres. This indicates that our participants had a preference for getting information through a secure online community, as they could post their questions at a time that suited them and then go about their day, knowing it would be responded to promptly.

In addition, participants built a trust relationship with the moderators: they knew they would get relevant and accurate answers, as the moderators took the time to understand people's circumstances and got to "know" them through the trial. Such a relationship is much harder to achieve through a phone call (or even a visit to an office), as one is unlikely to talk to the same person. In general, participants tended to verify in the community the information they had obtained via other means.

From the perspective of Human Services, the community enabled one-to-many targeted service delivery/information provision. As all community members were in similar situations, they often had the same questions or concerns. Moderators would answer questions individually, but these were visible to the whole community. It was evident through thumbs up ratings, multiple participants thanking moderators for answers, and people logging regularly to read the forum that answers benefited many members. Participants also mentioned relaying the information to others sites, other single parents and friends. Interestingly, as the community closed, some passive members (those who had never posted before) decided to comment in the community to say that they had visited it regularly to get up-to-date and reliable information, but that they had never needed to ask a question as others always did this for them. This shows that online communities can be a valuable service delivery channel, providing tailored information to a broad audience, helping customers, sometimes before they even need to ask. On the negative side, however, some members found the site depressing, because of the numerous sad stories expressed. But while there were sad stories shared, there were also stories of hopes, humour and success.

We also discovered an interesting tension. Some people expressed doubts about the usefulness of such a forum "run by the government", as it "meant they could not express themselves freely" (although, from what we observed, it seemed that people did not feel constrained in their posts, sometimes openly critisising Human services).[18] However, one of the aspects of the community people found most useful was that it gave them prompt access to information, precisely because it was run by the government and moderated by government employees. Finally, we note that the community was thriving when we had to close it.

6 Conclusions

In this work, we investigated whether an online community run by a government agency could be used to support specific target groups, in particular welfare recipients. We designed and deployed an online community whose aim was to provide informational and emotional support to its members. Our analysis of how participants used the forum and what posts they wrote leads us to believe that the community achieved its purpose, also providing a welcome voice to its participants who wanted to be heard by the government. Based on our experience, we believe a community might be an effective way to provide support to specific target groups. We observed that the moderators played a crucial role in engaging the participants, supporting them, and helping them support each other. They also were key to trust forming in the community, by always providing prompt and accurate information and by showing understanding, concern and compassion. Finally, we note that providing information through social media (as in an online community) can be a very effective way to provide information, as it is a one-to-many channel, as opposed to a one-to-one, as in call centres or office visits.

Acknowledgments This research has been partially funded under the Human Services Delivery Research Alliance (HSDRA) between the CSIRO and the Australian Government Department of Human Services. We would like to thank P. Aghaei Pour, B. Yan, S. Bista, and N. Colineau for their work on the project, all the staff at the Australian Government's Department of Human Services for their support in this work, and all our *Next Step* community members for their invaluable participation and engagement.

---

[18]It is also worth mentioning that the moderators did not censor any posts. The only constraint placed on participants (explained in the Terms and Conditions) was not to be abusive towards anyone in the community (a participant or a moderator).

References

1. Sensis. (2015). Available: https://www.sensis.com.au/content/dam/sas/PDFdirectory/Sensis_Social_Media_Report_2015.pdf
2. Palen, L., Hiltz, S. R., & Liu, S. B. (2007). Online forums supporting grassroots participation in emergency preparedness and response. *Communications of the ACM, 50*, 54–58.
3. AGIMO. (2008). *Consulting with Government—Online*. Australian Government, Department of Finance and Deregulation.
4. Bødker, S., Colineau, N., Gandrup Borchorst, N., Korn, M., & Paris, C. (2011). International Reports on Socio-Informatics (IRSI) (Vol. 8). *Proceedings of the 2011 Community and Technology (C&T 2011) Workshop on Government and Citizen Engagement*. IISI—International Institute for Socio-Informatics Brisbane.
5. Granoveter, M. S. (1983). The strength of weak ties: A network theory re-visited. *Sociological Theory, 1*, 201–233.
6. Skeels, M. M., Unruh, K. T., Powell, C., & Pratt, W. (2010). Catalyzing social support for breast cancer patients. In *28th International Conference on Human Factors in Computing Systems*, Atlanta, Georgia, USA, pp. 173–182.
7. Ma, M., & Agarwal, R. (2006, 18th July). *With a little help from strangers: Social support and smoking cessation in online communities*. Available: http://www.rhsmith.umd.edu/news/releases/2006/120406.aspx
8. Sweetser, K. D., & Lariscy, W. (2008). Candidates make good friends: An analysis of candidates' uses of facebook. *International Journal of Strategic Communication, 2*, 175–198.
9. Vargas, J. A. (2008, Septembre 17th). *Obama raised half a billion online*. Available: http://voices.washingtonpost.com/44/2008/11/obama-raised-half-a-billion-on.html
10. Williams, C., & Gulati, G. J. (2009). Facebook grows up: An empirical assessment of its role in the 2008 congressional elections. In *Midwest Political Science Association*, Chicago.
11. Mascaro, C. M., & Goggins, S. P. (2011). Challenges for national civic engagement in the United States. *International Reports on Socio-Informatics (IRSI)* (Vol. 8). Proceedings of the 2011 Community and Technology (C&T 2011) Workshop on Government and Citizen Engagement. Bodker et al. (Eds).
12. Muhamad, R. (2011). Political blogging and the public sphere in Malaysia. *International Reports on Socio-Informatics (IRSI)* (Vol. 8). Proceedings of the 2011 Community and Technology (C&T 2011) Workshop on Government and Citizen Engagement. Bodker et al. (Eds).
13. Toland, J. (2011). E-petitions in local government: The case of Wellington City Council. *International Reports on Socio-Informatics (IRSI)* (Vol. 8). Proceedings of the 2011 Community and Technology (C&T 2011) Workshop on Government and Citizen Engagement. Bodker et al. (Eds).15–22.
14. Cohen, S. (2004). Social relationship and health. *The American Psychologist, 59*, 676–684.
15. Maloney-Krichmar, D., & Preece, J. (2005). A multilevel analysis of sociability, usability, and community dynamics in an online health community. *ACM Transactions on Computer-Human Interaction, 12*, 201–232.
16. Shirky, C. (2008). *Here comes health*. Presented at the Health 2.0 Conference: User-Generated Healthcare, San Francisco, CA, USA.
17. Smith, K. P., & Christakis, N. A. (2008). Social networks and health. *Annual Review of Sociology, 34*, 405–429.
18. Welbourne, J. L., Blanchard, A. L., & Boughton, M. D. (2009). Supportive communication, sense of virtual community and health outcomes in online infertility groups. In *International Conference on Communities and Technologies (C&T'09)*, University Park, Pennsylvania, USA, pp. 31–38.
19. Baroni, A. (2011). Deliberation and empowerment in Rio de Janeiro's favelas. *International Reports on Socio-Informatics (IRSI)* (Vol. 8). Proceedings of the 2011 Community and

Technology (C&T 2011) Workshop on Government and Citizen Engagement. Bodker et al. (Eds).

20. Sawer, H. (2006). One fundamental value: Work for the dole participants' views about work and mutual obligation. In *Proceedings of the Road to Where? The Politics and Practice of Welfare to Work Conference*, School of Social Work and Applied Human Sciences, University of Queensland, Brisbane.

21. Cameron, H. (2006). Single parent family under welfare-to-work. In *Proceedings of the Road to Where? The Politics and Practice of Welfare to Work Conference*, School of Social Work and Applied Human Sciences, University of Queensland, Brisbane.

22. Cox, E., & Priest, T. (2008, Dec 15, 2010). *Welfare to work: At what cost to parenting?* Report available at: http://www.women.nsw.gov.au/women_and_work/partnership_projects/welfare_to_work

23. Cohen, S., & Hoberman, H. M. (1983). Positive events and social supports as buffers of life change stress1. *Journal of Applied Social Psychology, 13*, 99–125.

24. Ganster, D. C., Fusilier, M. R., & Mayes, B. T. (1986). Role of social support in the experience of stress at work. *Journal of Applied Psychology, 71*, 102–110.

25. Thoits, P. A. (1995). Stress, coping, and social support processes: Where are we? What next? *Journal of Health and Social Behavior, 35*, 53–79.

26. Dormann, C., & Zapf, D. (1999). Social support, social stressors at work, and depressive symptoms: Testing for main and moderating effects with structural equations in a three-wave longitudinal study. *Journal of Applied Psychology, 84*, 874–884.

27. Colineau, N., Paris, C., & Dennett, A. (2011). Exploring the use of an online community in welfare transition programs. In *25th BCS Conference on Human-Computer Interaction*, Newcastle-upon-Tyne, United Kingdom, pp. 455–460.

28. Colineau, N., Paris, C., & Dennett, A. (2011). Capitalising on the potential of online communities to help welfare recipients. In *International Reports on Socio-Informatics (IRSI)* (Vol. 8). Proceedings of the 2011 Community and Technology (C&T 2011) Workshop on Government and Citizen Engagement. Bodker et al. (Eds). pp. 59–65.

29. Bista, S. K., Colineau, N., Nepal, S., & Paris, C. (2012). The design of an online community for welfare recipients. In *Proceedings of the 24th Australian Computer-Human Interaction Conference*, Melbourne, Australia, pp. 38–41.

30. Colineau, N., Paris, C., & Nepal, S. (2013). Providing support through reflection and collaboration in online communities. In *Proceedings of the 16th ACM Conference on Computer Supported Cooperative Work and Social Computing (CSCW)*, San Antonio, Texas, pp. 471–476.

31. Paris, C., Colineau, N., Nepal, S., Bista, S. K., & Beschorner, G. (2013). Ethical considerations in an online community: The balancing act. *Ethics in Information Technology, Special Issue on Ethics of Social Networks for Special Needs Users, 15*, 301–316.

32. Terveen, L., & McDonald, D. W. (2005). Social matching: A framework and research agenda. *ACM Transactions on Computer-Human Interaction (TOCHI), 12*, 401–434.

33. Colineau, N. (2012). A buddy matching program to help build an online support network. In *OzCHI'12 Proceedings of the 24th Australian Computer-Human Interaction Conference* Melbourne, pp. 85–88.

34. McPherson, M., Lovin, L., & Cook, J. (2001). Birds of a feather: Homophily in social networks. *Annual Review of Sociology, 27*, 415–444.

35. Nepal, S., Paris, C., Pour, P. A., Freyne, J., & Bista, S. K. (2015). Interaction based recommendations for online communities. *ACM Transaction on Internet Technology (TOIT)*. 15 (2), article 6. June 2015.

36. Colineau, N., Paris, C., & Nepal, S. (2013). Designing for reflection and collaboration to support a transition from welfare to work. In *Proceedings of the 2013 conference on Computer Supported Cooperative Work (CSCW)*, San Antonio, Texas, pp. 471–476.

37. Bunchball. (2010). *Gamification 101: An introduction to the use of game dynamics to influence behaviour*. Available: http://www.bunchball.com/gamification101

38. Deterding, S., Sicart, M., Nacke, L., O'Hara, K., & Dixon, D. (2011). Gamification: Using game-design elements in non-gaming contexts. In *PART 2 Proceedings of the 2011*

Annual Conference on Human Factors in Computing Systems, Vancouver, BC, Canada, pp. 2425–2428.
39. Zichermann, G., & Cunningham, C. (2011). *Gamification by design: Implementing game mechanics in web and mobile apps*. Canada: OReilly.
40. Schein, A. I., Popescul, A., Ungar, L. H., & Pennock, D. M. (2002). Methods and metrics for cold-start recommendations. In *Proceedings of the 25th Annual International ACM SIGIR Conference on Research and Development in Information Retrieval*, Tampere, Finland, pp. 253–260.
41. Storm, C., & Storm, T. (1987). A taxonomic study of the vocabulary of emotions. *Journal of Personality and Social Psychology, 53*, 805–816.
42. Scott, W. A. (1955). Reliability of content analysis: The case of nominal scale coding. *Public Opinion Quarterly*.
43. Brooks, M. G., & Buckner, J. C. (1996). Work and welfare: Job histories, barriers to employment, and predictors of work among low-income single mothers. *American Journal of Orthopsychiatry, 66*, 526.
44. Oanziger, S., Corcoran, M., Danziger, S., Heflin, C., Kalil, A., Levine, J., Rosen, D., Seefeldt, K., Siefert, K., & Tolman, R. (2000). Barriers to the employment of welfare recipients. *Prosperity for all?: The economic boom and African Americans*, 245.
45. Meyers, M. K., Heintze, T., & Wolf, D. A. (2002). Child care subsidies and the employment of welfare recipients. *Demography, 39*, 165–179.

Gamification on the Social Web

Surya Nepal, Cecile Paris and Sanat Bista

Abstract The emergence of the social web has caused a significant movement in the way e-government initiatives are implemented and deployed. The focus of e-government has moved from delivering public services using information and communication technologies to enticing the active participation of citizens in service delivery through social web platforms, whereby people perform the role of partners rather than customers. The success of this new movement relies on the active participation and engagement of citizens on these platforms. A major question then arises: how to incentivise citizens to remain active and contribute as equal partner in the public service delivery. In recent time, gamification has emerged as a promising technique to enhance engagement, foster collaboration and induce desirable behaviour amongst people. Gamification is the use of gaming techniques in a non-gaming context. With a wide ranging application from business and marketing to social networks, health and well-being, gamification has proved to be effective in bootstrapping participation and improving collaboration amongst people while maintaining their motivation to remain engaged. Gamification could be equally valuable for government departments and agencies to incentivise citizens to engage with governments in their ever increasing presence on the social web. This chapter first provides a brief introduction on gamification and how it has been used in game dynamics. We then present our experience and observations on using gamification techniques in the public service delivery through the case study of NextStep, an online community described in Chap 9. Finally, we provide a review of some of the current popular techniques and service platforms for gamification.

S. Nepal (✉) · C. Paris · S. Bista
CSIRO Data61, Sydney, Australia
e-mail: Surya.Nepal@csiro.au

C. Paris
e-mail: Cecile.Paris@csiro.au

S. Bista
e-mail: Sanat.Bista@csiro.au

© Springer International Publishing Switzerland 2015
S. Nepal et al. (eds.), *Social Media for Government Services*,
DOI 10.1007/978-3-319-27237-5_10

Keywords Gamification · Enragement · Motivation Social Networks · Social Media

1 Introduction

Due to the ubiquitous nature of connectivity and the increasing popularity of social connectedness, budget-strapped government departments and agencies have started using a new way of delivering public services using the social web [46]. Most e-government initiatives were, at the beginning, focused on providing information to citizens on the Web [51]. With the advancement of information and communication technologies, there is now a movement from e-government to we-government, whereby citizens perform the role of partners rather than customers [53]. This is also termed as citizen co-production. Citizen co-production is classified into three categories: citizen to government (C2G), government to citizen (G2C) and citizen to citizen (C2C).

We have seen an increasing number of social web initiatives towards citizen co-production. For example, President Obama created the Change.gov website as a vehicle to engage citizens to collect input to set the agenda for his presidency, including for healthcare [1]. This website falls into the C2G category. Similarly, in the G2C category, governments around the world are making their data open through open data initiatives that enable citizens to be informed about useful information, such as health risks [27]. In the C2C category, citizens can form online communities to address their needs. These include, for example, communities for patient driven healthcare models, e.g., Yelp (http://www.yelp.com), Angie's List (http://www.angieslist.com), HealthGrades (http://www.healthgrades.com) and Physician Reports (http://www.physicianreports.com) [74].

A key challenge for all these initiatives is to keep citizens engaged on the social web. This has been recognised as a major issue. All communities on the social web experience some attrition (people failing to engage or leaving the community). For example, an online community to help with diet and healthy lifestyle, the Online Total Wellbeing Diet Portal, showed attrition rates of almost 50 % in the first weeks of membership [13]. It is thus highly likely that e-government initiatives that include the social web, online communities and rely on citizens participation and engagement will encounter similar issues. There are two important tools available to address this problem: recommendation and gamification. Recommendation systems have been well researched and used successfully to decrease attrition and increase participation in online communities [37]. This chapter focuses on gamification: what it is, what it is based on, and whether it might be applicable in e-government. We first define what gamification is, and look at its history and trends. We then briefly present gamification theory, followed by the main elements gamification typically employs. We then discuss applying gamification to government services, in the context of a case study. Finally, we present a review of gamification in other application domains, including its criticisms.

2 Gamification

2.1 Definition

The term gamification has its origin in the digital media industry, with its first encountered use in 2008 and a widespread acceptance in 2010 [24]. The following terms have also been used to mean something close to gamification [25]: "productivity games" [61], "surveillance entertainment" [41], "funware" [75], "playful design" [34], "behavioral games" [26], "game layer" [69], and "applied gaming" [4]. Montola et al. [64] have used the terminology "Achievement Systems" to describe a reward structure providing additional goals for users; the method itself is close to what is broadly covered by gamification.

The following two definitions broadly sum up gamification [25]: *"the use of game design elements in non-game contexts"* [24], and *"the process of game thinking and game mechanics to engage users and solve problems"* [88]. In addition, mentioning its role in changing the behaviour of users, Gartner IT glossary [45] defines it as *"the use of game mechanics to drive engagement in a non-game business scenarios to change behaviors for a target audience to achieve business outcomes"*. In 2014, to address market confusions leading to unrealistic expectations from gamification, Gartner redefined it as *"the use of mechanics and experience design to digitally engage and motivate people to achieve their goal"* [16]. An important addition here is the use of the term *"digitally engage"*. As opposed to person engagement, digital engagement here highlights the engagement of the user with digital devices such as computers or smartphones. *"Experience design"* as a key element of the definition underlines the importance of a good game play design that is capable of taking users through the experience journey.

2.2 History

A brief evolution of gamification is outlined by Professor Kevin Werbach in his coursera course on gamification [80] and Griffin [43] in the HRDirector. We present some highlights of this history from these two sources.

American Cracker Jack popcorn's inclusion of a free surprise toy in its packets in the year 1912 is seen as a first use of gamification idea in marketing. Earlier in 1910, through the use of ranks and badges for achievements in activities, the Scout movement introduced a form of gamification in education. Gamification in the form of frequent flyer programs was first used by Western Direct Marketing for United Airlines in 1972 [81] followed by others with variations in the following years.

Thomas Malone's publication of two books, *What Make Things Fun to Learn* [58] and *Heuristics for designing enjoyable user interfaces: Lessons from computer games* [59] from 1980s are considered the first academic publications around gamification of learning.

The 1990s saw the introduction of gamification techniques in the teaching of mathematics in classrooms through two games: *Math Blaster* and the *Incredible Machine*. The Serious Games Initiative[1] in 2002 aimed at bringing together the electronic games industry and people working on projects that used games in education, training, health and public policy. Conundra,[2] a UK based consultancy that had a short existence in 2003, is believed to be the first company that intended to introduce gamification in its current form. Its founder, Nick Pelling, wanted to make game-like user interfaces to make electronic transactions through ATMs, vending machines, etc., fun and fast; however, citing the lack of significant customer interest, the company was closed in 2006 [68].

Games for change (G4C)[3] in 2004 introduced social impact games to serve humanitarian and educational efforts.

Gamification as we know it today came into existence in 2007 with the release of the first gamification platform, Bunchball,[4] which introduced Points, Badges and Leaderboards (known in short as PBL). The popularity of the term gamification is due to the Design, Innovate, Communicate and Entertain (DICE) conference in 2010. The first gamification summit was held in San Francisco in 2011, and it attracted numerous participants. In the same year, the term gamification was added to Oxford dictionary.

As of 2015, gamification has seen a widespread application and has gone mainstream, largely due its corporate acceptance. Many organisations followed the trend of gamifying their websites or their internal human resource systems to incentivise people to participate corporate activities. However, not all these initiatives met with success, as stated by Gartner that gamification was being driven by "novelty and hype", and predicted that 80 % of current gamified applications would fail to meet their objectives [47]. Blame for failure was mostly attributed to poor game designs and to the focus on PBL implementations only, without appropriate attention to issues of competition, collaboration, skill and challenges. Spreading gamification in the social web is seen as the future of gamification. Gamification also has, of course, its critics. We present and discuss them in Sect. 5 of this paper.

2.3 Trend

Gamification has found its wide use in a diverse range of settings ranging from call centre employee engagement [18] to marketing [70, 71], education and health [50, 52], to innovation [15, 82], crowd sourcing [21] to Geographic Information System

---

[1]http://www.seriousgames.org/.

[2]http://www.nanodome.com/conundra.co.uk/.

[3]http://www.gamesforchange.org/about/.

[4]http://www.bunchball.com/.

(GIS) [62]. It is also used in social analytics [40]. Gamification has evolved as an effective method to enhance user engagement by inserting game dynamics, such as competition elements and rewards, into user interactions [14, 25, 88].

The trend in gamification adoption has been very positive. It has grown from media buzz in 2012 to its integration with mobile, social and collaboration platforms with the expectation that innovative uses of gamification analytics can influence behaviour [17]. M2 research estimated the market to reach to $2.8 billion by 2016 [56]. In 2011, Gartner thought that, by 2014, more than 70 % of Global 2000 organisations will have at least one "gamified" application" [38].

A gamification vendor survey of vertical market segments by M2 Research [63] shows that the uptake of gamification is spread amongst 11 different market segments, with enterprise, entertainment and media/publisher seeing most of the applications, with 25, 18 and 17 % of the market respectively. This is followed by consumer goods (10 %), retail (9 %), healthcare/wellness (4 %), financial (4 %), education (4 %), telecom (4 %), utility (1 %) and government (1 %). Though the use of gamification in the government sector is quite low, it is likely to increase as the social web is increasingly becoming the platform of choice to deliver government services to the citizens. Therefore, it is important to understand the gamification techniques and their potential uses in the government context to enable government departments and agencies to engage successfully with citizens through the social web.

3 Gamification Theory, Mechanics and Motivational Psychology

3.1 Gamification Theory

As stated above gamification is applying game theory in a non-gaming context. There are two main branches of game theory: cooperative and non-cooperative game theory. The cooperative theory is combinatorial and describes only the outcomes of the results, whereas the non-cooperative is procedural and describes all potential actions that can be taken. For example, providing group activities in an online community to achieve a certain goal [20] and awarding the group that completes the tasks on time is a cooperative game. On the other hand, providing an individual activity where a person can collaborate with buddies, but does not have to, in order to complete the task is an example of non-cooperative game.

One of the applications, where game theory has been studied, is economics [72, 73]. In economics, game theory is defined in three categories: decision theory, general equilibrium theory and mechanism design theory.[5] We briefly describe them below.

---

[5]http://levine.sscnet.ucla.edu/general/whatis.htm.

Decision theory: Decision theory is viewed as a theory of one person games, where the focus is on preferences and the formation of the best decision. Probability theory is widely used in order to represent the uncertainty of outcomes, and Bayes Law is frequently used to model the way in which new information is used to revise the decision making process [6]. Alternative theories such as fuzzy logic [85], possibility theory [29], and Dempster-Shafer theory [7] can be used to acquire information before making a decision.

General equilibrium theory: This theory deals with trade and production, and typically with a relatively large number of individual consumers and producers. The fundamental principal behind this theory is to explain the behaviour of supply, demand and prices in the economic context [78].

Mechanism design theory: This theory differs from game theory, but naturally relies on game theory. Unlike game theory that takes the rules of the game as given, the mechanism design theory asks about the consequences of different types of rules [48].

3.2 Motivational Psychology

A common objective of using gamification across all implementation scenarios is to drive user participation by making engagement with the *system* more fun and appealing, thus addressing the challenge of low contribution and attrition rate. At the same time, through careful design of the system, implementers are able to drive behavioural change of the engaged mass. Chamberlin sees behaviour change, improvement in collaboration, crowd sourcing of ideas, accelerated learning, increased participation and loyalty to be the drivers for the uptake of gamification, whereas games without proper motivation and poor game designs are labelled as some of the inhibitors to growth of gamification [17].

According to Gartner, gamification offers four principal means to drive engagement: (a) accelerated feedback cycle, through the increased velocity of feedback loops, (b) clear goals and rules of play, through simple, user friendly and well defined goals, (c) a compelling narrative that encourages user participation, and (d) challenging but achievable tasks offering thrill and enjoyment [39]. To engage users (who could be company employees or customers), a good design for gamification, would thus have to incorporate one or all of these principles. It must also find a balance between the users' skill level and challenge level. Radoff [70] mentions that a low challenge and high skill situation causes boredom, while the opposite triggers anxiety for the user.

3.3 Gamification Elements

Another important aspect to take into consideration when choosing the design for a gamification process is the likely desires of the users in the community, as it is those that the gamification targets to fulfill. For example, if users wish for a sense of achievement, a challenging task is appropriate; competition will be suitable in some contexts, appealing to altruism in others. Bunchball outlines six possible human desires (namely status, achievement, self expression, competition, altruism and reward) that a gamification model can target to motivate and engage users through the use of number of gamification elements [14].

A number of gamification elements have been used to inject game dynamics in non gaming environment [14, 25, 70, 88], including: Loyalty Points, Leader Boards, Badges, Progress Bars, Virtual Currencies and On Boarding, which will be introduced and described later. These elements, the scores the users obtain, the competition that might occur amongst players, championships, rewards, social recognition, self-satisfaction, feelings of achievement, intrinsic motivation, fan clubs, etc. all drive the level of passion and engagement. Understanding these elements and modelling them in their context of applications is thus the primary step towards the design of gamification.

Metrics or scores are the most important elements of gamification. They create a feeling of competition and help engaging the users. Thus, statistics lie at the core of gamification. They influence reward, status, achievement and competition [14].

Examples of statistics being related to status, achievement, competition and reward include eBay feedback profiles (transaction history), view records in YouTube, Facebook likes, run miles in Nike+IPod, performance measurements and goal achievements in Health Month plans, Four Square check-in counts, etc. All these elements of gamification have their roots in statistics.

We next describe some elements that have been popular and explain how they are used in different contexts. We will see later that not all of them are applicable in the government context.

Points System: Points System are now everywhere in online services, albeit in different forms. EBay's reputation, YouTube and Facebook's likes, friend numbers, online game scores, contribution scores, negative scores, virtual cash, etc. are all depicted in the form of points. Points are the basic metrics used in assessing quality of contributions and experiences of members online. Hence, they form a very important component of engagement game mechanics, and they are an absolute requirement for any gamified system [87]. Community behaviours can also be shaped by the notion of earning points, and different categories of points can be used to reward members in the community [14].

Badges: Badges are another way of rewarding members in a community. Studies have shown the positive impact of rewards in motivation. Antin and Churchill mention badges as a key element in gamifying social media experiences [2]. In their study, they deconstruct badges to five social psychological functions in social media context, namely: goal setting, instruction, reputation, status/affirmation and group identification. They further note that upcoming research should explore these psychological functions in specific application contexts.

Leader Boards: Leader boards are lists expressing a position of status in a community. For example, the most viewed video over YouTube, most rated videos, the best looking member of the community, the employee of the month, etc. Their presence is not only limited to online forum; they are often used to highlight player positions in video games. By giving people a position in the community, leader boards stand as an interesting and popular game mechanics. Positions help in driving users' motivation. The wish to gain a better position engages community members more in community activities.

Loyalty: Loyalty programs as a tool for marketing and holding customers are not new concepts. Airlines and Bank loyalty programs are by far the most known ones. There has been considerable debate over how effective loyalty programs are in retaining customers [28, 79]. However, the programs are still in practice and are increasingly being adopted. In the context of online communities, loyalty can be depicted in terms of the Visitor Return Frequency (VRF). By giving extra incentives to returning visitors and treating long standing members in a special way, loyalty programs can prove to be effective in engaging visitors.

On-Boarding: On-boarding is a behavioural mechanics of gamification. It has more to do with the quality of experience of the user than with a metric. It can be understood as the first experience of a user with the system. How welcoming and interesting did the user find the system in its first use? First impressions count a lot. This is also true with the first experience with a computer system or an online social network. If users experience difficulties in their first use, their chances of returning back get slimmer. So, it is very important to ensure that users are not exposed to the detailed complexities of the system in their first use. Zichermann and Cunningham mention that revealing the complexity of the system slowly, reinforcing the user positively, removing opportunities to fail and learning something about the player during first use are the key elements of a good on boarding process [88].

Challenges: Challenge can drive a user in continuing with the activities. Challenges can be skillfully presented in the form of games. It is, however, important to rightly assess the level of challenge posed to the user, as the appropriate balance of skill and challenge is an important aspect of engagement. Setting too high a challenge for the user's skills will lead to disinterest or anxiety. Conversely, lack of challenge can lead to boredom. Figure 1 from [70] illustrates this phenomenon:

Fig. 1 Balance of skill and challenge [70]

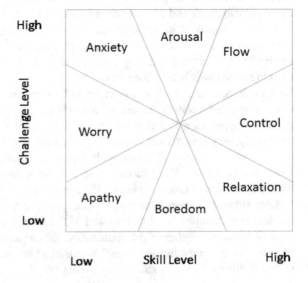

Lifecycle and Level: Presence of a lifecycle for users is another important aspect of engagement. Lifecycles are important in giving a feeling of progression to users, and this feeling keeps the user in a loop of continuous engagement. An example of such lifecycle could be: motivation, action, engagement and reward. Subsequently, the reward enhances the level of motivation, and the cycle continues. Zichermann and Cunningham [88] present a social engagement loop designed to maximise user engagement and re-engagement. It is shown in Fig. 2.

With an ongoing cycle of events, if users can see a difference in their presence in the community, their motivation to go forward remains high. With the progression in life cycle, different levels for the user can be designed, and, if desired, the status can be made public in the community.

Identity: Users like to have different possible identities over the social web. Identities can be chosen according to mood. This flexibility of representing self is another interesting gamification element, as this is something not available in the real world. Many online environments present a choice of Avatars to users. This has been one of the most popular elements of gamification.

Virtual Goods: Just like the possession of materials is significant in the real world, having virtual goods holds an importance in the virtual world. Points (like in the form of virtual cash) can be spent on buying virtual goods. Having more goods can remain a desire of the user, and thus the user engages with the system to acquire more. Possession of virtual goods can also define the identity of users online.

It is important to understand what might motivate users to get engaged with the gamification elements above. Incentives are typically a way to increase motivation. In the government context, incentives cannot be monetary as all citizens need to be treated equally. In social psychology, Liu et al. looked at non-monetary incentive mechanisms such as location based leader board based on points to increase

Fig. 2 Social engagement loop to maximise player engagement [88]

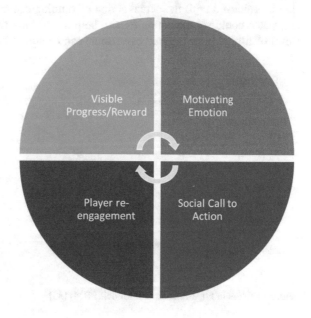

contributions to online systems [54]. The use of social psychological theories such as social loafing [49] and goal setting [3, 55] to tackle the under-contribution problem in online communities is studied in [5], in the context of the Movie Lens online community. Their findings show that reminding members of the uniqueness of their contributions and giving them specific challenging goals increased their contribution to the community. Gamification also offers visibility of one's performance in the community. For example, if someone is on the community's leader board, the whole community could be watching that individual [54]. This in turn could have a social facilitation effect [86], where people have a tendency to perform better when someone is watching than while doing it alone. Using computers and psychology to persuade and shape user behaviour and promoting the use of computers and games in instructional design are not new concepts [5, 36, 58, 66]. However, building mechanisms based on those resources through gamification is an upcoming idea that has started penetrating a variety of application domains.

Fogg's model for persuasive design [35] has been one of the popular works presenting a model of human behaviour as a product of three factors namely motivation, ability and trigger (refer to Fig. 3). The model has been widely referred to by the gamification community as a reference in game design.

The two axes of the model represent ability (also called simplicity) and motivation. Along the diagonal plane lies a target behaviour and triggers that are required to achieve the target behaviour. Typically, reaching a target behaviour is a balance between the motivation and ability. A high motivation and high ability ensures that the target behaviour is achieved. However, it would still need a trigger just before the user performs some action to achieve that behaviour. An example from real life could be, a person might be highly motivated to run and could have a high ability to do so as well. However, if fitness is the targeted behaviour, this may not be achieved until the actual action of running occurs. Trigger in the form of a race date could set the action on and help in reaching the targeted behaviour. The level of fitness (as a targeted behaviour) can occupy different position in the plane

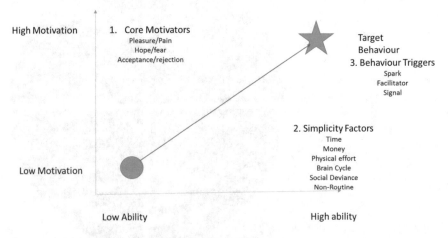

Fig. 3 Factors in Fogg Behavioural Model (FBM) [35]

Fig. 4 The flow channel [22]

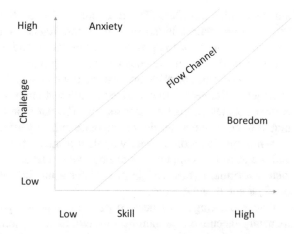

according to the ability and motivation of the individual. This means that the location of targeted behaviour in the plane can be varied to respond to variations in the ability and motivation.

Michael Wu from Lithium Technology used the Fogg Behaviour Model (FBM) to analyse the role of gamification in driving players above activation threshold and triggering them into specific action [83, 84]. Wu concludes that an effective gamification should facilitate the convergence of the three factors of FBM (motivation, ability and trigger).

Another psychological concept related to motivation is that of flow [22,23] as introduced by psychology professor Mihaly Czikszentmihalyi. It describes flow, *"as a state of absorption in one's work, characterised by intense concentration, loss of self-awareness, a feeling of being perfectly challenged (neither bored nor overwhelmed) and a sense that time is flying"* [84].

As shown in Fig. 4, flow occurs when there is a right balance between challenge and skill possessed by users. High skill and low challenge lead to boredom whereas high challenge low skill can trigger anxiety. Flow has been referred to as an important aspect in game designs. With gamification concerning the use of game mechanics, the concept of flow becomes important to gamification designers as well. For example, during the design phase, an appropriate reward component could only be outlined after understanding the skill level of the prospective users of the system. Challenges in the system could then be set against skill levels and reward offered at a right balance to preserve the flow.

4 Application in Government Services

The gamification has been widely used in both commercial world and social web. In the commercial world, major retailers in the world have loyalty programs for their members. The airline and hotel industries royalty programs are very popular among regular travellers. The discounts and one off benefits aim to incentivise people to use certain brand of airlines and hotels. In all these programs, there is a tangible benefit for the people to use certain brand of products or services. The situation is similar in the social web. The prime example is Foursquare, which offers mayorships for frequent visitors. Popular social networks such as LinkedIn also incentivise people to continue to participate in providing content by providing regular updates on visitor numbers, etc. The question is: can we apply these techniques to government services to increase citizen participation?

While gamification is readily applied in many forms in the commercial world and social web, its application to improve government services, offered via social web platforms, is not straightforward for a number of reasons. We next discuss briefly some of the reasons.

Government agencies need to treat all citizens equally. This limits the use of monetary incentive as a gamification tool in social web (e.g., online community), as not all citizens will be members in the community. As most of the government services are targeted for a certain group of citizens, providing equal opportunity for all members in the community to participate is not an easy task. Furthermore, Web based government services need to follow strict guidelines that can become hurdles for implementing some of the gamification techniques. For example, gamification mechanisms that require plugins in the standard browsers cannot be implemented, as many people do not have those plugins installed in their browsers by default. Implementing some gamification techniques require change in the government policies and guidelines. Another important aspect of government services is that it has to follow stricter security and privacy requirements than non-government organisations. One of the key challenges in implementing gamification mechanisms in government services is how to balance the privacy, equality and incentive to increase engagement.

In this section, we explain our work in which we used some of the gamification techniques in an online community *Next Step* (see Chaps. 2 and 9 for further detail on *Next Step*) [10, 11]. We were involved in designing, developing and deploying the *Next Step* online community. This was done in collaboration with the Australian Government's Department of Human Services, which is responsible for the welfare payments. The *Next Step* community was developed to help deliver government services to a specific group of welfare recipients [19]. The target group was parents in a transition phase, being asked, by legislation, from one type of welfare payment, a parental payment, to a new payment type, new start payment. The new payment type required the individuals to look for jobs and sometimes had a lower monetary value.

The transition is stressful and hard for many parents. The community, *Next Step*, aimed to help them in a number of ways.

- The community was built to bring people in similar situations together, hoping that they would share experiences, ideas and tips.
- The community was expected to provide social, emotional and moral support to its members.

- The community was built to be a place for the government to target its information and services when dealing with a specific group of welfare recipients.
- The community was expected to be a space in which individuals could go through a personal journey via a set of weekly activities, in order to better prepare them for the transition and their return to work [8, 9, 20].

Members in the community did not know each other before joining the community, and their privacy was protected through a double blinded registration process [67]. The members joined the community only on invitation, and all members were on the similar situation. Human Services explicitly invited a subset of the individuals which were in the target group.

One of the challenges in our community was to encourage engagement of the members in the community. In order to address this challenge, we took a number of approaches: recommendation, gamification and reflection journey. In the following, we describe our gamification approach in *Next Step*.

In the context of *Next Step*, we focused on four specific human desires, amongst those identified in [14]:

- Reward—for people who actively participate in the community;
- Self expression—for people to share their stories and obtain support;
- Achievement—to see people move along the transition process; and
- Altruism—to have people provide each other support, whether it be informational, moral or emotional.

However, providing gamification in a government-run online community offering support to its members in changing situations had its own unique constraints, including:

- Equality—the community needed to treat all members equally. This constraint prohibited us to categorise people into different membership groups, have leader boards, and offer tangible incentives, financial or otherwise.
- Judgment—the community members needed to be able to express their situations without fear and freely. This meant that the design element could not give members the perception of being judged. It also could not reveal their identity or their actions in the community.
- Single out—though the purpose of introducing gamification in the community is to encourage and promote people who engaged in the community, we could not single out others for not doing so.
- Perception—*Next Step* members were in changing and sensitive situations. It was thus possible that game elements would be inappropriate if they were perceived as fun.

These requirements thus posed significant challenges to implement the traditional game elements identified in the earlier section. However, the gamification is one of the important aspects to bootstrap, engage and retain community members in the community. The challenge was to find appropriate gamification elements for *Next Step*.

We decided to use points and badges as our main design elements for gamification. The decision was based on the positive recommendations given in [2, 88]. Points and badges were awarded to members based on their actions in the community. We next describe in brief the design of our gamification elements. For details about our implementation, please see [11].

Our design process consisted of six phases, as presented in Fig. 5:

1. In the first phase, we identified the set of contexts from the online community where gamification was to be introduced. In our implementation, we considered each activity in which a member could participate as a context. Example contexts included buddy, journey activities, discussion forum, etc.
2. In the second phase, we identified a set of actions that could be carried out in each context. For example, a member could initiate a new thread in the forum, reply to existing posts in the forum, like the comment given to a post, etc.
3. In the third phase, a range of points to be allocated for different actions were identified. For example, a member scored points if he or she liked a comment or read the discussion forum.
4. In the fourth phase, the rules to allocate these points to actions in different contexts were established. In some cases, a member could figure out what points were given to what actions, whereas in other cases points were aggregated over a number of actions and their derivation was not straightforward.
5. In the fifth phase, the set of badges to be awarded were identified. For example, a reader badge was defined for a member who regularly read the posts in the forum.
6. In the final phase, we defined the rules to allocate badges to points. For example, a reader badge was awarded to a member if the member accrued certain reader points.

Table 1 shows the number of badges offered by *Next Step* and the rules to obtain each of these badges. The badges can be categorised into four different groups.

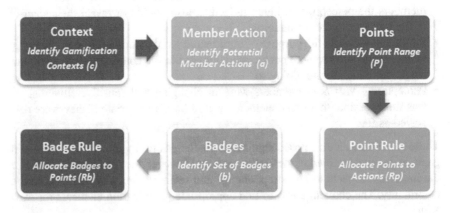

Fig. 5 Gamification design phases

Table 1 Badges and rules

Badge (b)	Awarded to (R_b)	Type
NextStep	All registered	Permanent
Early Bird	All registered within two weeks of community launch	Permanent
VIP	Fortnightly top ten scorers for unique sign-ins (two consecutive sign-ins are considered unique if they were separated by at least 2 h of time difference)	Temporary
VIP Plus	Members qualifying for the VIP badge twice in a row	Temporary
Social	Members sending out and accepting at least two buddy invitations	Permanent
Social Plus	Members sending out and accepting at least five buddy invitations	Permanent
Reader	Fortnightly top ten scores for reading and rating posts, resources and comments	Temporary
Reader Plus	Members qualifying for the Reader badge twice in a row	Temporary
Commenter	Fortnightly top 10 scorers for posting comments	Temporary
Commenter Plus	Members qualifying for the Commenter badge twice in a row	Temporary
Enthusiast	Top 10 scorers in Weekly Community Activities	Permanent
Scholar	Fortnightly top 10 scorers for balanced reading, rating and commenting activity	Temporary
Enlightened	Members whose contributions receive more positive ratings and less negative ratings (refreshed fortnightly)	Temporary

The first group of badges *(Next Step* and *Early Bird)* were given to all members who joined the community. The second set of badges (e.g., *Reader, Social* and *Commentator)* were given to members who were actively contributing in the community. The third set of badges (e.g., *Reader Plus, Social Plus* and *Commentator Plus)* was given to people who were active for a longer duration of time. The fourth set of badges (e.g., *VIP* and *VIP Plus)* were offered to encourage members to return to the community often. To prevent saturation, only some of the badges were conferred as permanent. Others lapsed after an interval of time and needed to be regained.

The community was run as a trial for about a year. It took a while to bootstrap the community. We noted that a group of members regularly visited the community after a few weeks. On average, 6.2 % of the members visited the community on a daily basis. Figure 6 shows some data on badges over a period of time. We discarded the early weeks as it took some time for members to register and start participating in the community. The badges also provided an important summary of the activities for the community provider. For example, any dip in the VIP badge curve indicated an attrition rate in visits since VIP badges were offered based on unique sign-ins.

The next challenging question for us was how to present the badges. There were two options: making badges public so that all community members could see them or making them private so that individual members could see their badges only. In many communities, individual member badges are made visible to the whole community, enabling members to see where other members stand in the community. However, in discussions with our ethics committee, we decided that it would be inappropriate to make badges visible in our community for the following reasons: (a) we feared that making badges visible would single out members who were active, and less active members visiting the community to seek information would feel discouraged, and (b) members might have felt that their privacy was breached and their actions too visible to everyone. Therefore, we implemented gamification with only local badge visibility, i.e., members could only see their own badges. Even then we needed to be careful that members would not feel that "someone was watching" their activities.

For the detailed analysis for the results and analysis, we refer readers to [11].

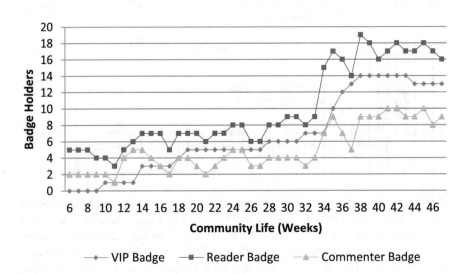

Fig. 6 Comparison of VIP, reader and commenter badges

5 Gamification Some Applications, Related Work and Criticisms

Gamification has been successfully used in many industries ranging from software industry to retailers to achieve different goals. We highlight some example success stories below:

- Marketers and product managers are using gamification to engage customers and influence desirable usage behaviour [70, 71, 88]. The application of gamification resulted in 20 % increase on time spent on Web sites by customers in comparison to that time spent before the application of gamification techniques [88].
- The technology development company, DevHub (www.devhub.com), has succeeded in increasing the number of users completing online tasks from 10 to 80 % by adding gamification elements such as points and levels [76].
- A New-York based food ordering website, Campusfood.com, experienced a 15–20 % increase in the return of new users after adding points and badges features to their site [57].
- A point-based gamification was used in crowd sourcing application to motivate people in a community to report issues in their surrounding environment [21]. Similarly, Martí et al. [60] introduced gamification into a mobile application to monitor noise pollution in the environment. In that work, users were able to use their personal smart phones to share important pollution data to relevant community.
- Gamification has been used in innovation as well. Quirky[6] makes use of gamified crowd sourcing to encourage members to submit innovative product development idea [15].
- In crowd sourcing applications, attracting and retaining good quality workers is a challenging task. In their work, Eickhoff et al. evaluated the use of a game to address this challenge [31]. Their model is shown to achieve high quality, with lower pay rate and fewer malicious submissions from the workers.
- Many organisations are using internal social networking sites to communicate with staff as well as collect ideas and concerns from staff. The impact of a point-based incentive system in a company-internal social networking site was conducted by Farzan et al. [33]. Their results show the positive impact of incentives in motivating staff to contribute to the company's social network. Similarly, Thom et al. studied the impact of gamification by removing point-based gamification in an enterprise social network. Their findings demonstrate that removing gamification from the enterprise network had a significant negative impact in the amount of user generated content [77].
- Is gamification a suitable mechanism to use in software systems? Herzig et al. [44] attempted to answer the question and their finding shows that gamification

---

[6]http://www.quirky.com/.

has a positive role in enhancing users' feelings like enjoyment and perceived ease of use of software systems. This finding is also supported by the study of Montola et al. that using a gamification element like reward is a viable option to add enjoyment for the system's users [64]. However, they note that not all users would appreciate it, so that there also needs to be an option to use the system without those gaming elements.

These applications are different to e-government ones, as government applications pose extra constraints as stated in the earlier section. However, the aims are similar as all these applications would like to use gamification to increase user participation. To present a summary of popular gamification applications of today against market segment and psychological characteristics, we obtained a list of ten from [30, 32]. Table 2 presents a list of these applications and classifies them according to their psychological characteristics.

Though gamification has been around for a while, its use in the social web driven services is still new and evolving. The success of gamification in different applications above may not be directly applicable to the social web in the context of government services. In addition, it is important to look at the failures of gamification and learn from them. There have been some criticisms of gamification techniques limited to use of points, badges and leaderboards (PBL). Robertson blames gamification (as it is practised) to be rather "poinstification" and a misrepresentation of games [72]. Many of PBL schemes ignore the *experience design* aspect of gamification, which is essential to motivate users. Providing points and scores alone may not be effective enough in motivating users to attain a desired behaviour. It has been reported that a score-based gamification could potentially reduce the internal motivation for users to engage [65]. There is a need of user-centred gamification that would provide intrinsic motivation to the users. This requires a good design that offers users a positive game-based experience though it may not be one of the main objectives of introducing gamification in applications.

The poor game design may lead to the negative consequences as people may feel that they are being manipulated through gamification [17]. How to change the perception of manipulation to challenge is the core challenge of good game design. Game designer Ian Bogost in his position statement at the Wharton gamification Symposium [12] criticised gamification to be "exploitation-ware" that replaces real incentives by fictional ones, striping away value and trust from the parties involved [84]. Griffin have pointed out some pitfalls of gamification such as intentional designs to promote addictive behaviour [42]. Finally, gamification also faces challenges from legal and regulatory perspective. Employment/Labour law, Deceptive Marketing, Intellectual Property, Virtual Property Rights are some legal issues, whereas Paid Endorsements, Banking Regulations, Games of Skills versus Chance are some regulatory issues [80].

Table 2 Ten popular gamification applications and their psychological characteristics

Application	Market segment	Game mechanics	Motivators	Ability	Trigger	Flow
eBay	eCommerce	Badges, points	Reputation	Business handling	Customer orders	Customer orders and supply
FourseSquare	Social networking (location checkin)	Badges, points	Sharing experiences	To checkin	Location checkin	Time and money
GetGlue	Social networking (sharing shows)	Recommendations, badges, rewards	Sharing experiences, recommendations	To view	View checkin	Time and money
Mint	Personal finance	Progress bar	Saving goal	To achieve goal	Expenditure	Need and want
Muchmusic.com	Entertainment	Points, rewards	Sharing experiences	To analyse and comment	Viewing and commenting action	Time and analysis skill
Nike+	Wellbeing/fitness	Points(nike fuel), awards(trophies)	Fitness/well being	Physical ability to achieve goal	Run	Goal and physical ability
Recycle Bank	Environment	Points, rewards	Conservation, experience sharing	To achieve goal	Conservation action	Goal and conservation
Samsung Nation	Corporate gamification	Points, badges, leaderboards	Loyalty	To analyse and comment	Viewing and com-menting action	Loyalty and usability
Sneakpeeq	Retail	Badges, rewards	Reward (discounted product)	To browse and purchase	Viewing and purchasing	Time and money
Xbox Live	Gaming	Points (gamer score), reputation	Reputation	Game skill	Game play	Time and skill

6 Conclusion and Future Work

This chapter provided a brief history and review of gamification, gamification theory, gamification elements and our experience of using gamification in an online community designed, developed, and deployed for a government department. Gamification has been widely used in the corporate world for a variety of reasons: providing different types of incentives for engagement, retaining customer base through loyalty programs, bootstrapping new products or services, competing in the marketplace, providing unique attributes to services or products, etc. We believe that the use of gamification on the social web is going increase in the coming years. Hence, the design and development of new gamification elements and techniques should get attention from the research community with the focus on good design of game elements that provides an enjoyable experience for users in a particular application context.

References

1. Abroms, L. C., & Craig Lefebvre, R. (2009). Obama's wired campaign: Lessons for public health communication. *Journal of Health Communication, 14*, 415–423.
2. Antin, J., & Churchill, E. F. (2011). Badges in social media: A social psychological perspective. In *Proceedings of the CHI 2011*, Vancouver, BC, Canada, ACM.
3. Austin, J. T., & Vancouver, J. B. (1996). Goal constructs in psychology: Structure, process, and content. *Psychological Bulletin, 120*, 338.
4. Baxter, N. (2012). Museum as game board. In *Fun is Not the Enemy of Work*, Natron Baxter, http://natronbaxter.com/museum-as-game-board
5. Beenen, G., Ling, K., Wang, X., Chang, K., Frankowski, D., Resnick, P., & Kraut, R. E. (2004). Using social psychology to motivate contributions to online communities. In *Proceedings of the 2004 ACM Conference on Computer Supported Cooperative Work*, Chicago, Illinois, USA, ACM, 1031642, pp. 212–221.
6. Berger, J. O. (1985). *Statistical decision theory and Bayesian analysis*. Berlin: Springer.
7. Beynon, M., Curry, B., & Morgan, P. (2000). The Dempster-Shafer theory of evidence: An alternative approach to multicriteria decision modelling. *Omega, 28*, 37–50.
8. Bista, S. K., Colineau, N., Nepal, S., & Paris, C. (2012). The design of an online community for welfare recipients. In *Proceedings of the 24th Australian Computer-Human Interaction Conference*, ACM, Melbourne, Australia, pp. 38–41.
9. Bista, S. K., Colineau, N., Nepal, S., & Paris, C. (2013). Next step: An online community to support parents in their transition to work. In *Proceedings of the 2013 Conference on Computer Supported Cooperative Work Companion*, ACM, San Antonio, Texas, pp. 5–10.
10. Bista, S. K., Nepal, S., Colineau, N., & Paris, C. (2012). Using gamification in an online community. In *CollaborateCom*, pp. 611–618.
11. Bista, S. K., Nepal, S., Paris, C., & Colineau, N. (2014). Gamification for online communities: A case study for delivering government services. *International Journal of Cooperative Information Systems,23*(2) 1–25.
12. Bogost, I. (2011). *Gamification is a Bullshit*, Wharton Gamification Symposium, http://www.bogost.com/blog/gamification_is_bullshit.shtml
13. Brindal, E., Freyne, J., Saunders, I., Berovksy, S., & Noakes, M. (2012). Weight tracking is predictive of weight loss for overweight/obese participants in a purely web-based intervention. *J Med Internet Research, 14* (6):e173.

14. Bunchball, I. (2010). Gamification 101: An introduction to the use of game dynamics to influence behaviour, Bunchball, While paper, Bunchball. http://www.bunchball.com/sites/default/files/downloads/gamification101.pdf

15. Burke, B. (2013). *The Gamification of Business*, Forbes, http://www.forbes.com/sites/gartnergroup/2013/01/21/the-gamification-of-business/

16. Burke, B. (2014). *Gartner redefines gamification*, Gartner, http://blogs.gartner.com/brian_burke/2014/04/04/gartner-redefines-gamification/

17. Chamberlin, B. (2013). Gamification: A 2013 HorizonWatching Trend Report. In *HorizonWatching: Emerging Business Issues, Trends and Technologies*, http://www.billchamberlin.com/

18. Citoresearch. (2013). It's no game: Gamification is transforming the call center. In *Advancing the Craft of Technology Leadership*, Evolved Media CITO Research, New York, USA.

19. Colineau, N., Paris, C., & Dennett, A. (2011). Exploring the use of an online community in welfare transition programs. In *25th BCS Conference on Human-Computer Interaction*, British Computer Society, Newcastle-upon-Tyne, United Kingdom, pp. 455–460.

20. Colineau, N., Paris, C., & Nepal, S. (2013). Designing for reflection and collaboration to support a transition from welfare to work. In *Proceedings of the 2013 Conference on Computer Supported Cooperative Work*, ACM, San Antonio, Texas, pp. 471–476.

21. Crowley, D. N., Breslin, J. G., Corcoran, P., & Young, K. (2012). Gamification of citizen sensing through mobile social reporting. In *IEEE International Games Innovation Conference (IGIC) 2012*, IEEE, Rochester, NY, USA, pp. 1–5.

22. Csikszentmihalyi, M. (1990). *Flow the psychology of optimal experience*. Chicago: Harper collins.

23. Csikszentmihalyi, M. (1997). *Finding flow: The psychology of engagement with everyday life*. New York: Basic Books.

24. Deterding, S., Dixon, D., Khaled, R., & Nacke, L. (2011). From game design elements to gamefulness: Defining gamification. In *Proceedings of the 15th International Academic MindTrek Conference: Envisioning Future Media Environments*, ACM, Tampere, Finland, pp. 9–15

25. Deterding, S., Sicart, M., Nacke, L., O'hara, K., & Dixon, D. (2011). Gamification: Using game-design elements in non-gaming contexts. In *PART 2 Proceedings of the 2011 Annual Conference on Human Factors in Computing Systems*, ACM, Vancouver, BC, Canada, pp. 2425–2428.

26. Dignan, A. (2011). *Using games as a strategy for success*. New York, USA: Free Press.

27. Ding, L., Difranzo, D., Graves, A., Michaelis, J. R., Li, X., Mcguinness, D. L., & Hendler, J. A. (2010). TWC data-gov corpus: Incrementally generating linked government data from data. gov. In *Proceedings of the 19th international conference on World wide web*, ACM, pp. 1383–1386.

28. Dowlin, G. R., & Uncles, M. (1997). Do customer loyalty programs really work? *Sloan Management Review, 38*, 71–82.

29. Dubois, D., & Prade, H. (1995). Possibility theory as a basis for qualitative decision theory. In *IJCAI*, pp. 1924–1930.

30. Duggan, K., & Shoup, K. (2013). *Business gamification for dummies*. New York: Wiley.

31. Eickhoff, C., Harris, C. G., De Vries, A. P., & Srinivasan, P. (2012). Quality through flow and immersion: Gamifying crowdsourced relevance assessments. In *Proceedings of the 35th international ACM SIGIR conference on Research and development in information retrieval* (pp. 871–880). Portland, Oregon, USA: ACM.

32. Enterpriseappstoday. (2013). 10 Great Gamified Sites and Apps. Enterpriseappstoday. (2013). 10 Great Gamified Sites and Apps. http://www.enterpriseappstoday.com/crm/10-great-gamified-sites-and-apps.html

33. Farzan, R., Dimicco, J. M., Millen, D. R., Dugan, C., Geyer, W., & Brownholtz, E. A. (2008). Results from deploying a participation incentive mechanism within the enterprise. In *Proceedings of the Twenty-Sixth Annual SIGCHI Conference on Human Factors in Computing Systems*, ACM, Florence, Italy, pp. 563–572.

34. Ferrara, J. (2012). *Playful design: Creating game experiences in everyday interfaces*. Brooklyn: Rosenfeld Media.

35. Fogg, B. (2009). A behavior model for persuasive design. In *Proceedings of the 4th International Conference on Persuasive Technology*, Claremont, California, ACM, 1541999, pp. 1–7.
36. Fogg, B. J. (2003). *Persuasive technology: Using computers to change what we think and do.* USA: Morgan Kaufmann Publishers.
37. Freyne, J., Saunders, I., Brindal, E., Berkovsky, S., & Smith, G. (2012). Factors associated with persistent participation in an online diet intervention. In *Proceedings of the 2012 ACM Annual Conference Extended Abstracts on Human Factors in Computing Systems Extended Abstracts*, Austin, Texas, USA, ACM, pp. 2375–2380.
38. Gartner. (2011). *Gartner predicts over 70 percent of global 2000 organisations will have at least one gamified application by 2014*, Gartner, Barcelona, Spain, http://www.gartner.com/newsroom/id/1844115
39. Gartner. (2011). *Gartner Says By 2015, More Than 50 Percent of Organizations That Manage Innovation Processes Will Gamify Those Processes*, Gartner, Stanford, USA.
40. Gigya. (2013). *Gamification Analytics: Track User Behaviors that Matter*.http://www.gigya.com/gamificationanalytics/
41. Grace, M. V., & Hall, J. (2008). Projecting surveillance entertainment. In *Proceedings of the Emerging Technology Conference ETech*, San Diego, California, O'Reilly.
42. Griffin, D. (2013). *Gamification in e-learning, Virtual Ashridge*, Ashridge Business School, Hertfordshire, UK, http://www.ashridge.org.uk/website/content.nsf/FileLibrary/8335DDE65 37E4C6480257CA60039399A/$file/Gamification%20in%20elearning.pdf
43. Griffin, D. (2014). *A brief history of gamification*, The HRDirector -Pure Strategic Media Ltd Englang, http://www.thehrdirector.com/features/gamification/a-brief-history-of-gamification/
44. Herzig, P., Strahringer, S., & Ameling, M. (2012). Gamification of ERP systems-exploring gamification effects on user acceptance constructs. *Multikonferenz Wirtschaftsinformatik* (pp. 793–804). Germany: Braunschweig.
45. ITGLOSSARY 2014. Gamification, GARTNER (Ed.), http://www.gartner.com/it-glossary/?s =gamification
46. Janssen, M., & Estevez, E. (2013). Lean government and platform-based governance—doing more with less. *Government Information Quarterly, 30*, S1–S8.
47. Knowledge@Wharton. (2014). *Gamification: Powering up or game over?* University of Pennsylvania, http://knowledge.wharton.upenn.edu/article/gamification-powering-game/
48. Krishna, V., & Perry, M. (1998). *Efficient mechanism design*. Available at SSRN 64934.
49. Latane, B., Williams, K., & Harkins, S. (1979). Many hands make light the work: The causes and consequences of social loafing. *Journal of Personality and Social Psychology, 37*, 822.
50. Lauby, S. (2012). Gamification coming to a workplace near you, Open Forum.
51. Layne, K., & Lee, J. (2001). Developing fully functional E-government: A four stage model. *Government Information Quarterly, 18*, 122–136.
52. Lee, J. J., & Hammer, J. (2011). Gamification in education: What, how, why bother? *Academic Exchange Quarterly, 15*, 146–150.
53. Linders, D. (2012). From e-government to we-government: Defining a typology for citizen coproduction in the age of social media. *Government Information Quarterly, 29*, 446–454.
54. Liu, Y., Alexandrova, T., & Nakajima, T. (2011). Gamifying intelligent environments. In *Proceedings of the 2011 International ACM Workshop on Ubiquitous Meta User Interfaces*, ACM, Scottsdale, AZ, USA, pp. 7–12.
55. Locke, E. A., Shaw, K. N., Saari, L. M., & Latham, G. P. (1981). Goal setting and task performance: 1969–1980. *Psychological Bulletin, 90*, 125.
56. M2research (2011). *Gamified Engagement*, M2Research, Gamification Summit, New York City, http://m2research.com/Gamification.htm
57. Macmilan, D. (2011). *Gamification: A growing business to invigorate stale websites*. San Francisco: Businessweek.
58. Malone, T. W. (1980). What makes things fun to learn? Heuristics for designing instructional computer games. In *Proceedings of the 3rd ACM SIGSMALL Symposium and the First SIGPC Symposium on Small Systems*, ACM, pp. 162–169.

59. Malone, T. W. (1982). Heuristics for designing enjoyable user interfaces: Lessons from computer games. In *Proceedings of the 1982 Conference on Human Factors in Computing Systems*, ACM, pp. 63–68.
60. Martí, I., Rodríguez, L., Benedito, M., Trilles, S., Beltrán, A., Díaz, L., & Huerta, J. (2012). Mobile application for noise pollution monitoring through gamification techniques. *Entertainment Computing-ICEC, 2012*(7522), 562–571.
61. Mcdonald, M., Musson, R., & Smith, R. (2007). *The practical guide to defect prevention.* Redmond, Washington: Microsoft Press.
62. Mckenzie, G. (2011). Gamification and location-based Services. In *Workshop on Cognitive Engineering for Mobile GIS In Conjunction with the Conference on Spatial Information Theory (COSIT'11)*, Belfast, Maine, USA.
63. Meloni, W. (2012). *Gamification in 2012: Trends in Consumer and Enterprise Markets*, M2Research, Gamification Summit, San Francisco, http://www.slideshare. net/wandameloni/gamification-in-2012-trends-in-consumer-and-enterprise-markets-13453048
64. Montola, M., Nummenmaa, T., Lucero, A., Boberg, M., & Korhonen, H. (2009). Applying game achievement systems to enhance user experience in a photo sharing service. In *Proceedings of the 13th International MindTrek Conference: Everyday Life in the Ubiquitous Era*, ACM, Tampere, Finland, PP. 94–97.
65. Nicholson, S. (2012). A user-centered theoretical framework for meaningful gamification. In *Proceedings of the Games + Learning + Society gls 8.0*, Madison, WI, June 13–15, 2012.
66. Niebuhr, S., & Kerkow, D. (2007). Captivating patterns—a first validation. In Y. De Kort, W. Ijsselsteijn, C. Midden, B. Eggen, & B. Fogg (Eds.), *Persuasive technology* (pp. 48–54). Berlin/Heidelberg: Springer.
67. Paris, C., Colineau, N., Nepal, S., Bista, S. K., & Beschorner, G. (2013). Ethical considerations in an online community: The balancing act. *Ethics and Information Technology, 15*, 301–316.
68. Pelling, N. (2011). The (short) prehistory of gamification. In *Funding Startups (& other impossibilities)*, http://nanodome.wordpress.com/2011/08/09/the-short-prehistory-of-gamification/
69. Priebatsch, S. (2010). *The game layer on top of the world.* TED, Boston: TED Talks.
70. Radoff, J. (2011). *Energize your business with social media games.* Indianapolis, USA: Wiley Publishing Inc.
71. Reeves, B., & Read, J. L. (2009). *Total engagement.* USA: Harvard Business Press.
72. Robertson, M. (2010). Can't play, won't play. In *Hide and seek inventing new kinds of play*, http://hideandseek.net/2010/10/06/cant-play-wont-play/
73. Shapley, L. S., & Shubik, M. (1974). Game theory in economics. Game Theory in Economics: Chapter 4, Preferences and Utility. Santa Monica, CA: RAND Corporation, 1974. http://www. rand.org/pubs/reports/R0904z4.
74. Swan, M. (2009). Emerging patient-driven health care models: An examination of health social networks, consumer personalized medicine and quantified self-tracking. *International Journal of Environmental Research and Public Health, 6*, 492–525.
75. Takahashi, D. (2008). *Funware's threat to the traditional video game industry*, VB, http://venturebeat.com/
76. Takahashi, D. (2010). *Website builder DevHub gets users hooked by "gamifying" its service*, Venture Beat VB, http://venturebeat.com
77. Thom, J., Millen, D., & Dimicco, J. (2012). Removing gamification from an enterprise SNS. In *Proceedings of the ACM 2012 Conference on Computer Supported Cooperative Work*, ACM, Seattle, WA, USA, pp. 1067–1070.
78. Tobin, J. (1969). A general equilibrium approach to monetary theory. *Journal of Money, Credit and Banking, 1*, 15–29.
79. Uncles, M. D., Dowling, G. R., & Hammond, K. (2003). Customer loyalty and customer loyalty programs. *Emerald Journal of Consumer Marketing, 20*, 294–316.
80. Werbach, K. (2014). Gamification. In *Gamification*, Coursera, Coursera, https://www.coursera.org/course/gamification

81. Wikipedia. (2014). *Frequent-flyer program*, Wikimedia Foundation, http://en.wikipedia.org/wiki/Frequent-flyer_program
82. Witt, M., Scheiner, C., & Robra-Bissantz, S. (2011). Gamification of online idea competitions: Insights from an explorative case. In *Proceedings of the Informatik schafft Communities*, Berlin, Lecture Notes in Informatics, Band, p. 192.
83. Wu, M. (2011). *The magic potion of game dynamics*, Lithium Science of Social Blog, http://lithosphere.lithium.com/t5/Building-Community-the-Platform/The-Magic-Potion-of-Game-Dynamics/ba-p/19260
84. Xu, Y. (2011). Literature review on web application gamification and analytics. In *CSDL Technical Report*, University of Hawaii, Honolulu, http://csdl.ics.hawaii.edu/techreports/11-05/11-05.pdf
85. Zadeh, L. A. (1997). Toward a theory of fuzzy information granulation and its centrality in human reasoning and fuzzy logic. *Fuzzy Sets and Systems, 90*, 111–127.
86. Zajonc, R. B. (1965). Social facilitation. *Science, 149*, 269–274.
87. Zichermann, G. (2010). *Game based marketing: Inspire customer loyalty through rewards, challenges, and contests*. New Jersey, USA: Wiley.
88. Zichermann, G., & Cunningham, C. (2011). *Gamification by design: Implementing game mechanics in web and mobile apps*. Canada: O'Reilly.

Improving Government Services Using Social Media Feedback

Stephen Wan, Cécile Paris and Dimitrios Georgakopoulos

Abstract Governments are making increasing use of social media technologies, both to inform citizens of available public government services, and to measure the effectiveness of existing services. We describe Vizie, a social media monitoring system designed to help analysts identify how current government services can be improved, by drawing on the commentary and feedback provided in social media by the public using those services. The Vizie system is designed to support the monitoring of arbitrary web and social media content, independent of topical domain and media type. It utilises a variety of natural language processing and information retrieval methods to highlight, distill, and present public feedback. We describe our analysis of the real-world constraints in which the system operates, based on a user requirements analysis which governed our research and development path, including our choice of text analysis methods. The end result is a system that (1) provides an ability to see an overview of the data as well as drill into explore the data in detail, (2) performs text analytics on the social media retrieved and (3) presents contextual information to enable users to decide when to engage with online communities.

Keywords Government communication · Data mining · Social media · Communication teams

S. Wan · C. Paris (✉)
CSIRO Data61, Sydney, NSW, Australia
e-mail: cecile.paris@csiro.au

S. Wan
e-mail: stephen.wan@csiro.au

D. Georgakopoulos
RMIT University, Melbourne, VIC, Australia
e-mail: dimitrios.georgakopoulos@rmit.edu.au

© Springer International Publishing Switzerland 2015
S. Nepal et al. (eds.), *Social Media for Government Services*,
DOI 10.1007/978-3-319-27237-5_11

1 Introduction

Social media has profoundly transformed online communications by empowering ordinary web users to become not just consumers but also producers of information, a combination sometimes referred to as a "prosumer". Such user-generated contributions, in turn, often spark further contributions from other users. For example, microblogs (e.g., Twitter), blogs, and discussion forums are often used to share advice, express opinions, ask questions and provide commentary that can elicit additional content from an online community whose members respond in turn. Crucially, these exchanges are there for the world to see, as they are publicly available and are often indexed by web search engines. By turning up in search results time and time again, online social media-based discussions have become a re-usable source of knowledge about different facets of life.

Once considered the realm of idle chatter, social media now complements the more traditional media forums, such as newspapers, television, and radio as a vehicle by which information is both disseminated and gathered [15]. It is now recognised as a first class source of intelligence and insight, and it is used widely by both governments and the private sector. For governments, social media now provides novel opportunities to listen to and engage with citizens. The benefits are several: (1) public social media can yield insights that are useful in refining business processes; (2) it can help departments improve the delivery of public services by improving the communications around them; (3) governments can obtain feedback from the public and engage with the public; and finally, (4) public social media is a many-to-many communication channel.

However, social media poses a tremendous burden on resources because of the sheer volume of content to analyse. For example, there are about 2.8 million Australian citizens that post in Twitter[1] on a regular basis. And this is only one of the available social media platforms. There is clearly too much data to monitor without computational support.

Considering that social media is big data, it presents unique challenges for its analysts in terms of grappling with its volume, velocity and variety (such as the language idiosyncrasies of social media content). Therefore, specialised tools are required to support social media analysts in their tasks. Our aim is to support such analysts through the design and development of tools building on different language technologies. This is a challenging task, however, as there is a need for data mining methods that can deal with issues such as the large quantity of streaming data (i.e., the velocity of posts) and the variations in language that social media typically contains (i.e., the variety of language expressions and related idioms).

This chapter describes our efforts to build such a tool. To maintain relevance with our intended user base, we worked with a social media monitoring team in a specific

---

[1]http://www.socialmedianews.com.au/social-media-statistics-australia-february-2015/. Accessed on April 26th, 2015.

government department. The system we produced is based on the analysis of the tasks performed by social media analysts, their needs and the challenges they faced.

The results from our task analysis informed the design and development of Vizie, a system that now supports social media monitors in a variety of organisation- and role-specific tasks. Vizie provides easy-to-use interfaces (a series of web-based dashboards) to present public feedback to the analysts, highlight major topics, issues, or questions that need to be answered. The data processing is done through a number of algorithms that have been developed for natural language processing and information retrieval. These are domain independent, to ensure the system could be used by a number of organisations, in different domains. Another important consideration in the design and implementation of the algorithms embodied in Vizie is their scalability—as noted earlier social media is big data. Finally, we sought to strike a balance between the sophistication of the processing and the requirements for real-time processing and the real-world constraints under which our intended users work. The resulting system has been trialled in over twenty organisations over the past two years, and continues to be in daily use by some of them.

In the remainder of this chapter, we will explore how social media can help improve the delivery of services (Sect. 2). We then describe our original user requirements analysis as well as later requirements we obtained once the Vizie system was trialled (Sect. 3). We present the Vizie system in Sect. 4, and its usage through specific case studies in Sect. 5. Related work is discussed in Sect. 6. Finally, we conclude in Sect. 7.

2 Improving Government Services

Being public, social media content is easily retrieved by web search engines. As a result, it may compete with official sources of information. For example, in answer to a query about a service, a search engine might return an answer from social media (such as a discussion forum or a question-answer site), just as easily as the service description on an official brand web site. In other words, a search about a service might return an answer that was contributed by someone in the public, as opposed to an official source. In addition, some research has shown that users often trust online information provided by friends above that of a company website [3, 20]. Thus, to ensure that people obtain accurate information about a service, governments must ensure that information provided via social media is correct. To do so, they must be able to monitor what is being published about their services on social media.

In general, social media is now an important, if not a dominant, communication and information dissemination channel. Governments are recognising the power of social media, not only to disseminate information but also to listen to their citizens and engage with them to obtain feedback, seek ideas for new policies and services, promote a more open and transparent government (e.g., [11, 13, 18, 19]), and even host their own social media forums (e.g., form online communities) for such purposes. Some of these efforts are described in other chapters of this book.

In this chapter, we are mostly concerned with the tasks of listening to and engaging with the community on their social media forum with the aim to better serve the community. We first sought to understand how engaging with social media could lead a government department to improve its services and the communication of information about them. We started our research in 2010 by working with the communications team of the Australian's Department of Human Services, which is the Department responsible for delivering a wide range of social and welfare services, as well as related payments, to the Australian public. The Department of Human Services (referred to in the remainder of this chapter as Human Services) is the largest government department in Australia. Through discussions and interviews with the Human Services team (described in more details in the next section), we found that listening to and engaging with social media enabled them to:

- Be aware of reactions to the content disseminated by the agency, and identify if the material was correctly understood by the public. This knowledge enables the Human Services staff to improve the content if/as required (for example if there are many questions about specific material), or provide additional content to address the issues or concerns that arise;
- Understand and potentially quantify the effectiveness of online information and campaigns;
- Check the accuracy of information contributed by the community. Because social media is a public many-to-many communication channel, a question posed on social media might be answered by anyone. It is important to Human Services that the answer provided is correct. By monitoring social media, Human Services staff can ensure the accuracy of responses and correct the information when necessary;
- Identify where to disseminate information to ensure it reaches its intended target;
- Identify (and intervene) when individuals have not received appropriate advice as to what services were available to them;
- Ensure citizens are not led by malicious individuals to provide private information in public fora;
- Collect feedback about services and policies to pass on to relevant entities; and
- Understand the language used by the community to refer to issues and services, and through this avoid language mismatches between official documents and widespread public understanding.

Through these actions, the Human Services communication team contributes to the improvement of service delivery and engages in trust-building dissemination of helpful information to the community that projects a government that is both concerned for its citizens and willing to help. This is crucial to the department, as public trust in governments and their agencies is often considered to be quite low.[2]

---

[2]See, for example, the report from PewResearchCenter for the USA http://www.people-press.org/2014/11/13/public-trust-in-government/, or, more generally, http://blog.ted.com/how-pervasive-has-government-distrust-gotten/–Both Accessed August 18th, 2015.

To understand how to support the Human Services communication teams in these tasks, we performed a task analysis in their workplace. This enabled us to design and develop our first social media monitoring system. It was then trialled by a number of communications teams, from which we obtained further requirements. This is described in the next section.

3 A Social Media Analysis User Requirement Study

3.1 Initial Analysis

In our first user requirements study with the Human Services communications team, we went to their workplace and employed qualitative methods to observe the activities. We first used a mixture of questionnaires, interviews and observations with talk-aloud protocols [23]. We then sought to understand the types of questions the Human Services team members were asking when looking at social media, the nature of the monitoring task (as least as instantiated at Human Services), the challenges encountered, and what tools the team members thought would be useful. In particular, we first asked each member of this team to fill in a questionnaire regarding their education and career background. We then conducted interviews to identify the social media monitoring tasks each individual Human Services team member performed and tools he/she used or desired. Next, we mapped both desired and used tools to a common set of functionalities that were required for each social media monitoring task and documented these. Finally, we captured the actions of team members while they performed their social media monitoring tasks using video recordings. In this way, we captured descriptions of the activities they performed, the content they accessed, and the specific social media sources they used (e.g., Facebook, Twitter, or a blog).

During these sessions, we noted that Human Services team members looked at a variety of data sources, each requiring a different tool. Sources included, for example, emails from alerting services (e.g., Google Alerts[3]) or services providing a digest of search results, lists of search results with specific search terms, material from various specific portals, and known websites.

Human Services team members would then scan the lists of posts obtained from these heterogeneous data sources to get an overview of the social media landscape and also to identify which posts were relevant. This often involved drilling down to specific posts and reading them carefully to decide whether an action was required. To judge what action was required, they considered:

- the post's topic and its importance,
- responses (i.e., answers or comments) from others in the same social media source,

---

[3]www.google.com/alerts.

- whether such responses where incorrect or negative, and
- what was the impact of negative responses (i.e., if somebody else had followed up with another comment, and whether that comment was negative or positive).

From this analysis, we determined that sequences of posts and responses formed important conversations that had to be considered together as they provided useful context in deciding what action Human Services team members needed to perform next [23].

The verbal explanations of their actions revealed that, typically, Human Services team members tried to (1) identify "hot topics"; (2) inform social workers of potential problems; (3) alert public relations teams when posts indicated a poor public perception (or lack of trust) for Human Services and related Human Services employees; (4) protect the personal information of citizens by watching for personal circumstances being posted (or requested) and intervening as appropriate; and (5) alert other Human Services staff about important posts or websites to watch.

On any given post, the staff member could take a number of actions, which were recorded. These included (1) responding directly in a forum (this action first required clearance by the appropriate authority); (2) passing responsibility to a colleague; (3) making a note to keep a watch on the discussion to see how it would evolve; (4) checking if reports of poor offerings of government services were accurate; and (5) providing an explanation when possible. When a Human Services response was posted, it was also archived to enable its re-use in the future. Finally, the communication team would generate regular reports, to inform Human Services about both what was happening in social media and what the team itself was doing, and also to plan future online engagements.

The workflow included a number of systems and processes that were not integrated. For example, notes were kept in Excel spreadsheets, separate from the messages. Replies were recorded separately to enable their re-use. No archives of the posts were kept, so that the Human Services communication team could not refer back to a specific post at a later time, which was identified as problematic. All records of engagement were made with different systems from the one used for monitoring the social media posts. Finally, it is interesting to note that, at the time, the computing environment itself added a few hurdles to the task. Visiting external posts required clicking through a number of security warning web pages, introducing delays in viewing the content. Additionally, team members had two types of computers available: those with mobile open internet access but no access to the Human Services' intranet, and Human Services computers with stricter access to web content. The latter was not amenable to social media monitoring but provided some enterprise resources. Alternating between computers and flicking between multiple web sites providing the social media data resulted in multitasking between scanning the digest and viewing the posts, adding cognitive load.

Through this first requirements analysis, we realised how complex the social media monitoring activity could be in the government context, as it served a variety of purposes, encompassed many tasks, and often resulted in a number of follow-up actions. To support such social media monitoring activity, we needed to develop a system that would fit into the Human Services communication team's workflow, offer an integrated suite of tools, and better support teamwork. The system also needed the ability to present an overview of all social media activity and enable the Human Services team members to access specific posts. This is what our first Vizie system aimed to achieve.

The first system we developed for the Human Services communication team used the API[4] of several popular social media sources (e.g., Twitter, forums, RSS feeds, etc.) to collect social media posts, and provided one interface to all the relevant data sources. This single interface lowered the cognitive load of Human Services team members by reducing several heterogeneous tools they previously needed to interact with to one. In addition to offering a single interface to access social media postings, the first Vizie system clustered social media posts in groups that were associated to a "topic". This was done using clustering and language analysis techniques. From any such topic, a social media analyst using this system could drill down to individual social media postings. Finally, this first system included the ability to record all activities performed by the Human Services team, together with its appropriate metadata (e.g., who had authorised specific responses). Overall, our first Vizie system addressed many of the requirements we uncovered in our requirements analysis study, and the Human Services communication team proceeded to use it on a regular basis.

3.2 Refining the System

Through regular meetings with the Human Services communication team, and another talk-aloud recording round after a few months of system use, we were able to refine the existing functionality in the initial system and identify new requirements. These included:

- The ability to supply the system with an external domain vocabulary (words to look for and words to ignore) that the language analysis modules can take into account to reflect a specific organisational context;
- The ability to obtain more contextual information for social media posts. One of the specific requirements in this category was the ability to reconstruct "important" conversations (as we described them in Sect. 3.1) to provide a richer context for understanding individual tweets. Another specific requirement was the ability to follow the links and references embedded in a tweet and include them in the post context together with the reconstructed conversations; and
- The ability to partition queries and resulting data into subsets that are meaningful from the perspective of a specific application. To give an example of meaningful subsets in the Human Services domain, consider different government services provided to parents and students. To satisfy this requirement, we introduced the

---

[4]Application Programming Interface.

notion of "monitoring activities", each with a different set of queries, resulting in a different data set. Each monitoring activity can be viewed and explored separately.

3.3 The "Early Adopters Group"

As explained in the previous section, the Vizie system was designed and developed initially for the Human Services communications team. Once it reached a level of maturity, we wanted to test its effectiveness for other organisations. To this end, we created in 2012 the "Early Adopters Group", which made Vizie available to several participating organisations. Through the programme, these organisations also served as evaluators and provided new input and requirements to the system. While we had one-to-one discussions with each organisation, we also organised quarterly user group meetings. These enabled our users to share their context, learnings, experiences, and success stories. Through the Early Adopters Group, we thus obtained new insights about the social media monitoring task and gathered new requirements for our system. The main new requirements are summarised below:

- Support to configure Vizie to access a number of social media platforms with the same query terms;
- Data exporting capability, as some of our users wanted to be able to use the data outside Vizie, and the creation of an API, to enable other systems to query Vizie for data;
- Additional filtering mechanisms for the collection, in particular in terms of language (e.g., posts in English) and locations (e.g., a specific state in Australia);
- Additional data sources, as new social media platforms were created (e.g., Instagram), when APIs were available;
- New interfaces to explore the data collected to gain yet more insights from it, with controls over the time period to be considered, in particular to look at shorter time periods than a week (e.g., hourly), the default in the original Vizie system; and
- System portability, in particular for mobile devices. For example, some tablets and smart phones could not produce (or did not had enough processing power to produce in real time) some of Vizie's elaborate graphical visualisations. Alternative simpler visualisations had to be developed.

Vizie now also addresses these requirements, as is described in detail in Sect. 4.

4 An Overview of the Vizie System

As discussed earlier, the Vizie system is specifically designed to provide social media mining support for social media monitoring for government services. Its design was informed by our original requirements analysis and our ongoing work

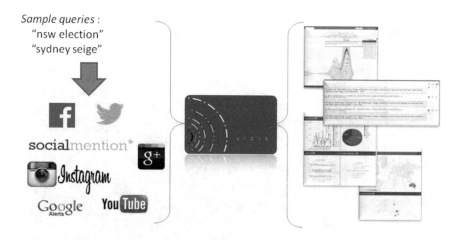

Fig. 1 The Vizie system: collecting and analysing social media data

with a number of digital communication teams, as explained above. In the implementation of the various modules required, we had to take into account real-time constraints (such as speed) [34].

The system is illustrated in Fig. 1. Vizie provides an integrated interface to access social media across all social media channels. It enables its users to have both overviews and details of the social media data collected, as well as contextual information to facilitate the analysts understanding and decision making.

Vizie focuses on providing two types of interfaces to help social media analysts. The first is an overview of aggregated search results, derived through text analysis and presented both textually and visually. The second enables an in-depth exploration of the data collected (an ability to "slice and dice" the data as desired). Both interfaces use natural language processing methods to, for example, cluster the posts, choose key phrases, or summarise the text. The text analysis methods deployed in our system are chosen considering the trade-off between computational overheads and data scalability versus the effectiveness at supporting an end-user task.

Figure 2 shows the architecture of the Vizie system. All interactions with the user are performed through a series of web components managed by the Web Presentation Layer. It is through this interface that the users specify query terms and interact with visualisations driven by data analysis. With these query terms, data collection occurs through a federated search interface [12].

As illustrated in the diagram, Vizie is built around data collection, contextualisation, and natural language analysis processes. More specifically, Vizie captures data from a variety of social media channels using either available APIs, or general purpose search engines such as SocialMention.[5] The collection of the posts is also

---

[5]www.socialmention.com.

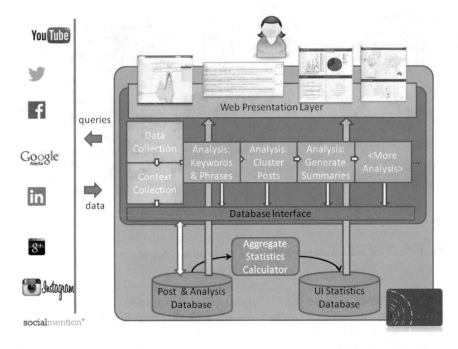

Fig. 2 Vizie architecture

coupled with "a Context Collection" step, explained below. As we noted earlier, Vizie provides one tool and interface to access all social media posts collected from different sources, thus addressing one of the challenges we identified in our user requirements analysis. The "context collection" or "contextualisation" step was also added in response to a requirement from our users. Once data is collected and contextualised, it is kept in the Posts and Analysis database, together with some meta-data.

Vizie's natural language analysis steps are illustrated in Fig. 2 and include keyword and phase identification, clustering of social media posts, and summary generation. Vizie's data analysis is extensible, i.e., additional natural language processing steps can be added, as/if needed (this is denoted by the "more analysis" step in Fig. 2). After each processing step, new meta-data is added to the post and stored in the Posts and Analysis Database.

We now illustrate various aspects of Vizie, with a running example of monitoring social media from our organisation, the CSIRO, also a government agency. To start the process of monitoring social media, queries need to be provided to the system. Vizie has a dedicated configuration interface for this purpose. The screen to specify a query is shown in Fig. 3. As can be seen from the figure, the user can select the platforms to which the query is to be sent.

A preview of the data that will be collected with the query is provided to help the user decide whether this is the right query term to obtain the desired data. It is

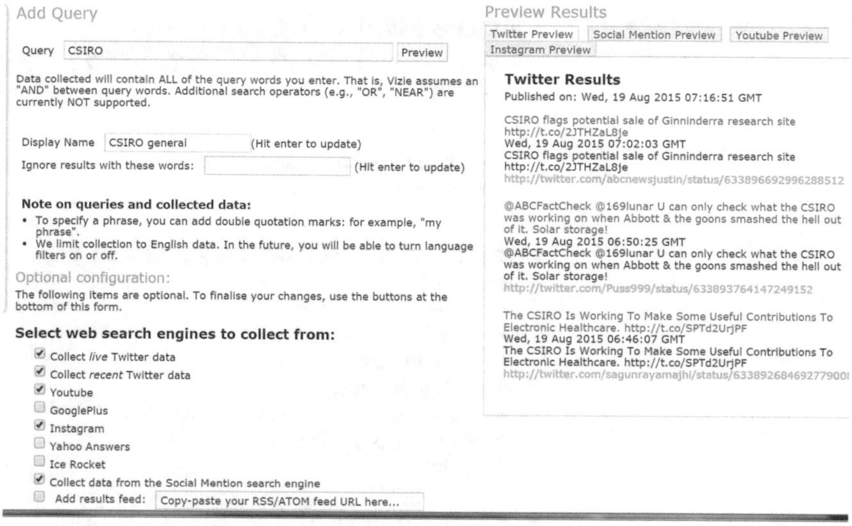

Fig. 3 Setting up the system: entering a query for the federated search

shown on the right of the figure. This enables the user to decide if the query needs refinement (for example, exclude posts with a specific word in it, a useful specification when the original query is ambiguous, or the addition of another word to specify a phrase instead of a word).

To enable the partition of queries and data into meaningful subsets (another requirement discussed in Sect. 3.2), we created "monitoring activities", which consist of multiple queries grouped for a specific monitoring purpose. To explain this concept further consider the need of organisations to monitor social media for different services, cohorts, and/or events. Monitoring any of these requires social media data to be partitioned respectively for further exploration. For example, the CSIRO communication staff have set up several monitoring activities for the organisation, including, as shown in Fig. 4: "*CSIRO General*", which gathers data about CSIRO as a whole, using queries such as "CSIRO", "@CSIRONews", and the name of the newly appointed CEO, "Larry Marshall"); "*enigma moth*", with queries such as "CSIRO moth" and "enigma moth", to see the public's reactions to the discovery of an insect of significance[6] (in which CSIRO researchers were instrumental), and "*campaign.csiro7*", with queries such as "csiro seven" and the names of the people involved, which gauges the effectiveness of a specific campaign. Like the queries, monitoring activities can be managed via the configuration interface.

At the request of the social media analysts who used Vizie, we also enabled the easy activation/deactivation of both monitoring activities and queries. This

---

[6]http://www.csiro.au/en/News/News-releases/2015/Enigma-moth-helps-crack-evolutions-code. Accessed August 19th, 2015.

Fig. 4 Monitoring activities

Active Monitoring Activities

- Activity - enigma moth (+Query , +Feed)
  Queries
    - #EnigmaMoth
    - CSIRO moth
    - enigma moth
    - primitive moth

- CSIRO General (+Query , +Feed)
  Queries
    - "Larry Marshall" ceo
    - #thankcsiroforthat
    - @BrianBoyleSKA
    - @CSIROnews
    - Australia "innovation catalyst"
    - PPL: "Larry Marshall"
    - csiro

- campaign.csiro7 (+Query , +Feed)
  Queries
    - "csiro seven"
    - #csiro7
    - #csiroseven
    - PPL: "Jane Bowen" csiro
    - PPL: "Matthew Hill" csiro
    - PPL: "Mibu Fischer"
    - PPL: "Nick Roden"
    - PPL: "Sam Movassaghi"
    - PPL: "Stephen Wan"
    - PPL: "Vivek Srinivasan"
    - PPL: Fischer csiro
    - PPL: Movassaghi csiro
    - PPL: bowen csiro
    - PPL: mibu csiro
    - PPL: roden csiro
    - PPL: vivek csiro
    - PPL: wan csiro
    - WHO csiro magazine
    - csiro @whomagazine
    - csiro sunday (Inactive)
    - csiro7
    - csiroseven
    - vice csiro
    - viceAU csiro
    - www.csiro.au/seven

is useful when one is monitoring a recurrent event. For example, the release of a budget is a major media event in Australia. It occurs twice in the year, and social media analysts need to monitor this only twice each year. Having defined appropriate queries/activities for it, they want to be able to simply de-activate them when it is no longer a current news item, and re-activate them at the appropriate time.

Once Vizie is configured with the appropriate queries, it starts collecting data from the various available social media channels. While collecting the posts, Vizie also attempts to obtain additional information which can form part of their context. For example, a post might contain a link to another site (e.g., a URL). Vizie will try to obtain the content of the URL. This provides the context in which to understand the post. Some examples are shown in Fig. 5. In Fig. 5a, the post merely mentions the title of a news article, with a pointer to it. To really understand the post, it is useful to also read the news article. In Fig. 5b, once again, the post makes little sense without knowing its context: the information CSIRO has been disseminating about its scientists, seen on a webpage below.

Similarly, Vizie attempts to present posts in the context of the discussion in which they occur, as a post in isolation might be meaningless. This illustrated in Fig. 6. The second post "Fantastic" is meaningless out of its context, represented by the post it answers.

To reconstruct discussions Vizie uses Twitter's API or extracts the posts from forum websites returned by a search engine with the unsupervised boilerplate removal approach described in [27]. All the data collected (the posts and their context) are stored in a database. At this point, analysis begins. The first step is a keyword and key phrases analysis to provide an immediate overview of current social media content. This is illustrated in Fig. 7. The next step is a cluster analysis that groups the data into topics. This new overview is presented to the user, either graphically or textually, as the user chooses.

Figure 8 shows an example of a textual visualisation, for the monitoring activity "*campaign.csiro7*". In Fig. 8a, the left hand side of the image shows the interface that enables a user to select a specific activity if desired, and choose the type of overview to be provided (textual or graphical). The overview is on the right. It presents social media postings from the same media type in cells organised in the same row. Each cell presents an overview of a group of postings that is labelled by an appropriate term or phrase. Overview rows are sorted by the date of social media posting. At the time of this screen shot capture, the campaign is in its 3rd day; so there is data for only three days. Vizie is using a sliding window, which is typically a week, to group posting into topics that are based on trending keywords and phrases. Hovering the mouse on a topic will bring up a pop-up window with the indicative phrases (that includes the keyword) for this topic, if there are any. This is shown in Fig. 8a for the topic: "inspiring", with the key phrase "inspiring future thinkers". The user can obtain additional information by clicking on a topic, which will result in all the posts for that topic to be presented on the right hand panel, as shown in Fig. 8b, again for the topic "inspiring". By placing the mouse on a post, the user can obtain more details about the post, as shown in the Fig. 8c. Vizie automatically relates identical topics from different social media sources/channels. This is achieved by correlating the topic name/phrase and dates of the postings, and it is visualised by highlighting all related topics when the user clicks the cell of any of them in the visualisation. The user can then drill down to the individual social post of the highlighted topic as illustrated in Fig. 8d. Finally, in Fig. 8 each line (channel) was fully filled. Some of our users wanted instead

Fig. 5 Retrieving the content of a URL to provide the context of a post. **a** A news article is the context for a post. **b** A website is the context of a post

Fig. 6 Showing the posts in their discussion context

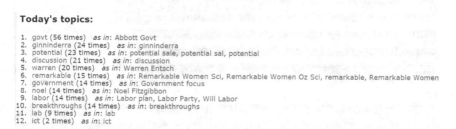

Today's topics:

1. govt (56 times) *as in*: Abbott Govt
2. ginninderra (24 times) *as in*: ginninderra
3. potential (23 times) *as in*: potential sale, potential sal, potential
4. discussion (21 times) *as in*: discussion
5. warren (20 times) *as in*: Warren Entsch
6. remarkable (15 times) *as in*: Remarkable Women Sci, Remarkable Women Oz Sci, remarkable, Remarkable Women
7. government (14 times) *as in*: Government focus
8. noel (14 times) *as in*: Noel Fitzgibbon
9. labor (14 times) *as in*: Labor plan, Labor Party, Will Labor
10. breakthroughs (14 times) *as in*: breakthroughs
11. lab (9 times) *as in*: lab
12. ict (2 times) *as in*: ict

Fig. 7 Results of the preliminary keyword and key phrases analysis

to have an idea of the varying amounts of data across days and channels. So we implemented the ability to show the proportion of data across the channels. This is shown in Fig. 9.

Topic labels and key phrases in these visualisations are computed through a text chunking algorithm that segments sentences using features such as the presence of closed-class words and capitalisation. The key phrase assigned to a post is chosen based on trending content over a time period. Our methods can also be parameterised to improve the diversity of key phrases, using methods such as Maximal Marginal Relevance (MMR) [7]. Once a key phrase is chosen, the word with the highest overall frequency over the week is chosen as the keyword. A cluster is then defined by a grouping of posts that have been assigned the same keyword. Given the way keywords are determined, the clusters visualise trending content over time.

The overview can also be presented as an interactive graphical visualisation (see Fig. 10, for the monitoring activity "*CSIRO General*"), in which each social media channel has its "river", and each river has "streams", corresponding to the different topics. As in the textual visualisation, the topic is represented by only one word because of space issues. The interaction is similar to the one for the textual visualisation: hovering on a topic provides additional details, clicking on it lists the posts, etc. This visualisation enables one to zoom in and out of it.

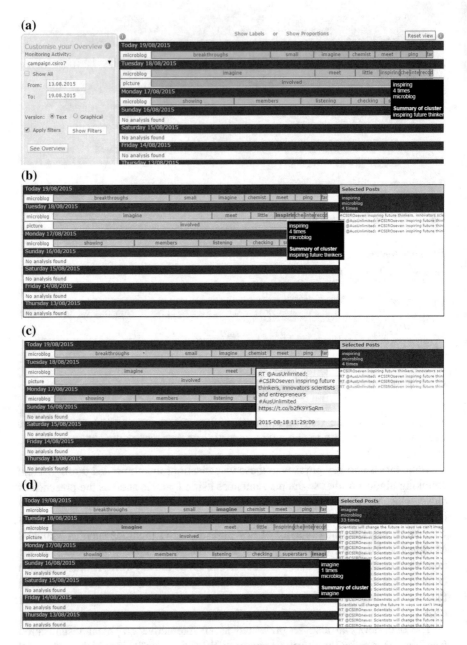

Fig. 8 Textual visualisation of the cluster analysis. **a** Requesting a visualisation of the data; key words and key phrases. **b** Obtaining the posts in a topic grouping. **c** Getting more details about a specific post. **d** Highlighting trends through the week and channels

Fig. 9 Showing the proportions of the data in the textual visualisation

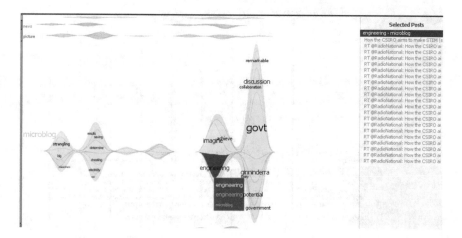

Fig. 10 Graphical visualisation of the topics of the captured data

The functionality described thus far supports setting up the system to obtain the appropriate data, scanning a list of collected posts, getting overviews and drilling into the data, and obtaining the appropriate context, all within an integrated interface.

The analyst can explore the data in depth ("slice and dice" the data) using the interface shown in Fig. 11. Within this interface, the user first selects the data to explore: this is done by selecting one or more monitoring activities, a time frame (with a slide window at the top of the screen), or one or more specific media types. The relevant data set is retrieved and presented to the user, together with various statistics about the data (e.g., the amount of data, the trending words, and media types). At this point, the analyst can study the data in detail, e.g., look at all the posts, or the posts with a specific word it in, obtain the shared posts, place them on a map, etc.

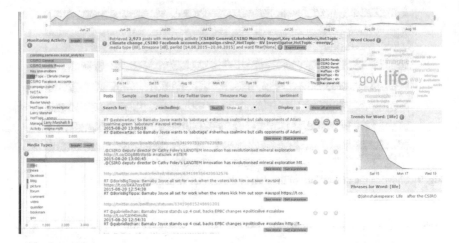

Fig. 11 Exploring the data

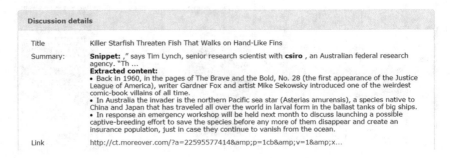

Fig. 12 Summaries about an article mentioning CSIRO

Figure 12 illustrates Vizie's summarisation capabilities, which use extraction techniques, as in [33].

To support the workflow of a team of users, Vizie also includes a reporting facility. Figure 13 shows portions of a report generated by Vizie. The user can select what to include in a report, and generate the PDF automatically. Reports can include post trends, broken down by monitoring activities or media type if required; time zone information for Twitter posts; insights about the content (e.g., top posts; major words and key phrases; etc.) and the posts' authors (e.g., key Twitter users, in terms of both retweets and mentions).

We are currently working on additional analysis modules. One, in particular, relates to discussions, providing more context to help with the relevance judgements needed to decide whether to engage with the public.

The discussion interface enables the social media monitoring analysts to look at the discussions in some priority order and get information enabling them to decide whether an action is required. An overall screen shot this triage interface is shown in Fig. 14.

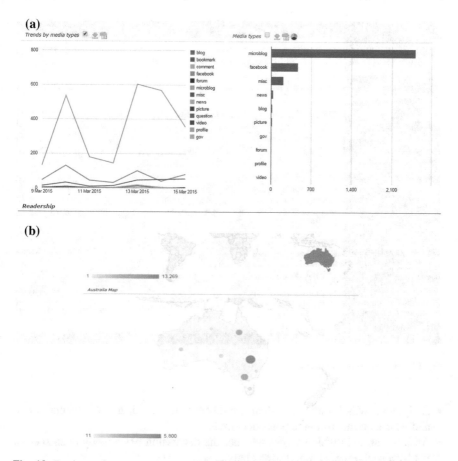

Fig. 13 Portions of a report generated by Vizie. **a** Volume by type and across time. **b** Data viewed on a map

The user chooses a priority order from the panel on the left. This can be based on time (chronological order, or reverse chronological order), or on other features such as most posts, most views, most read, most notes, most tags, or most connections. Once the priority order has been selected, each discussion is presented first as a summary, along with enough information to enable the user to make a decision as to whether there is a need to drill down and read the specific posts. The summary includes:

- A title for the discussion—The title is formed using the subject line of the first post in the discussion;
- Where the discussion comes from, and its media type;
- Tags associated with the discussion—these currently are automatically generated tags showing the label of the search engine query for provenance (e.g., SRC_ TWITTER_SEARCH_CSIRO and AUTO_SPIDERED (following embedded URLS)). In addition, keywords are automatically extracted from the post title and description;

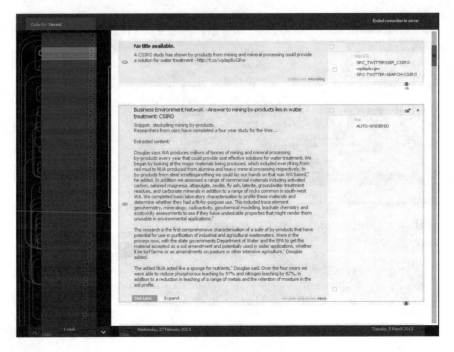

Fig. 14 The discussions interface

- A timeline which indicates when the discussion started, its current end-point, and where on this timeline posts occurred;
- An icon (an eye) which shows whether the discussion has already been seen or not by a social media monitoring analyst; and
- An indication of whether (Vizie) users have already provided comments about the discussion as a whole (via the drill down page for the discussion).

The discussion can be expanded, and all its posts are then shown. At this stage, the user can add comments or annotations to the discussion or the individual posts. This discussion interface, like the Overview functionality presented earlier, supports the main actions of the social media monitoring task: scanning a list of collected posts, viewing a social media post and scanning its text content, and making a relevance judgment as to whether to take further action.

5 Case Studies/System Usage

The Vizie system has been used by over twenty organisations over the past two years, and has received positive feedback [34]. We instrumented Vizie to capture various usage patterns, including logins, number of posts retrieved, specific interface usage patterns, etc.

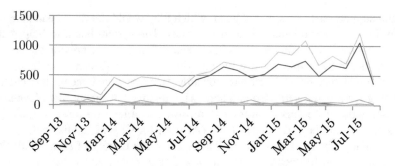

Fig. 15 Number of logins for the past two years

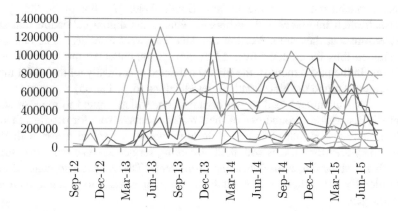

Fig. 16 Number of posts collected per organisation in the past two years

Figure 15 shows the number of logins in that time, with each line representing one organisation, and the top line the aggregate. As new features get added to the system, the number of logins usually increases. We noted that different organisations have different login patterns. Some organisations use Vizie on a daily basis, while others use it only when an event (such as a communication on their part) happens. This is reflected in the varying number of posts collected by the organisations in that time—see Fig. 16.

We now briefly mentioned three usage scenarios from our users:

- The Department of Human Services. The Human Services team with which we started our work on Vizie has grown significantly in the past few years, and it monitors social media for a variety of services. As a result, a multitude of monitoring activities (currently over 30 active activities) and queries has been set (a monitoring activity has typically at least 4–5 queries, with some activities regrouping a much larger number of queries, e.g., one activity has over 45 queries). The Human Services team uses the system on a daily basis to support their social media strategy. They have found that the system helps them find and support customers in real need, which they would not have been able to do by just tracking popular social media sites. The system has also helped them address misinformation in the public arena and proactively provide the information sought by people. Finally, by engaging actively with social media, the team has found that people's attitude towards them on social media has changed, going from being surprised and somewhat annoyed at seeing them listening to discussions in forums to waiting to receive the official response to their questions. This has helped increase trust. (Also see the Chap. 2 in this book.)

- The State Library of New South Wales. The State Library of New South Wales has a mission to document life in New South Wales, and it has realised that social media discussions provide an important record for the social scientists and historians of the future [9]. They use the Vizie system to collect and archive social media data about life in New South Wales [2]. For them, the system visualisation interfaces and dashboards enable the digital collection managers to ensure that they are collecting the data they want to collect. The collection obtained thus far contains over 17 million posts, collected through 964 query terms. In the past 4 months, the library collected specifically all the social media discourse around the New South Wales elections [6, 8, 17, 35].

- A major Australian broadcasting organisation, which wanted to monitor social media discussions around one of their major events: a vote for people's favorite band over one month period. It is through monitoring social media with Vizie that they identified issues with their streaming service at some point (as phrases such as "streaming issues" became prominent). The system also enabled them to identify how others were capitalising on their hashtag to promote their own messages.

6 Related Work

Systematic social media monitoring in the government context has mostly been in the area of disaster management—see [10]. Common solutions in this area involve monitoring and mining Twitter data to detect emergencies (e.g., a fire, flood, riot, etc.) that require government response and to collect information that will help mitigate them e.g., see [1, 29, 32, 36; Chaps. 12 and 13 in this book]. Researchers have also looked at monitoring and mining social media to obtain information that might be useful in the public health sector, for example to predict outbreaks, for syndromic surveillance or pharmacovigilance (identifying drugs side effects)—e.g., see [5, 14, 16, 21, 24, 28].

Our contribution in the development of Vizie has a more general scope since we cover any government service, and our aim is to help improve such services instead of simply detecting the need for such services in disaster management. Our goal is also to enable communication with social media users in their forum, while the related work in health only aims to mine health-specific data in social media posting.

A number of commercial social media monitoring tools are available. For example, some tools monitor specific social media channel (e.g., Tweetdeck[7] or Hootsuite[8]). These tools help monitor conversations on a given topic or present the frequency of mentions of specific terms in graph-based visualisations. Besides being limited to a specific media channel, these tools rarely support the data exploration task, which is required to gain insights from the data. Other tools (for example, Google Alerts[9] and Socialmention[10]) perform a wider search through the social media channels. These tools typically focus on a coarse-grained retrieval task, followed by a grouping of results by social media type and word trends analysis. No additional contextual information is retrieved, and the analysis of the returned data is usually limited to showing trending words (via a word cloud[11] or a ranked list) and presenting a visual dashboard of statistics about the data (e.g., most retweeted post, person post mentioned, etc.). Some tools (e.g., Twitter Map[12]) show Twitter content with geotagged data on maps, enabling one to identify what is being discussed in a particular region, while others perform some sentiment analysis (e.g., SocialMention).

It is difficult with current tools to get an overview of the discourse across all social media. To do so, one must employ several tools in an ad hoc manner (which is what we found in our requirement analysis), resulting in a multiplicity of views over the social media content. In contrast, Vizie enables the monitoring of all social media platforms through one tool, integrating the data so that an overview can be obtained, providing the analysts with a sense of the volume associated with major clusters of data, and how this changes across time. To our knowledge, such a federated search approach to social media monitoring, where a uniform query interface and a corresponding analysis is presented to the user, is not available through commercial tools and has not been explored in-depth within the research community. In addition, current tools typically do not support the data exploration task, and thus an analyst cannot gain insights beyond the statistics provided. Vizie supports such exploration. This not only leads to more insights into the data but also helps the government social media analysts decide whether to engage with the public.

Within the academic community, there has been much research to help identify what is of importance in social media—for example classifying tweets into news or junk, e.g., [30], or sorting tweets into generic categories such as news, events, opinions, and private messages [31]. Other work has studied topic modelling on social media (e.g., [4, 22, 25, 26]. These works tend to focus on Twitter data, and they are not aimed at supporting specific social media tasks. Our work

---

[7]www.tweetdeck.com.

[8]www.hootsuite.com.

[9]www.google.com/alerts.

[10]www.socialmention.com.

[11]For example, http://cloud.li/.

[12]www.twittermap.com

is concerned at social media data in general, and is designed to support the tasks involved in improving government services through social media monitoring. In addition, our Vizie system brings together a number of functionality (i.e., not just topic modeling) to offer the analyst an integrated system. Finally, as our system is being used in a real-work context, we had to balance the sophistication of the algorithms with real-time processing constraints.

7 Conclusions

In this chapter we looked at the task of social media monitoring in a government context, to understand both how such monitoring can help improve government services and how a tool might support the task. We presented requirements analysis from actual government social media analysts that spanned from an initial task analysis to subsequent trials of Vizie—our social media monitoring system. Vizie supports the social media monitoring task by:

- Providing access to all social media data through one interface;
- Presenting an overview of big social media content using content-driven and user-provided classification terms and across a variety of posts from heterogeneous social media sources; and
- Enabling in-depth data exploration.

Vizie combines natural language processing, information retrieval and machine learning algorithms and embodies them within an integrated interface that allows its users to interact with the data analysis and collection steps via the provided visualisations. The system has been in used in a number of organisations and has received positive feedback from them.

Acknowledgments This research has been partially funded under the Human Services Delivery Research Alliance (HSDRA) between the CSIRO and the Australian Government Department of Human Services, the CSIRO, and the "Early Adopters Group" Programme. We would like to thank P. Aghaei Pour, B. Jin, J. McHugh, A. Gall and H. Asghar for their work on the system, all the communications staff at the Australian Government's Department of Human Services for their support in this work, and all our other users for their invaluable support and feedback.

References

1. Abel, F., Hauff, C., Houben, G.-J., Stronkman, R., & Ke, T. (2012). Semantics+filtering+search=twitcident. Exploring information in social web streams. In *Proceedings of the 23rd ACM Conference on Hypertext and Social Media*, Milwaukee, Wisconsin, USA (285—294). ACM, New York, NY.
2. Barwick, K., Joseph, M., Paris, C., & Wan, S. (2014). Hunters and collectors: Seeking social media content for cultural heritage collection. In *Proceedings of the 7th VALA Biennial Conference*, Melbourne, Australia.

3. Bernoff, J. (2008). *People don't trust company blogs. What you should do about it.* http://blogs.forrester.com/groundswell/2008/12/people-dont-tru.html. Last viewed August 21, 2015.

4. Bernstein, M. S., Suh, B., Hong, L., Chen, J., Kairam, S., & Chi, Ed H. (2010). Eddi: interactive topic-based browsing of social status streams. *Proceedings of the 23nd annual ACM symposium on User Interface Software and Technology* (pp. 303–312). New York, NY, USA: ACM.

5. Bian, J., Topaloglu, U., & Yu, F. (2012). Towards large-scale Twitter mining for drug-related adverse events. In *Proceedings of the 2012 International Workshop on Smart Health and Wellbeing (SHB '12)*, New York, NY, USA, 2012.

6. Bielby, N. (2015). NSW state library wants how-to-vote cards and other election parphenalia. In *The Maitland Mercury, March 22nd, 2015.* http://www.maitlandmercury.com.au/story/3350977/word-watch-a-great-apostrophe-epidemic/?cs=179. Accessed September 15th, 2015.

7. Carbonell, J. G., & Goldstein, J. (1998). The use of MMR, diversity-based reranking for reordering documents and producing summaries. *The Proceedings of the 21st Annual International ACM SIGIR Conference on Research and Development in Information Retrieval (SIGIR'98)* (pp. 335–336). New York, NY, USA: ACM.

8. Donegan, J. (2015). *From Pamphlets to Tweets: Collecting New South Wales Election Material Through the Ages.* http://www.abc.net.au/news/2015-03-12/election-tweets-added-to-nsw-library-election-collection/6306490. March 12th, 2015. Accessed September 15th, 2015.

9. Gooch, D. (2015). *Library monitors Twitter Posts as Part of State's Social History. The Sydney Morning Herald, January 16th, 2015.* Accessed on line September 15th, 2015.

10. Griffin, G., Jones, R., Paris, C. (2013). Strategic implications of social media for emergency management. In M. Clarke., & G. Griffin (Eds.), *Next Generation Disaster and Security Management.* Canberra, Australia: Australian Security Research Centre. Publisher: Collaborative Publications. 213-240. ISBN: 978-0-9874332-0-6. 2013.

11. Government 2.0 Taskforce. (2009). *The Government 2.0 Taskforce's final report: Engage: Getting on with Government 2.0.* December 22nd 2009. http://www.finance.gov.au/publications/gov20taskforcereport/index.html. Last viewed April 15th, 2015.

12. Jacsó, P. (2004). Thoughts about federated searching, information today, *21*(9).

13. Janssen, M., & Estevez, E. (2013). Lean government and platform-based governance—Doing more with less. *Government Information Quarterly, 30*, S1–S8.

14. Karimi, S., Wang, C., Alejandro, M. J., Raj, G., Paris, C., & Harvey, B. (2015). Text and data mining techniques in adverse drug reaction detection. *ACM Computing Surveys, 47*, 2015.

15. Kulshrestha, J., Zafar, M. B., Noboa, L. E., Hummadi, K. P., & Ghosh, S. (2015). Characterizing information diets of social media users. In *The Proceedings of the 2015 International Conference on Web and Social Media* (pp. 218–227). UK:Oxford, AAAI.

16. Leaman, R., Wojtulewicz, L., Sullivan, R., Skariah, A., Yang, J., & Gonzalez, G. (2010). Towards internet-age pharmacovigilance: extracting adverse drug reactions from user posts to health-related social networks. In *Proceedings of the Workshop On Biomedical Natural Language Processing* (pp. 117–125), Uppsala, Sweden.

17. Ladiges, C. (2015). http://csironewsblog.com/2015/03/26/the-election-collection-tracking-trends-on-twitter/ March 26th, 2015. Accessed September 15th, 2015.

18. Layne, K., & Lee, J. (2001). Developing fully functional E-government: A four stage model. *Government Information Quarterly, 18*, 122–136.

19. Linders, D. (2012). From e-government to we-government: Defining a typology for citizen coproduction in the age of social media. *Government Information Quarterly, 29*, 446–454.

20. Nielssen. (2009). *Global Advertising Consumers Trust Real Friends and Virtual Strangers the Most.* Published 07/07/2009. http://www.nielsen.com/us/en/insights/news/2009/global-advertising-consumers-trust-real-friends-and-virtual-strangers-the-most.html. Last viewed April 15th, 2015.

21. Nikfarjam, A., Sarker, A., O'Connor, K., Ginn, R., & Gonzalez, G. (2015). Pharmacovigilance from social media: Mining adverse drug reaction mentions using sequence labeling with word embedding cluster features. *Journal of the American Medical Informatics Association*. The Oxford University Press.
22. Nugroho, R., Yang, J., Zhong, Y., Paris, C., & Nepal, S. (2015). Deriving topics in Twitter by exploiting tweet interactions. In *The Proceedings of IEEE Big Data Cloud 2015*.
23. Paris, C., Wan, S. (2011). Listening to the community: Social media monitoring tasks for improving government services. In *The Proceedings of CHI 2011 Work-In-Progress*. April 2011, Vancouver, Canada.
24. Paul, M., Dredze, M. (2011), You are what you tweet: Analyzing Twitter for public health. In *Proceedings of the International AAAI Conference On Weblogs and Social Media (ICWSM)* (pp. 265–272), Barcelona, Spain, 2011.
25. Ramage, D., Hall, D., Nallapati, R., & Manning, C. D. (2009). Labeled LDA: A supervised topic model for credit attribution in multi-labeled corpora. In *Proceedings of the 2009 Conference on EMNLP*. Singapore, August, 248—256. http://www.aclweb.org/anthology/D/D09/D09-1026.
26. Ramage, D., Dumais, S., & Liebling, D. (2010). Characterizing microblogs with topic models. In *Proceedings of the 4th AAAI International Conference on Weblog and Social Media (ICWSM 2010)* (pp. 130–137). Washington D.C., USA: AAAI Press.
27. Rowlands, T., Thomas, P., & Wan, S. (2009). Web indexing on a diet: template removal with the sandwich algorithm. In *The Proceedings of the Australasian Document Computing Symposium (ADCS)*. Available at http://es.csiro.au/adcs2009/proceedings/poster-presentation/06-rowlands.pdf.
28. Sadilek, A., Kautz, H. A., & Silenzio, V. (2012). Predicting disease transmission from geo-tagged micro-blog data. In *Proceedings of the Twenty-Sixth AAAI Conference on Artificial Intelligence*, 2012.
29. Sakaki, T., Okazaki, M., & Matsuo, Y. (2010). Earthquake shakes Twitter users: Real-time event detection by social sensors. *The Proceedings of the 19th International Conference on World Wide Web (WWW '10), Raleigh, North Carolina, USA* (pp. 851–860). New York, NY: ACM.
30. Sankaranarayanan, J., Samet, H., Teitler, B. E, Lieberman, M. D., & Sperling, J. (2009). TwitterStand: News in tweets. In *Proceedings of the 17th ACM SIGSPATIAL International Conference on Advances in Geographic Information Systems (GIS)* (pp. 42–51). Seattle, Washington. ACM, New York, NY, USA. doi:10.1145/1653771.1653781.
31. Sriram, B., Fuhry, D., Demir, E., Ferhatosmanoglu, H., & Demirbas, M. (2010). Short text classification in Twitter to improve information filtering. In *Proceedings of the 33rd Annual International ACM SIGIR (SIGIR'10)* (pp. 841–842). Geneva, Switzerland. ACM, New York, NY, USA. doi:10.1145/1835449.1835643.
32. Verma, S., Vieweg, S., Corvey, W., Palen, L., Martin, J., Palmer, M., Schram, A., & Anderson, K. (2011). Natural language processing to the rescue? Extracting "situational awareness" tweets during mass emergency. In *the Proceedings of the International Conference on Weblogs and Social Media (ICWSM)*, AAAI Press.
33. Wan, S., Paris, C., & Dale, R. (2009). Whetting the appetite of scientists: Producing summaries tailored to the citation context. In *Proceedings of the 2009 Joint Conference on Digital Libraries* (pp. 59–69), Austin, Texas (USA), June 15–19.
34. Wan, S., & Paris, C. (2014). Improving government services with social media feedback. In *Proceedings of the 19th International Conference on Intelligent User Interfaces (IUI 2014)* (pp. 27–36). Haifa, Israel, Feb 22–27, 2014.
35. Wan, S., & Paris, C. (2015). Ranking election issues through the lens of social media. In *Proceedings of the 9th Workshop on Language Technology for Cultural Heritage, Social Sciences, and Humanities*. Beijing, July 2015.
36. Yin, J., Lampert, A., Cameron, M., Robinson, B., & Power, R. (2012). Using social media to enhance emergency situation awareness. *IEEE Intelligent Systems, 27*(6), 52–59. IEEE Computer Society.

Using Crowd Sourced Content to Help Manage Emergency Events

Robert Power, Bella Robinson and Catherine Wise

Abstract The Emergency Situation Awareness (ESA) tool provides crowd-sourced information in near-real-time from Twitter about all-hazard events for emergency managers. ESA currently collects tweets from Australia and New Zealand and processes them to identify unexpected incidents, to monitor ongoing emergency events and provides access to an archive to explore past events. It is operated using a map based interactive web site and has processed over 2 billion tweets since September 2011. ESA has been developed by the Commonwealth Scientific and Industrial Research Organisation (CSIRO) and has been trialed by numerous emergency services organisations throughout Australia. Tweets are processed as a data stream using text mining techniques and natural language processing tools to identify content relevant to emergency managers. ESA is deployed as a distributed information architecture consisting of a combination of commodity open source technologies, such as an Apache Solr index, a relational database, messaging infrastructure, web servers and supporting software toolkits, as well as purpose built components for message burst detection, event identification and notification, message classification and clustering, geo-coding and searching. In this chapter, an overview of ESA is presented showing how tweets are gathered and processed. Three case studies are outlined explaining how ESA is used to detect earthquakes, monitor bushfire events and as a general all-hazard monitoring tool in a crisis coordination centre. We also note some of the issues we have encountered from using our tool and present an overview of our research road map noting the planned extensions and new features.

Keywords Disaster Management · Situation Awareness · Situation Reporting · System Architectures · Social Media · Twitter

R. Power (✉) · B. Robinson · C. Wise
CSIRO Data61, Canberra, Australia
e-mail: robert.power@csiro.au

© Springer International Publishing Switzerland 2015
S. Nepal et al. (eds.), *Social Media for Government Services*,
DOI 10.1007/978-3-319-27237-5_12

1 Introduction

According to the latest annual report on humanitarian crises and assistance from the United Nations Office for the Coordination of Humanitarian Affairs [1], 97 million people were affected worldwide by national disasters in 2013. This report also notes that over the past 10 years the global trend for the cost of disasters has been steadily increasing, and that in recent years the use of social media by affected people has become a common practice.

Significant Australian examples include: the 2010–2011 floods in Queensland that affected 70 towns, including the state capital Brisbane, and caused infrastructure damage of around A\$8 billion[1]; Cyclone Yasi in north Queensland which caused around A\$800 million in damage[2]; and Victoria's 2009 Black Saturday Bushfires, killing 173 people, impacting 78 towns and having an estimated A\$2.9 billion in total losses [2].

More recently in 2013, two major events in Australia were bushfires in New South Wales and significant floods in Queensland. The worst bushfires were in the Blue Mountains region starting in mid October. One of these, known as the 'State Mine Fire', was started accidently during an Army training exercise. This fire spread and merged with other nearby fires in the Blue Mountains area and remained a threat until mid November. The Insurance Council of Australia estimated the damage for these fires at over A\$183 million.[3]

The state of Queensland regularly encounters disaster events, the most significant usually being floods, severe storms, tropical lows and cyclones. In January 2013, Tropical Cyclone Oswald caused major damage throughout Queensland and further south into New South Wales. The resulting weather systems caused tornados, waterspouts and flooding in various town centers. In the Bundaberg region for example, three tornados downed power lines, trees, lifted roofs and smashed windows. There was also flooding in Bundaberg and over 2000 residents were evacuated. In total, natural disasters in 2013 cost Queensland A\$2.5 billion.[4]

The response and recovery activities to manage disaster events are typically performed by emergency services agencies that have personnel specifically trained to deal with the situation appropriately. Large scale disasters may involve the armed forces and coordinating the efforts of these multiple groups to achieve the best outcome in the shortest time frame is a challenging task. Central to these activities is effective and accurate information sharing: of the impact to the environment, the people affected and damage to infrastructure. This is referred to as situational awareness and it is vital that all those involved share a common operating picture.

---

[1]http://www.rba.gov.au/publications/smp/boxes/2011/feb/a.pdf.

[2]http://statements.qld.gov.au/statement/id/73637.

[3]https://www.emknowledge.gov.au/resource/?id=4781.

[4]http://www.parliament.qld.gov.au/Documents/TableOffice/TabledPapers/2013/5413T2788.pdf.

The use of crowd-sourced content provides crises coordinators with an opportunity to harness a new kind of previously unavailable information for decision making during emergency events. This is the goal of the Emergency Situation Awareness (ESA) tool.

2 Motivation

Social media has been recognised as an emerging source of information for emergency managers [3–5]. Twitter in particular is an important communication channel which can be used to source content from people experiencing disasters, and for emergency services agencies to inform the public of what's going on [6–10].

For example, UN OCHA [1] reports that on average 12 % of Tweets during natural disaster events were from eyewitnesses. After examining a sample of 100,000 tweets corresponding to 13 natural disaster events from around the world that occurred in 2013 they found 15 % of messages were from affected individuals, 14 % were offering caution and advice and 9 % noted information about affected infrastructure and utilities.

Similarly, research from the American Red Cross [11] found that 28 % of American citizens choose social media services to send messages after disaster events and that 20 % obtained emergency information from a mobile application. They also found that 40 % of citizens would use social media to inform their contacts they were safe if impacted by an emergency event and if they were to send a request for help via social media, 70 % expected help to arrive in less than 3 h of posting.

In order to manage emergency events effectively, it is critical that crisis coordinators have access to authoritative and verified 'official' information when they need it. The emergency services currently use social media, such as Facebook, Twitter and RSS feed content, to alert the community about known incidents, to inform them about the response activities underway and to provide advice to ensure community preparedness.

Social media has also been recognised as a new data channel to receive public crowd-sourced information about emergency events [12–14]. However, this use from the community to authority, referred to as 'C2A', is not yet widespread in Australia. One notable success has been the Queensland Police Service (QPS) Media Unit. During the South East Queensland floods in 2011, they found their use of Twitter played an important role in crisis communication. Specifically, they found Twitter to be useful for finding and disseminating information; it was effective in amplifying emergency content through retweets. Authoritative accounts were trusted, for example the QPS Media Unit and other news media accounts, so that myth busting of rumors and correcting misinformation was possible. Links to further relevant information and images from everyday citizens were also available [12].

Tweets about the NSW bushfires and Queensland floods mentioned above were investigated by Olteanu et al. [4]. They found that around 25 % of tweets contained content relating to caution and advice. This was similar to results from other disasters around the world. Most tweets originated from news media organisations, approximately 40 %, followed by the general public at around 30 %. Eyewitness reports came from 10 % of tweeters for the bushfires and 17 % for the floods. There were also reports of injured or affected people and information about affected infrastructure and utilities. These results are also summarised in the annual report on humanitarian crises and assistance from the United Nations Office for the Coordination of Humanitarian Affairs [1].

3 The Emergency Situation Awareness Tool

The ESA tool [9, 15] was developed for emergency managers and crisis coordinators to use information publically available on Twitter to detect and describe emerging and ongoing crisis situations. ESA uses the public Twitter Application Programming Interface (API) to collect tweets and performs further processing and filtering.

The ESA Home page, shown in Fig. 1, provides an overview of the Twitter content that has been recently analysed by ESA. The home page is available at http://esa.csiro.au and consists of a number of components including the Timeline at the top showing the volume of Tweets analysed over the last four days, the alert tag cloud showing the most recent alerts generated by ESA in reference to the background language model, the top 10 hashtags, users, mentions and links over the last 24 h, a listing of the tweets corresponding to a selected alert or top 10 feature and a map showing a heatmap of a selected alert's tweet locations and/or markers for any geo-tagged tweets. The full ESA system is available to registered users

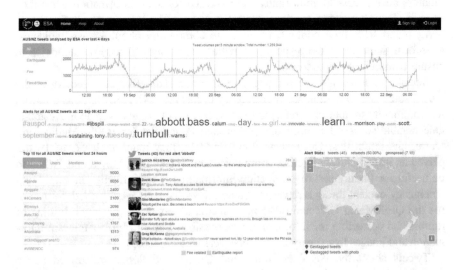

Fig. 1 The ESA home page: http://esa.csiro.au

while potential users in Australia and New Zealand that have an email account from a government department or university can self register for a free one month trial.

One of the key components of ESA is the near-real-time burst detector, used to generate the alerts. Bursting words are identified using a 5 min buffer of recent tweet words. The frequencies of the words in the buffer are compared against a background language model. When an observed word frequency is significantly different from the background language model, a burst is identified and an alert reported.

ESA also makes use of text mining techniques and machine learning algorithms and is currently in use by Australian government departments and emergency services agencies for: identifying and monitoring bushfires [16–18]; all-hazard monitoring in a crisis coordination centre [19]; and earthquake detection [8].

The ESA tool evolved from initial investigations of content published on Twitter during natural disaster events in Australia and New Zealand during 2010. Twitter was chosen because the API provided a useful and versatile method of obtaining public crowd-sourced content, and its uptake in Australia has been growing.[5]

The initial case studies sourced tweets for known emergency events by using both the stream interface filtering on target keywords as well as the search API focused at specific locations. For example, when Tropical Cyclone Ului (March 2010) was advancing on the coast of Queensland, the Search API was used to gather tweets originating from the impacted area. Similarly, after the two large Christchurch earthquakes (4 September 2010 and 22 February 2011), tweets from this region were collected and used as test data to refine our tools.

In late September 2011, search capture regions were established to cover all of Australia and New Zealand and we have been collecting tweets continuously since then. There have been some gaps in this process of gathering tweets as a result of issues with the Search API service from Twitter and IT infrastructure problems: power failures, scheduled data centre maintenance and internet outages.

During this time a comprehensive toolset has been developed that includes:

- a language model that describes the expected content on Twitter;
- a burst detector based on the language model;
- an alerting system that targets specific bursting words for notifications;
- clustering techniques to condense and summarise message content;
- classifiers to identify specific tweets of interest;
- interfaces to support users' investigative tasks.

The following sections briefly outline the ESA system architecture and describe its core components, including the backend tasks for gathering and processing tweets, the various user interfaces available to explore the live tweet stream and tools used to review previously processed tweets. Note that these components provide core

---

[5]https://www.business.qld.gov.au/business/running/marketing/online-marketing/using-twitter-to-market-your-business/who-uses-twitter.

functionality of the ESA tool and each has a specific web based user interface for users to explore its features. These components can also be readily assembled into targeted offerings to address specific user needs. Examples are described below for earthquake notification and monitoring ongoing fire events.

4 Architecture

The ESA architecture is shown in Fig. 2. Tweets are collected using the Twitter REST Application Programming Interface (API).[6] Capture regions are defined as latitude/longitude coordinate pairs, each with a search radius defined to cover Australia and New Zealand. A request is made for each capture region every 20 s with the resulting tweets published to the Java Message Service (JMS) middleware. JMS consumers then process the incoming tweets. There is some overlap with these regions and care is taken to only process the messages once. As noted above, tweets from these regions have been collected since late September 2011 and as of the end of January 2015 we have processed over 1.8 billion tweets at a rate of approximately 1500/min.

As noted above, alerts are generated by the burst detector in reference to a background language model, described in more detail below. The alerts and original tweets are cached in a repository for later reference. A Solr index is maintained for the previous four days of tweet content. Event detection is managed using a combination of keyword matching and machine learning classifiers. Only a small percentage of tweets are geo-tagged with precise latitude and longitude coordinates. Locations are estimated using the user's profile location for all other tweets. For tweets that are determined to be of interest, we have experimented with identifying toponyms in the message text and geo-coding with reference to gazetteer services.

There are a number of user interfaces available as web applications, the *Web Apps* in Fig. 2. The *Alerts Monitor* is the main user interface which provides an overview of the current Twitter activity. It can also be used to review historical alerts that have been stored in the *Repository*. The *Search Tweets* interface provides keyword search over tweets collected during the previous four days using the Solr index. This includes features to target geographic regions, predefined queries for common emergency management event types, continuous search and integration with the Emergency Response Intelligence Capability[7] tool. The *Search Alerts* interface searches the alert archive by keyword, date range and alert level. Tweets from official Australian emergency related Twitter accounts are available on the *Follow Users* page and there are other customised interfaces developed for specific users.

---

[6]https://dev.twitter.com/docs/api/1.1.

[7]Refer to Chap. 13 for details.

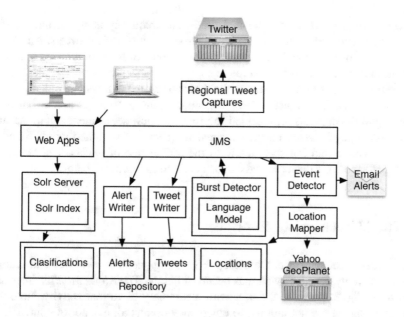

Fig. 2 ESA architecture

5 Generating Alerts

ESA produces alerts every minute by examining word frequencies within a rolling 5 min window of tweets. A word is said to be a 'bursting word', representing an alert, when its frequency in the 5 min window deviates from its frequency as recorded in the language model. This language model contains the frequencies for all words and other tokens historically encountered in the tweet stream. The scale of the deviation gives rise to the colour of the alert, ranging in order from green, blue, purple, yellow, orange to the highest alert colour: red.

The language model is created by processing the individual words contained in the tweets in 5 min intervals, called *bins*. This processing starts by tokenising the tweet text messages to remove punctuation which identifies the individual words. These words are then stemmed using the Porter Stemming algorithm [20]. For example the words 'play', 'plays', 'playing' and 'played' all have the same stem of 'plai'. Note the stem need not be a valid word. This is a common task in natural language processing as it reduces the problem space by conflating the words being processed. For each stemmed word found in the 'bin', the number of tweets containing a word matching the stem is counted. A frequency is then calculated in reference to the total number of tweets in the bin and a final frequency determined as the average for all bins processed [15].

The same processing is performed on the near-real-time message stream by buffering these tweets into a 5 min 'window' and calculating the stem frequencies.

A burst is found when the near-real-time stem frequency is significantly different to that recorded in the language model based on historical tweets. An alert is
determined by adjusting for uninteresting common words, often referred to as stop
words, and giving priority to words of interest for specific users. The alert colour
is determined by the relative size of the deviation from the language model.

The window is advanced every minute creating a 'sliding' 5 min buffer of
tweets and the contents reprocessed to produce a new set of alerts. Note that this
alert processing is based on the expected frequency of stemmed words found in
tweet messages and not specifically to the arrival rate of tweets. The generated
alerts are saved in a database and can be accessed as discussed below.

6 The Alerts Monitor Interface

The alerting mechanism is the central ESA component. It identifies and records
unusual activity based on what has occurred before. The *Alerts Monitor* interface,
shown in Fig. 3, provides the user with a summary of current activity. Note that
the alerts shown are not tailored to emergency events: all manner of content considered unusual can be alerted on. This frequently aligns with popular issues discussed by the Twitter community such as politics, sport, general news items and
celebrity gossip.

The example in Fig. 3 is from Saturday 1 November 2014 at 4:53 pm.
ESA found 97 alerts with 47 being red, 3 orange, 7 yellow, 6 purple, 12 blue
and 22 green. Note that not all the alerts are shown in this screen shot as the

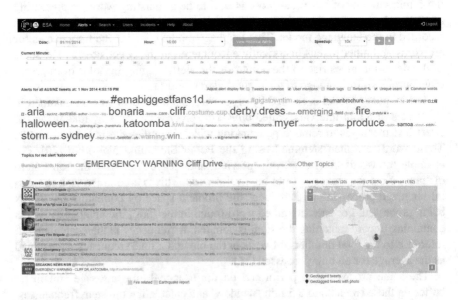

Fig. 3 The ESA alerts monitor user interface

'uninteresting' ones have been excluded by activating the *User mentions* and *Common words* check boxes. This was the day after Halloween (a red alert) and the weekend before an important horse race in Australia (the Melbourne Cup corresponding to the alerts: 'bonaria', 'cup', 'derby', 'field', 'finish', 'melbourne', 'win'). Some other alerts were due to the announcement that the band One Direction would be performing at the ARIA music awards ('#1dfouraus', '#ema-biggestfans1d', 'aria') and the results of a Four Nations Rugby League match ('kiwi', 'samoa').

During this time there was a fire near the town of Katoomba and a storm in Sydney. Fires in Australia are named by the responding agency and this one was called *Cliff Drive fire, Katoomba*; note the alerts 'cliff', 'emerging', 'drive', 'fire', 'katoomba' and 'warning' all relate to this event. Similarly, the storm event has been captured by the 'storm' and 'sydney' alerts.

The *Alerts Monitor* interface, accessed via the Alerts navigation menu, is designed for monitoring the latest ESA alerts. It is similar to the Alerts provided on the Home page, however additional options to customise the display are provided and there is a new Topics component. A similar page, *Alerts Historical* shown in Fig. 3, provides access to previous alerts. The web pages for these alert monitor interfaces are divided into three sections, top, middle and bottom. In the top section there are:

- date and time selection controls;
- playback controls to automatically advance the display of historical alerts at varying speeds;
- a time section consisting of a 60 min slider control with day and hour navigation links;
- an alert tag cloud.

The alert tag cloud can be adjusted using the *Tweets in common, User mentions, Hash tags, Retweet %, Unique users* and *Common words* checkboxes. The *Tweets in common* option groups together alerts with a significant proportion of common tweets. For example, for the alerts shown in Fig. 3, 'halloween' and 'costume' become grouped together. When the *User mention* option is selected, all the alerts consisting of a user mention are removed from the tag cloud. If the *Tweets in common* option is also selected, then the user mentions are still shown but the font becomes very small. When the *Hash tags* option is selected, all alerts that consist of a hash tag are removed from the tag cloud. Again, if the *Tweets in common* option is also selected, then the hash tags are still shown but the font becomes very small. Adjusting for *Retweet %* minimises alerts that are primarily due to significant retweets. The *Unique users* option reduces the influence of tweets from users who repeatedly post the same or similar content while the final checkbox hides common and normally uninteresting stop words.

Note that the user profile image associated with a Twitter account is displayed alongside the message text in ESA. When viewing historical tweets, the original image may have been subsequently deleted. This can be seen in Fig. 3 by the empty image for the fourth tweet. Other examples can be seen in subsequent

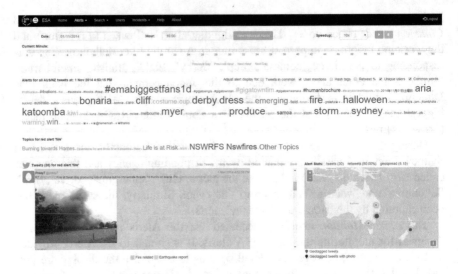

Fig. 4 ESA alerts monitor user interface showing cluster summary

figures below. Also, tweets containing fire or earthquake related words are processed by machine learning text classifiers. When a tweet is considered to be a positive example of someone describing a fire or earthquake event by this process it is highlighted in colour as indicated by the legend at the bottom of the list of tweets. The example in Fig. 3 has five highlighted tweets while Fig. 4 has one.

The *Alerts Monitor* page provides the user with an overview of what's unusual now. When a word in the alert tag cloud is clicked, the tweets contributing to that alert are processed by the Carrot2 clustering engine to produce a topic summary in the middle section of the *Alerts Monitor* page. The source tweets and alert heatmap, explained below, are also shown in the bottom section. An example can be seen in Fig. 4 when the 'fire' alert has been selected.

The aim of the tweet topic summary is to provide a high-level outline of topics contributing to the selected alert word. These topics can themselves be clicked to show the tweets contributing to the chosen cluster topic. An example is shown in Fig. 5 where the topic 'NSWRFS Nswfires' has been selected. Doing so updates the display to show the tweets contributing to this topic. There are 30 tweets contributing to the 'fire' alert in Fig. 4 while there are 10 tweets contributing to the 'NSWRFS Nswfires' topic in Fig. 5. Note that a tweet may belong to more than one topic.

The tweet display appears on the bottom left of the page and conforms to the Twitter Display Requirements.[8] The tweets displayed can be adjusted to hide the retweets, show or hide attached photos, reverse the ordering or export the tweet content to a CSV file.

---

[8]https://dev.twitter.com/terms/display-requirements.

Fig. 5   ESA alerts monitor user interface with a topic selected

The alert heatmap in the lower right hand corner gives an indication of the distribution of the locations of contributing tweets. The locations are determined from the geo-tagged coordinates, if present, or by geocoding the user's profile location using the Yahoo! GeoPlanet API. In the example of Figs. 4 and 5, most of the tweets originated from Sydney while some were from Brisbane and Melbourne. Icons are placed on the map corresponding to geo-tagged tweets and those with an attached photo are highlighted by giving them a different colour. This feature can result in cluttered icons on the map which is resolved for a specific geo-tagged tweet of interest by clicking on the location icon available as part of the tweet in the display at the bottom left. This only shows the single icon for that tweet of interest. All icons can again be displayed using the 'Map Tweets' link.

7   Search Alerts

As noted above, the alerts generated by ESA are saved in a database. These alerts can be searched using the *Search Alerts* web page so they may be reviewed at a later date. An example is shown in Fig. 6 where red 'fire' alerts from 1 November through to 16 November 2014 have been targeted.

The results are returned as a table which gives a quick overview of relative alert activity. In this example there are significant alert concentrations on the first and fourteenth of November. The table rows correspond to a continuous period of alerts that contain, in this example, a red 'fire' alert. Each row includes the alert word matching the search keyword, which is also a link back to the first alert for

Fig. 6 Example ESA search alerts results

the corresponding time period. This is followed by the timestamp of the first alert recorded in the row, the duration of the alerts shown and the number of tweets found. The profile is a band of coloured links back to the *Alerts Monitor* web page, grouped by contiguous alerts with the same alert level. The last two columns provide a link to the first tweet, useful for forensic examination, and a mechanism to export the identified tweets as a CSV file for further investigation.

As well as being able to search for specific alerts, this interface provides a useful mechanism to investigate trends in the alerts and identify periods of interest in terms of the alerts being searched.

8 Search Tweets

The *Search Tweets* web page provides a mechanism for searching recent tweets. This is achieved using a Solr[9] index of the previous four days which is updated every 2 min. The user can enter keywords to search for, optionally combined with conjunction and disjunction operators, with brackets used to set the desired precedence. Specific users and locations can also be searched for. Alternatively, predefined queries of interest for different emergency events and other categories of interest can be used.

---

[9]http://lucene.apache.org/solr/.

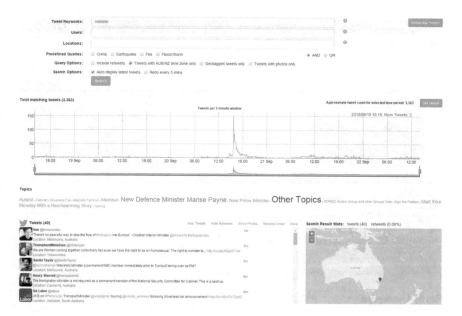

Fig. 7 ESA search tweets

In the example shown in Fig. 7, the word 'minister' has been searched for with the spike in activity corresponding to Australia's new Prime Minister Malcolm Turnbull announcing the new cabinet.

The matching tweets are retrieved, capped to the first 1000 found. These tweets are processed to identify the topics and indicate the geo-tagged tweets on a map. The search can be automatically repeated to update the display every 5 min. The timeline chart can be navigated to a period of interest by adjusting the side bars, and the corresponding tweets obtained and the content updated using the 'Get Tweets' button.

9 Users

The tweets available in ESA are from users deemed to be in Australia and New Zealand by Twitter. The information gathered from these people is primarily targeted for emergency services applications. This information is based on crowd-sourced content and is obviously not authoritative. The emergency services themselves are also contributing information on Twitter and this information should be seen as authoritative content.

In order to highlight this distinction between authoritative and non-authoritative content, the *Users* page tracks the tweets from approximately 350 official Australian emergency-related Twitter accounts. The accounts are grouped by

Fig. 8 Users page

geographic region and service category to allow a specific region or emergency event type to be targeted. Tweets from these accounts are gathered using the Twitter Streaming API which obtains content almost instantly. This is in contrast to the Search API which has a delay of about 20 s between repeated calls to gather the latest content. As well as demarcating the official and non-official content in this way, it is also useful to have a redundant source of these tweets, especially in times of emergency.

An example is shown in Fig. 8, again for the fire event in the Blue Mountains in early November 2014. The interface has been configured to only show the tweets originating from the emergency services, news agencies, police, transport agencies and utility companies in the state of New South Wales. A total of 299 tweets are found in a 24 h time period and these tweets have been scrolled to show an image published by the NSW Rural Fire Service of one home destroyed by the *Cliff Drive Katoomba* fire.

10 Feature Summary

The ESA tool suite includes a number of features as noted above. In summary, it gathers tweets via the public Twitter Search API from regions covering most of Australia and New Zealand. New tweets are retrieved every 20 s and passed onto the ESA burst detector for processing. A configurable alerting system notifies users when specific conditions are met, with the alerts saved into a database which can be subsequently searched.

User interfaces exist for:

- identifying previous historical alerts;
- finding tweets with specific keywords;
- restricting queries based on time intervals;
- restricting queries based on the geographic location of the tweet source;
- and near-real-time continuous tweet search.

The screen shots used in the examples above are based on the user interfaces that reference all the tweets currently collected from Australia and New Zealand. The same interfaces are also available but customised to be restricted to the tweets originating from the Australian states of Queensland, New South Wales, Victoria, Tasmania, South Australia and Western Australia. These interfaces are for state based users who are primarily interested in Twitter activity in a specific region of Australia. Note these interfaces use different language models based on the tweets originating from a single state based capture region.

The specific Twitter users that are currently being followed are those from official Australian emergency services agencies. Collecting and processing tweets has provided a large experimental dataset to explore natural language processing techniques such as text classification and clustering along with various algorithms for burst detection to improve the ESA system.

11 User Experiences

ESA was developed to extract useful public information posted on Twitter to help emergency managers and crisis coordinators. It has been trialed by over 30 government organisations from the emergency response agencies, police services and other government agencies in Australia. The following case study examples demonstrate that ESA is capable of providing additional, real-time situational awareness to enable more effective decision making. Further examples are reported in Power et al. [9].

12 Detecting Earthquakes

The detection, alerting, measurement, and recording of earthquakes in Australia is a service performed by Geoscience Australia (GA). This information is useful for earthquake hazard and risk assessment and is also used to identify potential tsunamigenic events. Earthquake information is traditionally collected using seismic monitoring equipment, however recent studies [8, 10, 21] have shown that earthquake events that occur in populated regions can be detected from tweets posted by people experiencing them. While the tasks performed by seismologists to verify, locate and characterise earthquakes remain, information from Twitter is useful

green 'earthquak' alert detected
Timestamp: Fri, 19 Sep 2014 21:30:15 +1000
View in the ESA Alert Monitor:

Statistics
Number of tweets (including retweets): 7
Retweets: 0%
Geographic spread: 1.36

Classification Results
Classifier used: Firsthand earthquake 'felt' reports
Percentage of tweets classified as positive: 100%
Geographic spread of positively classified tweets: 1.36

Location Summary (excluding retweets)

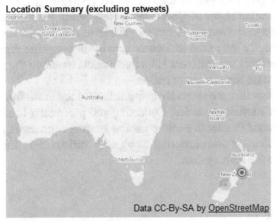

Data CC-By-SA by OpenStreetMap

Wellington (-41.28054,174.767136) - 3 tweets
New Zealand (-43.586578,170.371384) - 3 tweets
Wellington International Airport (-41.328869,174.81221) - 1 tweets

Cluster Topics
Other Topics - 7 tweets

Tweets (excluding retweets, +/- labels indicate classification result)
+ 19/09/2014 21:30:04 (Wellington, New Zealand) WAS THSAT AN EARTHQUAKE
+ 19/09/2014 21:30:05 (New Zealand) earthquake im shaking
+ 19/09/2014 21:30:07 (Wellington, New Zealand) Yikes. Earthquake in Wellington.
+ 19/09/2014 21:30:10 (NZ) Was that an earthquake :(((
+ 19/09/2014 21:30:11 (New Zealand) DID I JUST FEEL AN EARTHQUake or am I just high???
+ 19/09/2014 21:30:12 (Wellington, New Zealand) Earthquake!
+ 19/09/2014 21:30:14 (WLG) Earthquake!

Fig. 9 Example earthquake notification email

as both an alternative early warning and to provide evidence of the how the community has been affected by the event.

After the Christchurch earthquake in February 2011, the CSIRO ESA development team gathered a collection of tweets originating from the Christchurch area as a test corpus to explore how earthquakes could be detected in near-real-time using the ESA alerts monitor. This work was done in collaboration with Geoscience Australia who were one of the first regular users of ESA. The resulting notification system is based on a combination of ESA alert word filtering, location estimation, retweet percentage and message classification [8].

When a suspected earthquake event is detected, an email is sent to GA informing the duty officer. This email contains an overview of why ESA considers an earthquake to have occurred and the 'human in the loop' can then investigate this evidence further to make an informed judgment. Part of this process can involve referring to the ESA alerts monitor to review the ongoing record of tweets describing the earthquake event. An example notification email is shown in Fig. 9.

Figure 9 shows the contents of the email that was sent for an earthquake that occurred near Wellington on the 19th September 2014. The stemmed green alert 'earthquak' was generated by ESA based on seven tweets each classified as positive examples of messages from someone experiencing an earthquake. Note that this classifier has an accuracy of 91 % [8]. Further evidence that an actual earthquake event occurred is that the messages originate from the same geographic region, near Wellington, which can readily be seen on the map, and there are no retweets recorded. The duty officer can review this information directly in the email which includes the source tweets that generated the alert. A link directly to the ESA *Alerts Historical* web page is also included (redacted from Fig. 9) to review the current status of earthquake related content to monitor the event as it unfolds.

Most of the earthquakes detected by ESA have occurred in New Zealand since this is an area of high seismic activity. For this reason, New Zealand has a comprehensive network of seismic stations and can detect earthquakes quickly. Australia by comparison is geographically large, has fewer earthquake monitoring stations and consequently takes longer to determine when and where earthquakes occur. Regardless of the instrumentation supporting earthquake detection, social media still has a role to play to characterise the impact to the community. This information is reported on Twitter as calls for help and evidence of infrastructure damage. This information is useful to the emergency services agencies who are tasked with response activities and restoration of services.

13 Monitoring Fires

Australia has three levels of government (Federal, State or Territory, and Local) where each has complementary roles and responsibilities for disaster and emergency management. Bushfire management is generally the responsibility of State and Territory governments with agencies such as the New South Wales Rural Fire Services (NSW RFS) and the Queensland Fire and Emergency Services being responsible for responding to and managing fire events in non-metropolitan areas. During the Australian disaster season, October through to March, the fire agencies monitor weather conditions in preparation for responding to bushfire events. They inform the community about known incidents, providing updates of progress and the response activities undertaken on their web sites and in some cases through social media, such as Twitter and Facebook.

Most of the State and Territory emergency services agencies in Australia have map based web sites showing warnings and advice to the community about emergency events in progress. For bushfires, this information includes details of the fire alert level, the location, the severity, its status (for example 'contained' or 'out of control'), when an update was last reported, details of the response activities underway and sometimes specific instructions for those in the affected area.

The role of public information is recognised by the various fire agencies, however the focus to date has been on providing appropriate warnings to the community and liaison with news media outlets. While social media has been recognised as a means of communicating to the public, its use as a source of information from the public has not yet been widely adopted. This is due to numerous factors such as the difficulty in finding relevant information quickly and doubts about the veracity of the information found [13]. One of the goals of the ESA tool is to help overcome these issues: to obtain information useful to emergency managers from Twitter, and to help characterise the content found to give confidence to those using this information.

The NSW RFS have been actively using ESA to monitor community reaction to active bushfires. The initial approach was to repurpose the earthquake detector to check for fires. Fire related alert words were used as a filter and the contributing tweets processed by a fire tweet classifier developed to determine if a tweet was considered to correspond to an actual fire event. This approach did not work as well for fires as it did for earthquakes: the word 'fire' and its derivatives are often used with other meanings. The fire classifier has an 80 % accuracy, which is helpful in filtering out the non-fire related tweets, but is not as good as the earthquake detector [16–18].

A different approach was then investigated. Earthquakes occur with no warning but this is not the case for bushfires. Weather conditions combined with fuel loads in rural areas result in periods of known high fire danger. These regions need to be the focus of attention in terms of people tweeting from them in order to identify new fire events. Similarly, when a fire has been identified, its location and progress are often well known, and again the reaction from the community in the affected area needs to be monitored. This situation can occur for numerous different regions around the state.

For this reason we developed a new monitoring web application that allows incident controllers to monitor Twitter to identify evidence about fire events. The web application is user configurable to define the region of interest, the keywords to filter, a text classifier to identify tweets considered to be about actual fire events and provides access to photos posted by the public, which are of interest for fire responders. The tools can monitor up to four different fire events at a time and was motivated from a case study that examined a corpus of tweets posted during active bushfires [22].

An example is shown in Fig. 10 showing tweet streams of three fire incidents underway on 17 October 2013 in the state of New South Wales. A separate user

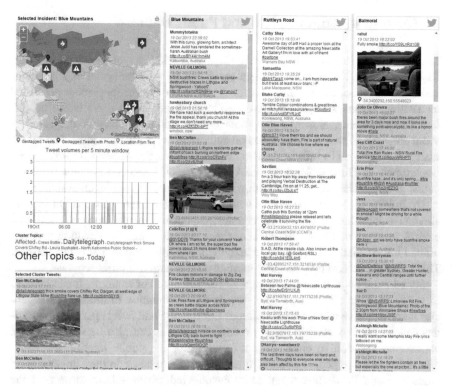

Fig. 10 The ESA incidents monitor [22]

interface, termed the 'Incidents Manager' is used to configure the process of identifying the tweets of interest: the keywords to filter and the geographic region of
interest. Each incident is given a name, displayed at the top of the tweet stream
on the 'Incidents Monitor' web site. One incident can be made 'active', showing
on the left the map of the event, the timeline chart, the cluster summary and the
tweets contributing to a user-selected cluster topic.

The 'Incidents Monitor' provides an overview of predefined events of interest
allowing the user to monitor the latest information from the public. When emergency events are underway, crisis coordinators are under time pressure to understand what is going on in order to make informed decisions. They don't have the
luxury to fine tune the configuration details of a user interface. This led to the
design decision to separate the process of managing an event and monitoring an
event.

While these interfaces were originally developed using bushfires as the case
study of investigation, they can also be used to monitor other emergency events.
This occurred in February 2015 when, unusually, two cyclones made landfall in
northern Australia at the same time.

14 Combining Authoritative and Public Data

The Emergency Response Intelligence Capability (ERIC) tool described in Chap. 13 is focused on authoritative content published by emergency services agencies while the ESA tool mostly gathers crowd-sourced social media content published on Twitter. These two systems were developed for different users based on different requirements. However they both deliver improved situational awareness about emergency events. ERIC relies on authoritative information published by the emergency services to inform decision makers within the Australian Government Department of Human Services. ESA gathers crowd sourced content from the public as a new channel of information to augment existing intelligence sources.

By linking these two systems together both sets of users gain insight into an alternative information source. Emergency responders operate in a command and control structure and it is important for them to have a clear demarcation between official information that should be acted upon, and information that is not verified. This is readily achieved by keeping these two information sources separate.

Social media is still a useful source of information. For example, it can be used to verify or contradict rumors spreading in the community. In times of emergencies there are those who spread malicious information and tweets from the authorities can be used to quickly set the record straight. It can also be used to gauge community reaction to emergency warnings. Are the public treating the situation seriously? Are people evacuating when told to do so or do they linger and go 'sight seeing'? While this is not to be encouraged, pictures from those near the event can provide useful information to incident controllers, especially if emergency responders are yet to arrive. In this way, an agency can find tweeters who appear to be in the vicinity and can communicate with them to verify information they have provided.

There have been situations where the emergency phone line, '911' in the United Sates and '000' in Australia, has been overwhelmed and people turn to social media to request help. This capability has not to date been endorsed by emergency services; they encourage the community to use the authoritative means of seeking help. When people need help they will use whatever means possible to seek it, and since social media has become an integral part of people's lives, this media will be used more to communicate in times of crises just as it has been adopted in people's day to day lives.

The ERIC system can be used to view the official record of previous events as published by the various emergency service agencies around Australia. Refer to Chap. 13 for details. In ERIC, when an event of interest has been navigated to and selected, the pop-up showing the event details includes a link to the ESA system for the user to explore the recent tweets from users considered to be in the nearby area.

An example is shown in Fig. 11. This is an ERIC screen shot of the fire in the Warrumbungle National Park which threatened the Siding Spring Observatory in January 2013. This fire went on to destroy over 50 properties and burned a region in excess of 53,000 ha. The extent of the fire reported by the NSW RFS is shown

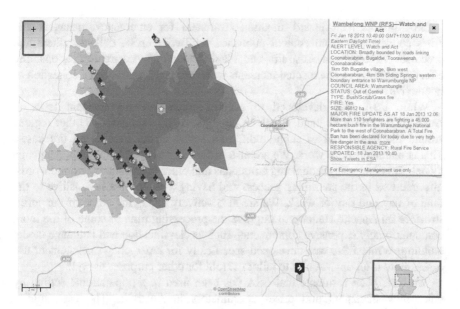

Fig. 11 The 'Wambelong WNP' fire on 18 January 2013 in ERIC

as the grey jagged polygon with a 'star' icon in the middle. Satellite 'hotspots' indicate where the active fire fronts were. Also shown is the popup of the details of the fire event reported by the NSW RFS.

The 'Show Tweets in ESA' link in the popup is set to the region and time of interest and selects those tweets that are positively classified as fire related. In this way users can see what the public is reporting about the event (if anything), as well as media and the official emergency services agencies. Note that this feature is currently only available for the Australian Government Department of Human Services users of ERIC.

Similar data integration has occurred linking ESA to ERIC. This is done in the 'Define Map Region' button available in the ESA *Search Tweets* page, shown in Fig. 7. When defining a region, the 'Show Events' icon displays the emergency events available in ERIC for the time and region of interest. This helps orientate the user to a region of interest based on the emergency events being reported by the official emergency services agencies. This feature is also available on the 'Incidents Manager' user interface described above.

15 Conclusions

The ESA tool applies text processing techniques to turn large amounts of raw tweet data into actionable information and provides effective visualisations for various user groups. The usefulness and effectiveness of the tool has been demonstrated by its use by several government agencies [9].

ESA provides all-hazard situation awareness for emergency managers and crisis coordinators from content published on Twitter. ESA collects, filters and processes tweets from Australia and New Zealand in near-real-time, enabling effective alerting of unexpected incidents with results accessible via a collection of interactive websites.

While ESA was developed to support emergency management tasks in Australia and New Zealand, it can be configured and deployed for other regions around the world and to support different social media monitoring use cases. This is planned future work. We are also exploring improvements to the language model. This includes recognising emoticons and other 'decorations' around words, informal text in the stemming process and having a model that is sensitive to the time of day and day of week. We are also actively deploying some of our infrastructure on Apache Hadoop to improve the processing time of some of the more computationally expensive components, such as classification and language model building. While ESA was developed specifically for emergency management use cases, there is an opportunity to tailor the tool for other purposes as well.

We have been fortunate that ESA has been used in an operational setting by emergency managers and crises coordinators in Australia. The case studies described above note the different ways the tool has been used to identify emergency events, notably earthquakes, and for monitoring ongoing potential disasters, specifically fires and cyclones. These experiences have allowed us to refine the tool to meet the specific needs of these users and to developed specialised user interfaces to support particular use cases.

There have been a number of lessons learned during this process. Apart from the technological challenges of identifying useful content published on Twitter, the main challenges have been organisational and sociological in nature. There is still some reluctance within operational centres, especially from senior management, to act on unverified and possibly incorrect or misleading information. We have had the advantage of working with individuals who recognise the potential of information published by the general public on social media for the purposes of informing situational awareness. These local champions and advocates of ESA are on the front line of emergency response and have been able to utilise its features during real emergency situations to provide improved outcomes to the community in need.

Acknowledgements There have been many CSIRO staff involved in the ESA project. The authors thanks the contributions of colleagues Mark Cameron, John Colton, Sarvnaz Karimi, Andrew Lampert, John Lingad, Peter Marendy, David Ratcliffe, Saguna, Brooke Smith, Gavin Walker, Allan Yin, Jie Yin and Emily Zhou. There has also been further CSIRO support of ESA from senior management and business development: thanks to Sarah Dods, Alan Dormer, Simon Dunstall, Dimitrios Georgakopoulos, Iftah Gideoni, Charlie Hawkins, Ron Jones, Michael Kearney, Ian Oppermann and Cecile Paris.

There have been numerous collaborators from agencies supporting this work, especially Anthony Clarke (New South Wales Rural Fire Service), Jim Dance and Andrew Grace (Attorney-General's Department), Daniel Jaksa (Geoscience Australia) and Adam Moss (Queensland Department of Community Safety).

Special note should be made to Bella Robinson who has been the main developer and architect of the ESA tool; Mark Cameron who originally came up with the concept for the tool, devised the alerting algorithm and has been responsible for gathering most of the user requirements; and John Colton who has provided oversight for the project and been the main contact point for user agencies.

The ESA project was originally financially supported by the Australian Government through the National Security Science and Technology Branch within the Department of the Prime Minister and Cabinet.

References

1. UN OCHA. (2014). *World humanitarian data and trends*. http://www.unocha.org/data-and-trends-2014/. Accessed January 21, 2015.
2. Stephenson, C., Handmer, J., & Haywood, A. (2012). *Estimating the net cost of the 2009 black saturday bushfires to the affected regions*. Technical Report, RMIT, Bushfire CRC, Victorian DSE, February 2012.
3. Hughes, A. L., Peterson, S., & Palen, L. (2015). Social media in emergency management. In *Issues in disaster science and management: A critical dialogue between scientists and emergency managers*. FEMA in Higher Education Program.
4. Olteanu, A., Vieweg, S., Castillo, C, (2015). What to expect when the unexpected happens: Social media communications across crises. In *Computer Supported Cooperative Work, CSWC 2015*, Vancouver, BC, Canada, March.
5. Thelwall, M., & Stuart, D. (2007). RUOK? Blogging communication technologies during crises. *Journal Computer-Mediated Communication, 12*(2), 523–548.
6. Abel, F., Hauff, C., Houben, G.-J., Stronkman, R., & Tao, K. (2012). Twitcident: Fighting fire with information from social web streams. In *Proceedings of the 21st International Conference Companion on World Wide Web, WWW '12 Companion* (pp. 305–308). Lyon, France: ACM.
7. Avvenuti, M., Cresci, S., Marchetti, A., Meletti, C., & Tesconi, M. (2014). EARS (Earthquake alert and report system): A real time decision support system for earthquake crisis management. In *Proceedings of the 20th ACM SIGKDD International Conference on Knowledge Discovery and Data Mining, KDD '14* (pp. 1749–1758). New York, USA: ACM.
8. Robinson, B., Power, R., & Cameron, M. (2013). An evidence based earthquake detector using Twitter. In *Proceedings of the Workshop on Language Processing and Crisis Information (LPCI) 2013* (pp 1–9). October 14, 2013, Nagoya, Japan.
9. Power, R., Robinson, B., Colton, J., Cameron, M. (2014). Emergency situation awareness: Twitter case studies. In *Proceedings of the 1st International Conference, ISCRAM-med, volume 196 of LNBIP* (pp. 218–231). Toulouse, France, October. Springer International Publishing.
10. Sakaki, T., Okazaki, M., & Matsuo, Y. (2013). Tweet analysis for real-time event detection and earthquake reporting system development. *IEEE Transactions on Knowledge and Data Engineering, 25*(4), 919–931.
11. American Red Cross. (2012). *More Americans using mobile apps in emergencies*. http://www.redcross.org/news/pressrelease/More-Americans-Using-Mobile-Apps-in-Emergencies. Accessed September 2, 2014.
12. Bruns, A., Burgess, J., Crawford, K., & Shaw, F. (2012, January). *#qldfloods and @QPSMedia: Crisis communication on Twitter in the 2011 South East Queensland Floods*.
13. Lindsay, B. (2011, September). *Social media and disasters: Current uses, future options, and policy considerations*. Congressional Research Service Report to Congress.

14. Verma, S., Vieweg, S., Corvey, W., Palen, L., Martin, J., Palmer, M., Schram, A., Anderson, K. (2011). Natural language processing to the rescue? Extracting 'situational awareness' tweets during mass emergency In *Fifth International AAAI Conference on Weblogs and Social Media (ICWSM)* (pp. 49–57). July 2011. Barcelona, Spain.
15. Yin, J., Lampert, A., Cameron, M., Robinson, B., & Power, R. (2012). Using social media to enhance emergency situation awareness. *IEEE Intelligent Systems, 27*(6), 52–59.
16. Power, R., Robinson, B., Ratcliffe, D. (2013). Finding fires with Twitter. In *Proceedings of the Australasian Language Technology Association Workshop 2013 (ALTA 2013)* (pp 80–89), December 2013. Brisbane, Australia.
17. Power, R., Robinson, B., Wise, C. (2013). Comparing web feeds and tweets for emergency management. *Social Web for Disaster Management (SWDM) Workshop 2013* (pp. 1007–1010). WWW 2013 Companion, May 13–17, 2013, Rio de Janeiro, Brazil.
18. Power, R., Robinson, B., Wise, C., Cameron, M. (2013). Information integration for emergency management: Recent CSIRO case studies. In J. Piantadosi., R. S. Anderssen., & J. Boland (Eds.), *MODSIM2013, 20th International Congress on Modelling and Simulation. Modelling and Simulation Society of Australia and New Zealand* (pp. 2061–2067). December 2013. ISBN: 978-0-9872143-3-1.
19. Cameron, M., Power, R., Robinson, B., & Yin, J. (2012). Emergency situation awareness from Twitter for crisis management. In *Social Web for Disaster Management (SWDM) Workshop 2012. WWW 2012 Companion* (pp. 695–698). April 16–20, 2012, Lyon, France. ACM 978-1-4503-1230-1/12/04.
20. Porter, M. F. (1980). An algorithm for suffix stripping. *Program, 14*(3), 130–137.
21. Earle, P., Bowden, D., & Guy, M. (2012). Twitter earthquake detection: earthquake monitoring in a social world. *Annals of GeoPhysics, 54*(6), 708–715.
22. Power, R., Robinson, B., Colton, J., & Cameron, M. (2015). A case study for monitoring fires with Twitter. In *Proceedings of the 12th International Conference on Information Systems for Crisis Response and Management (ISCRAM)*. Kristiansand, Norway, 24–27 May 2015. Springer International Publishing.

Improving Situation Awareness and Reporting Using the Emergency Response Intelligence Capability Tool

Robert Power

Abstract The Emergency Response Intelligence Capability (ERIC) tool automatically gathers data about emergency events from authoritative web sources, harmonizes the information content and presents it on an interactive map. All data is recorded in a database which allows the changing status of emergency events to be identified and provides an archive for historical review. ERIC is used by the Australian Government Department of Human Services Emergency Management team who is responsible for intelligence gathering and situation reporting during emergency events. Event information is combined with demographic data to profile the affected community. Identifying relevant community attributes, such as languages spoken or socioeconomic information, allows the department to tailor its response appropriately to better support the impacted community. An overview of ERIC is presented, including examples of its use by the department and the difficulties overcome in establishing and maintaining a nationally consistent harmonized model of emergency event information.

Keywords Disaster management · Situation awareness · Situation reporting · System architectures · Web feeds

1 Introduction

The Australian Government Department of Human Services' Emergency Management team is responsible for intelligence gathering and situation reporting during emergency events. This information is used by the department's senior management to make informed operational decisions to deploy appropriate staff into the affected region to provide services to the community on behalf of

R. Power (✉)
CSIRO Data61, Canberra, Australia
e-mail: robert.power@csiro.au

© Springer International Publishing Switzerland 2015
S. Nepal et al. (eds.), *Social Media for Government Services*,
DOI 10.1007/978-3-319-27237-5_13

government. This is done after the immediate threat to personal safety has passed and the emergency event is under control by response agencies. The movement of staff in this manner has an impact on the business as usual operations of the rest of the department as well as the front line services being deployed during an emergency.

These activities of intelligence gathering and situation reporting have traditionally been manual and time consuming, requiring several staff to obtain the required information and collate it into the appropriate structure and format to produce the situation report. Some of these tasks can be automated, improving the reliability and speed of situation reporting and allowing emergency coordinators to better utilize their time in the analysis of information to make recommendations to senior management.

This is the goal of the Emergency Response Intelligence Capability (ERIC) tool. It was developed as a collaboration between the Commonwealth Scientific and Industrial Research Organisation (CSIRO) and the Australian Government Department of Human Services (the department) as part of the Human Services Delivery Research Alliance. The Alliance was a five year collaboration between the department and CSIRO that ran from 2009 to 2014 to address research challenges and questions that support the department's national service delivery operations. The aim was to use innovative technologies and practices to increase the efficiency of government services, create options for future service delivery and improve the capacity for government to build better relationships with its customers.

ERIC supports the work practices of the department's Emergency Management team who are responsible for monitoring emergency events, performing intelligence gathering and situation reporting. It also demonstrates the utility of data integration for emergency managers by combining dynamic real-time web feed content describing ongoing emergency events with background static data characterizing the population affected to provide a national picture as a web map based single point of reference. A public version of the tool is available at http://eric.csiro.au/.

ERIC combines information from numerous sources: Australian Bureau of Statistics demographics; departmental customer details; 'live' web feeds describing emergency events in progress; the historical record of previous 'live' web feeds; social media; and an archive of previous situation reports.

This chapter presents background information about the role of the department's Emergency Management team and their operational needs that are addressed by the ERIC tool. Then the project process is briefly described followed by an overview of the features available in the tool. Examples of the use of ERIC by the department are discussed and the chapter concludes with a summary of our work and areas of possible future research and development.

2 Background

2.1 Australian Emergency Management Arrangements

Australia has three levels of government (National, State or Territory and Local) where each has complementary roles and responsibilities for disaster and emergency management. For example, the Department of Prime Minister and Cabinet is responsible for developing specific policies for different kinds of emergency events which are delivered as disaster plans. These plans cover preparation, preparedness, response and recovery (PPRR) for tasks such as bio-hazard, plane crashes, cyclones, floods and pandemics. Emergency Management Australia operationalize these plans from a national perspective, coordinating the crisis response and recovery efforts on behalf of the Australian Government as well as other duties such as protection for dignitaries and security for special events. Similarly, the States and Territories implement the plans for their level of jurisdiction.

The management of disasters and emergencies is the responsibility of the States and Territories and normally the police take command during the response phase where the initial concern is safety and shelter of citizens. When the scale of the event is beyond the capacity of the local authorities to respond, a request for assistance may be made to the Australian Government who provides financial and other support.

2.2 Department of Human Services Emergency Management Team

The Australian Government Department of Human Services provides access to social, health and financial support to the community. The department divides Australia into 15 Service Zones, some of which cross state borders. There are numerous offices located around the country of different types providing different service offerings. Figure 1 shows these Service Zone boundaries and the distribution of offices around Australia. Different icons are used to represent the different office types. Figure 1 is a screenshot of the map interface of the ERIC tool where the zoom level results in nearby icons being aggregated and annotated with a number indicating how many icons are grouped together. This aggregation may include different office types and the icon used corresponds to the office type with the maximum number of aggregate members.

The department's Emergency Management team is located in the national capital, Canberra. The team monitors emergency events across the country and coordinates the department's response during times of crisis. The Australian disaster season is from early October through to late March and often involves bushfires, floods and cyclones with many events often occurring at the same time across multiple Service Zone regions. The Emergency Management team has the responsibility of providing a single cohesive overview of all events in the situation report.

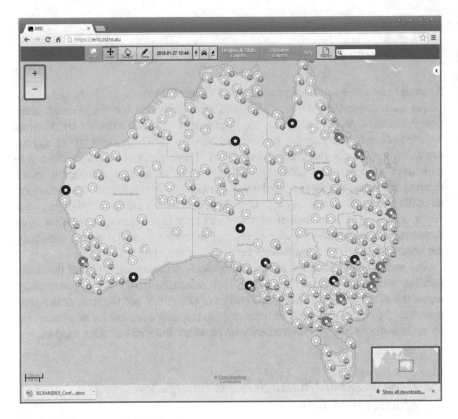

Fig. 1 Service zones and office locations

2.3 The Department's Emergency Management Arrangements

The process of responding to an event requires the department to make operational decisions to deploy staff into the affected region who will then provide services to the community. This deployment of staff has a business as usual impact on the rest of the department: it is crucial to respond appropriately to events so that the affected community is suitably supported and the department can maintain normal services to the rest of the country.

These decisions are made by the department's Emergency Response and Recovery Committee which is activated as the need arises. Membership consists of senior executives from specific business units from across the organization and they are responsible for the overall command, control and coordination of the response and recovery activities.

This committee is activated with a structure that depends on the nature and the scale of the event. A Zone Emergency Response and Recovery Committee is established for emergencies within a service zone that are outside business as usual activities while an Emergency Response and Recovery Committee is established for nationally significant large scale events or to provide assistance to one or more Zone Emergency Response and Recovery Committees.

A large scale event may require an Emergency Command Centre to be established by the department. The activities performed include the operational response as well as further considerations such as media relationships, communications, liaison with other Government agencies and logistics.

Note that an emergency event need not be a natural disaster. It may also be an event which has a significant impact on the service delivery requirements of the department, such as when a business closes that is a major employer for a town. Other examples are events that impact the ability of the department to operate normally, for example a power outage or data centre failure. The response by the department will be the same regardless.

3 Initial Requirements

The Emergency Management team is focused on delivering the right information in the right format to the right people in the right place at the right time. ERIC supports this aim by improving the current methods of the department's operational response during emergency events by providing the same services through improved delivery mechanisms.

In summary, the business goals of the ERIC tool are intelligence gathering and situation reporting. The purpose of these activities is to provide information as a situation report in a timely manner so that senior management can make informed decisions. These decisions are focused on the following five key questions:

1. Are the department's staff okay?
2. How is the community in the impacted region affected?
3. What is the Human Services business impact?
4. Does the department's Emergency Response and Recovery Committee need to be activated?
5. Is it anticipated that the event will turn into a Federal Government declared disaster?

The challenge for the ERIC tool is the ability to identify available intelligence to help inform the decision makers with respect to these key questions.

3.1 Operational Needs

Prior to and during an emergency event, Service Zone Emergency Management Coordinators (EMCs) have the responsibility to ensure their representative area is prepared to respond to the emergency event.

The department's head office Emergency Management team coordinates the response during emergency events. Examples of the specific responsibilities of the Management team are noted below, categorized in terms of the activities performed during the different phases of emergency response:

3.1.1 Preparedness

- Providing service delivery advice to policy/partner agencies on future emergency management policy.
- Ensuring departmental preparedness.
- Participation in emergency management committees at the Australian, State and Local Government levels.

3.1.2 Response

- Providing phone call centre assistance through the National Emergency Call Centre Surge Capability arrangements.
- Deployment of Family Support Teams in response to offshore emergencies as required.
- Priority service for Australian Organ Donor Register.
- Make arrangements for doctors to practice in different geographic locations and to implement different processes for pharmacists to dispense medications.

3.1.3 Recovery

- Delivery of Department of Human Services payments and services, for example, income support payments, Medicare approvals and processing, child support services including affected employers.
- Delivery of Australian Government disaster payments if activated by the Attorney-General.
- Delivery of State or Territory payments and services.

3.2 Maintaining Situational Awareness

Details about ongoing emergency events are mostly obtained by the department from public websites managed by State and Territory emergency services agencies. See for example the Rural Fire Service websites for New South Wales http://www.rfs.nsw.gov.au/ and Queensland https://ruralfire.qld.gov.au/map.html. These sites provide warnings and advice to the community and report information about the emergency event, such as its location, severity, status (for example 'contained' or 'out of control') and details of the relevant agency's response.

This information is reported by the agency at a point in time with the user responsible for maintaining 'context' of the information reported. For example, the user needs to identify when new events are reported or when the status of existing events changes. This can be a difficult task to perform by the department's Emergency Management team and is compounded by the need to do so for over a dozen websites for the different emergency service agencies across the country in the time frames required.

3.3 Mapping

The public State and Territory emergency services websites are map based to show where the events are occurring, but these maps do not include geographic information relevant to the Emergency Management team. This information, most notably Human Services office locations and evacuation centres, are produced as special purpose hard copy maps that are displayed in the department's Emergency Command Centre.

3.4 Intelligence Gathering

Members of the Emergency Management team obtain information about emergency events from various sources:

- Service Zone colleagues near where the events are underway.
- Australian Government agencies such as the Bureau of Meteorology, Emergency Management Australia and Geoscience Australia.
- State governments.
- Emergency Services Organizations.
- Not for profit agencies.
- Local councils.
- Media.

Table 1 Intelligence sources

Source	Method	Purpose
Service Zone Emergency Management Committee	Pers. comm.	Obtain firsthand accounts of the event; information about the impact to staff and clients; intelligence on the recovery effort
AGD CCC[a] all hazards report	Report	Obtain authoritative event specific information
Bureau of Meteorology	Websites; Pers. comm.	Weather forecasts, warnings and cyclone information
Geoscience Australia	Pers. comm.	Mapping information
Australian Bureau of Statistics	Websites	Demographic information; reporting regions, for example local government areas
Road traffic authorities	Websites	Road closures
Emergency services	Websites	Obtain event specific information (for example alerts and warnings and an indication of the severity of the event) and the response effort performed by these agencies
Australian Government Department of Human Services	Pers. comm.	BAU impact; emergency reserve deployed, departmental demographics
Traditional media	TV; websites	Understand the public perception of the event and further information about what is happening
Social media	Facebook; Twitter	As above: used informally by individual staff

[a]The Attorney-General's Department (AGD) Crisis Coordination Centre (CCC) is a 24/7 all-hazards facility providing whole-of-government situational awareness via a daily all hazards report

Communication is by phone, email, Instant Messaging within the department,[1] websites, and official lines of communication. The Emergency Management team also has access to 'departmental demographics': aggregate information noting how many people in the affected community are currently receiving different payment types such as Newstart Allowance, Parenting Payment, Age Pension, Disability Support Pension and so on. This information, along with publicly accessible census demographic data from the Australian Bureau of Statistics (ABS) for the affected region, such as the age profile, English language proficiency, other languages commonly spoken and average household income, is useful for preparing the appropriate response. These various sources of information are summarized in Table 1.

---

[1]Collectively referred to as personnel communication, pers. comm., in Table 1.

3.5 Situation Reporting

During large scale emergency events, the Emergency Management team creates a situation report as a Microsoft Word document based on the information noted above. The information recorded includes specific event details (the event type, its location, impact to the community) and the tasks undertaken by the department (the number of staff mobilized, the business as usual impact and statistics about the number of phone calls received and claims made by members of the community for disaster assistance payments). This information is tracked and reported on during the course of the emergency events and may continue well after the event has been responded to.

Social media is used informally by individuals within the Emergency Management team but is not currently recorded as a source of information in the situation report in terms of intelligence gathering. While this information is useful for the team as anecdotal evidence of intelligence, it is not considered an authoritative source and so is not currently considered for inclusion in the official reports.

The first situation report usually takes the longest to prepare. It includes detailed information about the event, or events, to initially orientate the reader. Subsequent situation reports can be produced faster by starting with the previous situation report and including the new information: this new information is highlighted, for example by marking up in italics, so the reader can quickly identify what the new information is. The reader is expected to have knowledge of the previous situation report; however the reports include all the relevant information from the previous reports.

3.6 Manual Data Integration

As noted above, one of the essential tasks in maintaining situation awareness and producing timely and effective situation reports is the ability to quickly assemble information from various sources. Prior to ERIC, this was done manually by members of the Emergency Management team, mostly by copying content from various sources such as word documents, websites, emails, previous situation reports, archive material and so on.

4 Related Work

The process of combining content from multiple web feeds is referred to as aggregation. There are numerous web feed aggregators, for example to combine news feeds, however they do not support the range of formats currently managed by ERIC. Also, the ERIC mapping and geospatial features are becoming commonplace on modern websites with tools and technologies available to help develop them. For example, Geospatial Information Infrastructures and Web 2.0 'mash-ups',[2] however they require the data providers to comply with specific data formats and web services standards which are not currently well adopted for the data sources in use by ERIC.

The main task of the department's Emergency Management team is to develop and sustain situational awareness throughout the response and recovery phases of disaster events. This knowledge is encapsulated in the Situation Report. A number of models and encodings exist to help characterize this process. For example, Endsley defines three levels of situation awareness: perception, comprehension and projection [3]. The first level involves understanding the environment. This leads to the second level, where the obtained data is combined to discover information. Finally, this information is used to predict possible future situations they may result. ERIC helps with the first two levels, perception and comprehension, by assembling information from various sources into a single coherent picture. Predicting possible future outcomes is the task of the user, although this could be an area of future work.

ERIC relies on public open government data. In Australia, a wide variety of government data is openly available and maintained in the http://data.gov.au/ repository which provides access to data that can be reused and combined with other datasets to gain new insights into research questions. Sharing data in this way is not only beneficial to research practitioners it is also a valuable resource for other groups such as governments, charity organizations, the not for profit sector and the general community. Some of this data has been used in ERIC by downloading the required data and loading it into the ERIC database system. In future we would like to move away from this data warehouse solution as it is better to retrieve the latest version of the data directly from the data custodian on demand. For this to be possible, the data custodians would need to provide web services to their data as well as data copies in data repositories. This is starting to occur in Australia. For example, the Australian Bureau of Statistics provides REST web services to some of the their data.[3]

---

[2]See GeoCommons: http://geocommons.com/.

[3]See for example: http://stat.abs.gov.au/itt/r.jsp?api.

5 The ERIC System

The motivation for ERIC was to demonstrate the benefits of web mapping and data integration for the purpose of monitoring emergency events around the country and to show that information from a wide collection of data sources could be rapidly combined into a single concise situation report for senior managers to make informed decisions.

ERIC was developed in two major project iterations with the first phase developed over the period July 2012 to June 2013 and the second over the period July 2013 to June 2014. The first phase was focused on CSIRO gaining an understanding of the existing work practices of the department's Emergency Management team, describing the business questions considered in scope for the project, documenting the capabilities of the planned ERIC tool and two iterations of software mock ups to communicate key features and capabilities. The first phase delivered an operational prototype for use by the department.

The second phased focused on improving the mapping features, implementing a new workflow to produce situation reports, investigating improved methods for data maintenance and establishing the ERIC tool on robust CSIRO IT infrastructure for operational use by the department.

5.1 Summary

The main features of the ERIC tool are:

- information from a range of dynamic data sources is automatically gathered;
- the information is integrated into a single place (a database);
- the information is available online using an interactive map based website;
- a large collection of static data provides context information for the user;
- information is easily available using 'popups' activated using a mouse click;
- the user is notified when new relevant information is available;
- the user can search for specific events by category, location and source;
- the user can review events that have occurred in the past;
- the database provides a cache of the web feeds which can be used as a backup;
- customized situation reports can be generated for different types of emergency events at specific locations;
- a collection of situation reports is maintained in an archive.

As of the end of 2014, ERIC has been in operation for over eighteen months. ERIC's primary interface is the map, allowing the user to navigate the information spatially. An example can be seen in Fig. 2 showing the fire warnings and satellite hotspots at 6:30 pm on 9 January 2015 across the country. While all this information is reproduced from existing sources, a simple benefit of ERIC is that it is

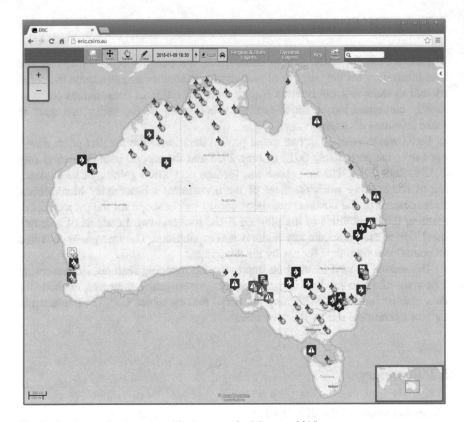

Fig. 2 Emergency events and satellite hot spots for 9 January 2015

available for the whole country at a single website and is available in a database so it can be reproduced as required. As noted above, the original web feed information only reports the current situation and cannot be used to determine the situation for events in the past.

Some of the visual elements in Fig. 2 should be noted. Different event types are represented using different icons and similar to Fig. 1, at this map resolution, it is not feasibly to show all the icons on the map. Nearby icons are aggregated and annotated with a number indicating how many icons are grouped together. The icon chosen for display is the most severe in terms of the corresponding emergency warning. In Fig. 2, there were over 1000 events to be displayed, with the majority (944) being satellite detected hotspot indicators. In the state of Western Australia, there was an Emergency Warning issued for a fire at Donnybrook, 200 km south of the state's capital, Perth. This fire burned about 100 ha of land and threatened 40 homes, but it was brought under control by the local rural fire service without loss of property.

A summary of the main benefits of ERIC are:

1. It provides a consistent national picture of emergency events.

   Emergency service organizations in each state and territory have their own website to provide information to the community about disaster events. The web feeds that provide the data content for these sites use different formats and content structure. The ERIC tool standardizes (harmonizes) this content resulting in a nationally consistent data collection [5].

2. ERIC records the current situation so that subsequent changes can be identified over time.

   By constantly monitoring the web feeds, ERIC identifies new events and changes to known events, such as an emergency warning escalation or descriptive changes about the response or community impact. This new information is summarized and notified to the user as a banner on the website and via an email message. This removes the onus on the user to constantly maintain situational awareness about the current status of emergency events across the country.

3. All information is recorded in a database enabling users to review the historical situation.

   The websites of emergency services agencies inform the community about current incidents, the agency's response and provides advice for people in the affected area. Their aim is to provide up to date information to the public about

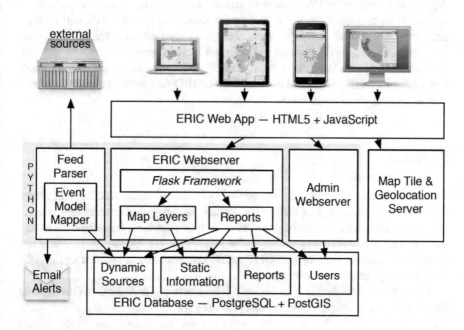

Fig. 3 ERIC architecture

the current situation. There is no facility for the public to find out information previously published. By recording all information in a database, the ERIC tool can be used to review what the situation was previously. This is valuable to the department's Emergency Management team when conducting post incident reviews to establish what information was available when as evidence for decisions that were made.

5.2 System Overview

The ERIC system is based on numerous open source components augmented by software developed for the web feed data aggregation and harmonization, web application functionality and report generation features. The user interface is operated using a standard web browser which makes use of features from Open Street Maps, the Apache web server, Apache Tomcat and Flask web application extensions. All data is stored in a PostgreSQL/PostGIS database with the web application server side code developed in a mixture of Java and Python and JavaScript for the client interface. This architecture is shown Fig. 3.

There are a number of different deployed versions of ERIC for reasons of redundancy, privacy, development, testing and training. Conceptually, there are two main versions of ERIC available: the public tool at http://eric.csiro.au/ and the secure one at https://eric.csiro.au/. The secure ERIC is for the sole use by the Australian Government Department of Human Services and includes departmental specific data and the situation reporting features. The public ERIC still demonstrates the benefits of data integration from numerous sources, but excludes data only applicable to the department and does not include situation reporting features. The department also has access to a 'sandpit' ERIC version for training purposes and a backup version deployed in a different CSIRO data centre to mitigate scheduled and unexpected down times.

5.3 Data

There are three categories of data available in ERIC: static data, departmental data and dynamic data. The static data consists of ABS statistical regions providing census data with details of population, industry profiles, household sizes and income, preferred languages and so on for various geographic scales. This data has been preloaded into the PostgreSQL/PostGIS database and is updated as the ABS incrementally releases further data.

The departmental data is information relevant only to the Australian Government Department of Human Services and includes the service zones, office locations and footprints (the geographic region under the jurisdiction of the office)

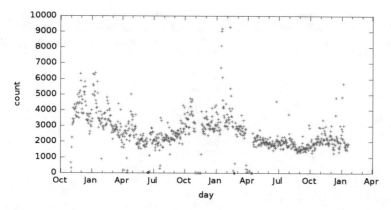

Fig. 4 Count of dynamic data obtained per day

and departmental demographics: aggregate information indicating the number of people in varying ABS statistical regions receiving certain benefit types as noted previously.

The dynamic data is from the emergency services web feeds and other organizations providing information about cyclones, fires, road closures, accidents, weather warnings and satellite 'hotspots'. This dynamic data is obtained by polling at 10 min intervals the web feeds and the Bureau of Meteorology FTP site. The newly obtained dynamic data is compared with the previous content from the same source and differences determined. This is the mechanism to notify the user of significant changes to the current situation, such as a new event or an escalation of an existing event to an 'emergency warning'.

A summary of the count of reports recorded in the ERIC database per day from all of the web feed sources for the period November 2012 through to mid January 2015 is shown in Fig. 4. Some days have a noticeable peak but otherwise there is a seasonal cycle to the number of reports found. There have also been periods of downtime due to supporting infrastructure issues when the internet was not available and the data centre was offline which can also be seen in Fig. 4 by the absence of reports recorded.

5.4 Map Interface

The ERIC map interface can be navigated by panning and zooming the map, turning layers of information on or off from the 'Region and Stats Layers' and 'Dynamic Layers' buttons, setting a specific day and time of interest and obtaining further information about the map icons and statistical regions by clicking them. The 'Key' defines what the icons mean. Figure 5 shows an example of the Wambalong fire in the Warrumbungle National Park (WNP) near Coonabarabran

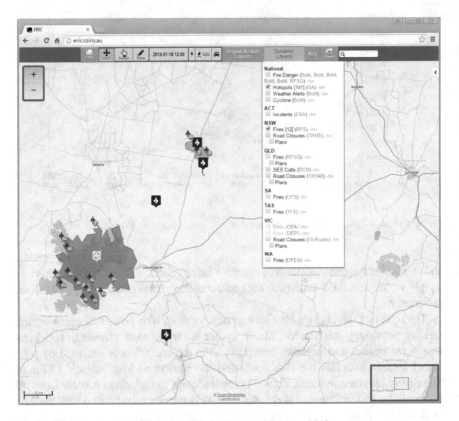

Fig. 5 ERIC showing the 'Wambelong WNP' Fire on 18 January 2013

at midday on 18 January 2013. This fire made international news headlines when it swept over the Siding Spring Observatory. Also shown in Fig. 5 is the list of available dynamic data layers indicating that the hotspots and New South Wales (NSW) state fire information is enabled.

In this example, the burn scar of the fire is provided by the NSW Rural Fire Service (RFS) along with details of the fire which are available in a pop up. Also shown are the satellite hotspots from Geoscience Australia. When viewed alongside the reported burn extent of the fire a visual depiction of where the current fire front is can be seen.

An example of the same event and region is shown in Fig. 6. Here the list of available static data layers is shown, with the postcodes enabled, shown as colored regions. The postcode covering the town of Coonabarabran, 2357, has been selected which is shown as the shaded region and the resulting popup is available. This provides a summary of demographic information available from the ABS with a link to the full information at the source website provided at the bottom of the popup. In the secure ERIC version, further information is shown specific to the Emergency Management team.

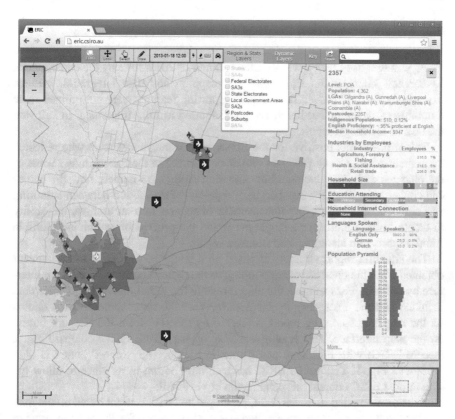

Fig. 6 ABS demographics summary for the postcode of Coonabarabran

As the map is zoomed different layers of information become available to the user. This can be seen in Fig. 6 by the top two static layer options (states and SA4s[4]) and the bottom one (SA1s) being inactive and unavailable to the user. In this example, showing this information at this screen resolution would either clutter the screen with too many regions to be able to discern (the SA1s) or the region is too large for the popup information to be relevant (states and SA4s).

ERIC employs a number of server side features to ensure a satisfactory user experience. For example, the speed of the map refresh is managed by 'simplifying' the boundary details to a level corresponding to the current map zoom level. This reduces the amount of information sent from the server to the client and, as noted previously, icons are aggregated depending on the zoom level. As the map is zoomed to show more detail, the icons separate. The map is also refreshed periodically to ensure the user has the most up to date content.

---

[4]The ABS releases demographics data into hierarchical regions called Statistical Areas (SAs), ranging from the largest SA4 down to the smallest SA1.

5.5 Report Generation

ERIC was first used over the Australian summer of 2012/2013 by the department's Emergency Management team with the mapping and data integration features extensively used. However, the situation reporting features were not utilized since a number of development iterations were required to fully implement in software the task of creating a report.

This process was positive for the Emergency Management team who reflected upon their existing work practices and made changes to their procedures. Some of the changes addressed include: how situation reports are named, how the names can change over time, the numbering of reports, the distinction between authoring and authorizing a report, the management of reports into an archive, the ability to create 'mini' reports for a single event and the process of combining multiple 'mini' reports into an aggregated situation report.

The situation report structure is based on a template with most of the content obtained from the database corresponding to the options enabled on the map interface by the user. For example, the map shown in the report, the demographics data included and the emergency events described are the same content that is shown on the map interface. The report is created by the user from the 'Report' button on the map interface. This is only available on the secure ERIC: compare Fig. 1 (secure ERIC) with Figs. 2, 5 and 6 (public ERIC). The 'Report' button is only present in Fig. 1. The public ERIC has a 'Share' button in its place to allow the user to post ERIC content on social media or via email.

A report is created as a web form, pre-populated with content based on the map interface settings as noted above, and has optional areas for the user to provide further details as free text or in tables. Once the report is complete it is published and saved on the web server. It can subsequently be viewed, but no further edits can be made. PDF or plain text versions of the report can be generated for printing or distribution by email.

6 Discussion

The ERIC tool streamlines the work practices of the Australian Government Department of Human Services Emergency Management team: it allows them to gather intelligence faster to support the generation of situation reports. The initial development was focused on features supporting the map interface. The seemingly simple task of combining information from various data sources, saving it in a database for later use, and providing a single map based website interface has proved a productivity improvement for the Emergency Management team for the purposes of quickly accessing relevant information.

When ERIC is used to manage the publication of situation reports, the repository of reports and the aggregate information they contain may provide insights into the department's response activities over the course of an emergency event. Examples are the call volumes relating to an event, number of staff attending evacuation and recovery centers, claims made and total payments. This information could be analyzed (correlated and plotted) and used as evidence for predictive modeling of expected behavior for future events. For example, during an emergency, the historical record could be used in conjunction with the current data for a specific event to anticipate what the expected call volume and payment rate will be for the next day.

Social media is playing an increasingly important role within the Emergency Management community. Chatfield et al. [2] describe how government engaged with citizens through social media during and in the aftermath of the Hurricane Sandy emergency event and highlights the potential benefits for both governments and affected communities. In a recent study [4], information ERIC retrieved via web feeds about a significant fire emergency in Australia was compared with Tweets about the same emergency. It showed that information was published on Twitter prior to the web feed, contained more specific incident information, was updated more frequently, included information from the public as well as official sources and was available after the web feed contents were removed. Anderson [1] discusses the challenges emergency service organizations face when dealing with social media as not only a new source of information but also a new avenue to distribute timely information to the public.

While ERIC was developed specifically for the department's Emergency Management team, there is an opportunity to extend its features for new purposes, for example to include crowd sourced social media. Some progress has been made in ERIC by linking to the CSIRO Emergency Situational Awareness (ESA) platform [6] described in Chap. 12. The secure ERIC was extended to generate a hyperlink to the ESA search interface for fire events, available in the ERIC event's popup. The search terms are pre-defined so that ESA will search for Tweets from the region surrounding the selected event that have been classified as positive fire related Tweets. Tweets from official agencies and the general public often contain extra information that is not available via the official web feeds. This extra information may include pictures or videos of the event and detailed impact information.

In future we would like to explore a more comprehensive integration of web feed and social media data. Instead of simply generating a hyperlink from ERIC to ESA, we would like to present the social media data within the ERIC tool. An identified issue to be resolved is the trustworthiness of this information source [7]. This is especially important for emergency managers who are mainly concerned with verifiable information.

A public version of the ERIC tool has been created to promote it to the wider emergency management community in Australia. All departmental information has been removed from the public version of the tool and the situation reporting features disabled. However, the public tool still demonstrates the utility of data integration for the purposes of emergency management.

Another area of research interest is to investigate a new data integration architecture. Currently, all data resides in a data warehouse which is appropriate for the department since they include sensitive information in the secure version of ERIC. However, maintaining the timeliness of the other datasets will become an issue over time. This is currently a manual process. In future we would like to source all content from the data custodian, keeping a cached copied locally only for efficiency and latency purposes. This goal may be achieved using semantic technologies and leveraging initiatives of open government data and Linked Open Data.

7 Conclusions

CSIRO have developed a web based tool to demonstrate the usefulness of data integration for emergency managers. The tool integrates information from real time web feeds with demographics data to provide a national picture that is available for historical review. The tool supports the intelligence gathering and situation reporting activities performed by the Australian Government Department of Human Services during emergency events and a public version is also available.

Preliminary versions of the ERIC tool were developed as proof of concept pilot systems to demonstrate to the department's Emergency Management team the benefits of data integration and the utility of a single point of access to a wide collection of information. These initial versions were consolidated and integrated into a single system providing a web based productivity tool that: automatically gathers dynamic data from a range of sources; stores it in a database; recognizes changes to the status of emergency events; presents the data in a map based website; includes references to further information managed by the data custodian; provides a backup of the fire agencies data; and assists in the generation of situation reports.

Further work is being considered to integrate new data sources, utilize social media information using the CSIRO ESA platform, extend the report generation features, analyze the dynamic data collected, deploy within the department's Service Zones and promote ERIC to other Federal government agencies involved in Emergency Management.

Acknowledgements ERIC was funded under the Human Services Delivery Research Alliance between the CSIRO and the Australian Government Department of Human Services. Thanks to the Human Services Emergency Management team for supporting the ERIC work, especially Lucy Knight and John Dickinson. The following CSIRO colleagues worked on the ERIC project: Michael Compton, David Ratcliffe, Bella Robinson, Geoffrey Squire and Catherine Wise. Special note should be made to Catherine and Geoff as the main developers for the tool and Catherine prepared Fig. 3.

References

1. Anderson, M. (2012, April 16–18). Integrating social media into traditional emergency management command and control structures: The square peg into the round hole? In *Disaster and Emergency Management Conference Proceedings* (pp. 18–34). Brisbane, Australia. ISBN: 978-0-9808147-4-3.
2. Chatfield, A. T., Scholl, H. J., & Brajawidagda, U. (2014, January). '# Sandy tweets: Citizens' co-production of time-critical information during an unfolding catastrophe. In *47th Hawaii International Conference on System Science (HICSS)* (pp. 1947–1957).
3. Endsley, M. R. (1995). Toward a theory of situation awareness in dynamic systems. *Human Factors, 37*(1), 32–64.
4. Power, R., Robinson, B., & Wise, C. (2013, May 13–17). Comparing web feeds and tweets for emergency management. In *Social Web for Disaster Management (SWDM) Workshop 2013. WWW 2013 Companion* (pp. 1007–1010). Rio de Janeiro, Brazil.
5. Power, R., Wise, C., Robinson, B., & Squire, G. (2013, December). Harmonising web feeds for emergency management. In Piantadosi, J., Anderssen, R. S. & Boland, J. (Eds.), *MODSIM 2013 20th International Congress on Modelling and Simulation. Modelling and Simulation Society of Australia and New Zealand* (pp. 2194–2200). ISBN: 978-0-9872143-3-1.
6. Power, R., Robinson, B., Colton, J., & Cameron, M. (2014, October). Emergency situation awareness: Twitter case studies. In *Proceedings of the 1st International Conference, ISCRAM-med* (Vol. 196 of LNBIP, pp. 218–231). Toulouse, France: Springer.
7. Thomson, R., Ito, N., Suda, H., Lin, F., Liu, Y., Hayasaka, R. et al. (2012, April). Trusting tweets: The fukushima disaster and information source credibility on Twitter. In *The 9th International Conference on Information Systems for Crisis Response and Management (ISCRAM)*. Vancouver, Canada.

A Lexical Resource for Identifying Public Services Names on the Social Web

Islam A. Hassan, Adegboyega Ojo and Lukasz Porwol

Abstract Discovery of government-related resources on the social web through mentions of government-related terms requires domain-specific lexical resources. This chapter describes an approach for developing a Lexical Resource for Public Services Names and how it could be exploited. Central to our technical approach is the development of a Semantic Alignment Algorithm, which organizes a set of public service names automatically captured from government websites in a semantic network based on a semantic relatedness measure (Explicit Semantic Analysis—ESA). To demonstrate the use of the developed lexicon, we: (1) clustered the United Kingdom and Irish Government public services catalogue for easier access to related services on citizens portals and (2) developed a Named Entity Recognizer (NER) to identify mentions of public service related information in a twitter stream. Evaluation of the semantic relations in the developed lexical resource computed by our semantic alignment algorithm showed the accuracy (specifically the F-Score ranged from 0.65 to 0.93.

Keywords Government 3.0 · Lexical resources · Linguistic linked data resource · Public service catalogues · Core public service vocabulary · Explicit semantic analysis

1 Introduction

With the adoption of the "Government 3.0" (Gov3.0) agenda by the Korean Government to create a *"transparent, competent and service-oriented"* government [74], there is a growing interest in both the policy and academic arena to

I. A. Hassan (✉) · A. Ojo · L. Porwol
Insight Centre for Data Analytics, National University of Ireland Galway,
IDA Business Park, Newcastle, Galway, Republic of Ireland
e-mail: islam.hassan@insight-centre.org

© Springer International Publishing Switzerland 2015
S. Nepal et al. (eds.), *Social Media for Government Services*,
DOI 10.1007/978-3-319-27237-5_14

deconstruct what this concept could mean. In the Korean framework, Gov3.0 is characterised by customized services tailored to various needs and demand. However, practitioners in general have associated the Gov 3.0 label with the next stage of e-government evolution (i.e. after Government 2.0 and Web 2.0). Like Government 2.0 that is associated with Web 2.0-based innovation, Web 3.0 or the Semantic Web is expected to play a major role in enabling Gov3.0 [74].

The emergence of the Semantic Web concept in 2001 marked an important stage in the Web's evolution. As stated in [14], Semantic Web is "an extension of the current Web in which information is given well-defined meaning, better enabling computers and people to work in cooperation". Providing the information elements that currently make up the Web with a well-defined meaning would, inter-alia, improve its contextual search capabilities, increase interoperability between systems in 'collaborative' contexts and, when combined with Web Services; ultimately enable near automatic composition of applications [84, 90].

Over the years many efforts have been made in this direction, and a number of semantic-web applications have emerged in different application domains. In the government domain, semantic web technologies have been applied to developing intelligent applications such as the semantic portal [60], linking of open government data [39, 48], modelling of e-government services and processes [45, 88], improving access to e-government resources on the web in general [53] and management of e-government services [69].

A fundamental aspect of all semantic web applications is the creation of semantic model and corresponding ontologies for describing resources central to the application. However, annotations or semantic description of resources (essential for populating the domain ontology) usually presents high human resource demands, given that automatic annotation is an exception rather than the rule. In our opinion, the diffusion of large-scale semantic web applications in general has been slow if not stagnated due in part to this challenge. Addressing this challenge requires developing tools and domain specific resources for automatic semantic annotation of existing government-related resources and contents on the web and social web to facilitate automatic creation of domain knowledge or ontology instances. A key part of the solution to this challenge requires the availability of Natural Language and Text analytics tools for automatic extraction of *domain-relevant* information from textual data and creating domain-specific annotation resources based on the extracted information.

A number of past efforts such as [59, 71] have aimed to tackle this challenge by developing domain ontologies that used along with Information extraction and Natural Language Processing (NLP) tools to identify structured information from the raw text. Specifically, in [3], the General Architecture for Text Engineering (GATE) components and relevant NLP tools were used to extract crime information automatically from police reports, newspaper articles, and victims' and witnesses' crime narratives, with the output presented as a meaningful summary for police investigators. This enabled quick comprehension of crime incidents without having to read an entire report. In [8], structural patterns expressed in terms of regular expressions combined with lexical conditions were used to detect the typologies of provisions contained in a normative document and extracted its related arguments.

Unfortunately, traditional approaches for developing domain specific NLP resources also require high manual engineering efforts. This has raised the interest in how to exploit domain independent or open information extraction (IE) techniques to create light-weight domain-specific IE tools. This article describes one of the first attempts at addressing this challenge in the domain of e-government.

This chapter describes how to create a domain-specific lexical resource for the domain of e-government to enable the automatic discovery of public services related information on the web and re-publishing such information with the necessary semantic annotations on the semantic web. The lexical resource consists of generic public service names, concrete instances of these names in two national public services catalogs, and semantic relatedness or similarities among the catalogued public services.

The rest of the paper is organized as follows: Sect. 2 presents a background on Semantic Web and NLP resources for the e-government domain. Section 3 presents a concrete scenario for applying the developed artefact and subsequently discusses our overall research approach for constructing such artefact. Section 4 presents the details of the Lexicon Development Process. Section 5 discusses the results from evaluation of semantic annotations in the resource. Summary and concluding remarks are provided in Sects. 6 and 7.

2 Background

The literature background for this work spans a few related domains. These domains include Semantic Web and Ontologies, Natural Language Processing (NLP), applications of semantic models to Electronic Government and Named Entity Extraction in Social Media. Our thesis in this chapter is that semantic and NLP technologies constitute enabling technologies for next generation government public services associated with the Government 3.0 phenomenon (see Fig. 1). The state-of-play in these domains is presented below.

Fig. 1 Literature review framework—social web

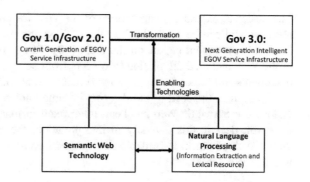

2.1 Social Media in e-Government

The last decade witnessed many attempts to harness the social software as an infrastructure to address some of the e-Government needs. Social software commonly referred to as Web 2.0 platform that enables social networking by offering capabilities for people to contact and interact with each other [82]. The main principle underpinning Web 2.0 is collective intelligence, collaborative content creation and composition by the user (here citizen) who contributes towards common knowledge [77]. Many e-Government solutions employed Web 2.0 introducing the GOV 2.0 mainly by leveraging tools like digital forums, blogs, wiki's and live-chat to provide dedicated e-Participation environment where citizens can express and discuss their needs, concerns and ideas. Those highly structured platforms, though supposedly well tuned to specific e-Government needs, in principle suffer from abysmally low citizen engagement. In contrast social media are widely used by citizens for spontaneous political discussions [61]. To increase citizens' engagement and reach, some emerging e-participation solutions now explicit support integration with social media platforms [21, 75]. Some more advanced solutions such as those presented in PADGETS [22] integrates social media widgets with dedicated e-participation platforms to provide citizen feedbacks. However, there are still major challenges with harnessing social media contents particularly in terms of filtering out salient contents for policy and decision makers [1]. Most of the proposed solutions such as in the WEGOV project [23] rely on generic Social Media analytics tools for topic detection, trends, sentiment analysis with no explicit or direct links to objects in the government domain. For instance, detected topics are usually not linked to governmental services, policy documents or specific regulations.

Other important uses of social-media in government include their use in disaster and crisis management [9, 37, 56]. Social media are also increasingly playing major role in crowdsourcing innovative ideas from citizens [62].

2.2 Semantic Web

The desire to extend the capabilities of the Web for publishing structured data is not new, and can be traced back to the earliest proposal for the World Wide Web [13] and subsequent papers on the topic [12]. Trends foreseen at the early stages of the Web included "Evolution of objects from being principally human-readable documents to contain more machine-oriented semantic information" [12], which can be seen as the seed of an idea that became known as the Semantic Web. The vision of a Semantic Web has been interpreted in many different ways [64, 14]. However, despite this diversity in interpretation, the original goal of building a global Web of machine-readable data remains constant across the original literature on the subject.

The Semantic Web provides a common framework that allows data to be shared and reused across applications, enterprises, and community boundaries. Its well-defined data semantics enable computer agents and humans to work in cooperation [14]. Recent efforts in the World Wide Web Consortium (W3C) to implement Semantic Web [42] have spurred interest in the use of ontologies for information modelling and knowledge representation. Ontologies provide shared domain models that are understandable to both humans and machines. They describe a set of concepts and relationships between them. Ontologies provide a controlled vocabulary of terms that can collectively provide an abstract view of the domain [83, 91]. Such a shared understanding of the domain greatly facilitates querying of data and increases recall and precision. Semantic Web technologies and ontologies are being used to address data discovery, data interoperability, knowledge sharing and collaboration problems. Software agents can then be used to construct and provide dynamic services on the web.

Ontologies can be described in RDF (Resource Description Framework) [33]. It provides a flexible graph based model for describing and relating resources. An RDF document is an unordered collection of statements; each with a subject, predicate and object (triples). These statements describe properties of resources. Each resource and property can be identified by a unique URI (Uniform Resource Identifier), which allows metadata about the resource to be merged from several sources. RDF has a formal specification and it is widely being used in a number of standards. It provides a common framework for expressing information, so it can be exchanged between applications without loss of meaning. RDF Schema (RDFS) adds taxonomies for classes and properties. It allows expressing classes and their relationships (subclass), and defining properties and associating them with classes. It facilitates inferencing on the data based on the hierarchical relationships.

OWL (Web Ontology Language) [43, 66] provides an extensive vocabulary along with formal semantics and facilitates machine interpretability. OWL is much more expressive than RDF or RDFS, allowing users to build more knowledge into the ontology. For example, cardinality constraints can be imposed on the properties of an OWL class. OWL is designed as a specific language to define and describe classes and properties within an ontology. It has many predefined built-in functionalities. For example, an ontology can import other ontologies, committing to all of their classes, properties and constraints. There are properties for asserting or denying the equivalence of individuals and classes, providing a way to relate information expressed in one ontology to another. These features, along with many others, are important for supporting ontology reuse, mapping and interoperability. OWL provides 3 sub languages with increasing levels of expressiveness and complexity. They are OWL Lite, OWL DL (Description Logics) and OWL Full. We have leveraged mostly OWL Lite due to lower complexity than DL and Full. Also it suffices for our purpose. More tool support is currently available for OWL Lite than others. A comprehensive list of OWL Lite language constructs is available at [66].

By publishing Linked Data, numerous individuals and groups have contributed to the building of a Web of Data, which can lower the barrier to reuse, integration and application of data from multiple, distributed and heterogeneous sources. Over time, with Linked Data as a foundation, some of the more sophisticated proposals associated with the Semantic Web vision, such as intelligent agents, may become a reality.

2.3 Natural Language Processing

This section presents an overview of the core and related aspects of Natural Language Processing application to our study. These are Information Extraction, Named Entity Recognition and Lexical Resources.

2.3.1 Information Extraction

To be able to manipulate vast amounts of unstructured data effectively, automated systems require efficient and accurate methods to derive information structures directly from text. The purpose of adding structure to otherwise flat text is to generate a partial representation of content in a form that can be effectively manipulated by the computer [86]. Specifically, most applications typically require representation that captures key events reported and the attributes of these events, including their role in analysing a corpus. Information extraction is the field that primarily deals with text.

Information Extraction addresses a variety of problems including: identifying relations from textual content [20, 29] and automatic instantiation of ontologies and building knowledge bases tools [2]. In domain specific context, information extraction could be used for obtaining information from specialized literature such as biomedical literature [52].

Traditional methods on IE have focused on the use of supervised learning techniques such as hidden Markov models [34, 85], self-supervised methods [31] and rule learning [87]. These techniques learn a language model or a set of rules from a set of hand-tagged training documents and then apply the model or rules to new texts. Models learned in this manner are effective on documents similar to the set of training documents, but extract quite poorly when applied to documents with a different genre or style. This process was expected to be simpler than manually creating patterns and rules by hand and therefore faster and more accurate than the pattern matching technique. BBN's statistical language model used this approach for their MUC system which performed extremely well [70] at MUC and is currently at the core of their leading IE system (Identifinder). However, the effort to annotate training data for each new domain was found to be more challenging than expected [86].

The semi-supervised learning (SSL) methods use smaller sets of annotated data than what is used in supervised learning (SL) methods, and they are augmented with large amounts of un-annotated data. The typical semi-supervised learning (SSL) process is that annotations of some examples, named entities, events, and relations can be used to find more examples and thus more patterns from unannotated text. Unsupervised learning (UL) methods attempt to glean information automatically from the texts themselves, also called Open Information Extraction [25, 30]. As the name suggests, this approach to IE does not require a pre-specified vocabulary or ontology [32], nor does it necessarily need training data or rules. Usually, this approach facilitates domain independent extraction of assertions. This paradigm is often considered to be liberal in a sense that essentially any texts between two entities' mentions are considered as a relation. Obviously, this implicitly promotes the recall while accepting a level of noise in the extraction results [59].

2.3.2 Named Entity Recognition

The Named Entity (NE) recognition and disambiguation problem has been addressed in different research fields and they agreed on the definition of a named entity, *which is an information unit described by the name of a person or an organization, a location, a brand, a product, a numeric expression including time, date, money and percent found in a sentence* [41]. The Supervised Learning (SL) techniques used a large dataset manually labelled. In the SL field, a human being usually trains positive and negative examples so that the algorithm computes classification patterns. SL techniques exploit Hidden Markov Models (HMM) [15], Decision Trees [18], Maximum Entropy Models [47], Support Vector Machines (SVM) [8] and Conditional Random Fields (CRF) [65]. The common goal of these approaches is to recognize relevant key-phrases and to classify them in a fixed taxonomy. The challenges with SL approaches are the unavailability of such labelled resources and the prohibitive cost of creating examples. Semi-Supervised Learning (SSL) and Unsupervised Learning (UL) approaches attempt to solve this problem by either providing a small initial set of labelled data to train and seed the system [50], or by resolving the extraction problem as a clustering one. Other unsupervised methods may rely on lexical resources (e.g. WordNet), lexical patterns and statistics computed on large annotated corpus [3].

The NER task is strongly dependent on the knowledge base used to train the NE extraction algorithm, for example by leveraging on the use of DBpedia [16], Freebase3 and YAGO [89] ontologies. In addition to detecting a NE and its type, efforts have been spent to develop methods for disambiguating information units with a URI. Disambiguation is one of the key challenges in this scenario and its foundation stands on the fact that terms taken in isolation are naturally ambiguous. These methods generally try to find in the surrounding text some clues for contextualizing the ambiguous term and refine its intended meaning. Therefore, a NE extraction workflow consists in analysing some input content for detecting named entities, assigning them a type weighted by a confidence score and by providing a list of URIs for disambiguation. Initially, the Web mining community has harnessed Wikipedia as the linking hub where entities were mapped [47, 55]. A natural evolution of this approach, mainly driven by the Semantic Web community, consists in disambiguating named entities with data from the linked open data LOD cloud. In [73], the authors proposed an approach to avoid named entity ambiguity using the DBpedia dataset.

2.3.3 Lexical Resources

Lexical resources and terminological databases are an essential part of modern NLP systems consisting of large amount of highly detailed and curated entries [67]. WordNet is arguably the most popular lexical resource available today. A Lexicon could be developed to be domain independent or to support a specific domain such as Medicine. For instance, in [92], a general purpose lexical database of Dutch was integrated with English lexical items and a formal ontology, to produce an information rich lexicon comprising lexical units, synonyms sets and ontology terms.

Domain specific applications of lexica particularly in the medical domain are available. For instance the role of lexical resources in extending the Unified Medical Language System (UMLS) with French vocabulary was described in [17]. While in [27], the application of a lexical resource partially derived from UMLS for identifying concepts within medical curricular documents was described. Another example employed UMLS based lexica for automatic annotation of microarray datasets for better search and high-throughput analysis [35]. Another category of applications of lexicon is in the sentiment analysis, where lexical items are associated with polarity tags [72].

There are several data models for lexicons making their reuse and integration difficult. Lately, open Lexica based on the Linked Data standards are emerging, see Fig. 2. Lemon—the Lexicon Model for Ontologies, is an emerging standard for representing lexical resources to foster interoperability and enable future integration of lexica [26, 67, 68].

2.4 Semantic Web and NLP in e-Government

We explore here past and ongoing efforts to exploit semantic web-enabled and information extraction technologies in the e-government domain. The application of semantic web technologies to e-government gained significant momentum between 2006 and 2010 with applications in at least four major areas including the use of ontologies to formally model different aspects of e-government; personalization of e-government services; interoperability and integration of services and to generally enhance e-government services. Some examples of the application of semantic web technologies in these areas are highlighted below.

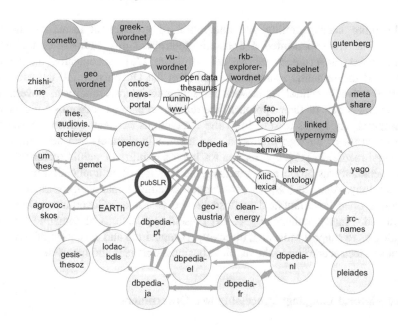

Fig. 2 Partial view of the linguistic linked open data (LLOD) cloud diagram (http://linguistics.okfn.org/resources/llod/)

2.4.1 Semantic Web in e-Government

Modelling e-government aspects—Research in this area covers development of ontologies to describe different aspects of the domains of public administration and e-government. We highlight three past efforts in this area. The first presents a formal PA domain ontology [40]. Specifically the paper describes public services using the Web Services Modelling Ontology based on the Governance Enterprise Architecture (GEA) model. This facilitates semantic interoperability of government web services to be provisioned by different government agencies. In the second, the authors sought to develop a legal ontology to underpin real-estate transaction provided by the Spanish Government [76]. This ontology will support the development of semantic applications to retrieve legal documents. The third paper presents the application of ontologies in the development of a semantically-enriched platform for the consistent composition, re-configuration and evolution of e-government services.

Enabling personalized service delivery—This stream of work employ ontologies for modelling citizens or users in the provision of services or retrieval of information. For instance, in [60] the authors described a project which leverages the Governance Enterprise Architecture (GEA) ontology for modelling public services and citizen needs to provide personalized dialog between the citizens and the government service portal. Authors of [63] described an intelligent search approach for statistical data services related to exports and import goods in European states.

Enabling interoperability and integration of government resources and services—The work presented a Semantic Interoperability Framework for social media based government service infrastructure [75]. Specifically, the authors examined the semantic issues associated with the Governance 2.0 networks and evolved an architectural framework for semantic interoperability in government agencies. As part of their approach, the authors generated scenarios for semantic interoperability issues arising from the interactions between citizens, businesses and government through traditional and electronic channels and different forms of social media. In [19], approaches for interoperability of public sector information metadata was proposed comprising the creation of an application profile and an ontology. Also, in [28], the challenges creating semantically enriched interoperable open government data (also known as Linked Government Data) was discussed. Finally authors of [38, 49] present applications of semantic web and ontologies to support browsing, discovery, composition and execution of e-government services according to the required business episodes and life events.

2.4.2 Natural Language Processing in e-Government

In general, there are very few applications of NLP and Information Extraction technologies in the e-government domain. In the first of the three works found in this space, the authors of [54] described an IE system to collect relevant crime information from the police and witness narratives using GATE components. The second example in [24] involves using NLP tools to facilitate the emails answering process by answering the re-occurring questions automatically or semi-automatically. The third work in this domain in [4] describes a novel model and information systems for integrating multimedia documents to support e-government activities.

2.5 Observations from Literature Review

Detailed review of extant literature appears to show that enthusiasm and interest in the semantic web applications to e-government is dropping. For instance, our bibliographic analysis of the literature in this area show very few papers published in 2013 and 2014. In our opinion, the decline in area is due to the challenges in providing the manual engineering resources required for scaling up initial ideas. For instance it is difficult to dedicate the highlight limited Information Technology (IT) human resources in government agencies to populating ontologies to drive innovative semantic web applications. We argue that overcoming this problem requires solution that enables automatic capture of contents into ontologies and knowledge bases. Such solution may be obtained by the integration of Natural Language processing and Semantic Web techniques. Our work leverages semantic web and NLP technologies to develop a lexical resource containing public services names (as "Things") and the relationship (the semantic relatedness of their names) among these services.

3 Methodology

Given that our goal is to construct a technical artefact—a Lexicon, we employed the Design Science Research (DSR) guidelines and process elaborated in [44, 79]. Design science in general creates and evaluates artifacts that define ideas, practices, technical capabilities and products through which the analysis, design, implementation and use of information systems can be effectively accomplished. Our objective includes creating an artifact; a lexicon for public services that will enable the development of intelligent e-government services. The development of the lexical resource provides the basis for generating a "Named Entity Recognizer" (NER) or "Spotter" for Public Service Names. With the availability of an NER for Public Services, the semantic discovery of public service names on the web and consequent acquisition of such information for populating a public service ontology or knowledge base becomes viable. In addition, by enabling clustering of public service names, opportunities for streamlining services into shared and integrated services across governments (vertically and horizontally) are revealed (as shown later in Sect. 4).

3.1 Scenario for the Use of Lexicon and Named Entity Recognizer

We briefly describe here a concrete scenario how an NER based the domain-specific lexicon could be employed in harnessing spontaneous discussions of citizens on the social media and networking sites.

John Smith (hypothetical character) is an Irish politician promoting legislation introducing restrictions on medical card applicants' eligibility.

John opens Dashboard with information on citizen discussions leveraging an NER solution underpinned by a Public-Service Lexicon. The NER is able to spot mentions terms related public services names in a twitter streams. Based on his specific request, the dashboard generates a dynamic report of places in Ireland which it appears that citizens express negative sentiments towards the healthcare services. From the information extracted from tweets (public service tweets spotted by our NER solution) it is apparent that Cork City (location detected) has the highest rate of negative opinions (sentiment analysis) oscillating around the institution of University Hospital—UH and Merlin Park Hospital—MPH (organisation entities detected). Moreover common topics found through topic analysis include: prenatal care, physiotherapy and medical card. John tries to identify the key arguments against his policy project therefore he explores the posts and

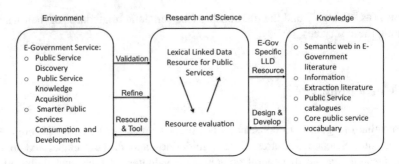

Fig. 3 The design research framework

discussions of highest popularity rank with negative sentiment associated with the medical card and public healthcare. After following selected discussions realises that the negative opinions come mainly from UH and MPH not accepting the medical card for particular services (prenatal care and physiotherapy) therefore he engages into discussion with citizens on Twitter and explains that the issues mentioned by citizens are of local character (but will be addressed) and ensures citizens that the upcoming legislation will not bring any harm but rather improve the current set of services covered. Moreover now, since John knows that the "hot" topics detected around Public Healthcare Services in Ireland are closely related medical card (based on semantic distance measures), he suggests relevant common strategy that should be developed in order to facilitate a solution for these problems.

We show in the subsequent sections how the public service lexicon underpinning the NER or spotter system in the scenario above was developed.

3.2 Research Framework

The research framework employed is an instantiation of the DSR Framework, comprising three core cycles—relevance, design and rigor [44]. As shown in Fig. 3, the research (i.e. development of the lexical resource for public services) is driven by the need to transform e-government services through better (semantically-enabled) discovery of services, automatic acquisition of public service information to populate government knowledge bases and provision of information that could underpin streamlining of services or development of integrated public services.

Our knowledge base here consists of the sources of information on the three underpinning domains described in Sect. 2. In addition, the research drew from the existing catalogue of services and the Core Public Service Vocabulary[1]—a simplified reusable and extensible data model that captures the fundamental

---

[1]https://joinup.ec.europa.eu/asset/core_public_service/description.

characteristics of a service offered by public administrations. Given the paucity of research on the development of lexical resources for the e-government domain and in the tradition of design science in Information Systems research, a major goal of the work is to contribute to literature on NLP and Semantic Web applications in e-government.

3.3 Design Process

In line with the DSR process model described in [79], the construction of the lexical resource design process proceeded in the following major steps:

- *Articulation of motivation for the development of the resource*—The context for the resource is to enable the automatic acquisition of public service related information from unstructured data sources into knowledge bases/ontologies to underpin intelligent e-government services and applications. Another context for the use of the artefact is the construction of "public service clusters".
- *Definition of objectives for the resource*—The goal of the resource is to provide a concrete named list of services (and their semantic relations) to enable NER parsing of Public Service names in unstructured data.
- *Development of an algorithm to construct the resource*—The third step involved the development of procedures to construct the lexical resource from datasets of public services names and align the various datasets by building a graph of services, where edges connotes semantic relatedness.
- *Application of the resource*—The developed resource was employed as a NER parser for identifying public services names from descriptions of public services published by governments of Canada and India.
- *Evaluation of framework*—Two levels of evaluation was carried out with respect to the lexical resource. The first involved determining the reliability of the semantic similarity and relatedness metrics underpinning our name matching and alignment actions. The second involved the degree of accuracy and recall provided by the lexical resource when used on two test datasets.
- *Communication of the framework*—The framework will be provided along with relevant libraries in the GitHub code repository in addition to dissemination through scholar channels such as this article.

3.4 Datasets

Two major datasets were employed as input resources to the development of the lexical resource—the United Kingdom and Irish Government Public Service Catalogues. A major reason for selecting the UK service catalogue is its quality as public services names were already assigned unique identifiers (or uniform resource identifiers—URI). The Irish service dataset was hinged on geopolitical and accessibility (from authors' research context) considerations. Given that the coverage of the resource is directly linked to the diversity of its entries, continued update to the lexical resource based on other government public service catalogues is important. We shall present in Sect. 4 how we intend to support the required continuous update to improve recall.

4 Developing the Lexical Resource

4.1 Context—Information Extraction Framework

As shown in Sect. 2, most of the current NER and IE tools provide only limited, generic capabilities for information extraction and do not support domain specific content processing. We describe here how we approach the problem (see Fig. 4). First we present the abstract Framework Architecture and focus on the semantic annotation and enrichment component. In our work, we propose to use the Open Information Extraction (OIE) tools to extract generic triples (statements) out of the raw text. Second, the triples will be used to generate a named entity recognition (NER) tool to extract and annotate the public services documents or corpus (see Fig. 5).

Thirdly, we populate ontology of public services, by mapping both the entity and the relations to the ontology to produce the RDF that will be used as domain specific semantic resources to be harnessed in our Gov 3.0 applications examples.

The main components of the proposed solution architecture include:

The Domain specific language resource—We started with building the domain specific language resource, this language resource will be used in extending the NER tool to recognize the public service terms. We built a seed corpus and worked

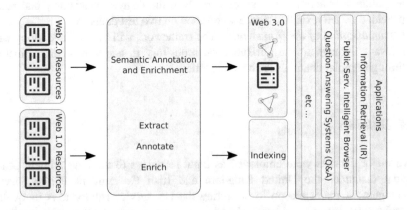

Fig. 4 Framework architecture

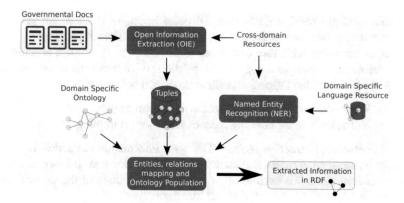

Fig. 5 The information extraction system architecture

on annotating it and semi-automatically transforming it from unstructured to structured form.

Domain Specific Ontology—This ontology is needed for building the graph by
mapping the correct relations to the extracted entities. We have used a conceptual
model for the public service, based on the public service ontology, being developed under the auspices of the ISA—the Interoperability Solutions for European
Public Administrations programme (Fig. 6).

Named Entity Recognition (NER)—As described in the background section, the
NER tool is the component that is responsible for recognizing and disambiguating the extracted entity by the open information extraction tuples, we tried to use

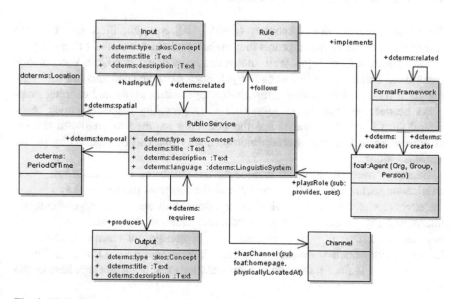

Fig. 6 UML diagram for the core public service vocabulary

DBpedia spotlight for doing this task. DBpedia Spotlight is a tool for automatically annotating mentions of DBpedia resources in text. Thus, it provides a generic domain independent NER tool that needs to be extended by domain specific language resource in order to recognize the public service terms; there are two possible ways to extend the DBpedia spotlight described below:

- Using Wikipedia Infoboxes and DBpedia extraction engine.
- Using N-Triples files for building indexes and Spotters training.

Open Information Extraction (OIE)—The open information extraction is mainly used for extracting the tuples automatically out of the raw text. It is a generic and domain independent. We explored three of the famous state of the art OIE tools ReVerb, OLLIE, and ClausIE during our literature review.

Tuples—This constitute the major outputs from the extracted information produced by the OIE tool. The tuples are represented in the traditional Subject, Predicate Object format (S, P, O) format.

Entities, Relations mapping and ontology population—This component is responsible for populating the ontology (public service ontology in our case) with the recognized entities by the NER, mapping the tuples into domain-specific relations based on the ontology, and producing the Extracted information in RDF/XML format.

4.2 Base Resources

4.2.1 The Core Public Service Vocabulary

The Core Public Service Vocabulary (CPSV) [80] is a simplified, reusable, and extensible data model that captures the fundamental characteristics of an entity in a context-neutral fashion [5]. Well-known examples of existing Core Vocabularies include the Dublin Core Metadata Set [6]. Such Core Vocabularies are the starting point for agreeing on new semantic interoperability assets and defining mappings between existing assets. Semantic interoperability assets that map to or extend such Core Vocabularies are the minimum required to guarantee a level of cross-domain and cross-border interoperability that can be attained by public administrations.

Semantic interoperability is defined as the ability of information and communication technology (ICT) systems and the business processes; they support the exchange of data and the sharing of information and knowledge: Semantic Interoperability enables systems to combine received information with other information resources and to process it in a meaningful manner ("European Interoperability Framework (EIF)—Towards Interoperability For European Public Services") [7]. It aims at the mental representations that human beings have of the meaning of any given data.

The Core Public Service Vocabulary (CPSV) is designed to make it easy to exchange basic information about the functions carried out by the public sector and the services in which those functions are carried out. By using the vocabulary, almost certainly augmented with sector specific information and organisations.

In the context of our work, the CPSV vocabulary is used as a lightweight ontology that is to be populated with public service names extracted from public services name catalogues. The public names in the lexicon are linked through the "related" relations as shown in Fig. 6.

4.2.2 Government Public Service Catalogues

If we consider the Public Service Name Lexicon as a lightweight ontology, the instances of this ontology are based on public service catalogues published by governments at different levels. In our work, we employed the public services catalogues published by the UK, Irish and Canadian Governments to bootstrap the lexicon. For each government catalog, the name, description and URL for the services are captured and transformed into concrete entries in the lexicon. These names are linked based on their semantic relatedness in the lexicon. We describe below our approach for organizing and linking the different public service names comprising the lexicon (Fig. 7).

4.2.3 Generating and Representing the Lexical Resource

The lexicon is represented in two different forms. In the first form, the lexical resource consists of public service names from the three catalogues organized into a graph with labelled edges representing semantic distances among different services based on different semantic distance measures. Like WordNet, the Lexicon allows users to query for distances between two public service names based on one or more measures. In the second form, the lexicon is presented as a graph with two kinds of connected nodes. The first type of nodes are labelled with abstract service names while the second type are labelled with concrete public service names. The abstract service name is an internal name constructed from child node names. For instance two child nodes with service names "Social Protection Services" and "Social Security Services" belonging originally from two different service catalogues (say Ireland and UK) could have an abstract or more general name such as "Social Security and Protection Services". This name is simply represented internally as a set of keywords such as "Social Security, Social Protection" as see Fig. 8.

The construction of the graph shown based on a simple alignment algorithm shown in Fig. 1. The process starts with an empty lexicon that is first initialized with one of the service catalogues. Next, each name in the second catalog is semantically matched with existing names in the lexicon. If a match is found,

Construct the lexical resource
Input: $C \neq \emptyset$ //C is the catalog of the public service names.
Output: R // R is the Lexical Linked Data (LLD) Graph of the service name.
begin
  $R \longleftarrow Initialize(c^*)$, where $c^* \in C$
  $c' = C - c^*$
  for $cg \in C'$ do
    $R = Align(R, cg)$
  end
Initialize:
Input: C_G //Dataset of public service names
Output: R //LLD graph contains only service names in C
$R = emptygraph$
for $ci \in C_G$ do
  Add node Si to R with new URI and same name with ci
  Create a child node $CiforSi$ in R with same identifier name in ci
  Create node ci in R
  Creat a directed edge from Si to ci
end
Align:
Input: R, C_G //C= Service Catalog
Output: R // C_G = Specific public service dataset, $C = C_G$
for $cg \in C_G$ do
  FoundSimilar = FALSE
  for $Si \in R$ do
    $V = $ Set of nodes in R with outgoing edges
    for $n \in V$ do
      if $SemanticRelatedness(cg, connectedNodes(n)) > T$
      then
        Create node cg in R
        Create a directed edges from node n to cg
        Update keywords in n
        foundSimilar = TRUE
      end
      if $!FoundSimilar$ then
        Add node Cg^* to R with new URI and same name
        with cg
        Create node cg in R
        Create a directed edges from node cg^* to cg
      end
    end
  end
end

Fig. 7 Lexicon construction algorithm

a new node is created and linked to the "parent" of the matching node as a new instance. The set of keywords for the parent nodes is then updated to accommodate the new child nodes. Parent and child relationships are implicitly established in the graph through the "*has_instance*" relations. All parent nodes have one or more outgoing edges with the "has_instance" label. However, if no matching node is found, a new node is created in the graph labelled the service name.

As a reusable resource for developers and NLP practitioners, the Lexicon is packaged as Linked Data to facilitate integration with other open lexicons (see Fig. 2). Linked Data provides a simple mechanism for combining data from multiple sources across the Web [10].

Fig. 8 Structure of public service lexical database

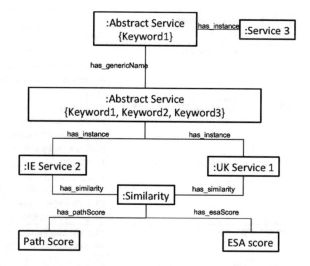

5 Evaluation

Before discussing the applications of the lexicon; we briefly present the correctness of the computed lexical terms and their relations. Following this, we also evaluate how well the lexicon performs when implemented as a look-up dictionary as part of a "spotting" or NER tool as discussed in Sect. 5.2.

5.1 Calculating Semantic Distances

Two broad approaches to semantic distances calculations were employed in the development of the lexicon. The first approach is based on calculating Semantic similarity based on the general purpose WordNet resource while the second employs a Semantic relatedness related approach—Explicit Semantic Analysis [36]. The WordNet based methods are described in Table 1.

After computing semantic distances among public services names from UK and Irish service catalogues, we also computed a correlation matrix for the measures. The results shown in Table 2 indicate that the Path measure could serve as a good proxy for the other WordNet based measures except JCN. At the same time, the ESA measure is not correlated with any of the seven WordNet based approach (Tables 3, 4 and 5).

Based on these results, subsequent evaluation of the accuracy of the semantic distance metrics was restricted to Path and ESA. Our goal in the evaluation is to verify if computed similarity values accurately reflects the semantic similarity provided by judgements of domain experts. To make judgements of what is significantly similar or related for a measure and what is not; two domain experts studied the

Table 1 Semantic similarity measures

ID	Publication	Description
HSO	Hirst and St-Onge [46]	Two lexicalized concepts are semantically close if their WordNet synsets are connected by a path that is not too long and that "does not change direction too often"
LCH	Leacock and Chodorow [57]	This measure relies on the length of the shortest path between two synsets for their measure of similarity. They limit their attention to IS-A links and scale the path length by the overall depth D of the taxonomy
LESK	Banerjee and Pedersen [10]	Lesk (1985) proposed that the relatedness of two words is proportional to the extent of overlaps of their dictionary definitions. Banerjee and Pedersen (2002) extended this notion to use WordNet as the dictionary for the word definitions
WUP	Wu and Palmer [93]	The Wu and Palmer measure calculates relatedness by considering the depths of the two synsets in the WordNet taxonomies, along with the depth of the LCS
RES	Resnik [81]	Resnik defined the similarity between two synsets to be the information content of their lowest superordinate (most specific common subsumer)
JCN	Jiang and Conrath [51]	Also uses the notion of information content, but in the form of the conditional probability of encountering an instance of a child-synset given an instance of a parent synset: 1/jcn_distance, where jcn_distance is equal to IC(synset1) + IC(synset2)—2 * IC(lcs)
LIN	Lin [58]	Equation is modified a little bit from Jiang and Conrath: 2 * IC(lcs)/(IC(synset1) + IC(synset2)). Where IC(x) is the information content of x. One can observe, then, that the relatedness value will be greater-than or equal-to zero and less-than or equal-to one

Table 2 Correlations among nine semantic similarity measures

Metric	ESA	Path	JCN	HSO	LCH	LIN	Lesk	RES	WUP
ESA	1								
Path	0.013567	1							
JCN	−0.01184	0.079086	1						
HSO	−0.0198	0.428895	0.102645	1					
LCH	0.015373	0.94971	0.04735	0.314014	1				
LIN	−0.03154	0.590723	0.058145	0.471453	0.610865	1			
Lesk	−0.02386	0.316054	0.344743	0.620139	0.197504	0.410536	1		
RES	−0.0053	0.657468	0.046148	0.577175	0.665562	0.87703	0.399397	1	
WUP	0.010856	0.884013	0.046338	0.377662	0.960225	0.726738	0.214114	0.806062	1

Table 3 Evaluation sample of ESA and PATH similarity scores for randomly selected cases

	Service 1	Service 2	ESA	Path	ESA comment	Path comment
1	Recycling sites	Pay the household charge	0.020405	0.3	Valid	Valid
2	Consumer advice	Register for energy advice and mentoring	0.080619	0.438034	Valid	False negative
3	Community centres	Access information on education training and career paths	0.014875	0.586538	Valid	Valid
4	Child protection	Read key documents from the commission for the support of victims of crime reports	0.011626	1.433333	Valid	False positive

Table 4 Evaluation sample of the top similarity scores for ESA

	Service 1	Service 2	ESA	Path	ESA comment	Path comment
1	Archives	Search for references to records held in the national archives	0.49117753	0.612745	Valid	False negative
2	Archives	Access national archives	0.489817676	0.183333	Valid	False negative
3	Cemeteries and crematoria	Watch county council meeting webcasts	0.48882719	0	False positive	Valid
4	Cemeteries and crematoria	Watch Mayo county council videos	0.399389612	0	False positive	Valid

generated distance values for pairs of public service names drawn from the UK and Irish catalogues. For ESA scores, values above 0.01 were considered significantly related while for Path, values over 1.0 were considered significantly similar. With these thresholds, we evaluated: (1) the generated score of 40 randomly selected pairs of public service names, (2) 20 top most similar service name pairs based on Path measures and (3) 20 top most related service name pairs based on ESA measures. Applying the threshold values, we remark for each computed score if the implied similarity judgment is valid, a false positive or a false negative. Consolidated comparative results for both measures are provided in the Tables 6 and 7.

Table 5 Evaluation sample of the top similarity scores for PATH

	Service 1	Service 2	ESA	Path	ESA comment	Path comment
1	Benefit fraud	Find out how to complain or give feedback about health and social care services in Ireland	0.013461889	3.892857	False negative	Valid
2	Birth registration	Find out how to complain or give feedback about health and social care services in Ireland	0.012666738	3.125	Valid	False positive
3	Benefit fraud	Access to crime and victimisation surveys from the national crime council	0.023621513	3	Valid	False positive
4	Copy certificates	Register for a reminder of your driving licence expiry date	0.023041065	3	Valid	False positive

Table 6 Summary of the results—raw score

	ESA			Path		
	Correct	False positive	False negative	Correct	False positive	False negative
40 random cases	35 [87.5 %]	1 [2.5 %]	4 [10 %]	34 [85 %]	3 [7.5 %]	3 [7.5 %]
Top 20 ESA cases	16 [80 %]	4 [20 %]	0 [0 %]	8 [40 %]	12 [60 %]	0 [0 %]
Top 20 path cases	15 [75 %]	5 [25 %]	6 [30 %]	6 [30 %]	0 [0 %]	14 [70 %]

Table 7 Precision and recall values for methods

	ESA			Path		
	Precision	Recall	F-score	Precision	Recall	F-score
40 random cases	0.9722	0.8974	0.9348	0.9189	0.9189	0.9189
Top 20 ESA cases	0.8000	1.0000	0.9000	0.4000	1.0000	0.7000
Top 20 path cases	0.7500	0.7142	0.7321	0.7321	1.0000	0.6500

Table 8 Evaluation of extracting public service terms out of twitter stream

Twit body	Twit link	Extracted public services	Extracted entities by Dbpedia spotlight	Extracted entities by alchemyAPI
Why Rwanda plans to issue biometric passport—Rwanda will start issuing biometric passports to her citizens which	https://twitter.com/m2sys/ status/538485285055922179	Passport: https://egov.deri. ie/PublicServices/Service/ CA_goc_passport	Rwanda: http://dbpedia.org/ resource/Rwanda biometric passports: http://dbpedia.org/resource/ Biometric_passport	Rwanda: Country
@HeraldNewsdesk that is why there is a reason they made the driver theory test more complicated. Crazy :(	https://twitter.com/JuditJkiss86/ status/579935117218594817	Driver theory test: https://egov.deri. ie/PublicServices/Service/IR_ apply-for-driver-theory-test		
@MikeBovill unfortunately I've found that a clothing allowance hasn't bought style, though…	https:// twitter.com/DonaldsonESPN/ status/582155654648987648	Clothing allow-ance: https://egov.deri. ie/PublicServices/Service/ CA_goc_clothing_allowance		
@SenatorLesniak no hfor ANYONE that hasn't com-pleted a gun safety course	https:// twitter.com/christwords199/ status/553672403046240256	Hunting licence: https://egov.deri. ie/PublicServices/Service/ UK_HUNTING_LICENCE	Gun safety: http://dbpedia.org/resource/ Gun_safety	
@TomLevenson @DonteStallworth firearms owned by law-abiding citizens being used in a way that would result in civic liability are rare	https:// twitter.com/CaptDavidRyan/ status/456189036638773248	Civic liability: https://egov.deri. ie/PublicServices/Service/ UK_CIVIC_LIABILITY		DonteStallworth: company

(continued)

Table 8 (continued)

Twit body	Twit link	Extracted public services	Extracted entities by Dbpedia spotlight	Extracted entities by alchemyAPI
#auslaw #legal super death benefit and suicide—Hi I just have a question. My husband recently suicided at 34 years	https://twitter.com/LawAnswersAU/status/581652155481911296	Death benefit: https://egov.deri.ie/PublicServices/Service/CA_goc_death_benefit	Suicide: http://dbpedia.org/resource/Suicide	
Polls and Surveys] open question: 770 account death benefit maximum that can be purchased?	https://twitter.com/zpravycz/status/581952421187874816	Death benefit: https://egov.deri.ie/PublicServices/Service/CA_goc_death_benefit		
#endocrine #hormone: Federal Court Overseeing Testosterone Treatment Lawsuits Schedules April Case Management Conf… http://ow.ly/2WCFlq	https://twitter.com/Endocrine_bio/status/582151836045574144	Case management: https://egov.deri.ie/PublicServices/Service/CA_goc_case_management	Endocrine: http://dbpedia.org/resource/Endocrine_system Federal court: http://dbpedia.org/resource/United_States_district_court Testosterone: http://dbpedia.org/resource/Testosterone	Federal court: organization testosterone: drug
#University 61 % of international students surveyed would consider setting up a business in Ireland: "A new sur… http://bit.ly/1FdZkw0	https://twitter.com/dcustudentlife/status/575964176641748992	International students: https://egov.deri.ie/PublicServices/Service/UK_INTERNATIONAL_STUDENTS setting up a business: https://egov.deri.ie/PublicServices/Service/IR_set-up-a-business	Ireland: http://dbpedia.org/resource/Ireland	University: organization

(continued)

Table 8 (continued)

Twit body	Twit link	Extracted public services	Extracted entities by Dbpedia spotlight	Extracted entities by alchemyAPI
That clothing allowance does hit this month look at Gawd	https://twitter.com/Heartbreak_Rell/status/574648994296557569	Clothing allowance: https://egov.deri.ie/PublicServices/Service/CA_goc_clothing_allowance		
Anyone who knows how and where I can apply for an Irish visa? #help	https://twitter.com/iSa3oood/status/430146950743465984	Apply for an Irish Visa: https://egov.deri.ie/PublicServices/Service/IR_apply-for-an-irish-visa	Visa: http://dbpedia.org/resource/Visa_(document)	
Apparently I haven't been getting my civilian clothing allowance for the last 4 years, so I'm getting a nice bonus from the Army as I leave	https://twitter.com/NewKindOfClown/status/581587474281054210	Clothing allowance: https://egov.deri.ie/PublicServices/Service/CA_goc_clothing_allowance		Army: organization 4 years: quantity
Apply for taxi licences, public entertainment licences, street trader licences and more online	https://twitter.com/HighlandCouncil/status/423061295240589312	Licences, public entertainment: https://egov.deri.ie/PublicServices/Service/UK_LICENCES_PUBLIC_ENTERTAINMENT		
Are you joining us tonight? Global citizenship education work: a look at Uganda in EME2202 with @Mrs_KV and Dr. Broom 4:15-4:45	https://twitter.com/UBCedO/status/575774662719762432	Citizenship Education: https://egov.deri.ie/PublicServices/Service/UK_CITIZENSHIP_EDUCATION	Uganda: http://dbpedia.org/resource/Uganda	Uganda: Country Dr. Broom: person

From Tables 6 and 7, the Path semantic similarity measure produces better recall than the ESA metrics (from 0.9189 to 1.0). However, ESA outperforms the Path measure in terms of precision (0.75–0.97). These results somewhat indicate the conditions under which the two semantic metrics could be used.

5.2 Evaluation of the NER Implementation

Our goal here is to determine the level of recall and accuracy of the NER tool built upon our lexicon. Specifically, for demonstration purposes we encoded our lexicon as a simple dictionary to support the identification of mentions of public service names in tweets from a filtered Twitter stream. Specifically, we compared the performance of our NER against two well-known general purpose NER tools—Alchemy and Dbpedia Spotlight. Table 8 presents the comparison of the performance of the three tools. Based on the results, our NER implementation outperforms the two generic tools. However these tools identify other named entity types such as: organizations, persons, country and location that, when combined, provides rich contextual information for the identified public services. Thus, simultaneous use of the generic tools to support NER implementations based on our lexicon is recommended. We elaborate on the implications of this approach further in the next section.

6 Summary

In this paper we have investigated the use of Semantic Web and Natural Language Processing technologies in the context of e-government. In particular, the last decade has seen a big shift in e-government from simple Web 2.0 solutions to more advanced platforms integrating information from external sources such as social media, blogs and variety of e-government websites. This implies the use of certain Web 3.0 and NLP technologies, enabling effective information extraction, dealing with information overload and low quality contributions. Although many solutions applying automatic information extraction methods for analyzing external e-government, related content have been deployed, these solutions demand significant manual engineering efforts (manual annotations) to build. Moreover the expensive, manual annotations pose a significant limitation to scaling the information extraction solutions to address the ever-growing demands of the web content processing.

In this paper we have shown that dedicated lexical resource can significantly boost the information extraction capabilities in the domain of government and at the same time ensure scaling into a domain-ontology. The lexicon was constructed using two datasets comprising public service names in UK and Ireland with the relations in the graph calculated based on specific similarity measures between public service names. The resulting lexicon or knowledge graph is constructed in a way that can be easily expanded to include new external data sources. Central to our approach is the development of a Semantic Alignment Algorithm, which organizes a set of public service names automatically captured from input websites in a semantic network based on a semantic relatedness measures. We also investigated several similarity measures to determine the best distance measures for building the lexicon. Our analysis shows strong correlation between investigated measures, in particular in the case of solutions based on WordNet dictionary. Here the results provided by PATH are strongly correlated with all the other results. However the only measure that does not apply WordNet called Explicit Semantics Analysis (ESA) presented significantly better performance in terms of precision. However, PATH measure more robust in terms of recall with respect to ESA.

Results from our work, show that a dedicated NER tool powered by the domain-specific lexicon could provide a first significant step towards building scalable and effective, next-generation NER solutions for e-government applications as well as contributing towards building extensive semantic map for e-government domain concepts. We have also shown that dedicated our NER solution outperforms the generic, of-the-shelf analytical solutions in identifying public services names on the web; therefore further development of custom solutions (based on the generic methodology presented in Sect. 3) is recommended. Moreover as shown in our results, a combination of the dedicated NER, supplied with rich contextual information provided by generic NER solutions can be assembled into very powerful tool for e-government information analytics. The example use of the NER tool for identifying mentions of public service names on social media discussions opens up a possibility for completely new set of capabilities for public services' and citizen-perception evaluation.

7 Conclusions

Motivated by the need to provide the necessary step towards facilitating identification and extraction of e-government related information from the web, we have described the process for developing a domain-specific lexicon and a dedicated NER solution for public services. The solution enables consolidation and enrichment of information on public services from variety of government catalogs, websites, blogs and social media in a single knowledge graph. Results described in this chapter show the immediate opportunities for developing and consolidating the domain-specific lexical resources, Semantic Web and NLP technologies into a rich analytical infrastructure for e-government. However, there are more rooms for a larger scale evaluation of the resources and associated semantic alignment algorithms. Next steps in the research include development of rich lexical resources and associated NER tools for other aspects of the e-government domain such as policy and regulations followed by the respective NER tool in different e-government subdomains. We also intend to further improve our Semantic Alignment Algorithm and consolidate the developed lexica into a comprehensive e-government semantic map or knowledge map to be used by variety of domain-specific applications.

References

1. Agichtein, E., et al. (2008). Finding high-quality content in social media. In *Proceedings of the International Conference on Web Search and Web Data Mining—WSDM '08* (p. 183).
2. Alani, H., et al. (2003). *Web based knowledge extraction and consolidation for automatic ontology instantiation*. Available at: http://eprints.soton.ac.uk/258325/1/Alani-SEMANNOT-camera-ready.pdf. Accessed June 5, 2014.
3. Alfonseca, E., & Manandhar, S. (2002). An unsupervised method for general named entity recognition and automated concept discovery. In ... *Conference on General ....* Available at: http://www-users.cs.york.ac.uk/~suresh/papers/AUMFGNERAACD.pdf. Accessed July 1, 2013.
4. Amato, F., et al. (2009). Semantic management of multimedia documents for e-Government activity. In *2009 International Conference on Complex, Intelligent and Software Intensive Systems* (pp. 1193–1198). Available at: http://ieeexplore.ieee.org/lpdocs/epic03/wrapper.htm?arnumber=5066947. Accessed September 20, 2014.
5. Anon. (2015). *DCMI Metadata terms, Dublin core metadata initiative*. Available at: http://dublincore.org/documents/dcmi-terms/. Accessed April 10, 2015.
6. Anon. (2015). *e-government core vocabularies: The SEMIC.EU approach*. Retrieved from European Commission—Directorate-General Informatics. Available at: http://www.semic.eu/semic/view/documents/egov-core-vocabularies.pdf. Accessed April 10, 2015.
7. Anon. (2010). *European interoperability framework (EIF)—Towards interoperability for European public services*, p. 6. Available at: http://ec.europa.eu/isa/documents/isa_annex_ii_eif_en.pdf. Accessed April 10, 2015.
8. Asahara, M., & Matsumoto, Y. (2003). Japanese named entity extraction with redundant morphological analysis. In *Proceedings of the 2003 Conference of the North American Chapter of the Association for Computational Linguistics on Human Language Technology—NAACL '03* (pp. 8–15). Morristown, NJ, USA: Association for Computational Linguistics. Available at: http://dl.acm.org/citation.cfm?id=1073445.1073447. Accessed June 5, 2014.
9. Ashley, H., et al. (2009). Change at hand: Web 2.0 for development. *Participatory Learning and Action, 59*, 8–20.
10. Banerjee, S., & Pedersen, T. (2002). An adapted Lesk algorithm for word sense disambiguation using WordNet. In *Computational linguistics and intelligent text processing* (pp. 136–145). Berlin Heidelberg: Springer.
11. Bernadette, H., Atemezing, G., & Villazón-Terrazas, B. (2014). *Best practices for publishing linked data*. Available at: http://www.w3.org/TR/ld-bp/. Accessed April 10, 2015.
12. Berners-Lee, T. J. (1992). The world-wide web. *Computer Networks and ISDN Systems, 25*(4–5), 454–459. Available at: http://www.sciencedirect.com/science/article/pii/016975529 290039S. Accessed June 2, 2014.
13. Berners-Lee, T. (1989). *The original proposal of the WWW, HTMLized*. Available at: http://www.w3.org/History/1989/proposal.html
14. Berners-Lee, T., Hendler, J., & Lassila, O. (2001). The semantic web. *Scientific American*. Available at: http://www.scientificamerican.com/article/the-semantic-web/
15. Bikel, D. M., et al. (1997). Nymble. In *Proceedings of the Fifth Conference on Applied Natural Language Processing* (pp. 194–201). Morristown, NJ, USA: Association for Computational Linguistics. Available at: http://dl.acm.org/citation.cfm?id=974557.974586. Accessed June 5, 2014.
16. Bizer, C., et al. (2009). DBpedia—A crystallization point for the web of data. *Web Semantics: Science, Services and Agents on the World Wide Web, 7*(3), 154–165. Available at: http://www.sciencedirect.com/science/article/pii/S1570826809000225. Accessed May 24, 2014.
17. Bodenreider, O., & McCray, A. T. (1998). From French vocabulary to the unified medical language system: A preliminary study. *Studies in Health Technology and Informatics, 52* (1), 670–674. Available at: http://www.ncbi.nlm.nih.gov/pubmed/10384539

18. Borthwick, A., & Sterling, J. (1998). NYU: Description of the MENE named entity system as used in MUC-7. ... *Conference (MUC-7.* Available at: http://citeseerx.ist.psu.edu/viewdoc/summary?doi=10.1.1.108.6430. Accessed June 5, 2014.

19. Bountouri, L., et al. (2008). Metadata interoperability in public sector information. *Journal of Information Science, 35*(2), 204–231. Available at: http://jis.sagepub.com/cgi/doi/10.1177/0165551508098601. Accessed September 19, 2014.

20. Buitelaar, P., & Ramaka, S. (2005). Unsupervised ontology-based semantic tagging for knowledge markup. *Workshop on Learning in Web Search at 22nd ....* Available at: http://cosco.hiit.fi/search/learninginsearch05/ICMLW4-LWS.pdf#page=34. Accessed July 9, 2013.

21. Chang, A. (2008) Leveraging web 2.0 in government E-government/technology series leveraging web 2.0 in government.

22. Charalabidis, Y., & Loukis, E. (2011). *Transforming government agencies' approach to eParticipation through efficient exploitation of social media.*

23. Claes, A., et al. (2010, December). *WeGOV project: Where eGovernment meets the eSociety, initial WeGov toolbox* (pp. 1–65).

24. Dalianis, H., Rosell, M., & Sneiders, E. (2010). Clustering e-mails for the Swedish social insurance agency—What part of the e-mail thread gives the best quality ? (pp. 115–120).

25. Dalvi, B., Cohen, W., & Callan, J. (2012). Websets: Extracting sets of entities from the web using unsupervised information extraction. In ... *ACM international conference on Web ....* Available at: http://www.cs.cmu.edu/~bbd/wsdm2012.pdf. Accessed June 5, 2014.

26. Davis, B., et al. (2010). Squeezing lemon with GATE.

27. Denny, J. C., et al. (2003). "Understanding" medical school curriculum content using KnowledgeMap. *Journal of the American Medical Informatics Association: JAMIA, 10*(4), 351–62. Available at: http://www.pubmedcentral.nih.gov/articlerender.fcgi?artid=181986&tool=pmcentrez&rendertype=abstract

28. Ding, L., Peristeras, V., & Hausenblas, M. (2012). Government data. *IEEE Computer,* (January 2010), 11–15.

29. Embley, D. W., et al. (1998). Ontology-based extraction and structuring of information from data-rich unstructured documents. In *Proceedings of the Seventh International Conference on Information and Knowledge Management—CIKM '98* (pp. 52–59). New York, New York, USA: ACM Press. Available at: http://dl.acm.org/citation.cfm?id=288627.288641. Accessed June 5, 2014.

30. Etzioni, O., et al. (2008). Open information extraction from the web. *Communications of the ACM, 51*(12), 68. Available at: http://dl.acm.org/ft_gateway.cfm?id=1409378&type=html. Accessed June 5, 2014.

31. Etzioni, O., et al. (2005). Unsupervised named-entity extraction from the web: An experimental study. *Artificial Intelligence, 165*(1), 91–134. Available at: http://www.sciencedirect.com/science/article/pii/S0004370205000366. Accessed May 26, 2014.

32. Fader, A., Soderland, S., & Etzioni, O. (2011). Identifying relations for open information extraction. In *Proceedings of the Conference on ...,* (pp. 1535–1545). Available at: http://dl.acm.org/citation.cfm?id=2145432.2145596. Accessed June 5, 2014.

33. Frank, M., & Eric, M. (2014) *RDF primer.* Available at: http://www.w3.org/TR/rdf-primer/

34. Freitag, D., & McCallum, A. (1999). Information extraction with HMMs and shrinkage. In ... *on machine learning for information extraction.* Available at: http://www.aaai.org/Papers/Workshops/1999/WS-99-11/WS99-11-006.pdf. Accessed June 5, 2014.

35. French, L., et al. (2009). Application and evaluation of automated semantic annotation of gene expression experiments. *Bioinformatics (Oxford, England), 25*(12), 1543–1549. Available at: http://www.pubmedcentral.nih.gov/articlerender.fcgi?artid=2687992&tool=pmcentrez&rendertype=abstract. Accessed September 19, 2014.

36. Gabrilovich, E., & Markovitch, S. (2007). Computing semantic relatedness using wikipedia-based explicit semantic analysis. In: *IJCAI International Joint Conference on Artificial Intelligence* (pp. 1606–1611).

37. Gao, H., Barbier, G., & Goolsby, R. (2011). Harnessing the crowdsourcing power of social media for disaster relief. *IEEE Intelligent Systems, 26*, 10–14.
38. García-Sánchez, F., et al. (2011). Applying intelligent agents and semantic web services in eGovernment environments. *Expert Systems*, p.no–no. Available at: http://doi. wiley.com/10.1111/j.1468-0394.2011.00586.x. Accessed September 19, 2014.
39. Gheorghiu, C., & Nicolescu, R. (2011). SIGMA-semantIc government mash-up application: Using semantic web technologies to provide access to governmental data. ... *(ISPDC), 2011 10th* .... Available at: http://ieeexplore.ieee.org/xpls/abs_all.jsp?arnumber=6108280. Accessed June 5, 2014.
40. Goudos, S. K., et al. (2007). Public administration domain ontology for a semantic web services e-government framework 2. In *Related work : E-government models and 3. The governance enterprise architecture., (Scc)*.
41. Grishman, R. (1996). Message understanding conference-6: A brief history. In *Proceedings of COLING*, 96.
42. Gruber, T. R. (1995). Toward principles for the design of ontologies used for knowledge sharing? *International Journal of Human-Computer Studies, 43*(5–6), 907–928. Available at: http://www.sciencedirect.com/science/article/pii/S1071581985710816. Accessed June 2, 2014.
43. Hayes, P. F. P.-S. P., & Ian, H. (2004). *OWL web ontology language semantics and abstract syntax*. Available at: http://www.w3.org/TR/owl-semantics/
44. Hevner, A., & Chatterjee, S. (2010). Design research in information systems. In *Integrated series in information systems. Integrated series in information systems* (pp. 9–23). Boston, MA: Springer US.
45. Hinkelmann, K., Thönssen, B., & Probst, F. (2006). *Reference modeling and lifecycle management for e-government services., (Imi)*.
46. Hirst, G., & St-Onge, D. (1998). Lexical chains as representations of context for the detection and correction of malapropisms. *WordNet: An electronic lexical database, 305*, 305–332.
47. Hoffart, J., et al. (2011). *Robust disambiguation of named entities in text*, (pp. 782–792). Available at: http://dl.acm.org/citation.cfm?id=2145432.2145521. Accessed June 5, 2014.
48. Hoxha, J., & Brahaj, A. (2011). Open government data on the web: A semantic approach. *Emerging intelligent data and web* .... Available at: http://ieeexplore.ieee.org/xpls/abs_all.jsp?arnumber=6076428. Accessed June 5, 2014.
49. Hreňo, J., et al. (2011, April). Integration of government services using semantic technologies. *Journal of theoretical and* .... Available at: http://www.scielo.cl/scielo.php?pid=S0718-18762011000100010&script=sci_arttext&tlng=pt. Accessed April 2, 2014.
50. Ji, H., & Grishman, R. (2006). *Data selection in semi-supervised learning for name tagging*, (pp. 48–55). Available at: http://dl.acm.org/citation.cfm?id=1641408.1641414. Accessed June 5, 2014.
51. Jiang, J. J., & Conrath, D. W. (1997). Semantic similarity based on corpus statistics and lexical taxonomy.arXiv:preprint cmp-lg/9709008.
52. Kamegai, S. (2002). Toward ontology-based knowledge extraction from biomedical literature. *Genome informatics ...*, 577(2002), 576–577. Available at: http://jsbi2013.sakura. ne.jp/pdfs/journal1/GIW02/GIW02P078.pdf. Accessed July 9, 2013.
53. Klischewski, R. (2003). Semantic web for e-government. *Electronic government*. Available at: http://link.springer.com/chapter/10.1007/10929179_52. Accessed June 5, 2014.
54. Ku, C. H., et al. (2006). Natural language processing and e-government: Crime information extraction from heterogeneous data sources. In *The proceedings of the 9th Annual International Digital Government Research Conference* (pp. 162–170). ACM International Conference Proceedings Series, ACM Press.
55. Kulkarni, S. et al. (2009). Collective annotation of Wikipedia entities in web text. In *Proceedings of the 15th ACM SIGKDD International Conference on Knowledge Discovery and Data Mining—KDD '09* (p. 457). New York, New York, USA: ACM Press. Available at: http://dl.acm.org/citation.cfm?id=1557019.1557073. Accessed May 28, 2014.

56. Kuzma, J. (2010, March). Asian Government Usage of Web 2. 0 Social Media. *Sites The Journal Of 20th Century Contemporary French Studies* (pp. 1–13).
57. Leacock, C., Miller, G. A., & Chodorow, M. (1998). Using corpus statistics and WordNet relations for sense identification. *Computational Linguistics, 24*(1), 147–165.
58. Lin, D. (1998). An information-theoretic definition of similarity. In ICML(Vol. 98, pp. 296–304).
59. Lin, T., Etzioni, O., & Fogarty, J. (2009). Identifying interesting assertions from the web. In *Proceeding of the 18th ACM Conference on Information and Knowledge Management—CIKM '09* (p. 1787). New York, New York, USA: ACM Press. Available at: http://dl.acm.org/citation.cfm?id=1645953.1646230. Accessed June 5, 2014.
60. Loutas, N., Lee, D., & Maali, F. (2011). The semantic public service portal (S-PSP). In G. Antoniou (Ed.), *ESWC 2011*. LNCS 6644 (pp. 227–242). Springer-Verlag. Available at: http://link.springer.com/chapter/10.1007/978-3-642-21064-8_16. Accessed August 19, 2014.
61. Macintosh, A., Coleman, S., & Schneeberger, A. (2009). *eParticipation: The research gaps* (pp. 1–11).
62. Makinen, M., & Wangu Kuira, M. (2008). Social media and postelection crisis in Kenya. *The International Journal of Press/Politics, 13*(3), 328–335.
63. Markellos, K., et al. (2007). Semantic web search for e-government: The case study of intrastat 1 introduction. *Journal of Internet Technology, 8*(4), 457–468.
64. Marshall, C. C., & Shipman, F. M. (2003). Which semantic web? In *Proceedings of the Fourteenth ACM Conference on Hypertext and Hypermedia—HYPERTEXT '03* (p. 57). New York, New York, USA: ACM Press. Available at: http://dl.acm.org/citation.cfm?id=900051.900063. Accessed June 5, 2014.
65. McCallum, A., & Li, W. (2003). Early results for named entity recognition with conditional random fields, feature induction and web-enhanced lexicons. In *Proceedings of the Seventh Conference on Natural Language Learning at HLT-NAACL 2003* (pp. 188–191). Morristown, NJ, USA: Association for Computational Linguistics. Available at: http://dl.acm.org/citation.cfm?id=1119176.1119206. Accessed June 5, 2014.
66. McGuinness, D. L., & van Harmelen, F. (2004). *OWL web ontology language overview.* Available at: http://www.w3.org/TR/owl-features/
67. Mccrae, J., et al. (2012). Interchanging lexical resources on the semantic web. *Language Resources and Evaluation, 46*(4), 701–719.
68. Mccrae, J., Spohr, D., & Cimiano, P. (2011). Linking lexical resources and ontologies on the semantic web with lemon. In *ESWC'11 Proceedings of the 8th Extended Semantic Web Conference—Volume Part I* (pp. 245–259).
69. Medjahed, B., Bouguettaya, A., & Ouzzani, M. (2003). Semantic web enabled e-government services. In *Proceedings of the 2003 ....* Available at: http://dl.acm.org/citation.cfm?id=1123287. Accessed June 5, 2014.
70. Miller, S., Crystal, M., & Fox, H. (1998). Algorithms that learn to extract information BBN: Description of the sift system as used for MUC-7. ... In *Conference (MUC-7).* Available at: http://aclweb.org/anthology//M/M98/M98-1009.pdf. Accessed June 5, 2014.
71. Misuraca, G., Broster, D., & Centeno, C. (2012). Digital Europe 2030: Designing scenarios for ICT in future governance and policy making. *Government Information Quarterly, 29,* S121–S131. Available at: http://www.sciencedirect.com/science/article/pii/S0740624X11000724. Accessed June 5, 2014.
72. Moreno-ortiz, A., & Hernández, C. P. (2013). *Lexicon—Based sentiment analysis of twitter messages in Spanish* (pp. 93–100).
73. Nadeau, D., & Sekine, S. (2007). A survey of named entity recognition and classification. *Lingvisticae Investigationes, 30*(1), 3–26. Available at: http://www.ingentaconnect.com/content/jbp/li/2007/00000030/00000001/art00002. Accessed June 3, 2014.
74. Nam, T. (2013). Government 3.0 in Korea: Fad or fashion? In *Proceedings of the 7th International Conference on ....* Available at: http://dl.acm.org/citation.cfm?id=2591896. Accessed August 19, 2014.

75. Ojo, A., Estevez, E., & Janowski, T. (2010). Semantic interoperability architecture for Governance 2.0. *Information Polity, 15*(1), 105–123.
76. Ortiz-rodr, F., & Villaz, B. (2006). *Legal Ontologies for the Spanish e-Government* (pp. 301–310).
77. O'reilly, T. (2007). What is web 2.0: Design patterns and business models for the next generation of software. *Communications & Strategies, 65*(4578), 17–37.
78. Panopoulou, E., Tambouris, E. & Tarabanis, K. (2010). eParticipation initiatives in Europe : Learning from practitioners. *Ifip International Federation for Information Processing* (pp. 54–65).
79. Peffers, K., et al. (2007). A design science research methodology for information systems research. *Journal of Management Information Systems, 24*(3), 45–77.
80. Phil, A., Stijn, G., & Nikolaos, L. (2013). *Core public service vocabulary specification.* Available at: https://joinup.ec.europa.eu/sites/default/files/72/94/04/D5.1.2—Core Public Service Vocabulary specification v0.05.pdf. Accessed April 10, 2015.
81. Resnik, P. (1995). Using information content to evaluate semantic similarity in a taxonomy. arXiv:https://preprint cmplg/ 9511007
82. Reuter, C., & Marx, A. (2011, May). Social software as an infrastructure for crisis management—A case study about current practice and potential usage. In *Proceedings of the 8th International ISCRAM Conference* (pp. 1–10).
83. Schreiber, R., & Swick, G. (2006). *Semantic web best practices and deployment working group.* Available at: http://www.w3.org/2001/sw/BestPractices/
84. Sheth, A., et al. (2002). Managing semantic content for the Web. *IEEE Internet Computing, 6*(4), 80–87. Available at: http://ieeexplore.ieee.org/lpdocs/epic03/wrapper.htm?arnumber=1020330. Accessed June 5, 2014.
85. Skounakis, M., Craven, M., & Ray, S. (2003). Hierarchical hidden markov models for information extraction. *IJCAI.* Available at: http://papercut.googlecode.com/hg-history/98464a c0efb47c55159b313c89b0b305ba1d83f9/PaperCutTesting/targetPDF/success/hhmm.pdf. Accessed June 5, 2014.
86. Small, S., & Medsker, L. (2013). Review of information extraction technologies and applications. *Neural computing and applications.* Available at: http://link.springer.com/article/10.1007/s00521-013-1516-6. Accessed June 5, 2014.
87. Soderland, S. (1999). Learning information extraction rules for semi-structured and free text. *Machine learning, 34*(1–3), 233–272. Available at: http://link.springer.com/article/10.102 3/A:1007562322031. Accessed June 5, 2014.
88. Stadlhofer, B., Salhofer, P., & Tretter, G. (2009). Ontology driven E-government. In *2009 Fourth International Conference on Systems, 7*(4), 251–255. Available at: http://ieeexplore.ie ee.org/lpdocs/epic03/wrapper.htm?arnumber=4976353
89. Suchanek, F., Kasneci, G., & Weikum, G. (2007). Yago: A core of semantic knowledge. In *Proceedings of the 16th ...* (p. 697). Available at: http://dl.acm.org/citation.cfm ?id=1242572.1242667. Accessed June 5, 2014.
90. Tsai, T. -M., et al. (2003). Ontology-mediated integration of intranet web services. *Computer, 36*(10), 63–71. Available at: http://ieeexplore.ieee.org/xpls/abs_all.jsp?arnumber=1236473. Accessed June 5, 2014.
91. Uschold, M., & Gruninger, M. (2009). Ontologies: Principles, methods and applications. *The Knowledge Engineering Review, 11*(02), 93. Available at: http://journals.cambridge.org/abstract_S0269888900007797. Accessed June 5, 2014.
92. Vossen, P., & Rambousek, A. (2008). A distributed database system for developing ontological and lexical resources in harmony. In *Computational linguistics and intelligent text processing* (pp. 1–15).
93. Wu, Z., & Palmer, M. (1994). Verbs semantics and lexical selection. In Proceedings of the 32nd annual meeting on Association for Computational Linguistics (pp. 133–138). Association for Computational Linguistics.

Transport Policy: Social Media and User-Generated Content in a Changing Information Paradigm

S.M. Grant-Muller, A. Gal-Tzur, E. Minkov, T. Kuflik,
S. Nocera and I. Shoor

Abstract Rapid and recent developments in social media networks are providing a vision amongst transport suppliers, governments and academia of 'next-generation' information channels. This chapter identifies the main requirements for a social media information harvesting methodology in the transport context and highlights the challenges involved. Three questions are addressed concerning (1) The ways in which social media data can be used alongside or potentially instead of current transport data sources, (2) The technical challenges in text mining social media that create difficulties in generating high quality data for the transport sector and finally, (3) Whether there are wider institutional barriers in harnessing the potential of social media data for the transport sector. The chapter demonstrates that information harvested from social media can complement, enrich (or even replace) traditional data collection. Whilst further research is needed to develop automatic or semi-automatic methodologies for harvesting and analysing transport-related social media information, new skills are also needed in the sector to maximise the benefits of this new information source.

Keywords Social media · Transport planning · Transport policy · Text mining

S.M. Grant-Muller (✉)
Institute for Transport Studies, University of Leeds, 36–40 University Road,
Leeds LS2 9JT, UK
e-mail: S.M.Grant-Muller@its.leeds.ac.uk

E. Minkov · T. Kuflik
Department of Information Systems, University of Haifa, Haifa, Israel

S. Nocera
Department of Architecture and Arts, IUAV University of Venice,
Dorsoduro 2206, I-30123, Venice, Italy

A. Gal-Tzur
Transportation Research Institute, Technion - Israel Institute of Technology,
Technion City, Haifa, Israel

I. Shoor
Department of Computer Science, University of Haifa, Abba Khoushy Ave 199, Haifa, Israel

© Springer International Publishing Switzerland 2015   325
S. Nepal et al. (eds.), *Social Media for Government Services*,
DOI 10.1007/978-3-319-27237-5_15

1 Introduction and Definitions

The cultural revolution of social media is the first of the 21st century [28] and a central pillar of the new Information Age [16]. In considering the role of social media in the transport context, it is useful to first review the definitions and scope of this phenomena and how the general functionality presents an opportunity for the transport sector. This forms the backdrop to the remainder of the chapter, where the methods of extracting information and current uses of social media in transport are given detailed attention, using examples from recent research and real-life practice.

Many definitions of social media can be found in literature. Kaplan et al. [44] defined it as a group of Internet-based applications that build on the ideological and technological foundations of Web 2.0 that allow the creation and exchange of User Generated Content. Gartner Inc.[1] described it as an online environment where content is created, consumed, promoted, distributed, discovered or shared for purposes that are primarily related to communities and social activities, rather than functional, task-oriented objectives.

Millions of people now make use of a variety of online Web platforms to express their opinions, thoughts and experiences. Once a topic is raised by a participant in a social media network, typically others react and a "conversation" may develop. The nature and depth of the conversation largely depends on the application or web site providing the infrastructure for the social interaction, as reflected by the seven categories defined in Sterne [85]. As a result, it has already been shown that these platforms can serve as a reliable resource for public opinions as well as factual information across several disciplines.

Social media has created an opportunity for transport stakeholders and policy makers, where information flow has strategic importance both in long term planning and short term tactical system management. The important role that information plays in transport decision making ranges from understanding choices and preferences (e.g. on routes and modes) to participatory scheme evaluation [7]. Giannopoulos [37] defined seven categories of information use in transport at a more disaggregate level, whilst Kenyon and Lyons [46] highlight the role of traveller information in encouraging mode switch for more sustainable transport systems.

Existing research has already illustrated how social media may serve as a near real-time information source in the transport sector for tactical measures that require travel times, network demand or incident detection [56, 75, 33, 96]. Social media data may also support the development of strategic policies, such as those concerning levels of service quality and the study of activity-travel patterns [15, 22, 80]. Whilst previously various traditional tools such as surveys and interviews were used to obtain such data, this information is now freely available and easily accessible. The potential of the social media platform as a means to conduct transport surveys has already been recognized [5] and briefly demonstrated [30].

The general characteristics of social media that are of particular value for the transport sector include: the potential for all users to contribute content,

---

[1]http://www.gartner.com/it-glossary/social-media/.

dematerialization of data collection, community facilities (such as discussion boards/blogs, video sharing) and virtual meetings. Information harvesting may be: (1) dynamic, informing short-term decisions by system operators and users, or (2) off-line, supporting policy makers and stakeholders in forming improved policies.

Social media data could be harvested on-line directly from other transport users in a type of Advanced Traveller Information System, influencing important travel choices: departure time, route and mode choice. The information harvested might also have secondary influences on traveller destination choice and activity patterns, whilst the framework developed might assist policy makers and stakeholders in an understanding those choices. Social media is a new and effective means for organisations to communicate with customers and members of the public. Increased engagement with social media has happened from both bottom up (the public and users of the transport system) and top down (by the transport system stakeholders who operate, provide services and develop policies for the system). A number of transport sector organisations use social media as a strategic tool to reach out to customers, using social media as a 'help line' for customer service or for real time information. Users' perceptions of the transport service may not reflect the outcomes of rational planning choices, but may be influenced by sensations [29, 59]. The collection of user views and perceptions is therefore essentially a commitment to evaluate differences between expected and perceived results and correct process deficiencies, rather than simply measure outcomes. The ability of social media to capture this dynamically at the time of the experience is a further source of added value.

Overall, the rapid and recent developments in social media networks are providing a vision amongst transport suppliers, governments and academia of 'next-generation' information channels. Policy makers in many countries have high expectations of the possible effects of such information services on, for example, network efficiency (e.g. [32, 87]), with the view that strategic policy may reduce transport impacts significantly [68]. These expectations provide momentum for transport research and development in the field of personal mobility and information provision, particularly in understanding customer perceptions in order to provide a new generation of travel information services.

However, the harvesting and processing of textual messages into meaningful and actionable information is not without its challenges. Relevant data must be identified from a very large data mass and social media content is mostly in natural language form, which cannot be readily interpreted, queried, or aggregated. For these reasons, relevant information must be 'harvested' using text mining techniques [58, 73]. A key question is whether social media information is of sufficient quality to meet the needs of the system operators/policy makers and travellers who, through traveller information systems, may also be end-users of the information.

This chapter identifies the main requirements for a social media information harvesting methodology in the transport context and highlights the challenges involved. Specifically, the goal is to address the following questions:

(1) In which ways can social media data be used alongside or potentially instead of current transport data sources?
(2) What technical challenges in text mining social media data create difficulties in generating high quality data for the transport sector?

(3) Are there wider institutional barriers in harnessing the potential of social media data for the transport sector in addition to the technical challenges?

The answers to these questions will enable policy makers to assess the challenges in obtaining information from social media text sources and properly assess the ways in which it can then be used, for example in either fusing the data with that from other sources or processing it as an additional data stream.

The remainder of the chapter is organised into the following sections. Following an overview of the role of data in transport planning and policy in Sect. 2, the sources of social media transport data and rationale for harvesting the data are given in Sect. 3. An overview of the text mining process in general is provided in Sect. 4, with an illustration of a method for harvesting useful social media information for transport policy in Sect. 5. This draws on a multidisciplinary interface between transport science and text mining expertise, establishing 'what' should be harvested and 'how' it can be harvested. A review of the specific challenges and the state-of-the-art and in text mining techniques to obtain transport-related data from social media text sources is then provided in Sect. 6. A top-down perspective is then taken to illustrate the manner in which different selected transport providers currently use social media in Sect. 7. Within this a reflection on institutional issues is given, considering whether technical or institutional issues are the greater obstacle and informing the direction for future research directions. Finally, concluding remarks are provided in Sect. 8.

2 The Role of Data in Transport Planning and Policy

Information flow plays a central role in the decisions made by transport system users in how, when and whether to travel. It also supports recovery in cases of unexpected disruption [66, 67]. The question is therefore whether current data streams can be either integrated with (or replaced by) new sources, to provide cost effective and potentially more complete information.

In order to answer this question, it is first useful to assess the needs for information as part of transport sector policy and operational objectives. These vary between countries, modes and potentially regions and operators, but typically include a mixture of objectives such as efficiency, safety, reliability, environmental sustainability and traveller experience (including information). Table 1 provides example objectives and more detailed service provision for firstly highways and secondly public transport (adapted from Innovateuk [43], Metro [60]).

A typology of primary data needs, data sources and the potential role of social media is given in Table 2, which draws on sources including the CHARM specifications [43] and other public transport (PT) service performance specifications (for example [66]). The first column of Table 2 is cross-referenced with the higher level policy objectives summarised in Table 1, indicating the link between the different data sources and both operational and policy objectives.

Existing transport systems often comprise layers of technologies and monitoring equipment that have accumulated as technology has advanced [39]. However

Table 1 Archetypal objectives for highways and public transport

Highways objectives	Service outcomes
(1) To deliver a *safe* journey on the road network	• Dynamic traffic warnings
	• Control traffic (e.g. speed signals)
	• Incident management—protect event scene
	• Continuity management
	• Operate tunnels
	• Maintain safety in operation of hard shoulder lanes
	• Provide safe roadworks
	• Maintain safety during technical failures
(2) To deliver a ***reliable and smooth*** journey on the road network	• Set detours
	• Incident management
	• Deploy traffic scenarios
	• Set traffic management measures
	• Operate hard shoulder lanes
	• Limit disturbance of road works
	• Maintenance, tuning and configuration of traffic management systems
	• Maintain road functions in case of failures and blockades
(3) To deliver ***reliable and useful*** information to road users	• Traffic management messages
	• Traffic information through service providers and dedicated channels
	• Information via VMS and other roadside equipment
	• Information on road works
	• Information through social media
(4) To operate the road network in a ***sustainable*** way	• Dynamic speed control
	• Virtual patrolling
	• Decision making supported by intelligence
Public transport objectives	Service outcomes
(1) Reduced congestion	• Optimising the use of the existing road space through traffic management, regulation and enforcement
	• Encouraging modal shift to public transport, walking and cycling
	• Manage demand for travel including promotion of land use policies and practices to reduce the need to travel
	• Effective and efficient management of road works, events and other potential sources of delay and disruption on the road network
	• Providing information to enable more informed travel choices
(2) Better control of street works and incident management	• Ensure safety is not compromised by unplanned events
	• Minimise the impact of unforeseen incidents
	• Ensure co-ordination in the management of unplanned events
	• Develop resilience to ensure that the existing network can be used to its full capacity, reducing the demands on other less suitable routes

(continued)

Table 1 (continued)

Public transport objectives	Service outcomes
(3) Reduced bus journey times	• Optimising the use of the existing road space through traffic management, regulation and enforcement
	• Monitoring trends in the growth of traffic
	• Identifying appropriate policy actions
	• Implementing initiatives and schemes which support sustainable travel
(4) Reduce the cost of disruption and congestion	• Effective and efficient management of road works, events and other potential sources of delay and disruption
(5) Increase journey time reliability	• Effective and efficient management of road works, events and other potential sources of delay and disruption
(6) Encourage mode shift to more sustainable modes of travel	• Encouraging modal shift to public transport, walking and cycling
(7) Ensure service quality, passenger comfort, cleanliness	• Effective passenger information
	• Monitor overcrowding
	• Monitor cleanliness
	• Effective customer services

the distribution of instrumentation can be patchy, resulting in some geographic areas with dense data collection and others with sparse data (typically rural). This gives rise to two challenges: the first is whether new data forms can be integrated with other data sources to create new or better quality knowledge [15] and the second is whether there is the possibility to adopt various 'user generated data' where current data collection is sparse [14].

The many sources of new technology-enabled data include textual social media, Geographic Information Systems (GIS) and digital data from Intelligent Transport Systems (ITS). The potential for information enrichment arises from data collection at various levels of aggregation and with some sources providing associated 'clues' to the socio-economic characteristics associated with individual data units.

Uses may include monitoring system performance, informing new policies based on expected demand, providing cost effective, more detailed and potentially more complete information on context, improving understanding of behavior and perceptions that underlie mode choice [52] and enriching the understanding of scheme impacts [68]. They may serve to improve the efficiency and effectiveness of current databases, for example through reconciling data contradictions and reducing redundant data collection. To answer both challenges fully a further significant tranche of research is needed.

3 The Role of Social Media Information in Transport

This section begins by providing an overview of some archetypal sources of transport related social media data, including sources that are not specific to the transport domain. The features available in these, together with the analysis reported in

Table 2 Overview of current and new transport data sources

Data purpose	Data issues	Potential role of social media or new technology data
Speed monitoring Provides estimated travel time for traffic management and ATIS (Highways objectives 1 and 3, PT objectives 1, 2, 3, 4, 5, 7) **Current data sources:** 1) ANPR camera 2) Loops (e.g. MIDAS) embedded in the highway	**1) ANPR** • Automatic data collection following installation (Fixed location) • Can capture large proportion of population at location Costly to maintain • Accuracy in plate reading and matching, e.g. in poor weather • Data is obtained without explicit consent • No user characteristics for each trip • Applicable to motorized vehicles only **2) Loops (MIDAS)** • Automatic data collection following installation (Fixed location or temporary loops) • Can capture large proportion of population at location • Faulty loops generate data gaps and errors, which can be substantive • Loop maintenance costs and costs of downloading/processing data • Speed is inferred and smoothed, missing spikes in actual vehicle speed • No user characteristics for each trip • Applicable to vehicles only	**GPS tracking** (e.g. on mobile phone) • Can generate speeds • Tracking has some errors in measurement • Data is generated automatically • GPS data is given by consent • Basic user characteristics possible • Can be applied to non-motorized modes (such as bike riders and pedestrians) **Cellular based monitoring** • Less accurate than GPS based (accuracy is usually proportional to cell size) • However it does not require activation of a GPS-based app • The number of samples is much higher (to compensate for the accuracy of identification of any single probe) • Cellular operators provide the data to the companies calculating speeds/travel time • Privacy is preserved by assigning each probe an ID which is different than the original ID of phone

(continued)

Table 2 (continued)

Data purpose	Data issues	Potential role of social media or new technology data
Constructing O-D movements Provides estimates of demand to policy decisions and traffic management strategies (Highways objectives 2 and 4, PT objectives 1, 6, 7) **Current data sources:** 1) ANPR camera and 2) RP/SP questionnaires	1) **ANPR** (Issues as above) 2) **RP/SP** • Allows bespoke design and can collect user characteristics • Resource intensive • Potential sampling and other sources of bias e.g. in administration of complex design • Response rate/participation may not be high	**Social media text content** • Content can contain O-D data, but coverage may be limited • Depends on users choosing to contribute content • Socio-economic and contextual data may be present alongside O-D **GPS tracking** • Can generate individual O-D movements for full trip
Link demand Provides estimates of demand to policy decisions and traffic management strategies (Highways objectives 1, 2, 3, 4, PT objectives 1, 2, 3, 4, 5) **Current data sources:** 1) Roadside counts, 2) Loops (e.g.MIDAS) embedded in the highway, 3) RP/SP questionnaires **PT Mode demand** Provides information on demand for PT services to policy making and/or commercial decision making by suppliers (PT objectives 6,7) **Current data sources:** 1) In-mode counts, 2) Patronage data (e.g. ticket sales), 3) RP/SP questionnaires	1) **Roadside counts** • Manual process, resource intensive therefore limited sample possible • Human and other errors 2) **MIDAS** • Inaccuracies in vehicle classification • Other Issues as above 3) **RP/SP** (Issues as above) 1) **In-mode counts** • Can be targeted to areas/services of interest • Manual, therefore resource intensive • Limited sampling practical 2) **Patronage data** • Automatically collected • Large proportion of population can potentially captured • Commercially sensitive • Some inaccuracies e.g. in cross mode tickets 3) **RP/SP** (Issues as above)	**Social media text content** • May generate additional data on demand, but unlikely to capture total demand • Unlikely to identify specific link within a journey as part of content **GPS tracking** • Can generate link demand, but would need large scale monitoring to estimate total demand **Social media text content** • Useful for understand mode choice rationale • Unlikely to capture total • Demand • May capture evidence on demand for responsive services **GPS tracking** • Can generate evidence on mode demand • Large scale monitoring needed to estimate mode demand with confidence

(continued)

Table 2 (continued)

Data purpose	Data issues	Potential role of social media or new technology
Service quality and driver comfort Provides estimates of actual and perceived level of service to policy planning and operations (PT objectives 6,7) **Current data sources:** 1) RP/SP questionnaires	1) RP/SP (Issues as above)	**SM text content** • Analysis of text content effective in generating service quality data
Public opinion (e.g. new schemes or services) Inputs to long term policy development and planning decision (Highways objective 4, PT objectives 6,7) **Current data sources:** 1) Focus groups, Committees, Consultation meetings, 2) Household Questionnaires	1) Groups and meetings • Resource intensive • Limited samples possible • Sources of bias e.g. in participation 2) Household questionnaires • Resource intensive • Some biases e.g. in response rates	**Social media text content** • Analysis of text content effective in supplementing or replacing public opinion data sources
Detection of abnormal or undesirable event (various modes of transport) Inputs to day-to-day operations and ATIS. Includes incidents along the road network, train delays, packed bus, missing rental bikes etc. (Highways objectives 1 and 3) **Current data sources:** 1) Various types of physical devices (e.g. Video cameras, Loops, in mode counters etc.) and 2) Systems (such as patronage data, bike rental systems etc.)	1) Physical devices • Continuous monitoring • Level of accuracy is usually sufficient • High coverage is often costly 2) Management/operational/control systems • Systems often belong to private operators and the quality of data sharing is often a challenging issue • Such systems don't necessarily enable real time data processing which is required for event detection	**Social media text content** • Low cost for authority • Even a small number of similar reports constitute a solid basis for verifying the event • Many types of events can be detected in the same manner • Depends on human reporting • Time constraints require the use of very efficient text mining techniques

Source Adapted from Grant-Muller et al. [34]

early research form the basis for the rationale to harvest the data from these and other sources, presented in Sect. 3.2.

3.1 Sources of Transport Related Social Media Information

Transport-related information can be found in most forms of social media. HelloPeter.com, a platform dedicated to reviews and opinions, enables individuals to report the quality of service in many domains including transport (for example, on a late running bus service[2]). This platform also allows the service providers to respond. Transport-related forums often focus on a specific mode of transport, such as bikeforums[3] (serving the community of bicycle riders), and the Transport forum within Topix[4] that deals mainly, but not exclusively, with air transport issues. Transport-related information also appears in more general forums, such as those in Tripadvisor that focus on a specific city (for example, concerning transport to a national airport).[5] Social media applications also served as a catalyst for the emergence of social networks aimed at improving both participants personal mobility and general transport provision through shared information. As is the case with forums, these communities mostly focus on a specific mode of transport, such as the Facebook open group TRAFFIC UPDATE **LONDON-ESSEX-KENT**.[6] Facebook pages dedicated to traffic information updates or seeking a ride-share partner enable the users not only to post free text messages, but also to use "Like" and "Share" functions, expressing their approval of the message posted and their desire to reveal its content to their friends.

For the transport sector, the distinction between real-time or near real-time information and historic information is highly relevant. Forums, often containing and storing information over time, provide a different point of view on the transport system compared with social networks. The latter are often based on information exchange via mobile applications, and are mainly directed at real-time information. WAZE[7] is an example of a well-established application targeted towards users of private vehicles. It uses geo-spatial information automatically obtained from community members to infer current traffic conditions, which forms the basis on which to calculate the fastest route. The geo-spatial information is enhanced by user reports, either regarding pre-defined irregular events (such as

---

[2]3/12/14 traveller complaint on late running bus service in South Africa. http://hellopeter.com/greyhound/complaints/ruined-our-holiday-1577792.

[3]http://www.bikeforums.net/forum.php.

[4]http://www.topix.com/forum/business/transportation.

[5]27/4/14 a question in the Tel Aviv Forum within Tripadvisor asking about transport to national airport late at night http://www.tripadvisor.com/ShowTopic-g293984-i3332-k7406231-Getting_to_Ben_Gurion_middle_of_the_night-Tel_Aviv_Tel_Aviv_District.html.

[6]http://www.facebook.com/groups/369684789781652/?fref=ts.

[7]http://world.waze.com/?redirect=1.

accidents or a vehicle stopping on the hard shoulder) or any other unstructured textual information. Moovit[8] is a similar application focusing on PT journeys.

Twitter,[9] the wide-spear Micro Blogging application, is extremely effective for short real-time information delivery and status updates. Travellers use Twitter to report events related to different transport modes and different events. *"Traffic Lights All Out at the junction where the eastbound Westgate meets with the westbound offslip coming off the A58(M) Inner Ring Road"* is an example of an individual sharing information about malfunctioning traffic lights, whilst *"With no Central Line at Liverpool St youd think the Hammersmith/Circle lines might be working too. Obvs not#RAGE"* is expressing a complaint about the underground.

These examples provide the initial basis for the notion that content voluntarily contributed through social media by the public can assist in understanding users' needs, which is a precondition for developing and implementing user-led transport services. Analysing structured content (such as pre-defined reports sent by clicking a button or by tagging an item) is far more straightforward. Understanding free, unstructured text is a much more technically challenging task. This is especially true when dealing with text on social media. Such content often contains typographical errors, uses specialized language and lacks contextual information [62], especially in the case of short messages (such as micro-blogging).

As experts estimate that approximately 80 % of the data posted on social media is unstructured [53], it is therefore not surprising that research is increasingly turning towards the development of methods to analyse unstructured data. From this point forwards, this chapter focuses on the potential contribution of unstructured content towards improving transport planning and management.

3.2 Rationale and Hypothesis in Mining Social Media for Transport Policy

In recent years, researchers have made the first steps in addressing the challenge of applying text mining techniques to analyse transport related social media content. Gao et al. [35] demonstrated the potential of text mining techniques in analysing accident reports for the purposes of crash classification. Mai and Hranac [56] evaluated the use of data from Twitter as a potential complement to traffic incident data. They focused on Tweets that included geographic information and used semantic analysis (which assigns values to words with different connotations) then computed an overall ranking to identify tweets that are more likely to concern a traffic incident. The incident-related Tweets identified appeared to correlate with traffic incident records and were able to provide agencies with a user-centric perspective, namely context and sentiments, to the roadway incident reports.

---

[8]http://tripplan.moovitapp.com/?selectCity=false.
[9]https://twitter.com/.

Research by Schulz et al. [79] demonstrated the ability to increase situational awareness by harvesting additional information about small scale incidents from Twitter. By using a machine-learning algorithm combining text classification and semantic enrichment of microblogs, they detected valuable and previously unknown information during crisis situations. Such information could contribute to enhance situational awareness for decision-making and improve crisis management.

Schweitzer [80] implemented similar techniques to mine customer opinions on the quality-of-service of transport services (including air transport) with promising results. The research used Twitter data, seeking insights on customer sentiments concerning mobility services. The findings indicated that mining could detect both major trends in satisfaction and opinions arising around irregular events (for example, a heat wave that affected comfort on public transport). Collins et al. [22] used Twitter to evaluate transit rider satisfaction by implementing a machine-learning program to detect the sentiment value. Results indicated that transit riders are more inclined to assert negative sentiments to a situation than positive ones. Several phenomena identified by the Twitter analysis could also be explained by irregular events, such as exceptional delays caused by power outages at one station.

Steiger et al. [83] proposed a framework for inferring public transport flows from unstructured georeferenced social media data. They combined social media datasets from Twitter and textual information associated with Instagram and Flickr photos, while analysing only geotagged messages. Semantic topic modelling and spatial clustering techniques were applied in a case study in London. The research demonstrated that public transport hubs and public transport flows can be successfully extracted from these data sources.

It is therefore clear that the use of text mining techniques to extract specific types of transport-related information is possible. The broader potential of text mining to automatically (or semi-automatically) abstract transport-related information from social media is still to be explored however. In developing a methodology to explore the potential of social media for transport policy, three questions need to be addressed:

Q1: To what extent do social media contain valuable information for transport planning and management, e.g. information that improve the decisions taken by transport planners and operators?
Q2: How can the value of such information be evaluated?
Q3: Can such information be practically harvested either automatically or semi automatically?

High quality harvesting methodologies (Question 3) are essential to understand the scope and quality of transport related information from social media platforms (Question 1). An assessment of the value of harvested information (Question 2) can be achieved using complementary approaches. The first is to quantify the results of any action taken, e.g. measuring the outcomes of the improved transport service. A second parallel approach can be an on-going analysis of social media information to reveal changes in trends concerning the level of satisfaction with the transport service. If a positive trend in the level of satisfaction is revealed, then it can be inferred that harvesting the information and acting in response to the content is an effective tool to address travellers' needs. In order to implement the second approach, efficient extraction of transport-related information should be possible (Question 3).

A starting position to address these related questions is by inference from the use of social media in other domains i.e. an initial assumption that valuable information is indeed contained within this data source. It is therefore the purpose of this chapter to focus on Question 3 and the development of an information harvesting methodology that converges text-mining and transport context.

Question 3 should be approached in the light of the characteristics of unstructured text data within social media (i.e. informal language), where syntax rules are often overlooked and the use of slang is common. Two criteria are commonly used to test hypotheses of this type involving automatic text processing:

- The information that is automatically extracted should be highly relevant. Domain experts are used to evaluate the relevance of each item of information extracted. The ratio of the correctly extracted items to the total number of extracted items is then calculated (this measure is known as **Precision**).
- The extracted information should be complete. Domain experts fully identify the relevant information within a finite set of text sources. The ratio of the relevant information found by automatic text mining to the total number of relevant information items can be calculated (this measure is known as **Recall**).

The key to a successful development of a transport-related harvesting methodology is to specify the searching goals based on the general characteristics of social media content. Specifically, the searching goals should be defined in light of three main characteristics of social media content, reflecting its nature and the examples of its use in various domains:

- Social media content created by an individual usually refers to a specific event that the individual has experienced or a specific action that the individual intends to preform;
- The event or action the individual comments on occurs either shortly before or shortly after the time point at which the content is created;
- The issue raised by the individual creating the content is of importance to him/ her.

These characteristics form the basis for specifying the goals of harvesting transport service related information, where the term "transport service" is used here to describe any service that enables a person to make a journey from an origin to a destination. A "transport service" includes the transport mode used (e.g. private vehicles, public transport, walking) and physical facilities such as parking spaces, bike rental stations and others. It also includes a range of auxiliary services such as route planning applications, information dissemination, payment and reservation services. The goal of the harvesting process is therefore to find three types of transport-related information, as illustrated by the following examples:

- Travellers' needs and queries concerning a journey. The content might refer to a specific transport service or remain as a general wish to perform a journey. One example is the Tripadvisor message: *"which bus goes from Ataturk Airport to Bakirkoy?"*[10] and a message in Ride Share USA" *"... I need a ride to work!! (enfield to ludlow): I will pay you and gas too!! ..."*[11]
- Detection of an irregular event that has an impact on mobility, such as an accident, a malfunctioning traffic light or a hazard at a train station. An example Twitter message is as follows: *"fire at Station Part-Dieu; police informed us that access to train may be disrupted"*[12]
- Travellers' opinions on the quality of a transport service, for example the Hellopeter message: *"Travelled on bus ... from Braamfontein to Elandspark, driver .... Driver was rude from the time we boarded..."*[13]

Such information can serve as the basis for at least three types of actions to be taken by transport planners and operators and is therefore relevant in terms of policy development and delivery:

- Creating a new transport service or enhancing an existing one in order to better comply with travellers' needs where high latent demand emerges. An example may be to increase the frequency of a shuttle from a main train station to a high-density employment area.
- Undertaking an ad hoc solution for a problem reported through social media applications, for example, evacuating a vehicle that has broken down and is blocking a lane before congestion forms.
- Improving the level-of-service of an existing service, for example improving the cleanliness of PT vehicles.

These definitions and searching goals, in conjunction with the opportunities offered by text mining, serve as the basis on which to demonstrate the harvesting process for transport-related content. This is described as a general process in Sect. 4, whilst a specific case study illustration is given in Sect. 5.

4 Overview of the Text Mining Process

In order to begin to meet the challenges involved in automatic information extraction from ever growing volumes of free text, a number of text mining techniques have developed over recent years. These techniques are based on classic information retrieval techniques, for which improved algorithms continue to emerge [76].

---

[10]http://www.tripadvisor.com/ShowTopic−g293974−i368−k6532611−Which_bus_goes_from_Ataturk_Airport_to_Bakirkoy−Istanbul.html.

[11]https://twitter.com/Rideshare_USA/status/537044332667101184.

[12]https://twitter.com/fabien_gandon/status/193355911643926529.

[13]http://hellopeter.com/metrobus/complaints/rude-bus-driver-1563736.

They enable automatic identification of meaningful keywords and their use in training classifiers to automatically identify relevant content from streams of text. Text mining techniques have been applied with considerable success with social media to gain knowledge and understanding of public opinion across several areas of the social sciences (e.g. politics, entertainment and business). For example, Twitter messages have been analysed as an alternative to presidential approval rating data and presidential election polls, where results showed a high correlation with these polls [70]. In other recent work, market-structure insights for specific products were obtained from online user-generated content [64]. There is also much interest in using social media as a source of information on health issues, such as the early tracking of disease outbreaks [23].

The remainder of this section provides an overview of the various steps involved in mining social media text in general and how these relate to the transport specific context. The adaptation of aspects of the text mining process to transport-related tasks is illustrated in more detail in Sect. 5. Figure 1 outlines a general flow of the text mining process, with the main steps as follows:

Message filtering. A set of potentially relevant messages must first be extracted from the social media message stream. Meta-data is often useful for this purpose if available. For example, Twitters' streaming API (an interface provided by Twitter for access to the real-time tweet stream) allows message filtering using criteria such as date and geographical meta-data. In addition, keyword specification allows the extraction of messages that contain pre-specified words. Asserting message relevancy based on keyword matching is highly effective in some contexts. In the political arena for example, messages containing 'Obama' were first filtered and then analyzed with respect to the sentiment that they expressed in order to assess presidential approval rates [70].

In the transport domain [15], a list of train names was used to filter social media message content, with the goal of eliciting user opinions on the rail system from social media. Further research by Mai and Hranac [56] involved the collection of incident statistics from social media. A set of word collocations was used to filter potentially relevant messages including the collocations "traffic accident" and "car crash".

The task here, however, is to distil social media content into a stream of messages that are related to transport, concerning multiple aspects of interest to transport policy makers. Message relevancy in this case therefore requires that texts are related to a broad range of transport issues. A reasonable strategy for keyword specification would be to use keywords that are typical for the transport sector, possibly deriving them from an existing transport lexicon or ontology. In addition, keywords may be selected specifically targeting messages that concern an event of interest (such as a concert) or a specific transport type.

Whilst some keywords have unique meaning (such as "Obama" or "influenza"), typical words used in the transport sector may be highly ambiguous. For example in the phrases "cross the bridge when we get there", or "wash the car", the terms "bridge" and "car" are associated with transport but are used with an irrelevant meaning or context. Filtering messages by keywords may therefore yield

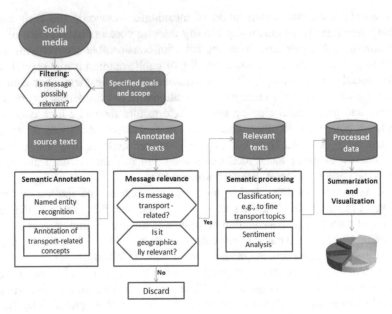

Fig. 1 Overview of text mining process (*Source* Gal-Tzur et al. [34])

very noisy results. However, having identified candidate messages using the initial criteria, an improved assessment of relevance and more detailed interpretation of content can be performed using further text mining steps, as described below.

Semantic Annotation. The initial pool of filtered raw texts ("source texts", Fig. 1) can be further annotated with useful semantic information [79]. Specifically, named entity recognition (NER) techniques annotate the scope and types of entities of interest, including place names, facilities, organisations and person names. Recent NER models have been adapted to handle informal text such as social media [19, 78]. It is also useful to annotate transport-related concepts in the text, linking textual phrases to domain ontology. This level of annotation can be used to assist in further decoding the meaning of the whole message, whilst place names provide evidence on the location orientation of the message.

Message relevancy. The relevance of annotated messages to the transport authority can then be more thoroughly evaluated. The automatic association of text with a topic—transport in this case—typically uses supervised machine learning approaches. In supervised settings, a model is learned based on labelled examples; this implies that a *dataset* must be constructed that contains example texts with their correct labels. Manual labelling is generally costly, especially if domain expertise is required. However, when relevant texts can be obtained from known transport-related contexts, for example social media messages posted to the account of a transport authority, these can be assumed to be relevant and used to automatically construct a dataset. To learn a classification model that fits labelled examples and generalises to new examples, example texts are abstracted into pre-defined *feature* values. In the popular 'bag-of-words' feature schema a document is represented as an unordered set of the words [58]. This simple representation can give good performance, for example, documents containing the terms "train", "bus", and "ticket" are likely to be transport-related. Similarly, word bigrams, or trigrams, may be modelled as features, capturing collocations such as "car accident". Various classification paradigms are known to give good performance on text categorization problems, including Support Vector Machines, Bayesian models and more [58]. Similar classification techniques are well established in other fields of transport modeling, for example [71]. Once classified, messages that are identified as irrelevant to transport will be discarded at this stage. Finally, another aspect of relevancy is the location orientation of a message.

Semantic Processing. Messages judged as relevant can then be classified into finer semantic categories of interest to the transport context; for example messages that report accidents or messages in which users express a wish to travel to a particular destination. In addition to features encoding word occurrences, enhanced feature schemes may be useful for such classification tasks, for example indicating whether location names or transport-related terms are observed in the text, as indicated by the semantic annotation of the messages [79]. Similarly, messages may be automatically associated (using dedicated classifiers) with transport modes and subjectivity classification (using sentiment analysis [19]).

Summarization and Presentation. The final stage is to aggregate and present the text mining outcomes so as to support decision making [69]. For example, providing graphical presentations of positive versus negative public sentiment [45] towards a service, showing map or location based demand for a transport service, etc.

Measuring the Accuracy of the Text Mining Results. A quantitative evaluation of the text mining process is needed to tune the system and evaluate the degree of success. Evaluation generates common performance measures originating from the information retrieval domain [22], namely precision and recall. Precision measures the accuracy of the predictions made by the system (i.e. how many of the texts classified as relevant are indeed relevant). Recall corresponds to coverage ratio (how many of the total transport relevant texts were classified as relevant). Given a dataset of examples associated with correct class labels on the one hand and automatically inferred labeled on the other, it is possible to evaluate the system's performance both in terms of precision and recall.

The individual components of the text processing pipeline, including the classifier and text annotators can be evaluated using labeled examples that were set aside for testing purposes. Each component is typically tuned until the output performance measures are considered satisfactory. In general, an important factor affecting the performance of learning systems is the size of the labelled data that is available to learn from. Rather than manually label large amounts of data, which is costly, automatic and semi-automatic methods for labeling examples can be applied. Using the pseudo relevance feedback approach, for example, texts that are classified with high confidence at early iterations are processed as labelled examples to retrain improved models [22]. Automated text mining is inherently imperfect, however this should not imply the data cannot be used within the transport information cycle. To the contrary, an appreciation of where data quality is either strong or weak allows a more confident utilisation of the data.

The infinite nature of the message stream in social media is challenging from several perspectives. From a performance perspective, as the content posted on social media changes rapidly over time, periodic monitoring and possibly re-tuning of the system is required. From an evaluation perspective, it is impossible to identify all relevant messages in the data stream and as a result one cannot compute recall precisely. The large mass of data on social media however also carries an important advantage. Social media information is characterised by a high degree of redundancy, having multiple messages that are phrased differently conveying similar content. This means that while some relevant messages may be overlooked by the text mining process this may not have a drastic effect on the output of the text analysis process [2].

In summary, text mining provides a means for automatic identification of transport-relevant messages in a stream of incoming messages. Specific challenges remain and solutions are needed where the user must be in the loop for periodic monitoring and enhancement of the system.

5 Illustration of Text Mining for Transport Related Content

To illustrate the various steps involved in text mining in the context of searching for transport related information, a particular case study is reported here. This draws on research reported in Gal-Tzur et al. [34] and Grant-Muller et al. [38] with further additions.

5.1 Background

An exploratory study designed to investigate the use of text mining for transport relevant content (and guided by the goals and hypotheses defined in previous sections) is used for illustration here. Due to the complexity of information harvesting from social media, a focused task was defined, i.e. to extract transport-related information concerning trips to and from mass events such as sports and cultural events. Liverpool (UK) football games were chosen for the case study here as they are recurrent events (almost 40 matches per season) and are well defined by date and location. This choice also allows clear and meaningful interpretation of the information harvested, and assessment of its relevance to transport services.

Twitter was chosen as the social media information source, given that it is a real time information channel that it is widely used in the UK. Past research has also shown that Twitter can be used as a source of information regarding sports events in real time [49].

The general approach can be summarised as follows. Firstly messages that appeared to be generally related to the Liverpool football games were filtered from the general Twitter message stream. Transport related messages were then identified using a dedicated classifier and extracted from this initial pool. A supervised learning approach was used to create models that associated messages with pre-specified categories of interest. Each message was then represented as a 'bag-of-words', that is, as a collection of the terms it contained, weighted by term counts. In addition to word unigrams (single words), word multigram features were also used (representing unigram, bigram and trigram word sequences), which allowed expressions to be captured. Several learning methods were explored in the study using the Weka learning suite [41]. The results reported here were obtained using an SVM classifier [84], which was found to give the best performance in the experiments.

A more detailed elaboration of the steps involved in the text mining pipeline and the results is given below, alongside discussion of the challenges identified with particular tasks.

5.2 The Text Mining Pipeline

Message filtering: the first task was to collect messages that were likely to refer to the events of interest. Three consecutive matches of the Liverpool football team were targeted in this study. Twitter's streaming application program interface (API) enables access to the real time Tweet stream with some limitations (such as a limitation on the percentage of tweets retrieved from the real time stream based on a privilege level). The *filter* API allows the filtering of messages using a set of keywords (currently up to 400) or geo-location specifications[14]. As football matches were the event of interest, keywords were specified for message filtering including names of the football clubs that played in each of the three targeted matches, stadium names and other relevant names. The goal was to assure high recall level, i.e. identifying as many messages as possible out of all relevant ones. Messages were retrieved over a period of approximately one week per match, starting three days before each event. Overall this yielded an initial corpus of more than 3 million messages.

Only a small fraction of the millions of messages retrieved, however, may have included relevant transport issues. Rather than applying costly processing to all messages, efforts were focused on messages that were likely to be relevant. To achieve this, a lexicon of transport-related terms was constructed with the goal of identifying messages that used transport terminology. While such a lexicon could be potentially derived from domain ontology, there is currently no large scale ontology (to the best of the authors' knowledge) that is publicly available and can

---

[14]Extracted from https://dev.twitter.com/streaming/reference/post/statuses/filter (Dec 2014).

be used to reliably identify transport-related terms. Instead, a lexicon was constructed semi-automatically using the following process. A total of 35 documents from the transport domain, including scientific articles, Websites, and user forums, were processed into a list of terms ranked by their frequency in this document collection. The most frequent terms (excluding terms known to be highly common in general language, known as "stop-words") were further scored using a 6-point scale by domain specialists according to their perceived relevance to the transport domain (a score of 0 meant that the term was not related to transport and a score of 5 meant that the term was highly relevant or related to transport). The resulting lexicon included approximately 500 high-scoring terms (scored 3 and above), including the terms "traffic", "bus", "congestion", "vehicle", and "passengers". This weighted lexicon was used to obtain a rough estimate of message relevancy, computed as the sum of scores associated with the terms that the message contains.

Identifying transport-related messages: In order to identify transport-related messages, two classifiers were learned in the study, where the output of the first classifier served as the input to the second classifier:

Classifier I: filtering 'authority' messages. Many transport-related messages concerning traffic updates are posted by authorities or other organizations. Since the objective is to harvest information that is generated by the public, such messages need to be discarded. A classifier was therefore trained with the purpose of automatically filtering such messages. A dataset was constructed of example Tweets labelled as 'authority-authored' vs. 'individual-authored'. The dataset consisted of the top 1500 messages ranked using the newly derived lexicon from the pool of messages retrieved. This size of dataset was sufficiently large to support effective learning whilst also meeting the research resource constraints, given that all messages were manually annotated. Overall, about 45 % of the messages in the dataset were labelled as having been written by individuals. According to the learned models, messages posted by individuals are characterized with word usage such as "I" or "we" and informal words such as "lol". In contrast, formal language was found to be indicative of messages posted by organisations; for example, the term "due" is apparently frequently used by authorities when providing the reasons for irregular events in the transport network. The corresponding precision and recall metrics (defined in Sect. 4) were high, with a precision of 0.88 and recall of 0.92.

Classifier II: identifying transport-related messages. Another dataset of example messages was constructed and annotated for the purpose of training a classifier that predicts whether a message did in fact contain transport-related issues. In this case, the first classifier had been applied to the initial pool of messages. A further set of top-scoring 1500 examples was then obtained from the resulting messages that were predicted by classifier I as having been posted by individuals. These messages were then labelled by three annotators as being transport-related or not. The average pairwise inter-annotator agreement rate was evaluated at 80.9 %, indicating that this categorization task is subjective in some cases. Cross-validation showed good results, with precision and recall ratios of 0.8 and 0.78, respectively. The prominent terms used by the classifier to distinguish whether a Tweet is transport related or not include "train", "to", "bridge", "from", "bus" and "station". Although some of the words are common words (for example "to") others are specific to the domain of transport (for example, the terms "bus" and "station").

Message categorisation: The next step in the message processing pipeline involved the classification of messages that were automatically found to be transport-related into finer categories. In this study, a three-level hierarchical annotation scheme was followed defined according to the planning tasks that could be supported. The **first level of annotation** was selected to reflect the purpose of the message. Three main purposes were defined:

1. Expressing a need for a transport service
2. Expressing an opinion regarding a transport service
3. Reporting a transport related incident or event (which may be a planned or unplanned disruption to the 'normal' transport service)

In general a message may be associated with more than one category, for example expressing both a need for travel and an opinion.

The **second annotation level** aimed to identify the category of transport service that the message concerns, for example the train, private car, subway or other services. Specific service categories of interest were defined in the hierarchy according to the message purpose. For example, a message posted by an individual complaining about the quality of service when repairing a private car was irrelevant for the harvesting process of this study. As a result, the service sub-categories of the category "expressing an opinion" did not include private vehicles. However, when reporting an event (the third category), private vehicles were relevant items as events concerning closed road sections or congestion are valuable input for traffic management decisions. Again, a data set of example labelled messages was established for learning purposes. Having applied classifiers (I) and (II) and having removed duplicate messages (re-tweets), a dataset of 1174 messages was constructed. These messages were annotated by two domain experts with respect to the purpose of message and transport service type. Inter-annotator agreement rates for the categories of reporting an event, expressing an opinion and need for travel, were 94, 84 and 78 %, respectively.

A k-fold CV learning process involves splitting the labelled dataset into k roughly equal parts. Different learning models are then trained using $(k - 1)$ subsets of the examples, where each example is tested once overall [57]. In this case study a 10-fold CV learning evaluation was used. The results indicated that out of the three message purpose categories, messages expressing an opinion were the easiest to identify (with precision of 0.68 and recall of 0.79). Opinions can often be tracked based on sentiment-bearing words; the words 'excellent' or 'terrible' are clear examples. Identifying messages expressing a need for travel was found to be the most difficult task (precision 0.53 and 0.58 recall). Indeed, inter-annotator agreement rate on this latter category was the lowest, indicating the complexity of identifying this need and given it is sometimes stated implicitly in the message. Evaluation of the classification of a tweet as reporting an event resulted in 0.63 precision and 0.6 recall, indicating it to be a relatively difficult classification task.

Interpreting the precision and recall values depends on a number of factors that determine what 'good' rates should be, however a score of 1.0 on both indicators represents perfect performance. Performance rates depend (among other factors) on the difficulty of the task, where precision and recall of 0.8 and above for text processing tasks are typically considered to be high. The rates given above are comparable or better than those found in the analysis of social media texts in other research in non-transport domains (see for example [27]). Considering that the reported study is preliminary, these results are encouraging. Improvements can be achieved by leveraging unlabelled data using semi-supervised learning schemes [17], for example. Furthermore, performing initial semantic processing of messages, including named entity recognition of location names transport-related concepts and representing this information as features, should support the automatic association of messages into fine semantic categories. For example, the presence of source and destination location names in a message indicates a wish to travel. Annotating mentions of transport facilities may enable the identification of the focus of an opinion, or the underlying transport mode. Finally, while the results are imperfect the output predictions may be directly used in noise-tolerable settings. They can be further refined in a semi-automatic scenario, being post-processed by humans.

6 Challenges in Text Mining for Transport Information Needs

While social media information may be useful, the processing of textual messages into meaningful data is not straightforward. Crucially, only a proportion of social media messages concern genuine transport issues. In this section further attention is given to three challenging areas of particular relevance to uses of social media in transport. The aim is to highlight the state of the art in the technical process and reflect on the implications for increased uptake of social media as a transport information source.

6.1 Transport Ontology

A main barrier to automating text processing in general (and micro-blogs such as Twitter in particular) is the lack of accompanying context. By way of illustration, to infer that the text "The 61C was late this morning" is relevant to transport, it must be known that "61c" is the name of a bus line. One of the most effective ways to represent background (world) knowledge is through *ontologies*. Ontologies serve as a methodological framework for representing objects or concepts as a networked structure, with related items linked by labeled relationships. Freebase [9] is a popular example of a general-purpose ontology. The mining process would ideally involve semantic annotation, linking text segments to concepts in the ontology, thus enabling semantic search and processing. Following the example above, an ontology is needed that represents the term "61c" as an entity, connected with an "is-a" (hyponymy) relation to the concept "bus", where "bus" in turn is mapped as a hyponym of the "transport mode" concept etc. This allows an association of the text with transport categories at various granularities; e.g. "transport", "transport mode", "bus" etc.

A literature review of transport-related ontologies reveals two main categories. The first concerns the type of activity for which the ontology was created. Some work has focused on very specific tasks such as the transmission of communication between in-vehicle and external systems [54]. Others have targeted more general processes such as micro-simulation [20] or journey planning [65]. Generally, an ontology required for specific activities is narrower than one for more general processes. The second category concerns the transport mode the ontology covers, with some focusing on a single mode whilst others cover multi-modal travel. Combining both categories of ontology-related transport research means that all combinations appear in the literature:

- **Ontologies addressing a specific activity and a single mode**—Private vehicle context-aware services [54]; Customer satisfaction of travellers of Mass Transit System [89]; Situation Awareness of City Tunnel Traffic [51].
- **Ontologies addressing a specific activity and multi-modal journey**—Military transport planning and scheduling [6].
- **Ontologies addressing a general activity and a single mode**—Personalised private vehicles route planning [91]; Activity-based Carpooling Microsimulation [20].
- **Ontologies addressing a general activity and multi-modal journey**—Public Transport Query System [91]; Journey Planning [42].

Despite the substantial contribution of existing research, there is no comprehensive transport ontology currently available (see also [40]). Constructing such ontology would be resource intensive as it involves the abstraction and conceptualization of the transport domain, tasks typically conducted by domain experts. Fusing existing ontological resources may alleviate this effort and some attempts in this direction have already been made, for example [94]. The dynamic and geography dependent nature of transport-related content on social media further contributes to the complexity in creating ontology. A full scale ontology should, for example, capture the reality in which the underground system in London (UK) is called "tube", while at the same time "T" is commonly used for informally referring to the underground in Boston (USA). At present this aspect is therefore a topic for further research in the field. Ideally, a transport ontology would also be maintained using collaborative intelligence and drawing on contributions by non-experts, in a similar fashion to Wikipedia. Future research activities are likely to include modelling relevant semantic information given pre-specified tasks and consolidating dictionaries that are available in different formats.

6.2 Sentiment Analysis

Sentiment analysis (or 'opinion mining'), is the process of identifying and extracting opinions from a given text. The recent upsurge of user generated content on social media has boosted research efforts in this area [72, 73]. Sentiment analysis of social media has been used to estimate public mood [10], trends such as stock market behaviour [11] and political elections results [21]. Sentiment analysis is important to address some of the information needs of transport policy makers. Previous research in the transport sector has explored Twitter as an information source for evaluating transit rider satisfaction [22]. Using the rapid transit system of the Chicago Transit Authority as a case study, a correlation was found between irregular events (such as extreme delays) and the volume of postings expressing negative sentiment. This correlation supports the notion that Twitter is a valid source of information for inferring transport-related sentiments. In general, relevant subjective data in the transport domain includes opinions expressed by bus, train or plane passengers (e.g. on service quality), as well as public attitudes towards new transport schemes [55].

Sentiment analysis typically makes use of a dedicated lexicon of words marked with their prior polarity i.e. negative/positive [93], matching a given text with the lexicon in order to analyse emotions in the text [82]. It has been shown however that expressions of negative/positive sentiment in natural language are highly context dependent [92]. For example, "busy" may be positive in describing some transport contexts e.g. 'the road is busy and should qualify for upgrade' but negative in others 'the road is busy and unsuited for further housing development'. A text may say that a policy is "not at all desirable" (negative sentiment), or a product is "terribly good" (positive sentiment). Natural language may also include irony and sarcasm, which adds to the challenge [25]. Analysis of transport sentiment data [34] illustrated the difficulty with sarcasm in service quality related text. The message 'train service is just fantastic' needs the surrounding context for interpretation. In this case clues in the preceding or subsequent content (e.g. relating to late running trains) may indicate whether it is genuine or sarcastic. Inferring sentiment can therefore be posed as a text classification task [10], enabling the consideration of contextual clues in identifying sentiment [82]. It has been claimed that ideally, the learned models should be trained using labelled data within the domain of interest; however, even when this is not the case, contextual learned models can achieve accuracy level of 80 % or more [73]. Results reported for the Liverpool football case study in Sect. 5 support this claim.

Following the discussion in Sect. 6.1, the consideration of specialised transport lexicons (either mode specific or task specific) in the learning process may be appropriate. The social media platform from which the content is harvested might also influence sentiment analysis. For example, sites dedicated to complaints, such as Hellopeter.com, are likely to be biased towards negative sentiments [55].

6.3 Location Data

Most transport operators and managers are likely to be primarily concerned with identifying transport related information from social media that is closely associated with the transport services for which they have responsibility. It is a reasonable assumption that most messages posted on the formal websites for a transport authority (or supplier) will have relevance to their locality. However, the transport system inherently contains networks (e.g. of roads, PT services) and as a result, both upstream and downstream transport activity may be of relevance to a particular geographic location. The governance of particular sections of the transport system that together form networks may be undertaken by different authorities with different websites. For example, complaints about connections between inter-city and local services may be posted on the web site of inter-city service operators but be of interest to local providers seeking to improve connection services.

It is therefore necessary to identify those messages (from the very many that will be available) relevant to the location and/or specific transport services for the task. Two possible location identification approaches are either (a) to identify the current location of the person posting the message and/or (b) to correctly identify locations from message content. Figure 2 outlines the process involved for an example case of PT messages based on the fusion of information either within the message or attached to it.

A primary source of information on the location of the person posting the text message is voluntarily posted geo-meta-data associated with the social media user account. In practice, many users do not provide this information (9) and even if a message is geo-tagged, it may be inaccurate. The message may also relate to transport in locations distinct from the users home town, e.g. whilst traveling. Mobile device GPS coordinates offer further implicit meta-data indicating the users' location, but is only a portion of all social media traffic and user consent is required for this functionality. Research continues to maximize the precision of location inference from pervasive devices [8]. Given current limitations in coverage of these types of meta-data [44, 50], other implicit information sources have been investigated for potential location inference. Social network structures can be used for this purpose as users tend to live in close geographic proximity to their social network peers [26]. An estimate of user location may be inferred based on the message content [77]. In particular, it has been shown that fine geographical distinctions are possible based on local language characteristics [31, 48].

The second approach to identifying location data is from the contents of the message. This task is especially challenging when considering the high ambiguity of place names. For example, "Liverpool" is the name of a UK city, a London rail station (Liverpool Street), a city in the USA and an Australian suburb. Several approaches have been proposed for identifying geo-location based on message content. Named entity recognition techniques can automatically annotate the text with mentions of entity names. Having extracted candidate location names, disambiguation is needed to align inferred location with any other contextual information, in conjunction with relevant sources of location names.

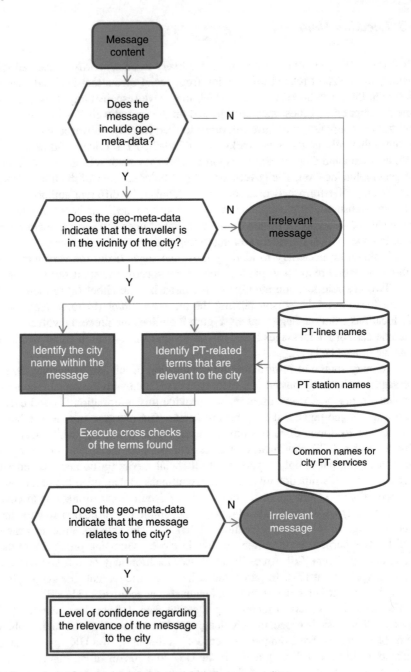

Fig. 2 Analysis of geo-location data in social media transport data

Web-a-Where, a system for associating geography with Web pages was one of the early works that have tackled this problem [3]. TwitterTagger [74] geotags tweets by comparing their content with the United States Geological Survey (USGS[15]) database of locations. Another approach for content-based geo-location of multilingual tweets is based on collating contextual tweets into a document using a user-tweeting-frequency based temporal window [86]. An approach based on "local" words, e.g. words that are typical to specific location such as "Hoody" for Texas, was proposed by Cheng et al. [18] to estimate a Twitter-user city level location.

The availability of data sources containing transport-related entities (e.g. PT line identifications, station formal and informal names, names of parking facilities) may constitute a valuable asset for identifying locations for transport-related messages. Bry et al. [13] provide interesting examples of the use of such data sources in building a world model for geospatial data. The world model consists of concrete data (such as train connections) plus logically formalised ontologies of transport networks. Following conjectures on the location of the message based on the different approaches, the data analyst can check for possible inconsistencies and choose whether to discard messages where there is low confidence in geographical orientation.

In summary, three main challenges are currently evident in mining transport social media data: the construction of ontology, sentiment analysis and location identification. These are not specific to the transport domain, but the third is arguably the most crucial for the transport context. However this should be viewed in the context of the accuracy requirements for the intended use case. This general principle applies to user generated content as a whole, where an improved understanding of the level of accuracy needed to turn harvested data into actionable data is an issue for future research.

7 Engaging with Social Media Information in Practice

This section provides a short overview of the evidence on how the transport stakeholders are currently using social media, specifically:

- How social media is being used in terms of the apparent function, for example for publicity of the new initiatives introduced by the organisation, for customer relations (CR), for up to date information notices or other purposes
- Whether there is evidence on the extent of engagement with the public (such as the number of 'followers', the number of 'likes') and whether there is any apparent trend in this, for example according to the size of the organisation.

This section also seeks to address the final question: are there wider institutional or other barriers in harnessing the potential of social media data in transport in addition to the technical issues? A review of institutional attitudes to social media use is therefore followed by some findings on social media use by transport authorities in practice.

---

[15]http://geonames.usgs.gov/.

Whilst there is a growing tranche of literature concerned with the attitudes and perceptions of individuals on social media use, rather less has been published on the formal stance of organisations on their use of social media. This is particularly the case for those in a governmental (or public sector) role, which is a significant number of organisations in the case of the transport sector. Given the important role of information in both operational activity and strategic planning [55] improved understanding of the barriers and enablers in accelerating the effective uptake of social media in the transport sector is needed. Part of the appeal to transport agencies of using social media to disseminate service alerts is that it is inexpensive and quick to implement, as some social networks (e.g. Facebook, Twitter, and Google) sometimes provide and maintain the infrastructure for free. Initial attempts to provide authorities with guidelines for effective use of social media have already been made [36, 58]. Based on more general social media literature, the following arise as possible organisational stances.

A reluctance to engage with social media may be a result of the need to be active as a 'key requirement of success' [44], potentially related to the need for resource input (see also [5, 23, 34, 80, 95]). Social media platforms facilitate brief, focused communication, which may make customer service more efficient. There may also be concerns about safeguarding corporate image, given the dynamic nature of messaging. Less opportunity for 'lagged' responses may give rise to fears around 'sending out the wrong messages'. Gal-Tzur et al. [34] outline evidence of a 'code of conduct' having been established in the case of one heavily engaged transport supplier (KLM). Lack of formal evaluation and 'proof of concept' may be a further issue as a body of evidence on the benefits for the transport sector has yet to be established [5], although anecdotally they may be substantive. Conducting customer service conversations "in the open" gives the impression to customers that the transport agency is accountable and transparent. A common refrain is that this may help customers feel that their concerns are taken seriously. Further research to in-fill the formal evidence basis may be needed. A willingness to engage with social media may be a result of perceived advantages in closing the perceptual distance between public and governmental services, resulting in increased public satisfaction and trust [24, 86, 89]. Social media can be used to create a positive image (e.g. for PT use and encouraging PT use through building a community of customers) and to support operational objectives (see Table 1). Finally, authorities may benefit from promoting and connecting related activities—social media can act in an integrative way for organisations that have a range of activities rather than just transport.

The willingness of transport authorities to engage with social media as a working tool is reflected by the interest of the state Departments of Transport (DOTs, USA) to improve the effectiveness of their social media programs [1]. Not all agencies publish reports concerning social media related activity and therefore the evidence found is not complete. However descriptions within social media sites, articles, interviews with officials and surveys conducted by various organisations reveal a set of typical activities conducted either frequently or occasionally. Table 3 contains some examples of such activities.

Table 3 Summary of findings on the use of social media by authorities

Authority	Summary of findings
Buckinghamshire and City of Edinburgh [4]	Using Twitter to give timely information to drivers about conditions on the road network
Transport Safety Board of Canada [88]	Mainly used as an alternative method for accessing the material shared through the TSB's RSS feeds and website
AASHTO [1], Third Annual State DOT Social Media Survey	Just less than 90 % of states are using Twitter. More than three-quarters of states are using Facebook
Minnesota's Local Road Research Board [61]	25 cities and 25 counties were selected for closer examination. Among the 50 governments sampled, Facebook was found to be the most common social media outlet (used by 19 for any reason and by 10 for transport communications) followed by Twitter (used by 15 for any reason and by 9 for transport). Across all social media channels, the most common transport-related topics for communication were planning, zoning, road construction and street closures
New York regions' major transport providers [63]	Links to social media accounts from the homepage, in tandem with service alert tools. This feature allows riders to comprehend urgent information in the context of social media's engagement, showing the complementary nature of the different resources
Various US Authorities [81]	While it should be noted that social media could greatly enhance a transport organisation's public outreach, there are also some potential dangers. Some aspects of social media are beyond the authority's control: hackers are a threat, people may post old or false news and leaks can occur
Virginia DOT [90]	The Virginia Department of Transportation is expanding its use of social media to communicate with the 7.5 million Virginians who depend on us to connect them with the things that are most important in their lives
Local Authorities in California [95]	Cities are generally more interested in information-sharing through social media than constituent engagement
Bay Area Rapid Transit (BART), Oakland, CA [24]	Facebook page is mostly used to promote contests, highlight agency news and make followers aware of upcoming public hearings. The Twitter account mostly includes service alerts
Ministry of Transport (MIT), Italy	The Ministry of the Italian Infrastructure and Transport has only a twitter profile that is used for official communications and information on projects, works and funding
MOT, Israel	The Ministry of Transport and Road Safety has a Facebook profile (the most used) and Twitter account. The information often refers to the official government site

Following the approach of Bregman et al. [12], a selection of transport providers of different types (size, location, business type) were chosen and their current use[16] of social media reviewed using publically available information. The sample chosen is only a small, preliminary snapshot determined by a number of factors and not intended to be either random or fully representative. The availability of a website with English language was one restriction and in general, medium to large sized organisations were chosen. The sample is shown in Table 4, comprising a local authority, three national transport policy/decision makers, two airports, one transnational ticket sales and schedule information companies (rail, ferry), two railway companies, one ferry service provider and four airlines. The two types of social media observed were Facebook and Twitter.[17] The nature of the business of most of these stakeholders involves dynamic interaction with the public—for example in providing timely information or sales. These two media inherently function in such a way as to facilitate this and bring the possibility of a two way exchange—the main advantage over most standard websites. However during the course of the research it did become clear that some were also using Youtube as a third source of social media particularly for one-direction communication of new company initiatives or campaigns. Different models of use of the media were observed:

(1) The public were strongly invited to engage with either Facebook, Twitter within a section of the company website and the use of the media was purposeful,
(2) The public were invited to engage with tailored and welcoming messages, the purpose of use was general or multifunctional,
(3) Links to social media were given on the main website page but were small in size and the invitation to engage was simple/generic (e.g. 'follow us') and;
(4) Logos were present on the main website or there were links to a twitter stream, but there was no direct link to the Facebook page or no Facebook page was available.

Whilst most organisations had a Facebook page and Twitter line that was focused around their core business, some webpages gave links to Facebook/Twitter that were shared between organisations within a larger group (e.g. the Gran Canaria airport and Leeds City Council). Gran Canaria is part of a larger group of airports, whilst Leeds city council has a single Facebook and Twitter line for a number of departments (transport, city cleansing, housing and more). One advantage of a dedicated social media line or page would be an improved ability to conduct further analysis on public postings, e.g. picking up trends in sentiments or information requests. With sites that cover multifunctions or several organisations this may well become more difficult with a wider variety and relevance of messages. The main advantage of the shared social media function however is the reduced

---

[16]December 2014.

[17]www.facebook.com and www.twitter.com.

Table 4 Review of transport stakeholder social media use

Transport stakeholder	Business type	Approx. turnover	Facebook page/likes	Bespoke invitation to engage in social media	Twitter account Followers/Tracking start date
	Airline (international travel)	2011: KLM Group carried 25.2 M passengers, 484.100 tonnes of freight. Income 6.985 M Euros	http://www.facebook.com/KLM 8,001,571 likes	Yes	@KLM 1545,801 Followers Tracking: 13/07/2009
Ryanair	Low cost airline	2012: 75.8 M passengers Income 4.324.9 M Euros	Strategic decision on no Facebook account	N/A	@Ryanair 114,265 Followers Tracking: not found
voyages-sncf.com	Rail ticket service provider at trans european level	Not readily available (four independent companies in distinct geographical areas)	https://www.facebook.com/VoyagesSncf.uk 318.131 likes	No	@Vsncf_UK_agents 80 Followers, Tracking: 25/07/2012
Direct Ferries	Ferry services provider at international level	2011: Turnover £46.5 M	https://www.facebook.com/directferries?sk=app_4949752878 21,842 likes	Yes	@directferriesuk 872 Followers Tracking: 8/12/09
Frankfurt airport	Air Transport node (3rd busiest airport)	2012: 57.52 M passengers	https://www.facebook.com/FrankfurtAirport 239,226 likes	Yes	@Airport_FRA 23,072 Followers Tracking:06/04/09
Gran Canaria airport	Air Transport node (38th busiest airport—tourism)	2011: 10.5 M passengers, 23.7 million tonnes of cargo	https://www.facebook.com/AenaAeropuertos 7553 likes	No	@aenaaeropuertos 50,523 Followers Tracking: 4/12/10
Department for Transport (UK)	NGO—Transport strategy and planning (national)	N/A	No Facebook page	No	@transportgovuk 44,353 Followers Tracking: 11/06/09

(continued)

Table 4 (continued)

Transport stakeholder	Business type	Approx. turnover	Facebook page/likes	Bespoke invitation to engage in social media	Twitter account Followers/Tracking start date
Leeds City Council (UK)	LGO—Transport policy and planning (local)	N/A	https://www.facebook.com/Leedscouncil 4478 likes	No	@leedscc 12,196 Followers Tracking: 19/6/09
NS (Netherlands transport service)	National transport supplier	2011: 396 M passengers Income €272 M	https://www.facebook.com/nederlandsespoorwegen 111,637 likes	No	@NSonline 119,705 Followers Tracking: 09/03/10
National rail enquiries (UK)	National information service on rail times and disruptions	N/A	https://www.facebook.com/nationalrailenq?group_id=0&filter=2 42,211 likes	No	@nationalrailenq 271,057 Followers Tracking: 20/04/09
Alitalia	Airline (international travel)	2013: 2399 M passengers	https://www.facebook.com/alitalia/timeline 1.257.108 likes	No	@Alitalia 72,660 Followers Tracking: 01/2010
Ferrovie dello Stato, Italy	Railway company	N/A	No Facebook page	No	@fsnews_it 93,600 Followers Tracking: 11/2010
Italo, Italy	Railway company	2013: 6.2 M passengers	https://www.facebook.com/ItaloTreno 925.061 likes	No	@ItaloTreno 107,935 Followers Tracking: 04/2010
El al, Israel	Airline (international travel)	2005: 3.5 M passengers	http://www.facebook.com/ELALAirlinesIL 367.727 likes	No	@EL_AL_AIRLINES 13.472 Followers Tracking: 12/2008

cost in maintenance and active CR input. It may well be the case that over a period of time, the use of the media for organisations currently on model 2–4 above may develop and step increasingly towards the more directed use such as model 1.

As can be seen from Table 4, the organisation with the largest number of Facebook likes and highest Twitter tracking was KLM. This was not the largest airline in the survey but was the first from this group to establish a Twitter line. KLM use model (1) above, with Facebook and Twitter prominently used for CR purposes. Links to both media were provided from their customer services webpage. One of the organisations with a low social media presence is the low cost carrier Ryan Air, which in 2013 carried 81.3 M passengers, one of the world's top 10 largest carriers according to the International Air Transport Association criteria. Ryan Air took a strategic decision not to engage with social media: 'such accounts would result in too many customer queries and would require more resources from the airline'. "A Facebook account would not be helpful to us, as we would have so many people looking for a response", "two more people just to sit on Facebook all day". The proposition was that passengers could get in touch through Ryanair's customer care line [47]. More than one Twitter line was found on searching and it wasn't entirely clear which was the 'official' line. In a similar stance to Ryanair, Trenitalia does not use an official Facebook page, but uses two Twitter accounts instead (@fsnews and @LeFrecce) in order to separate information for different customers. In the first account, general information concerning train operations may be found; the second one is specifically dedicated to offers and discounts for the high-speed trains. The concurrent railway company Italo uses its Twitter profile to disseminate aggressive offers, whilst holding a Facebook profile for interactions with customers. Bregman et al. [12] note that also some US-organisations deliberately use more than one twitter line, but the purpose is to direct customers towards a line of chatter or posted material most appropriate to their needs. This is a more developed version of model 1 above.

The Italian National Company Alitalia has also a Facebook page and a Twitter account: the latter is basically used for interacting with the customers, providing a fast and personalised reply. In its Facebook page, Alitalia has reconstructed the major historical events that made the history of the company. Examples of organisations using model 2 above were Direct Ferries and Frankfurt Airport, with examples of tailored invitations as follows. KLM was the only site to advise users not to share personal information.

> 'Visit Frankfurt Airport on the popular social network platforms Facebook, Twitter and just recently also on YouTube. Connect with other guests and passengers and stay informed about what is happening at Frankfurt Airport' 'Contact us. Please share your personal details via private messages only. Ask KLM a question 27/7 via Facebook > Ask KLM a question via Twitter.'

In general the style of communication from the organisation was far more informal than that used on the main website. Facebook and Twitter generally had a 'person' who was responding i.e. someone with a first name and responses that appeared to have been written by a human rather than a computerised/automated response. In this respect these media represent a far more accessible and welcoming interface with the organisation than some customer relations websites which, at best, may offer a menu of FAQ or what appear to be computer generated responses to standard customer enquiries. The main functions of social media use across the organisations sampled were as follows (not in order of priority or frequency of function):

(1) Information/updates on main website—this was a common type of message on Facebook from organisations, generally informing travellers that a problem or updating process was happening with the main website. This type of message was mainly one-directional i.e. the main webpage would not advise of changes to Facebook and the public did not appear to respond to this type of message:

> "Hi Facebook! Just to let you know that we're continuing to update information on our service disruptions page of the website, so you can find out about school closures, bin collection and gritting plans on the site. Thanks, Rob"

(2) Advising the public on Travel Disruption—this function is very much part of the core business for many of the organisations surveyed, particularly those concerned with scheduling, timetables and ticket sales. The type of information posted by the stakeholders included 'best knowledge' on the current or expected weather conditions and signposting to other sites that would hold the 'official' news on the disruptions.

> "Hi Facebook World! I'm going to be heading off for the weekend shortly, but just to confirm that although the snow seems to have eased off for now—it's likely to be back with a vengeance! We have updated the service disruption page on our website listed below, and you can follow us on Twitter for updates on gritting (@LCCPressOffice). Keep wrapped up this weekend. Thanks, Rob"

(3) Handling travel queries and complaints—the stream of interaction between the organisation and members of the public showed the different approaches used to deal with either straight forward or general questions, personal queries or complaints. Questions which didn't refer to a particular travel booking and which didn't involve a complaint were generally responded to on-line. Where the public asked about specific bookings, the organisation generally advised that they would be contacted off-line using the individual's personal Facebook account (in order to preserve security/privacy). For complaints about travel, the organisations generally offered a public apology and offered to speak with the individuals off-line by phone or in email correspondence. This 'code of practice' seemed to work well in general, although there were some issues aired around the use of social media (see 4 below). Some organisations appeared to ignore negative comments from the public. This may have avoided lengthy public correspondence but then left the comments 'hanging in the air' on the social media site and unsatisfied.

> "I can't find how much KLM charge per extra kilo on a flight from Dublin to Hong Kong? The limit is 23 k, what happens if your bag is 25 kg? It seems to cost €200 extra for an additional bag? Can you confirm how much in Euro it is?"

"That sounds like quite an interesting and nice route, Mairead. In regards to your question, we can inform you that we don't charge extra weight as per the kilo concept but as per piece. If you decide to take one additional luggage, then it will cost €100 for that route, for the 2nd piece (on top of your free allowance) and €200 for each piece in addition of those two. Let us know in case you have further doubts."

(4) Responding to queries around use of social media—inevitably some members of the public commented on the way in which the organisation was using social media. This included positive messages concerning the speed of responses, but also comments concerning non-response or unwanted presence on the users own social media site. The most constructive responses from organisations were to offer a route to addressing these issues. This type of customer query is analogous to customers asking for their telephone number to be removed from the databases of direct marketing organisations. Interactions of this type may be dealt with effectively through published policies on how the organisation uses social media and how customers can choose to end the social media relationship.

"You were absent from my FB page for one wonderful week now you're back again! Please go away and stay away nothing I can do this end makes any difference"

"Like explained before, our posts will only show on the people who likes us, pages. If you don't wish to see them, you need to unlike us (same place as you liked us)…….. Kind regards, Camilla"

"Why do you delete the posts from people airing their opinions? You should be taking action, not ignoring them." (no response from the organisation/CR team)

(5) Seasonal goodwill messages—the final category of dialogue and one present on many of the sites was that of the seasonal message of goodwill. This was consistently informal in nature and seemed to be aimed at promoting the concept of timeliness, community and friendly service.

"Happy Easter to all our followers! We hope you have a great day, enjoy your Easter eggs! The Frankfurt Airport Team wishes all fans very wonderful and happy holidays"

Some general observations from this short study were as follows. The size of the organisation overall didn't solely determine the degree or type of social media use. The largest organisation didn't use social media as a strategic stance. Four main levels of use of media were observed, ranging from highly focused and directed use, to a low level social media presence with general material posted. It is conjectured that a combination of the length of time the organisation has used social media, along with the nature of their core business may determine the extent to which it is used and how. The two governmental organisations for example demonstrated different use to the airports. The longer the social media sites have been established, the more likely the use becomes focused. A pattern of interaction was seen with some organisations that used social media in a highly interactive fashion, which may set an example for other organisations seeking to either the social media arena or increase their level of activity.

The evidence presented in this section concerning organisational uptake supports previous findings [34] on both the volume and pertinence of the information contained in social media textual data. It also highlight potential uses of social media information that have not yet been explored by authorities. The most prominent concerns the potential to aggregate traveler's information. Aggregated information can serve as a basis for identifying major needs and perceived satisfaction that serve as a vital input for decision making in the medium and long term. Figure 3 depicts the principle data flows to and from official transport authority social media sites, covering those reported as currently implemented and additional potential future flows.

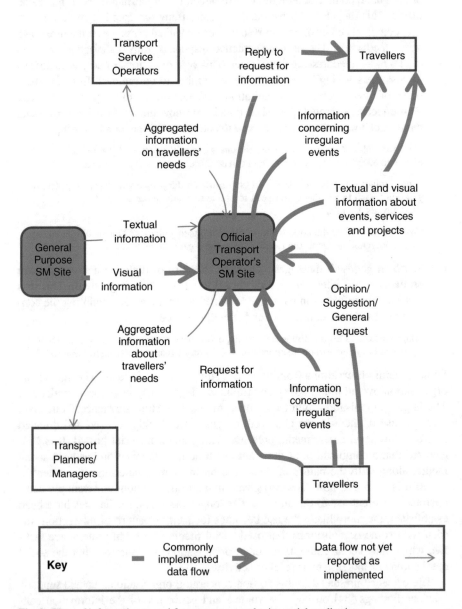

Fig. 3 Flow of information to and from transport authority social media sites

8 Concluding Remarks

The most important cultural revolution of recent times has undoubtedly been the introduction of web 2.0 enabled technologies to everyday life. Social media has been at the core of this massive social change and now acts a substitute for traditional shared spaces (such as bars, associations, cultural societies) as the place where individuals exchange facts, experiences and perceptions.

The increasingly central role of social media in modern life (in conjunction with the aim for many parts of the transport sector to provide user-led services) has provided the motivation for many transport stakeholders to consider the value of social media data. As an information-driven sector, the issues of cost, accuracy, robustness and bias in both current data sources and social media have risen to the fore.

As illustrated in this chapter, recent research and the community of practice indicate that information harvested from social media can compliment, enrich (or even replace) traditional data collection. It can be accessed freely and at relatively low cost, often containing user generated data from sections of the population that can be difficult to capture using more established forms of data collection. Whilst the data is not without issues of bias, these may be comparable with the biases typically associated with traditional survey techniques.

Many organisations in the transport sector are still taking their first steps on the path to engaging directly with members of the travelling public using social media and some barriers are still in evidence. In particular the availability of dedicated staff resources to effectively engage with the public through social media appears to be a significant barrier to harnessing the full potential. Further research is needed to develop automatic or semi-automatic methodologies for harvesting and analysing transport-related social media information.

However the combination of the evidence to date and the future potential of social media suggests that transport stakeholders would be wise to reflect on the skills needed in their employee base to 'future proof' their organisation. Alongside the traditional skills of transport engineering, transport economics and transport planning, new skills in webscience, data fusion, the management and analysis of 'Big Data' and direct interaction with the travelling public will be at a premium in the next stage of evolution for the transport sector.

References

1. AASHTO (2012, September). *Third annual state DOT social media survey.* http://communi-cations.transportation.org/Documents/Social_Media_Survey_2012.pdf
2. Aggarwal, C. C., & Zhai C. -X. (2012). *Mining text data.* Berlin: Springer.
3. Amitay, E., Har'El, N., Sivan, R., & Soffer, A. (2004). Web-a-Where: "Geotagging Web Content". In *SIGIR '04 Proceedings of the 27th Annual International ACM SIGIR Conference on Research and development in Information Retrieval* (pp. 273–280).

4. Austin, J. (2013). Use of social networking to promote public transport and sustainable travel. http://www.analytics.co.uk/resources/Use+of+Social+Media+to+promote+PT+$2 6+Sustainable+Travel.pdf. Accessed August 1, 2013.
5. Barron, E., Peck, S., Venner, M., & Malley, W. G. (2013, September). Suggested practices guidance resource. NCHRP 25–25 TASK 80.
6. Becker, M., & Smith, S. F. (1997). *An ontology for multi-modal transportation planning and scheduling.* Technical report CMU-RI-TR-98–15, Robotics Institute, Carnegie Mellon University.
7. Bickerstaff, K., & Walker, G. (2001). Participatory local governance and transport planning. *Environment and Planning A, 33*(3), 431–452.
8. Bie, J., Bijlsma, M., Broll, G., et al. (2012). Move better with tripzoom. *International Journal on Advances in Life Sciences, 4*, 125–135.
9. Bollacker, K., Evans, C., Paritosh, P., Sturge, T., & Taylor, J. (2008). Freebase: A collaboratively created graph database for structuring human knowledge. In *Proceedings of the ACM SIGMOD International Conference on Management of Data*, Vancouver, BC, Canada (pp. 1247–1250). ACM (2008). ISBN 978-1-60558-102-6.
10. Bollen, J., Pepe, A., & Mao, H. (2011a). Modeling public mood and emotion: Twitter sentiment and socio-economic phenomena. In *Proceedings of the 5th International AAAI Conference on Weblogs and Social Media (ICWSM)* (pp. 450–453), Barcelona, Spain, July 17–21.
11. Bollen, J., Mao, H., & Zeng, X. J. (2011). Twitter mood predicts the stock market. *Journal of Computational Science, 2*, 1–8.
12. Bregman, S. (2012). Uses of Social Media in Public Transportation, TCRP SYNTHESIS 99.
13. Bry, F., Lorenz, B., Ohlbach, H.J., & Rosner, M. (2005). A geospatial world model for the semantic web. In *Principles and Practice of Semantic Web Reasoning*, Vol. 3703. Lecture Notes in Computer Science (pp. 145–159). Berlin: Springer.
14. Caceres, N., Romero, L. M., Benitez, F. G., & del Castillo, J. M. (2012). Traffic flow estimation models using cellular phone data. *IEEE Transactions on Intelligent Transportation Systems, 13*(3), 1430–1441.
15. Carrasco, J. A., Hogan, B., Wellman, B., & Miller, E. J. (2008). Collecting social network data to study social activity-travel behavior: An egocentric approach. *Environment and Planning B: Planning and Design, 35*(6), 961–980.
16. Castells, M. (2011). The power of identity: The information age: Economy, society, and culture, Vol. 2. Wiley-Blackwell.
17. Chen, M., Jin, X., & Shen, D. (2011). Short text classification improved by learning multi-granularity topics. In *Proceedings of the Twenty-Second International Joint Conference on Artificial Intelligence* (IJCAI).
18. Cheng, Z., Caverlee, J., & Lee, K. (2010). You are where you tweet: A content-based approach to geo-locating twitter users. In *Proceeding of CIKM '10 Proceedings of the 19th ACM International Conference on Information and Knowledge Management* (pp. 759–768). New York.
19. Chenliang, L., Weng, J., He, Q. et al. (2012). TwiNER: named entity recognition in targeted twitter stream. In *Proceedings of the International ACM SIGIR Conference on Research and Development in Information Retrieval.*
20. Cho, S., Kang, J. Y., Yasar, A., Luk, Knapen L., Bellemans, T., Janssens, D., et al. (2013). An activity-based carpooling microsimulation using ontology. *Procedia Computer Science, 2013*(19), 48–55.
21. Chung, J., & Mustafaraj, E. (2011). Can collective sentiment expressed on twitter predict political elections? In *Proceedings of the Twenty-Fifth AAAI Conference on Artificial Intelligence.* San Francisco, CA, USA (pp. 1770–1771).
22. Collins, C., Hasan, S., & Ukkusuri, S. V. (2013). A novel transit rider satisfaction metric: Rider sentiments measured from online social media data. *Journal of Public Transportation, 16*(2), 21–45.

23. Corley, C., Cook, D., Mikler, A., & Singh, K. (2010). Text and structural data mining of influenza mentions in web and social media. *International Journal of Environmental Research and Public Health, 7*(2), 596–615.
24. Cotey, A. (2011). Social media: Transit agencies connect with riders in new ways. Progressive Railroading, January 2011. http://www.progressiverailroading.com/passenger_rail/article/ Social-media-Transit-agencies-connect-with-riders-in-new-ways–25447
25. Davidov, D., Sur, O., & Rappoport, A. (2010). Semi-supervised recognition of sarcastic sentences in Twitter and Amazon. In *Proceedings of the Fourteenth Conference on Computational Natural Language Learning* (pp. 107–116). Uppsala, Sweden.
26. Davis Jr, C. A., Pappa, G. L., de Oliveira, D. R. R., & de L Arcanjo, F. (2011). Inferring the location of twitter messages based on user relationships. Transactions in GIS, *15* (6), 735–751.
27. Denecke, K., & Nejdi, W. (2009). How valuable is medical social media data? Content analysis of the medical web. *Information Sciences, 179*(12), 1870–1880.
28. DuBose, C. (2011). The social media revolution. *Radiologic Technology, 83*(2), 112–119.
29. Eboli, L., & Mazzulla, G. (2012). Performance indicators for an objective measure of public transport service quality. *European Transport/Trasporti Europei, 51*, 1–21.
30. Efthymiou, D. & Antoniou, C. (2012). Use of social media for transport data collection. Procedia—Social and Behavioral Sciences, Vol. 48, pp. 775–785. doi:http://dx.doi.org/10.1016/j.sbspro.2012.06.1055. ISSN 1877-0428.
31. Eisenstein, J., O'Connor, B., Smith, N. A., & Xing, E. P. (2010). A latent variable model for geographic lexical variation. In *Proceedings of Empirical Methods in Natural Language Processing*, Stroudsburg, PA, USA, pp. 1277–1287.
32. European Commission. (2001). *A sustainable Europe for a better world: A European Union strategy for sustainable development*. Belgium: Brussels.
33. Gal-Tzur, A., Grant-Muller, S. M., Minkov, E., & Nocera, S. (2014). The impact of social media usage on transport policy: Issues, challenges and recommendations. *Procedia—Social and Behavioral Science, 111*, 937–946.
34. Gal-Tzur, A., Grant-Muller, S. M., Kuflik, T., Minkov, E., Nocera, S., & Shoor, I. (2014). The potential of social media in delivering transport policy goals. *Transport Policy, 32*, 115–123.
35. Gao, L., & Wu, H. (2013). Verb-Based Text Mining of Road Crash Report, TRB 92nd Annual Meeting.
36. Gao, L., Zhang, Z., & Wu, H. (2013b). Analyzing the Use of Facebook Page Among State DOTs. In *TRB 92nd Annual Meeting Compendium of Papers*.
37. Giannopoulos, G. A. (2004). The application of information and communication technologies in transport. *European Journal of Operational Research, 152*(2), 302–320.
38. Grant-Muller, S. M., Gal-Tzur, A., Minkov, E., Nocera, S., Kuflik, T., & Shoor, I. (2014a). Enhancing transport data collection through social media sources: Methods, challenges and opportunities for textual data. IET Intelligent Transport Systems. doi:10.1049/iet-its.2013.0214.
39. Grant-Muller, S. M., & Usher, M. (2013). Intelligent transport systems: The propensity for environmental and economic benefits. *Technological Forecasting and Social Change*. doi:10.1016/j.techfore.2013.06.010
40. Grosenick, S. (2012). Real-time traffic prediction improvement through semantic mining of social networks. Thesis (Master's)—University of Washington. url:http://hdl.handle.net/1773/20911
41. Hall, M., Frank, E., Holmes, G., Pfahringer, B., Reutemann, P., & Witten, I. H. (2009). The WEKA data mining software: An update. *SIGKDD Explorations, 11*(1), 10–18.
42. Houda, M., Khemaja, M., Oliveira, K., & Abed, M. (2010). A public transportation ontology to support user travel planning. In *Proceedings of the Fourth International Conference on Research Challenges in Information Science (RCIS)* (pp. 127–136). Nice, France.
43. Innovateuk.org. (2013). Common Highways Agency Rijkswaterstaat Model (CHARM) (online). Available at: https://www.innovateuk.org/documents/1524978/1866952/CHARM+business+specification/b5f6281d-8701–4287-84e9-c00d266a15b3. Accessed 11 Dec 2013.

44. Kaplan, A. M., & Haenlein, M. (2010). Users of the world, unite! The challenges and opportunities of SocialMedia, Business Horizons, *53*(1), 59–68.
45. Kaur, A., & Gupta, V. (2013). A survey on sentiment analysis and opinion mining techniques. Journal of Emerging Technologies in Web Intelligence, Vol. 5, No. 4, November 2013.
46. Kenyon, S., & Lyons, G. (2003). The value of integrated multimodal traveller information and its potential contribution to modal change. *Transportation Research Part F: Traffic Psychology and Behaviour, 6*(1), 1–21.
47. Kiely. (2013). http://businessetc.thejournal.ie/facebook-social-media-ryanair-robin-kiely-783104-Feb2013/. Accessed 1 April 13.
48. Khanwalkar, S., Seldin, M., Srivastava, A., Kumar, A., & Colbath, S. (2013). Content-based geo-location detection for placing tweets pertaining to trending news on map. In *4th International Workshop on Mining Ubiquitous and Social Environments* (*MUSE*), Prague, Czech Republic, September 2013.
49. Lanagan, J., & Smeaton, A. F. (2011). Using twitter to detect and tag important events in live sports. In *Proceedings of the Fifth International AAAI Conference on Weblogs and Social Media* (*ICWSM*).
50. Leetaru, K., Wang, S., Cao, G., Padmanabhan, A., & Shook, E. (2013). Mapping the global Twitter heartbeat: The geography of Twitter. First Monday, *18* (5), doi:10.5210/fm. v18i5.4366
51. Li, L., Wu, W., & Liu, N. (2013). Ontology model for situation awareness of city tunnel traffic. In *Proceedings of the 2nd International Symposium on Computer, Communication, Control and Automation* (*ISCCCA-13*) (pp. 601–603). Paris, France: Atlantis Press.
52. Libardo, A., & Nocera, S. (2008). Transportation elasticity for the analysis of Italian transportation demand on a regional scale. *Traffic Engineering and Control, 49*(5), 187–192.
53. Liu, X., Lang, B., Yu, W., Lou, J., Huang, L. (2011). AUDR: An advanced unstructured data repository, pervasive computing and applications (ICPCA). In *2011 6th International Conference, Conference Publication*, pp. 462–469.
54. Madkour, M., & Maach, A. (2011). Ontology-based context modeling for vehicle-aware services. *Journal of Theoretical and Applied Information Technology, 34*(2), 158–166.
55. Musakwa, W. (2014). The use of social media in public transit systems: the case of the Gautrain, Gauteng Province, South Africa: Analysis and Lessons Learnt. In *Proceedings REAL CORP 2014 Tagungsband*, 21–23 May 2014, Vienna, Austria. http://www.corp.at
56. Mai, E., & Hranac, R. (2013). Twitter Interactions as a Data Source for Transportation Incidents. In *TRB 92nd Annual Meeting Compendium of Papers*, 2013.
57. Manning, C., & Schütze, H. (1999). *Foundations of statistical natural language processing.* Cambridge, MA: MIT Press.
58. Manning, C., Raghavan, P., & Schtze, H. (2008). *Introduction to information retrieval.* New York, USA: Cambridge university Press.
59. Mazzulla, G., & Forciniti, C. (2012). Spatial association techniques for analysing trip distribution in an urban area. *European Transport Research Review, 4*(4), 217–233.
60. Metro. (2011). West Yorkshire LTP3 Network Management Plan, 2011. http://www.wymetro.com/uploadedFiles/WYMetro/Content/aboutmetro/Local_Transport_Plan/20121003Network ManagementPlan.pdf. Accessed January 2015.
61. Minnesota Department of Transportation, Office of Policy Analysis (2011). Use of Social Media by Minnesota Cities and Counties. Transportation Research Synthesis.
62. Minkov, E., Wang, R. C., Cohen, W. W. (2005). Extracting personal names from email: applying named entity recognition to informal text. In *Proceedings of the conference on Human Language Technology and Empirical Methods in Natural Language Processing*, pp. 443–450.
63. Moss, M. L., & Kaufman, S. (2013). How Social Media Moves in New York—Final report. http://www.utrc2.org/sites/default/files/pubs/Final-Report-Social-Media-NYC.pdf. Accessed August 1, 2013.

64. Netzer, O., Feldman, R., Goldenberg, J., & Fresko, M. (2012). Mine your own business: market-structure surveillance through text mining. *Marketing Science, 31*(3), 521–543.
65. Niaraki, A. S., & Kim, K. (2009). Ontology based personalized route planning system using a multi-criteria decision making approach. *Expert Systems with Applications, 36*, 2250–2259.
66. Nocera, S. (2010). An operational approach for quality evaluation in public transport services. *Ingegneria Ferroviaria, 65*(4), 363–383.
67. Nocera, S. (2011). The key role of quality assessment in public transport policy. *Traffic Engineering and Control, 52*(9), 394–398.
68. Nocera, S., & Cavallaro, F. (2011). Policy effectiveness for containing CO_2 emissions in transportation. *Procedia—Social and Behavioral Science, 20*, 703–713.
69. Nugroho, A. S., Endarnoto, S. K., Pradipta. S., & Purnama J. (2011). Traffic condition information extraction and visualization from social media twitter for android mobile application. In *Proceedings of the International Conference on Electrical Engineering and Informatics* (*ICEEI*).
70. O'Connor, B., Balasubramanyan, R., Routledge, B. R., & Smith, N. A. (2010). From tweets to polls: Linking text sentiment to public opinion time series. In *Proceedings of the Fourth International AAAI Conference on Weblogs and Social Media* (*ICWSM*).
71. Oppenheim, N. (1995). *Urban travel demand modeling: From individual choices to general equilibrium*. New York: Wiley.
72. Pak, A., & Paroubek, P. (2010). Twitter as a corpus for sentiment analysis and opinion mining. *Computer, 10*, 1320–1326.
73. Pang, B., & Lee, L. (2008). Opinion mining and sentiment analysis. *Foundations and Trends Information Retrieval, 2*(1–2), 1–135.
74. Paradesi, S. (2011). Geotagging Tweets Using Their Content. In *Proceedings of the Twenty-Fourth. International Florida Artificial Intelligence Research Society Conference, 2011* (pp. 335–356).
75. Pender, B., Currie, G., Delbosc, A., & Shiwakoti, N. (2014). Social Media Use in Unplanned Passenger Rail Disruptions—An International Study. IN *TRB 93rd Annual Meeting, 2014*.
76. Piskorski, J., & Yangarber, R. (2013). Information extraction: past, present and future. In *Theory and Applications of Natural Language Processing* (pp 23–49).
77. Priedhorsky, R., Culotta, A., Del Valle, S. Y. (2014). Inferring the origin locations of tweets with quantitative confidence. In *Proceedings of the 17th ACM conference on Computer Suppostive Cooperative Work and Social Computing* (*CSCW*), Baltimore, MD, Feb 15–19.
78. Ritter, A., Clark, S., Mausam, & Etzioni, O. (2011). Named entity recognition in tweets: an experimental study. In *Proceedings of the Conference on Empirical Methods in Natural Language Processing* (*EMNLP*).
79. Schulz, A., Ristoski, P., & Paulheim. H (2013). I see a car crash: Real-time detection of small scale incidents in microblogs. In P. Cimiano, M. Fernández, V. Lopez, S. Schlobach, J. Völker, (Eds.), *The Semantic Web: ESWC 2013 Satellite Events*, Vol. 7955. Lecture Notes in Computer Science, pp. 22–33. Berlin: Springer.
80. Schweitzer, L. (2012). How are we doing? Opinion mining customer sentiment in US transit agencies and airlines via twitter. In *TRB 91th Annual Meeting*.
81. Shepherd, P. A. (2013). The transportation world should embrace social media… carefully. In *Eno Center of Transportation*. http://www.enotrans.org/ctp-blog/the-transportation-world-should-embrace-social-media-carefully. Accessed August 1, 2013.
82. Sood, S., Owsley, S., Hammond, K., & Birnbaum, L. (2007). Reasoning through search: A novel approach to sentiment classification. In *WWW2007, North Western University, Electrical Engineering and Computer Science Department Technical Report NWU-EECS-07-05*, Banff, Canada, July 21, 2007. http://infolab.northwestern.edu/media/papers/paper10171.pdf. Accessed July 7th, 2013.
83. Steiger, E., Ellersiek, T., Zipf, A. (2014). Explorative public transport flow analysis from uncertain social media data. In *GeoCrowd '14 Proceedings of the 3rd ACM SIGSPATIAL International Workshop on Crowd sourced and Volunteered Geographic Information* (pp. 1–7).
84. Steinwart, I., & Christmann, A. (2008). *Support vector machines*. New York: Springer.

85. Sterne, J. (2010). Social media metrics: How to measure and optimize your marketing investment, books.google.com.
86. Tapscott, D., Williams, A. D., & Herman, D. (2013). Government 2.0: Transforming government and governance for the twenty-first century, New Paradigm, January 2008 http://mobility.grchina.com/innovation/gov_transforminggovernment.pdf
87. Transportation Research Board [TRB] (2004). User information systems; developments and issues for the 21st century. In *TRB Millennium Papers* (Washington, DC: National Academy of Sciences).
88. Transportation Safety Board of Canada (2013). Social media terms of use. http://www.bst-tsb.gc.ca/eng/social. Accessed August 1, 2013.
89. Trappey, C., Wu, H. Y., & Liu K. L. (2012). Knowledge discovery of customer satisfaction and dissatisfaction using ontology-based text analysis of critical incident dialogues. In *Proceedings of the 2012 IEEE 16th International Conference on Computer Supported Cooperative Work in Design*, Wuhan, 2012 (pp. 470–475).
90. Virginia Department of Transportation (2013). VDOT on Social Media. http://www.virginiadot.org/newsroom/social_media.asp. Accessed August 1, 2013.
91. Wang, J., Ding, Z., & Jiang, C. (2005). An ontology-based public transport query system. In *Proceedings of the First International Conference on semantics and Grid, SKG, 2005*.
92. Wiegand, M., Balahur, A., Roth, B., Klakow, D., & Montoyo, A. (2010). A survey on the role of negation in sentiment analysis. In *Proceedings of the Workshop on Negation and Speculation in Natural Language Processing (NeSp-NLP '10)*, Association for Computational Linguistics (pp. 60–68). Stroudsburg, PA, USA, 2010.
93. Wilson, T., Wiebe, J., & Hoffmann, P. (2009). Recognizing contextual polarity: An exploration of features for phrase-level sentiment analysis. *Computational Linguistics, 35*(3), 399–433.
94. Yang, W. D., & Wang, T. (2012). The fusion model of intelligent transportation systems based on the urban traffic ontology. *Physics Procedia, 25*, 917–923.
95. Zimmer, C. G. (2012). Social media use in local public agencies: A study of California's cities. Master Thesis, Department of Public Policy and Administration, California State University, Sacramento.
96. Grant-Muller, S. M., Gal-Tzur, A., Minkov, E., Nocera, S., Kuflik, T., & Shoor, I. (2014). Efficacy of mining social media data for transport policy and practice. In *Proceedings of the 93th Transportation Research Board Meeting*, paper no. 14–1716. Washington, D.C., USA, January 12–16, 2014.

'Garbage Let's Take Away': Producing Understandable and Translatable Government Documents: A Case Study from Japan

Rei Miyata, Anthony Hartley, Kyo Kageura and Cécile Paris

Abstract Government departments increasingly communicate information to citizens digitally via web sites, and, in many societies, the linguistic diversity of these citizens is also growing. In Japan, a largely monolingual society, municipal governments now routinely address the necessity of providing practical and legal information to residents with limited Japanese by machine-translating their public service web sites into selected languages. Cost constraints often mean the translation is left un-edited and, as a result, may be unclear, misleading or even incomprehensible. While machine translation from Japanese is particularly challenging because of its structural uniqueness, the state of the art in the field generally is such that poor output is a universal problem. The solution we propose draws on recent advances in controlled authoring, document structuring and machine translation evaluation. It is realised as a prototype tool that enables non-professional writers to create documents where individual sentences and overall flow are both clear. The tool is designed to enhance machine-translatability into English without compromising the readability of the Japanese original. The originality of the tool is to provide an interactive sentence checker that is context-sensitive to the individual functional elements of a document template specialised for the public administration domain. Where natural Japanese sentences give bad translation results, we pre-process them internally into a form which yields acceptable machine translation output. Evaluation of the tool will target three concerns: its usability by non-professional

R. Miyata (✉) · K. Kageura
Graduate School of Education, The University of Tokyo, Tokyo, Japan
e-mail: rei@p.u-tokyo.ac.jp

A. Hartley
College of Intercultural Communication, Rikkyo University, Tokyo, Japan

C. Paris
CSIRO, Data61, Sydney, Australia

A. Hartley
University of Leeds, Leeds, UK

© Springer International Publishing Switzerland 2015
S. Nepal et al. (eds.), *Social Media for Government Services*,
DOI 10.1007/978-3-319-27237-5_16

367

authors; the acceptability of the Japanese document; and the comprehensibility of the English translation. We suggest that such an authoring framework could facilitate government communication with citizens in many societies beyond Japan.

Keywords Government communication · Controlled language · Document structure · Authoring tool · Machine translation · DITA

1 Introduction

In this digital age, government information too is typically disseminated digitally, for example via web sites and social media, such as Facebook[1] accounts that, increasingly, government departments maintain to communicate with the online citizenry. In the case of Japan, a recent survey [27] shows that 46.7 % of Japanese municipalities use commercial Social Networking Services (SNS) such as Facebook, mixi[2] and Myspace,[3] and 38.3 % use mini- and micro-blogs such as Twitter[4] and Ameba なう.[5] Municipalities publish on their web sites and social media information about not only events or tourism of the regions, but also a number of procedures that must be complied with when living in Japan (e.g., registering residency in the local district; sorting and recycling garbage; taking action in case of emergencies). Importantly, we observed that in many cases texts disseminated in social media are based on or extracted from existing web site texts, which justifies our taking web site documents as our preferred starting point.

In general, such texts are produced in the national language(s). In many countries, however, some residents do not speak the local official language(s), possibly because they have not been in the country for a long time. In Japan, the case in point, there are many foreign residents who do not have the Japanese skills necessary to understand official documents written in Japanese. Although some large municipalities provide translations of their web site into various other languages spoken by local communities, the target languages are limited, often only English. Moreover, the scope of the translated versions is usually much more restricted than the original Japanese since, as [9] points out, 'to expect local governments with limited resources to translate their entire web sites into one or more foreign languages would be unrealistic.' In most of the small municipalities, conditions are worse. These then typically rely on automated machine translation (MT) tools, or the residents themselves rely on MT, such as Google Translate,[6] somehow to grasp the meaning of the texts.

---

[1]http://facebook.com/.

[2]https://mixi.jp/.

[3]https://myspace.com/.

[4]https://twitter.com/.

[5]http://now.ameba.jp/.

[6]https://translate.google.com/.

Several issues arise. These documents are typically created by non-professional writers, since local councils often do not have the money to hire trained authors. Machine translation tools are known to be imperfect, in particular for languages with greatly differing structures, such as Japanese and English (as opposed to French and English, or Japanese and Korean, for example). The documents are often embedded in html (since they are web pages), which may further complicate the automatic translation by fragmenting sentences. As a result, the translated texts are often misinterpreted or not understandable by their intended audience.

Our work builds on prior research in controlled natural languages, document structuring and authoring environments to design and develop a system that will assist people in creating documents that are more amenable to machine translation, without impairing the understandability of the source text. Although our research is done specifically in the context of generating web site text about municipal procedures in Japan, it is nonetheless applicable to the contents of social media and other types of documents, as well as other countries and languages.

This chapter introduces our scenario, providing specific examples of the problems encountered both in Japanese-to-English translation and document structuring. We then introduce the notions of controlled natural language, functional document structure and authoring environment, reviewing prior work in these areas. We present (with examples in English) an analysis of procedural texts from Japanese municipalities, and show how a standard document structure can be specialised and instantiated to cover these texts. We then argue for the need to contextualise the rules of a controlled natural language within that document structure. We propose an authoring environment, named *MuTUAL*, that exploits these concepts to support the writing of municipal procedures such that they are easily translatable by automated tools. The system is currently a work-in-progress. It is designed to employ a variety of mechanisms, including guidance on document structure and on appropriate syntax, and automatic pre-translation processing where necessary. We also aim for our system to easily integrate in the future other mechanisms related to machine translation, such as terminology databases and translation memories, to provide yet more support. Finally, we draw conclusions for future work.

2 Problems and Scenario

Imagine that you have just started life in Japan. You seek information on the web, in particular on the web site of your local municipality, to ensure you are complying with various regulations. We identified that you might encounter two difficulties, at two different linguistic levels. We outline them below.

2.1 Sentence-Level Issues

We continue our scenario. Suppose you have not yet gained sufficient operational command of Japanese to understand the instructions when they are provided only in Japanese. While some information is provided in such languages as English, Chinese, Korean, or Portuguese, these versions are usually created in part by machine translation (MT). Also, in many municipalities there remains information vital for completing necessary administrative procedures or leading your daily life which is provided only in Japanese. In such a situation, having recourse to free, online and thus readily available MT may seem an attractive option. However, while the quality of MT output is very reasonable for many language pairs, this is unfortunately not the case with Japanese-into-English (and into most languages, except for Korean). On not-so-infrequent occasions, you may encounter such MT outputs as:

> (a)   Garbage let's take away.
> (b)   From July 2013, you will not be able to use only the specified garbage bag.

The Japanese input for (a) is 'ごみは持ち帰ろう,' the sensible translation of which is 'Please take your garbage home.' This MT error stems from differences between Japanese and English in expressing public requests.

The Japanese input for (b) is '2013年7月からは、指定ごみ袋しか使えません,' which is correctly translated as 'From July 2013 you can use only the specified garbage bags.' In this case, the MT system has mis-translated the Japanese construction 'しか…ない,' which is something like a double negation.

While, as a native- or non native-speaker of English, you may be able to guess what (a) means, you may equally be misled into thinking this notice is a call for community volunteers to clean up garbage in, for instance, a nearby park. In the case of (b), what the MT output says is just the opposite of what the Japanese says. You are therefore at risk of completely misinterpreting the message or, even if you suspect its true intended meaning, being left in a state of uncertainty. Such misunderstandings and doubts can pose critical problems for your new life.

Given that MT systems are being and will continue to be widely used in this domain, considering the cost of having all municipal information translated solely by human translators, improving the quality of the output to a reliable level is an urgent—but arduous—task.

From the point of view of MT technologies, MT systems dealing with Japanese as source language (SL) or target language (TL) are not behind the state-of-the-art. Japanese natural language processing (NLP) researchers have historically invested much energy in MT research and sometimes played a world-leading role, e.g., in proposing the paradigm of example-based machine translation (EBMT) [30, 46]. Moreover, there are many commercially or freely available Japanese MT systems developed in Japan and based on different architectures and technologies: rule-based machine translation (RBMT), which uses (manually-constructed) rules to transform SL into TL; EBMT, which uses analogical reasoning based on translated examples; and statistical machine translation (SMT), which relies on statistical learning from large aligned bi-lingual text corpora [8]. Although R&D has recorded a steady advance in MT performance, it does not point to a massive breakthrough in the near future.

An alternative approach to improving the performance of MT is to impose restrictions on the form and/or length of SL texts or using controlled natural language (CNL). If we can diagnose what MT can and cannot do and embed MT within the overall framework of information flow, we anticipate being able to use MT for producing reliable outputs.

2.2 Document-Level Issues

In Japanese municipal documents, we often find cases in which individual sentences make sense, but directions provided by the document as a whole are confusing.

Figure 1 provides an example: the instructions for registering personal seals[7] (for signing documents) in Shinjuku-city, Tokyo, which is one of the largest municipalities in Japan and provides human-translated information in multiple languages.

Reading this document, you may be at a loss, wondering whether you are eligible for seal registration or not, since the eligibility conditions for registering a personal seal are stated only at the bottom of the document, and then in an unclear manner, namely: 'Those Who Are Not Eligible for a Residence Records.' The requirements for re-registering a seal are similarly unclearly signposted: 'If You Move Out of Shinjuku City'; 'If You Leave Japan.' Moreover, section 'Personal Seals Registration Certificate,' which is a different task, offers no explanation as to why you would need to obtain such a certificate and whether it is required or optional, although this is alluded to at the end of 'Personal Seal (*Inkan*).'

2.3 Solution Scenario

We thus have two different but related problems. On the one hand, we have poor MT output. On the other hand, we have ill-organised document structure, which may well aggravate the situation, as readers have no reliable context to aid 'guessing' the actions actually required. This observation led us to realise the necessity of pursuing a unified solution to the overall issue of multilingualisation of municipal procedural information, namely, introducing controlled authoring of documents, where this control is applied consistently and seamlessly at both sentence- and document-level.

---

[7]http://www.city.shinjuku.lg.jp/foreign/english/guide/todoke/todoke_7.html. Accessed 11 June 2015.

Seal Registration

■ **Personal Seal (*Inkan*)**

In Japan, personal seals are used as a symbol of agreement or approval, like a signature, to verify official documents, such as contracts.

You can order a personal seal for your name at a stamp engraving outlet and register the imprint at the City Office. You must certify that the personal seal is registered, when necessary.

■ **Personal Seal That Cannot Be Registered**

• Stamps with letters that do not combine to form part of your full name, last name, or first name as registered in your residence record
• [...]
• Stamps that are inappropriate for registration (for example, stamps without an outer rim, cracked stamps, ready-made stamps, ring stamps, etc.)

■ **Personal Seal Registration Procedures**

Please bring the personal seal you wish to register along with your valid residence card [...] and complete the application procedures [...] Some registration restrictions apply, such as those on age (must be 15 years of age or older).

[...] bring the following items:
• The response sheet
• [...]

When registration has been completed, you will be issued a personal seal registration card. [...]

■ **Personal Seals Registration Certificate**

To apply for a certificate, please complete application procedures [...] and show your personal seal registration card. You will be issued a personal seal registration certificate, which certifies that your personal seal has been registered. [...]

■ **When Notification Is Necessary (for Personal Seal Registration)**

(1)   If you lose your personal seal [...]   Notification of Discontinuation
[...]

■ **If You Move Out of Shinjuku City (Personal Seal Registration)**

If you have completed personal seal registration but are moving out of Shinjuku City, please return the personal seal registration card. You will need to complete personal seal registration procedures at the municipal office of your new address. Even if you move back to the same address, you must still complete procedures for seal registration again.

■ **If You Leave Japan (Personal Seal Registration)**

If a person with personal seal registration leaves Japan, the personal seal registration becomes invalid and is deleted.

Even if you move back to the same address, you must complete personal seal registration again.

■ **Those Who Are Not Eligible for a Residence Record**

Anyone who is not eligible for a residence record—[...]—cannot register a seal.

Fig. 1 Personal seal registration procedure

As we will elaborate in later sections, we find that this integrated approach of embedding controlled sentences within a well-designed document structure has clear benefits in further improving MT output. Take, for instance, '文書を印刷する,'

which may naturally appear as a task title or as a step in a procedure. A given MT system may translate this as 'To print the document,' which is an appropriate wording for a title but not for a step, where 'Print the document' (imperative) is needed. If we knew the functional element in which a Japanese expression occurs, we could exploit this knowledge to pre-process expressions where necessary by transforming them such that the MT system is coerced into producing a contextually appropriate English translation (see Sect. 5.4). Since the pre-processing would be an internal operation which does not change the Japanese text seen by readers, the readability of the SL text would not be degraded by TL-oriented writing rules designed to improve MT output quality, which can happen (e.g., [18]).

3 Foundational Work

As mentioned above, we propose to solve the problem of producing translatable documents with an integrated approach of embedding controlled sentences within a well-designed document structure. We review below the work on which we build our approach.

3.1 Controlled (Natural) Language—C(N)L

A wide-ranging survey of the field offers the following short definition: 'A controlled natural language is a constructed language that is based on a certain natural language, being more restrictive concerning lexicon, syntax, and/or semantics, while preserving most of its natural properties' [26]. Since we are not concerned here with artificial, formal languages, for the sake of brevity we talk simply of controlled languages (CLs).

CLs can be categorised according to the problem they have been constructed to address: 'to improve communication among humans [...]; to improve [...] automatic translation; and to provide a natural and intuitive representation for formal notations' [26]. This third problem lies outside of our interests here. However, the ambition of the current work is to improve *both* monolingual communication *and* automatic translation, and thereby multilingual communication. In our case the constructed language is based on Japanese and the target language of translation is, in the first instance, English.

CLs can be further categorised according to whether they support communication among specialists or with 'lay' readers. Many CLs are designed for a specific domain—for example, AECMA [2] for aircraft maintenance, and Caterpillar Technical English [22] for engineering—and are characterised by a closed lexicon. SMART Controlled English [49], while imposing unchanging syntactic restrictions, can accommodate different lexicons to make it usable in a range of domains, although each is assumed to be specialised. In contrast, PLAIN [42] is designed to make official US government documents easier to understand for the general public.[8] The present application of CL has the same goal of promoting 'lay' understanding in a multilingual society.

With respect to language properties, Kuhn [26] identifies four largely independent dimensions for categorising CLs, each divided into five non-overlapping classes, 1–5. First, Precision (P) captures the degree to which meaning can be directly retrieved from textual form. Languages where every sentence is vague to some degree (like natural languages) are categorised as *Imprecise languages* (P^1). Our aim is to construct a *Less imprecise language* (P^2) with lower ambiguity and context-dependency. Second, Expressiveness (E) describes 'the range of propositions that a certain language is able to express.' Our CL needs to be on a par with PLAIN [42], classified as a *Language with maximal expressiveness* (E^5); the same goal holds for the English translated text. Third, Naturalness (N) describes the CL's proximity to a natural language in terms of readability and understandability. Again, our goal with the Japanese CL is to achieve the categorisation (N^5) of PLAIN—'complete texts and documents can be written in a natural style, with a natural text flow.' However, we may have to accept that, without editing, the English translated document may appear as (N^4) where, although single sentences have a natural flow, the text as a whole may not. Fourth, Simplicity (S) measures the simplicity or complexity of an exact and comprehensive description of the language. While natural Japanese—like any natural language—is classified as *Very complex* (S^1), we are attempting to eliminate many of the complex structures by specifying restrictions on it, while taking its description (knowledge, from the author's perspective) for granted. Crucially, achieving greater simplicity (S^2) requires implementing a tool that can identify violations of these restrictions and, ideally, propose legitimate alternatives (see Sect. 5.3).

CLs intended for communication and translation comprise a lexical component and a syntactic component. The former ideally respects the principles of 'one term—one meaning' and 'one meaning—one term,' to eliminate ambiguity and synonymy. Thus, for example, the AECMA standard [2] allows the use of 'free' only as an adjective meaning 'moves easily' (e.g., *Ensure the fasteners are free.*); its use as a verb is proscribed in favour of 'release' (e.g., *Release the fasteners.*). The syntactic component typically comprises between 30 and 60 rules, stated, depending on the particular CL, to varying degrees of specificity; thus it is not always possible to identify shared rules [36]. It is possible, however, to distinguish a common underlying ambition, which is to eliminate syntactic complexity and ambiguity by restricting sentence length and complexity. So, sentences are limited to 20 words and the maximum number of clauses is normally two, with constraints on the connectives that are used. Local dependencies are flagged by such devices as obligatory use of the complementiser 'that' and of pronouns (e.g., 'which'). This synthesis (Table 1) of the rules of Perkins Approved Clear English [44] typifies many English-based CLs designed for domain-specific communication.

---

[8]See http://www.plainlanguage.gov/. For a similar UK initiative, but one not backed by legislation, see http://www.plainenglish.co.uk/.

Table 1 Perkins Approved Clear English rules

1. Keep sentences short	6. Avoid elliptical constructions
2. Omit redundant words	7. Do not omit conjunctions or relatives
3. Order the parts of the sentence logically	8. Adhere to the PACE dictionary
4. Do not change construction in mid-sentence	9. Avoid strings of nouns.
5. Take care with the logic of 'and' and 'or'	10. Do not use '-ing' unless the word appears thus in the PACE dictionary

The fundamental problem with the current formulation of CL rule sets is that they are almost exclusively specified at the level of the sentence rather than at the level of the document [17]. This is because the notion of document element is itself very coarse-grained; the AECMA standard, for example, recognises only three document elements: procedures (instructions for use or action), descriptions and warnings/cautions. There is a very sparse linkage between syntactic rules and document elements; for example, the constraint of 20 words per sentence is relaxed to 25 in descriptions, while warnings are required to begin with a simple, clear command.

Generalising the principles of CL across languages requires a language-independent model of document structure that has been lacking hitherto. Such a model is necessarily functionally-oriented; it needs also to be sufficiently fine-grained to allow rules to be tied to functional elements that can provide context-sensitive guidance both to authors and to an MT system in its translation decision making. DITA (Darwin Information Typing Architecture) [35], an XML standard for defining documents in terms of their functional constituents, affords just such a framework [15], as we will see in Sect. 4.1.

Kittredge [24] and Nyberg et al. [34] provide overviews of CLs designed for translation. Evidence of reduced post-editing costs when a CL is employed is provided by, e.g., [4, 44, 45]. Improved comprehension by readers of the source documents themselves is demonstrated by, e.g., [37].

3.2 Japanese-Based CLs

In the case of Japanese CL, Nagao et al. [31] devised a controlled grammar to syntactically disambiguate Japanese sentences. Other pioneering work on Japanese CL was conducted by Yoshida and Matsuyama [52]. Although these researchers advocated the need for a Japanese CL in parallel with MT development, no practical implementation resulted from their efforts.

From the 1990s to the 2000s, research in computational linguistics focused on automatic rewriting (or pre-editing) and paraphrasing [19, 47, 48, 53]. However, this work on the automatic processing of natural language could not deal with highly complex or difficult expressions and the scope of variations of linguistic patterns was, therefore, limited.

More recently, Ogura et al. [38] proposed 'Simplified Technical Japanese' to improve MT performance, specifying six linguistic patterns to be regulated. Requirements for controlling Japanese texts, however, have not been examined sufficiently, and only a few studies, such as [18], have empirically measured the effectiveness of CL using qualitative human evaluations. In addition, the practical application of controlled Japanese has advanced little.

In contrast, Japanese technical writing methods and guidelines intended for human communication have been developed in the field of practical writing [20]. In recent years, the on-going 'Technical Japanese' (産業日本語) project has focused mainly on documents related to industry, such as patents. The aim of Technical Japanese is to improve readability and machine tractability [51]. Hartley et al. [18] also investigated the efficacy of CL for technical documents in Japanese, with respect both to the readability of the Japanese source and the quality of the English machine-translated output. Meeting both goals requires combining the wisdom of technical writing and CL.

While the recent studies mentioned above focused mainly on technical documents of industry and business, such as patents and manuals, Tatsumi et al. [50] formulated 22 CL rules for municipal web site documents (Table 2).

Table 2 Japanese CL rule set for municipal documents

1. Try to write sentences of no more than 70 characters. In no case use more than 100 characters
2. Do not interrupt a sentence with a bulleted list
3. Do not use parentheses to embed a sentence or long expression in a surrounding sentence
4. Ensure the relationship between the subject and the predicate is clear
5. Ensure the relationship between the modifier and the modified is clear
6. Use the particle が only to mean 'but'
7. Do not use the preposition ため to mean 'because'
8. To express 'from,' use the particle から. Use particle より only in comparisons
9. Avoid using multiple negative forms in a sentence
10. Use れる/られる only for the passive voice, and not to express the potential mood or honorifics
11. Avoid using words that can be interpreted in multiple ways. Use words with a narrowly defined meaning
12. Avoid using the colloquial expression になります (become)
13. Avoid using the expression という (as/like)
14. Avoid using the expressions ような, こと and もの (such as)
15. Do not double-up on words with the same meaning in a single sentence
16. Avoid using the expression 思われる (seems to be) and 考えられる (be considered)
17. Avoid using the verb 行う (do) with Sahen-nouns
18. Avoid the single use of the form したり (do … and)
19. When listing items, make sure they are syntactically parallel
20. Use words from a general Japanese-English dictionary
21. Avoid using compound Sahen-nouns
22. Ensure there are no typos or missing characters

They proceeded by (i) extracting writing guidelines and rules from books and documents about technical writing, and (ii) conducting a preliminary assessment of their efficacy. This work also empirically evaluated human readability of the source text (Japanese) and usefulness of MT output (English). The results showed that, overall, only about 30 % of the MT output was deemed useful even after CL rules were applied, although most of the rules improved or at least preserved Japanese readability. This tells us that CL itself alone is not enough to raise MT performance to an immediately usable level (without human editing). Thus, we need to complement the CL with other mechanisms, which we propose in Sect. 4. More interestingly, there is still a significant gap between technical writing and CL, which is counter-intuitive, since both share the same principle, that is, controlling the complexity and ambiguity of the linguistic expressions in texts.

In addition, comparing the outputs of RBMT and SMT systems revealed 'architectural' differences between them in terms of the impact of specific CL rules on their performance. This gives us the insight that it is important to formulate not only CL rules generally applicable to all MT systems, such as 'avoid long sentence,' but also rules specifically tuned to a particular system.

3.3 Authoring Environments for Multilingual Instructional Text

The idea and implementation of CL checkers is not new (e.g., [1]). Commercial tools are currently available to check conformity to general or to company-specific writing standards, for example, MAXIT,[9] which works only for English, and Acrolinx,[10] which caters for several languages, including English and Japanese.

The leading example of CL authoring linked to MT is the KANTOO system [33], which was designed for producing multilingual documentation in a range of technical domains.

A number of research projects explored the feasibility of generating multilingual instructional text from an underlying conceptual model of the task to be performed (e.g., [7, 16, 25, 39, 40, 43]). While the output could in principle be constrained to conform to CL rules, since these systems used rule-based text generation, in practice this was not the case. Moreover, they required a full ontological model of the target domain, which is not practicable for the relatively diffuse scope of Japanese municipal documents.

A related although different body of work relates to the broader field of Document Automation (DA). Commercial DA systems exist (e.g., HotDocs,[11]

---

[9]http://www.smartny.com/maxit.html/.

[10]http://www.acrolinx.com/.

[11]http://www.hotdocs.com/.

Exari,[12] LogicNets[13] and Arbortext[14]). They have been used in technical documentation to produce model-specific product documentation and decision support systems, and in the legal profession to automate the production of custom-built legal documents (e.g., standardised agreements). These systems provide an environment in which one can specify a document template to produce a set of documents with some degree of variability, thus enabling personalisation. These tools provide mail-merge-like features extended with conditional inclusion/exclusion of coarse-grained text units generally of the order of sections, paragraphs or perhaps sentences. They make use of a document structure, as we do, but do not explicitly address issues of multilinguality or translation.

Other authoring environments of interest include environments designed specifically to produce personalised documents [11, 12, 14]. Like commercial DA systems, HealthDoc, which generates tailored health-education documents, enables the authoring of a 'master document' which includes conditions that specify when to include various aspects of the document (e.g., for which intended user). Colineau et al. [11, 12] present a system interesting for our work because of its domain of application: the generation of public administration documents. All these environments make use of a document structure. They open for us the possibility of eventually having an environment which enables not only the production of understandable multilingual texts in the public administration domain but also their personalisation, so that readers obtain only those parts that are relevant to them. In the domain of public administration, such personalisation was shown by Colineau and her colleagues to be effective in terms of information seeking and a feature citizens might appreciate.

3.4 Document Structure: DITA

DITA (Darwin Information Typing Architecture) is an XML architecture for authoring and publishing technical information. DITA supports topic-based authoring which helps writers compose the modularised information covering not more than one concept, one procedure or one unit of referential information [3].

DITA was first developed at IBM and donated to the OASIS standards organization in 2004 [13]. DITA version 1.0 was approved by the OASIS DITA TC in 2005, and the latest version (1.2) was approved in 2010. Although DITA is not as widely used in Japan as in Europe and the US, DITA Consortium Japan[15] was established in 2008 to promote the DITA standard and develop the DITA market in Japan.

---

[12]http://www.exari.com/.

[13]http://www.logicnets.com/.

[14]http://www.ptc.com/products/arbortext/.

[15]http://dita-jp.org/en/.

DITA has two basic components: topic and map. Topic is a self-contained informational unit. Map is a mechanism for creating different deliverables from a single source, in other words, organising multiple topics as a document according to the output media or document purpose. The focus of this chapter is, however, chiefly on topic, although map is a useful mechanism for compiling and publishing documents both for web sites and for social media, given that the contents of the web site and those of social media overlap, as we mentioned in Sect. 1.

A topic is composed of functional elements which guide authors as to what kind of contents should be included and in what way these contents should be organised. At the highest level, the functional elements of a topic are predefined as follows [35]:

- *Title* 'contains the subject of the topic.'
- *Short description* is 'used both in topic content (as the first paragraph), in generated summaries that include the topic, and in links to the topic.'
- *Prolog* is 'the container for topic metadata, such as change history, audience, product, and so on.'
- *Body* 'contains the topic content: paragraphs, lists, sections, and other content that the information type permits.'
- *Related links* 'connect to other topics.'

DITA defines by default three basic topic types. *Concept topic*, which answers the question 'What is it?' is used to provide conceptual information. *Task topic*, which answers the question 'How to do it?' is used to describe a step-by-step procedure. *Reference topic* is used to present reference information which guides readers to other related documents or web sites.

These topics are defined by specialising the *Body* element of the generic topic. Task topic, for example, contains the following functional elements to cover the necessary information for describing certain tasks (ibid):

- *Prereq* (prerequisite) 'describes information that the user needs to know or do before starting the immediate task.'
- *Context* 'provides background information for the task.'
- *Steps* 'provides the main content of the task topic. A task consists of a series of steps that accomplish the task.'
- *Result* 'describes the expected outcome for the task as a whole.'
- *Example* 'provides an example that illustrates or supports the task.'
- *Postreq* (postrequisite) 'describes steps or tasks that the user should do after the successful completion of the current task.'

However, the functional elements of task topic as defined in DITA are still too coarse-grained to afford specific guidance to authors of municipal procedural documents. It becomes necessary to instantiate each element and specialise certain elements to match the needs of municipal procedures.

4 Case Study

In this section, we describe a DITA instantiation for municipal procedural documents. Although procedural documents include 'concept' and 'reference' as well as 'task,' as a starting point we focus on the task topic, which forms the core of procedural documents. We present a set of CL rules for administrative documents, corresponding to a list of features to be controlled to improve MT performance, and discuss ways of contextualising the rules to the document structures. Furthermore, to attain a higher MT performance, we suggest combining the contextualised CL rules with pre-translation processing.

4.1 DITA Instantiation

To instantiate each element of the *Body* of the task topic, we first investigated 123 Japanese municipal procedural documents collected from the Council of Local Authorities for International Relations (CLAIR), Shinjuku-city, and Hamamatsu-city. We comprehensively extracted the functional elements and categorised them according to a fine-grained scheme based on [23]. We then assigned these functional elements to DITA elements (Table 3).

Prereq can be specialised into three types of conditions for municipal procedures: *Personal condition*, *Event condition*, and *Item condition*. *Personal condition* defines conditions for social status of applicants such as 'those who are 15 years of age or older,' 'those who do not have Japanese nationality' and 'those who live in Shinjuku-city.' *Event condition* defines conditions related to life events such as 'when you enter Japan,' 'when you get married' and 'when you come into

Table 3 Instantiation of the DITA task topic

DITA element (default)	Specified functional element
Prereq	Personal condition
	Event condition
	Item condition
Context	Explanation (Summary, Purpose, Expiration of validity, Penalty, Related concept)
Steps	Necessary items to bring
	Place to go
	Form(s) to complete
	Payment
Result	Result (Period for procedure, Items to be issued, Contact from local government)
Example	(N/A)
Postreq	Guidance to other procedures

Shinjuku-city from other municipalities.' *Item condition* defines conditions for physical objects such as 'Stamps with imprints that are smaller than an 8-mm^2 or larger than a 25-mm^2,' which is a constraint on registering a personal seal.

Context plays an important role in helping readers understand and facilitating smooth conduct of procedures. In this element, explanations such as 'why you need to complete the procedure' (*Purpose*) or 'the consequences of not completing the procedure' (*Penalty*) are presented.

Steps, an essential element for properly carrying out municipal procedures after satisfying the conditions, can be specified into four main functional elements shown in Table 3. This element directly specifies readers' actions (*bring, go to, submit* and *pay*).

DITA also defines the *Result* of the task. Although this element is not necessarily required by procedural tasks, it is useful for readers to know in advance the expected results, such as 'when and what will happen after the procedure is completed.'

Example is often used in technical documents such as software manuals and is specified in DITA by default. However, we rarely found this element in the municipal procedures and decided to omit it.

Finally, as for *Postreq*, in some cases municipal procedures refer to other related procedures. For instance, documents explaining 'Personal Seal Registration' tend to contain the procedure for 'Personal Seals Registration Certificate' as we saw in Fig. 1. While this kind of related information is of practical use in real life, it can confuse readers' understanding of the current procedure to be completed. Therefore, it is effective to group related procedures together separately from the main procedure, labeled as *Guidance to other procedures*.

Using this DITA framework helps us to diagnose existing documents and decide how to reorganise them. Figure 2 is an excerpt of the Shinjuku-city 'Seal

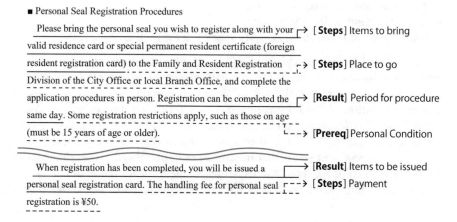

Fig. 2 Analysis of an existing municipal document using our DITA framework

Fig. 3 Model example of the seal registration procedure

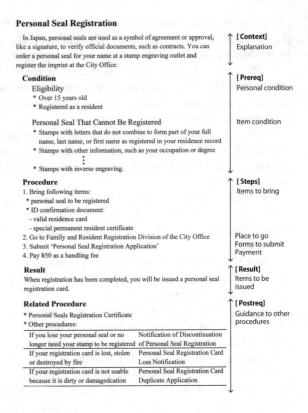

Registration' document presented in Fig. 1, here annotated in accordance with our DITA elements to highlight several problems.

- *Steps* are scattered in the text.
- *Results* are also scattered in the text.
- *Forms to submit* of *Steps* is missing.
- *Prereq* (*Personal condition*) abruptly appears in the middle of the text.

Our ultimate objective in applying DITA is to offer document models that non-professional authors can use easily to create municipal documents from scratch. Figure 3 shows a sample task topic of 'Seal Registration' procedure we created as a reformulation of the information in Fig. 1 following the analysis of documents from CLAIR, Shinjuku-city and Hamamatsu-city. Since our aim here is to illustrate the advantages of a well-structured document, this sample text is created by 'recycling' text spans that instantiate our specialised DITA elements in the publications of these three municipalities. Sentence-level issues of clarity and simplicity are left unaddressed here but are a major focus of our development effort.

4.2 CL Formulation and Contextualisation

The DITA specialisation described above has provisionally established a specific task topic for municipal procedures and enabled us to know 'what contents should be written and in what order they should be organised.' Now, given that MT deals only with linguistic expressions, we go on to specify 'how they should be written in the text.' What is important here is to define CL rules to regulate linguistic patterns in relation to each functional element.

We first formulated CL rules by (i) translating existing sentences extracted from municipal web sites using three MT systems, (ii) specifying the linguistic and textual features which tended to degrade MT performance, and (iii) defining CL rules to control these features. While Tatsumi et al. [50] constructed rather 'general purpose' rules based on insights from technical writing targeting linguistic features that may not in fact occur in our domain, we focused on finer-grained linguistic and textual features actually occurring in our corpus of municipal documents and formulated 'domain specific' CL rules. A list of features to be controlled is shown in Table 4. Although we noted that the presence of terminology (technical expressions, proper nouns) in municipal documents hinders MT performance to a nonnegligible degree, we have deferred work on this issue to a future time.

At this stage, we have, on the one hand, a specialised DITA structure and, on the other hand, a set of CL rules (linguistic or textual features to be controlled). The next task is to connect these CL rules to the DITA structure.

The Japanese source segment '日本に入国したとき,' for example, occurs as a DITA *Event condition* and corresponds to linguistic feature no. 11, 'Lack of subject,' in Table 4. This may be mis-translated as 'When I entered Japan' instead of 'When you entered Japan.' This indicates that the lack of an explicit subject in the *Event condition* degrades the MT output. In contrast, in the *Steps* context, the lack of a subject does not cause a problem. Indeed, it can be desirable if you want to produce a target English sentence in an imperative form, such as 'Bring the ID.' Thus, defining which CL rules apply to which DITA elements, which we term *CL contextualisation*, is a requirement for the effective use of MT.

In particular, Japanese stylistic features such as 'Imperative/persuasive form' and 'Voice' are closely tied to specific DITA elements: in *Steps*, for instance, we find various sentence-final endings, including '〜してください' ('please do'), '〜しましょう' ('let's'), and '〜しなさい' ('do'). We next plan to tune our CL rules to sanction particular linguistic patterns for each functional element. To achieve this goal, we will identify and categorise the patterns existing in a corpus of real documents, adopting the approach of register analysis [6]. We will then define what should be written in a prescriptive manner with reference to both MT errors and knowledge of technical writing and formulate specified CL rules. For example, we might tentatively formulate the rule that, within the *Steps* element, the imperative style '〜しなさい' should be used at the end of the sentence.

Table 4 Features to be controlled to improve MT performance

Mood/modality

1. Imperative/persuasive form	5. Tense
2. Interrogative	6. Voice
3. Prohibition	7. Ending sentence with particle O (を) + Noun
4. Possibility	

Structural

8. Long sentence	19. Inserted adverbial clause
9. Dependency relation	20. Ending clause with noun
10. Multiple verbs in a sentence	21. Sahen-noun + Desu (です)
11. Lack of subject	22. Attributive use of Shika ~ Nai (しか〜ない)
12. Lack of object	23. Inconsistency between subject and object
13. Conjunction	24. Verb + You (よう)
14. Connection	25. A or not
15. Unbalanced connection	26. Sahen-noun + O (を) + Suru (する)/Okonau (行う)
16. Particle Ga (が) for object	27. Ni-Naru (になる)/To-Naru (となる)
17. Enumeration A-Mo, B-Mo (Aも、Bも)	28. Possible auxiliary verb Reru/Rareru (れる・られる)
18. Te-kuru (てくる)/Te-iku (ていく)	29. Sahen-noun + Sareru(される)

Lexical

30. Particle Nado (など・等)	40. Expression Kangae-rareru (考えられる)
31. Formal noun Koto (こと)/Mono (もの)	41. Expression Ni-tsuki (につき)
32. Giving and receiving verb	42. Particle Te (て)
33. Redundant word	43. If particle To (と)
34. Compound word	44. Particle E-Wa (へは)
35. Omission	45. Particle Ni-Wa (には)
36. Suffix	46. Particle No-Ka (のか)
37. Particle Made (まで)	47. Demonstrative pronoun (ko-so-a-do)
38. Particle De (で)	48. Particle Ni (に)
39. Particle No (の) to mean 'by' or 'from'	

Textual/orthographic

49. Japanese Kana/Chinese Kanji/number	53. Parentheses
50. Bullet mark	54. Square bracket
51. Unit	55. Wave dash
52. Punctuation (sentence separation)	

4.3 Pre-translation Processing

We now illustrate our observation at the end of Sect. 2.3 that TL-oriented CL rules for MT do not necessarily ensure the quality of the source text. Here is an example.

> [JA1]　身分証明書を持参する。
> [MT1]　The ID is brought.

The Japanese source sentence [JA1] is written in the declarative style '〜する,' which has been translated by using the passive voice in English when in fact the imperative form is more natural in this context. So we can apply the tentative rule formulated at the end of Sect. 4.2 to rewrite '〜する' as '〜しなさい' (imperative form *do*), as seen in [JA2].

> [JA2]　身分証明書を持参しなさい。
> [MT2]　Bring the ID.

[MT2] is, as expected, better than [MT1]. However, we now face the problem that, in terms of appropriateness and naturalness, [JA1] is more suitable for municipal documents than is [JA2]. To meet the requirements of both source text quality and MT performance, we have to complement CL rules with subsequent pre-translation processing. In this example, we in fact define the rule for authors as 'use declarative form' then process this source sentence in accordance with the 'use imperative form' prior to translating it. What is more, this processing can be automated, providing we control the linguistic patterns of source texts strictly enough, an issue which we address in the next section.

5 MuTUAL: An Authoring Support System

Considering the fact that most Japanese municipalities cannot afford to hire technical writers, it is crucial to provide non-professional authors with tools that support the structuring and writing of municipal documents. In this section, we propose an authoring support system for municipal documents, *MuTUAL* (Municipal Text multilingUALisation), which implements the framework described in the preceding sections and explain the system configuration. We then elaborate on the core modules, introducing the prototype we are currently developing.

5.1 Document Structuring Mechanism

Our system comprises the following modules (see Fig. 4).

- *Topic template* is a user interface for municipal staff to author a particular topic from scratch or by reusing previously written topics from the *topic database*, seamlessly invoking *CL checker* and with access to the *terminology database*.

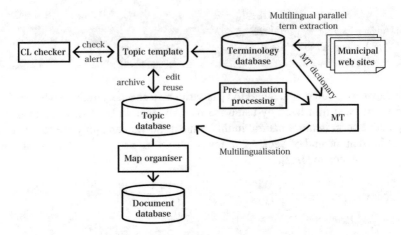

Fig. 4 Modules of *MuTUAL*

- *CL checker* is a background process that analyses the source text in the topic template, displays the diagnosis and suggestions for rewriting, and supports the editing task.
- *Terminology database* registers multilingual parallel terms extracted from existing municipal web sites authors can or should refer to, and also constitutes an MT dictionary.
- *Topic database* archives the topics written in the source language (i.e., Japanese).
- *MT* with *pre-translation processing* automatically translates the topics in the *topic database*.
- *Map organiser* helps authors to assemble multiple topics from the *topic database* and compose documents tailored for different purposes, which will finally be preserved in *document database*.

5.2 Topic Template

The topic template is the core interface for authoring topics. Figure 5 shows the prototype task topic template. It provides the basic DITA task topic structure on the left-hand side of the screen. Authors can populate (or delete) the additional elements such as *Step 1*, *Step 2* and *Step 3* in *Steps*, and instantiate each element by selecting an appropriate one from the list of detailed functional elements shown in Table 3. It also provides tool tips for guidance on DITA elements.

The principal means to enhance authoring and translation is to invoke different CL checkers tailored to each functional element. For example, the CL checker for the *Steps* element implements the rule 'use declarative form 〜する at the end of the sentence,' while others do not.

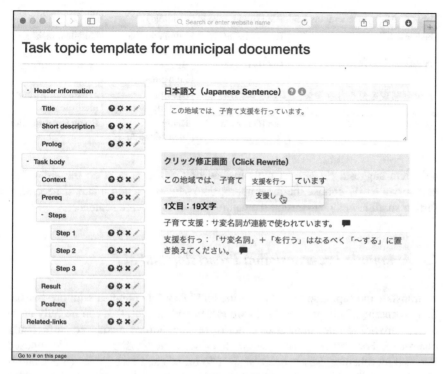

Fig. 5 Prototype of the task topic template with CL checker

5.3 CL Checker

On the right-hand side of the interface in Fig. 5, authors enter Japanese text for each functional element in the simple text box on the top of the screen, referring as necessary to writing instructions and guidelines about implemented CL rules.

The system automatically splits the input text by sentence, counts and shows the number of characters in each sentence, and displays warning messages if it exceeds the threshold levels of 30 characters ('long') and 50 characters ('too long'). The system then analyses each sentence and displays any sentence that violates the CL, together with diagnostic comments and suggestions for rewriting below.

In addition, we have implemented a preliminary rewriting support function with several of the features implemented by Mitamura and Nyberg [28] and Mitamura et al. [29]. It shows the original input sentence with the offending expression high-lighted and alternatives displayed on mouse-over. If the author clicks a suggestion, the original sentence in the text box above is automatically rewritten. Figure 5 shows a violation of the CL rule 'Avoid using the verb 行う (do) with Sahen-nouns,' which corresponds to the linguistic feature no. 26 in Table 4. The system detects the rule violation in the initial draft '支援を行っています' ('is doing the

Table 5 MT system outputs contrasted (imperative form in bold)

Japanese ST	TransGateway	Minna no Jido Hon'yaku	Google translate
身分証明書を持参する	The ID is brought	**Bring identification**	I bring identification
身分証明書を持参しなさい	**Bring the ID**	Brought identification	**Please bring your identification**
身分証明書を持参	The ID is brought	**Bring identification**	**Bring identification**

aid') and suggests '支援し' ('aid') instead of '支援を行っ' ('do the aid'). The author can easily choose the most appropriate suggestion and make, if necessary, further small revisions to ensure the naturalness of the source sentence.

5.4 Automatic Pre-translation Processing and MT

To translate the Japanese text, we employ an MT system coupled with pre-translation processing. This processing, as we mentioned in Sect. 4.3, can be fully automated providing the linguistic patterns of the source texts are sufficiently controlled. For instance, the CL-compliant segment '持参する' is decomposed into two morphemes, Sahen-noun '持参' ('to bring') and verb 'する' ('do'), and is changed into '持参しなさい' through transformation of the latter morpheme. This is accomplished by defining simple transformation rules and using a Japanese morphological analyser such as MeCab.[16]

Since Hartley et al. [18] and Tatsumi et al. [50] revealed that the efficacy of CL rules is sensitive to the particular MT system being used, it is also critically important in this phase to cope with the variability of the systems. Let us take another look at the example sentence shown in Sect. 4.3, '身分証明書を持参する,' which we now rewrite in two different versions: '身分証明書を持参しなさい' and '身分証明書を持参' (see Table 5). The desired translation uses an imperative form, such as 'Bring ID' or 'Bring identification.'

TransGateway, an RBMT system widely used on web sites of Japanese local governments, generated an imperative from '身分証明書を持参しなさい,' only, while Minnano Jido Hon'yaku, the freely available SMT developed by the National Institute of Information and Communications Technology (NICT), generated the same imperative 'Bring identification' from both '身分証明書を持参する' and '身分証明書を持参.' Finally, Google Translate, one of the most widely used SMT systems, generated differing imperative translations—'Bring identification' from '身分証明書を持参' and 'Please bring your identification' from '身分証明書を持参しなさい.' This problem of variance in MT can be resolved in this pre-translation process by tuning the transformation rules to the MT system downstream.

---

[16]http://mecab.googlecode.com/svn/trunk/mecab/doc/index.html.

It should be added that RBMT has a higher affinity with CL rules and pre-translation processing than does SMT because RBMT, in using linguistic rules and a dictionary, is consistent in its treatment of the linguistic patterns of the source texts. In comparison, SMT using statistical models automatically calculated from corpus data is relatively unpredictable, although we can improve predictability by training the models.

6 Conclusions, Discussion and Future Work

This chapter has illustrated the problems encountered in using MT to translate the web sites of municipal offices in Japan into English, that is, ill-organised documents that result in unserviceable translations. It has sketched out a road map to address these problems by creating a novel document authoring environment. Introducing the document structure, particularly DITA, is of primary importance to our work. It contributes not only to creating well-organised documents but also to improving MT performance by contextualising the CL rules to enable better guidance and pre-translation processing. We also proposed an authoring support tool which implements these mechanisms with non-professional municipal authors in mind.

This is ongoing work and much is still to be done: to investigate and specialise the concept topic and reference topic for municipal documents as we have with the task topic; to fully contextualise the CL rules according to DITA elements; and to implement the CL checker and other modules of the authoring support system. Furthermore, in order to make best practical use of MT, it will be necessary to integrate other tools such as post-editing and translation memory.

Evaluation is an important part of developing a workable system. For the authoring process, it will be necessary to assess the system's usability [32] by non-professional authors in municipal offices. This will help us refine the functions and the interface. For the system output, we plan to evaluate the quality of both the Japanese source documents and the English target documents. While previous work has tended to assess sentence-level text quality [18, 50], our focus will be more on document level quality. In this respect, adopting task-based methods [10] and user-focused methods [21], for example, will be beneficial in gauging whether the documents created by using the system actually help readers achieve their goals of carrying out selected municipal procedures.

Let us now focus specifically on social media and government, the theme of this book. Bertot et al. [5] look at the impact of (US) government policies on social media usage, discussing in particular the requirements for 'access and social inclusion.' They note the challenges raised by *Executive Order 13166—Improving access to Services for Persons with Limited English Proficiencies*, which applies to all 'federal conducted programs and activities, including social media communication.' While this policy applies only in the USA, many governments choosing social media to communicate with the public will have similar concerns (being understood by people with limited understanding of the national language). We suggest that our work, in particular the proposed framework, could scale well to social media and make an impact in this respect, enabling government employees to write social media messages in such as way as to make them translatable by automatic tools.

Extending our framework specifically to social media necessitates taking into account the following aspects: (i) the linguistic characteristics peculiar to each medium and domain [41], (ii) the frequent update of the contents, and (iii) the interaction between citizens and the government. Firstly, although the texts disseminated by social media tend to be extracted from the corresponding web sites, we note some features characteristic of certain social media. Consider the sentences below: [JA], an excerpt of a *tweet* posted by Shinjuku-city on their official Twitter account; [MT], machine translated sentence of [JA]; and [EN], human translation of [JA].

[JA]	【学校や子育てについて悩んでいたら相談を】区教育委員会では、いじめ、教員の指導や親子関係などについての相談をお受けしています。
[MT]	The District Board of Education [consult when I worried about school and child care], bullying, we have accepted the advice of such faculty guidance and parent-child relationship.
[EN]	[Please consult if you are concerned about schooling or child rearing] Consultation is available about bullying, teaching and parent-child relationship at the board of education of the ward.

The limitation of the 140-character space imposed on *tweets* often induces the omission of linguistic elements and use of the special symbols for emphasis or punctuation. In this case, the first sentence omits a verb phrase, such as 'してください' or 'しましょう,' and ends with the particle 'を.' In addition, it is wrapped in black lenticular brackets, both of which degrade MT performance. Such linguistic or textual patterns characteristic of social media need to be specified if we are to apply our CL approach. Secondly, the contents of social media are frequently updated, which sometimes denies authors and translators sufficient time to polish their writing or craft fluent translations. In this situation, we believe that *MuTUAL* will facilitate the production of texts that can then be felicitously translated by the public using MT services freely available on the web. Finally, interaction via social media between citizens and the government would be a challenging dimension to handle since textual communication *from* citizens *to* the government would require accommodating various source languages, in particular Chinese, Korean and Portuguese. In addition, it would be necessary to provide a sufficiently simple interface to the authoring tool that everyone can use easily. For the time being, however, we focus on FAQs for Japanese speakers only, which, if translated, can be equally useful for foreign residents. A possible next development is a structured question form to enhance two-way communication and multilingualisation.

Tokyo will host the Olympic and Paralympic Games in 2020. Accordingly, many prospective and actual visitors to Japan will access municipal web sites and social media and many more Japanese texts will need to be multilingualised both by humans and by machines. The problematic sentence from municipal web sites shown in the title 'Garbage let's take away' recalls the old computing axiom 'Garbage in, garbage out.' MT and other language processing technologies have difficulty in dealing with poorly written or organised texts, so human authors should take responsibility for preparing machine processable texts from the outset. Thus, we would argue, our framework and the implementation of controlled authoring upstream of multilingualisation are the keys to improving the situation of Japanese municipal documents. Our mantra is 'Garbage let's take away from the source.'

Acknowledgments This work was supported by the Research Grant Program of KDDI Foundation, Japan. The MT system J-SERVER Professional TransGateway V3 was offered by Kodensha Co. Paris's stay in Japan to work with Miyata, Kageura and Hartley was funded by the Japanese Society for the Promotion of Science and CSIRO.

References

1. Adriaens, G., & Schreurs, D. (1992). From Cogram to Alcogram: Toward a controlled English grammar checker. In *Proceedings COLING1992*, Nantes, France.
2. AECMA (1995). A guide for the preparation of aircraft maintenance documents in the aerospace maintenance language AECMA Simplified English. *AECMA Document*, PSC-85-16598, Paris: AECMA.
3. Bellamy, L., Carey, M., & Schlotfeldt, J. (2012). *DITA best practices: A roadmap for writing, editing, and architecting in DITA*. Upper Saddle River, NJ: IBM Press.
4. Bernth, A., & Gdaniec, C. (2001). Mtranslatability. *Machine Translation, 16*(3), 175–218.
5. Bertot, J., Jaeger, P., & Hansen, D. (2012). The impact of policies on government social media usage: Issues, challenges and recommendations. *Government Information Quarterly, 29*(2012):30–40. (Elsevier).
6. Biber, D., & Conrad, S. (2009). *Register, genre, and style*. New York: Cambridge University Press.
7. Bouayad-Agha, N., Power, R., & Belz, A. (2002). PILLS: Multilingual generation of medical information documents with overlapping content. In *Proceedings LREC 2002*, Las Palmas, Spain.
8. Brown, P., Della Pietra, S., Della Pietra, V., & Mercer, R. (1993). The mathematics of statistical machine translation: Parameter estimation. *Computational Linguistics, 19*(2), 263–311.
9. Carroll, T. (2010). Local government websites in Japan: International, multicultural, multilingual? *Japanese Studies, 30*(3), 373–392.
10. Colineau, N., Paris, C., & Linden, K. V. (2002). An evaluation of procedural instructional text. In *Proceedings International Natural Language Generation Conference*, New York.
11. Colineau, N., Paris, C., & Linden, K. V. (2012). Government to citizen communications: From generic to tailored documents in public administration. *Information Polity, 17*(2), 177–193.
12. Colineau, N., Paris, C., & Linden, K. V. (2013). Automatically producing tailored web materials for public administration. *New Review of HyperMedia and MultiMedia, 9*(2), 158–181.
13. Day, D., Priestley, M., & Schell, D. (2005). *Introduction to the Darwin Information Typing Architecture: Toward portable technical information*. IBM Corporation. http://www.ibm.com/developerworks/xml/library/x-dita1/x-dita1-pdf.pdf. Accessed 18 Jan 2015.

14. DiMarco, C., Bray, P., Covvey, H. D., Cowan, D., DiCuccio, V., Hovy, E., & Yang, C. (2008). Authoring and generation of individualised patient education materials. *Journal on Information Technology in Healthcare, 6*(1), 63–71.

15. Hartley, A. (2010). Enabling multilingual applications of 'controlled language': The DITA framework. *Asia-Pacific Association for Machine Translation Journal, 48*, 15–18.

16. Hartley, A. F., & Paris, C. (1997). Multilingual document production: From support for translating to support for authoring. *Machine Translation, 12*(1997), 109–128.

17. Hartley, A., Paris, C. (2001). Translation, controlled languages, generation. In E. Steiner, C. Yallop (Eds.), *Exploring translation and multilingual text production: Beyond content* (pp. 307–325), Berlin: De Gruyter Mouton.

18. Hartley, A., Tatsumi, M., Isahara, H., Kageura, K., & Miyata, R. (2012). Readability and translatability judgments for 'Controlled Japanese.' In *Proceedings EAMT2012*, Trento, IT.

19. Inui, K., & Fujita, A. (2004). 言い換え技術に関する研究動向 (A survey on paraphrase generation and recognition). *Natural Language Processing, 11*(5), 151–198.

20. Japan Technical Communicators Association (Ed.). (2011). 日本語スタイルガイド *(Style guide for Japanese documents)* (2nd ed.). Tokyo: JTCA Publication.

21. Jong, M., & Schellens, P. J. (2000). Toward a document evaluation methodology: What does research tell us about the validity and reliability of evaluation methods? *IEEE Transactions on Professional Communication, 43*(3), 242–260.

22. Kamprath, C., Adolphson, E., Mitamura, T., & Nyberg, E. (1998). Controlled language for multilingual document production: Experience with Caterpillar Technical English. In *Proceedings CLAW1998*, Pittsburgh, PA.

23. Kando, N. (1997). Text-level structure of research articles and its implication for text-based information processing systems. In *Proceedings. 19th British Computer Society Annual Colloquium on Information Retrieval Research*, Aberdeen, Scotland, UK.

24. Kittredge, R. (2003). Sublanguages and controlled languages. In R. Mitkov (Ed.), *Oxford handbook of computational linguistics* (pp. 430–437). Oxford: Oxford University Press.

25. Kruijff, G.-J., Teich, E., Bateman, J., Kruijff-Korbayova, I., Skoumalova, H., Sharoff, S., Sokolova, E., Hartley, T., Staykova, K., & Hana, J. (2000). Multilinguality in a text generation system for three Slavic languages. In *Proceedings COLING2000*, Saarbruecken, Germany.

26. Kuhn, T. (2014). A survey and classification of controlled natural languages. *Computational Linguistics, 40*(1), 121–170.

27. Ministry of Internal Affairs and Communications. (2014). 地域におけるICT利活用の現状等に関する調査研究 報告書 (Report of survey on utilisation of ICT in the regions). http://www.soumu.go.jp/johotsusintokei/linkdata/h26_07_houkoku.pdf. Accessed 24 May 2015.

28. Mitamura, T., & Nyberg, E. (2001). Automatic rewriting for controlled language translation. In *Proceedings NLPRS2001 Workshop on Automatic Paraphrasing: Theory and Application*, Tokyo, Japan.

29. Mitamura, T., Baker, K., Nyberg, E., & Svoboda, D. (2003). Diagnostics for interactive controlled language checking. In *Proceedings EAMT2003 Workshop on Controlled Language Applications*, Dublin.

30. Nagao, M. (1984). A framework of a mechanical translation between Japanese and English by analogy principle. In A. Elithorn & R. Banerji (Eds.), *Artificial and human intelligence*. New York: Elsevier North-Holland Inc.

31. Nagao, M., Tanaka, N., & Tsujii, J. (1984). 制限文法にもとづく文章作成援助システム (Support system for writing texts based on controlled grammar). *Information Processing Society of Japan, NL-44*, 33–40.

32. Nielsen, J. (1993). *Usability engineering*. San Francisco: Morgan Kaufmann.

33. Nyberg, E., & Mitamura, T. (2000). The KANTOO machine translation environment. In *Proceedings AMTA2000*, Cuernavaca, Mexico.

34. Nyberg, E., Mitamura, T., & Huijsen, W. (2003). Controlled language for authoring and translation. In H. Somers (Ed.), *Computers and the translator*. Amsterdam: Benjamins.
35. OASIS. (2010). *Darwin Information Typing Architecture (DITA) Version 1.2*. http://docs.oasis-open.org/dita/v1.2/os/spec/DITA1.2-spec.html. Accessed 31 May 2015.
36. O'Brien, S. (2003). Controlling controlled English: An analysis of several controlled language rule sets. In *Proceedings EAMT2003 Workshop on Controlled Language Applications*, Dublin.
37. O'Brien, S. (2010). Controlled language and readability. *Translation and Cognition, 15*, 143–165.
38. Ogura, E., Kudo, M., & Yanagi, H. (2010). シンプリファイド・テクニカル・ジャパニーズ 英訳を視野に入れて日本語を作る (Simplified Technical Japanese: Writing translation-ready Japanese documents). *Information Processing Society of Japan, DD-78*(5), 1–8.
39. Paris, C., Linden, K. V., Colineau, N., & Lu, S. (2005). Automatically generating effective on-line help. *International Journal on E-Learning, 4*(1), 83–103.
40. Paris, C., Colineau, N., Lampert, A., & Linden, K. V. (2010). Discourse planning for information composition and delivery: A reusable platform. *The International Journal of Natural Language Engineering, 16*(1), 61–98.
41. Paris, C., Thomas, P., & Wan, S. (2012). Differences in language and style between two social media communities. In *Proceedings ICWSM2012*, Dublin.
42. PLAIN (Plain Language and Information Network). (2011). *Federal Plain Language Guidelines*. http://www.plainlanguage.gov. Accessed 31 May 2015.
43. Power, R., Scott, D., & Hartley, A. (2003). Multilingual generation of controlled languages. In *Proceedings EAMT2003 Workshop on Controlled Language Applications*, Dublin.
44. Pym, P. (1990). Pre-editing and the use of simplified writing for MT. In P. Mayorcas (Ed.), *Translating and the computer 10* (pp. 80–95). London: Aslib.
45. Roturier, J. (2009). Controlled language for MT in action. In *Proceedings Translingual Europe*, Prague.
46. Sato, S., & Nagao, M. (1990). Toward memory-based translation. In *Proceedings COLING1990*, Stroudsburg, PA.
47. Sato, S., Tsuchiya, M., Murayama, M., Asaoka, M., & Wang, Q. (2003). 日本語文の規格化 (Standardization of Japanese sentences). *Information Processing Society of Japan, NL-4*, 133–140.
48. Shirai, S., Ikehara, S., Yokoo, A., & Ooyama, Y. (1998). Automatic rewriting method for internal expressions in Japanese to English MT and its effects. In *Proceedings CLAW1998*, Pittsburgh, PA.
49. Smart, J. F. (2006). SMART Controlled English. In *Proceedings CLAW2006*, Cambridge, MA.
50. Tatsumi, M., Miyata, R., Hartley, A., Kageura, K., & Isahara, H. (2013). Towards acceptable quality machine translation without post-editing for municipal websites: An evaluation of Japanese controlled language rules. *MT Summit 2013 QTLaunchPad Workshop on Human-Centric Machine Translation and Evaluation*, Nice, France.
51. Watanabe, T. (2010). 産業日本語プロジェクトの概要 特許・技術情報の利用性向上のために (Outline of the 'Technical Japanese' project: Activity for acceleration of patent technological information utilization). *Information Processing and Management, 53*(9), 480–491.
52. Yoshida, S., & Matsuyama, A. (1985). 日本語の規格化:係り受け関係の規格化とそれへの変換ルール (Standardizing Japanese: Standardizing dependency relations and transformation rules). *Information Processing Society of Japan, NL-31*, 1–6.
53. Yoshimi, T., Sata, I., & Fukumochi, Y. (2000). Automatic preediting of English sentences for a robust English-to-Japanese MT system. *Natural Language Processing, 7*(4), 99–117.

Multi-hazard Detection by Integrating Social Media and Physical Sensors

Aibek Musaev, De Wang and Calton Pu

Abstract Disaster Management is one of the most important functions of the government. FEMA and CDC are two examples of government agencies directly charged with handling disasters, whereas USGS is a scientific agency oriented towards disaster research. But regardless of the type or purpose, each of the mentioned agencies utilizes Social Media as part of its activities. One of the uses of Social Media is in detection of disasters, such as earthquakes. But disasters may lead to other kinds of disasters, forming multi-hazards such as landslides. Effective detection and management of multi-hazards cannot rely only on one information source. In this chapter, we describe and evaluate a prototype implementation of a landslide detection system LITMUS, which combines multiple physical sensors and Social Media to handle the inherent varied origins and composition of multi-hazards. Our results demonstrate that LITMUS detects more landslides than the ones reported by an authoritative source.

Keywords LITMUS · Social media · Physical sensor · Disaster management · Landslide detection

1 Introduction

Government through its agencies plays a critical role in disaster management. There are multiple government agencies dealing with various aspects of disasters, including FEMA and CDC. The Federal Emergency Agency (FEMA) is a

A. Musaev (✉) · D. Wang · C. Pu
College of Computing, Georgia Institute of Technology, 266 Ferst Drive,
30332 Atlanta, Georgia
e-mail: aibek.musaev@gatech.edu

D. Wang
e-mail: wang6@gatech.edu

C. Pu
e-mail: calton.pu@cc.gatech.edu

© Springer International Publishing Switzerland 2015
S. Nepal et al. (eds.), *Social Media for Government Services*,
DOI 10.1007/978-3-319-27237-5_17

federal agency under the Department of Homeland Security, which is responsible for coordinating the response to a disaster. The Centers for Disease Control and Prevention (CDC) is a federal agency under the Department of Health and Human Services. It is responsible for emergency preparedness and response. Unlike these two major agencies that are directly charged with handling disasters, the United States Geological Survey (USGS) is a scientific agency. It studies the landscape of the United States, its natural resources and the natural hazards that threaten it. But regardless of the type or purpose, all of these agencies utilize Social Media as part of their activities.

The agencies maintain a number of Social Media accounts as part of their mission to disseminate information to the public and even offer digital toolkits to integrate such information into third party tools.[1] USGS uses Social Media channels to inform the public about various natural hazards, including earthquakes, landslides and volcanoes.[2] However, Social Media itself can be used as a source of data for disaster management instead of solely relying on physical sensors. A good example of exploring the data from Social Media is Twitter data streams functioning as social sensors [1]. Also, many existing disaster management systems adopt multiple information sources, including news channels. However, they all face the challenge of integrating multiple information sources in the way that preserves the useful information while limiting the amount of noise. We cannot depend on a single information source to make decisions, since each information source has its advantages and disadvantages. For instance, Social Media sources can provide real-time streaming information, but not all of such information is related to disasters that we are interested in. In fact, there is a high amount of noise in Social Media, which has been elaborated in our previous research study on denial of information [2–4]. Also, one interesting example of the noise about "landslide" is the 70s rock song "Landslide" by Fleetwood Mac. Twitter filter for the word "landslide" gets more tweets on this song than landslide disasters that involve soil movement. News channels provide reliable and mostly verified information sources. Unfortunately, they normally have high latency that may be up to several days after the occurrence of a disaster.

Besides, disasters like multi-hazards present more significant challenges, since there are no effective physical sensors that would detect multi-hazards directly. Landslide, which can be caused by earthquakes, rainfalls and human activity among other reasons, is an illustrative example of a multi-hazard. After investigating existing approaches using physical and social sensors, we proposed a new landslide detection service—LITMUS [5–7] and also implemented a prototype system in practice, which is based on a multi-service composition approach to the detection of landslides. More concretely, LITMUS has the following benefits compared with traditional or existing approaches for natural disaster detection:

---

[1]http://www.cdc.gov/socialmedia/tools/guidelines/socialmediatoolkit.html.

[2]https://twitter.com/usgsnewshazards.

- It composes information from a variety of sensor networks including both physical sensors (e.g., seismometers for earthquakes and weather satellites for rainfalls) and social sensors (e.g., Twitter and YouTube). Besides providing wider coverage than a system relying on a single source, it improves detection accuracy and reduces the overall latency.

- It applies state-of-art filters for each social sensor and then adopts geo-tagging to integrate the reported events from all physical and social sensors that refer to the same geo-location. Such integration achieves better landslide detection when compared to an authoritative source. Meanwhile, the geo-location information not only provides the base for the integration, but also enables us to do real-time notification in the future.

- It provides a generic approach to the composition of multiple heterogeneous information services and uses landslide detection as an illustrative example, i.e. it is not tied to disaster detection and can be applied to other application areas involving service composition. Traditional approach to the composition of web services makes strong assumptions about services, which it then uses to select services when composing a new service, such as quality of service [8] or service license compatibility [9]. In practice, the real world services do not satisfy such assumptions. The claim we make is that more information services should provide a more solid result and we demonstrate that it is the case with LITMUS.

The rest of the chapter is organized as follows. Section 2 provides an overview of the LITMUS system. We introduce the supported physical and social sources, and describe implementation details of each system component. In Sect. 3, we present an evaluation of landslide detection using real data and compare the results generated by LITMUS with an authoritative source. We summarize related work in Sect. 4 and conclude the chapter in Sect. 5.

2 System Overview

There are several stages in the LITMUS prototype that are implemented by the corresponding software components—see Fig. 1 for an overview of the system pipeline.

The data collection component downloads the data from multiple social and physical sources using provided API. The data from Social Media requires additional processing as it is usually not geo-tagged and contains a lot of noise. That is why the data from Social Media is geo-tagged followed by the filtering out of irrelevant items using stop words/phrases and classification algorithms. The integration component integrates the data from social and physical sources by performing grid-based location estimation of potential landslide locations followed by the computation of landslide probability to generate a report on detected landslides. This report includes all of the data related to detected landslides, i.e. the physical sensor readings as well as all tweets, images, and videos that were used to detect them.

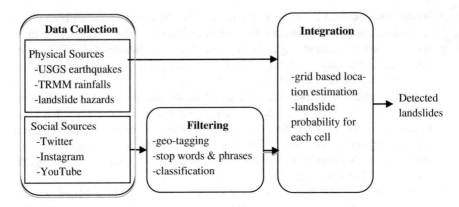

Fig. 1 Overview of system pipeline

2.1 Data Collection Component

Social Media feeds. There is a separate data collection process based on the capabilities provided by each data source. Among the currently supported data sources, Twitter has the most advanced API for accessing its data. In particular, it provides a Streaming API, which returns tweets in real-time containing the given keywords. Instead of storing the incoming tweets directly into a data store, LITMUS writes the tweets to a set of intermediate files first. The intermediate layer was introduced for two reasons. On the one hand we wanted to increase overall robustness, such that even if the data store failed we would still have the original files that we could restore the data from. On the other hand it allows us to easily switch to another data store if needed. The file structure of the intermediate layer is as follows:

```
<source_type>_< event_type>_<year>/<month>/<day>/<hour>/<min>.json
```

Note that when there are multiple incoming items per minute, then they get appended to the same file. The item IDs are used to make sure there are no duplicate records. The rate of incoming items containing landslide keywords is moderate, but we plan to add support for other types of events that would have a much higher rate of incoming items, such as "ebola" for instance. So, a file structure as this makes sure that the data is broken into manageable chunks.

The next step is to upload the incoming items to a data store. We use Redis, because it is an in-memory data store that is widely used and it is open source [10]. We keep the latest 30 days worth of data in the data store to maintain a fixed memory footprint. The new data is periodically uploaded into Redis and obsolete items are removed. The rest of the system works with Redis directly instead of files.

Both YouTube and Instagram provide a pull type of API that LITMUS uses to periodically download items containing landslide keywords. Again, the items from these Social Media get stored into the described file structure and the new items are periodically uploaded into Redis.

The rainfalls data is available due to the Tropical Rainfall Measuring Mission (TRMM) [11]. TRMM is a joint space project between NASA and the Japan Aerospace Exploration Agency (JAXA). The mission uses a satellite to collect data about tropical rainfalls. TRMM generates various reports based on its data, including a list of potential landslide areas due to extreme or prolonged rainfall. In particular, it generates reports of potential landslide areas after 1, 3, and 7 days of rainfall. The data is provided in HTML format, which LITMUS periodically downloads, parses and saves extracted content into data storage for further analysis. TRMM project has been operating since December 1997. However, on July 8, 2014 pressure readings from the fuel tank indicated that the TRMM satellite is near the end of its fuel. The satellite is estimated to be shutdown in February 2016, but JAXA may stop distribution of the radar data prior to that date. As of January 1, 2015 the data is still available.

The seismic feed is provided by the United States Geological Survey (USGS) agency [12]. USGS supports multiple feeds of earthquakes with various magnitudes. The data is provided in a convenient GeoJSON format, which is a format for encoding a variety of geographic data structures. LITMUS uses a real-time feed of earthquakes with 2.5 magnitude or higher, which gets updated every minute. USGS includes event id, which is used to avoid duplicate records in the system.

Global Landslide Hazards Distribution is another physical source that LITMUS supports [13]. It provides a 2.5 min grid of global landslide and snow avalanche hazards based upon the work of the Norwegian Geotechnical Institute (NGI). This source incorporates a range of data including slope, soil, precipitation and temperature among others. The hazard values in this source are ranked from 6 to 10, while the values below are ignored. The reason why this particular source is supported is because the landslides detected by LITMUS to occur in the landslide hazardous areas are more likely to be determined correctly as opposed to the landslides detected to occur in other areas.

2.2 Filtering Component

Geo-tagging. All Social Media supported by LITMUS allow users to disclose their location when they send a tweet, post an image or upload a video. However, based on the evaluation dataset collected in November 2014 very few users actually use this functionality. In particular, less than 0.77 % of all tweets are geo-tagged in our dataset. That is why we analyze the textual descriptions of the items from Social Media to see if they mention geographic terms in them.

A common approach implementing this idea is based on the use of a gazetteer. A gazetteer is a dictionary that maps geographic terms to geographic coordinates. An exact match of a sequence of words is performed against the gazetteer. Since we do not know in advance which particular word or sequence of words is a geographic term, all possible sequences are considered. This approach requires the presence of a local and relatively small gazetteer, since requests to remote or large gazetteers will significantly slow down the system, as the number of sequences of words in a text is very high.

Another weakness of this approach is that gazetteers often have geo terms that are common nouns, so they are used in texts a lot. For example, "Goes" is a city in Netherlands and "Enterprise" is a city in the United States. Most likely both words will be useless geo terms for the purposes of landslide detection and would have to be excluded from consideration by the system. Also, many news sources contain geographic terms in them, such as "Boston Globe" or "Jamaica Observer". A geo-tagging algorithm would have to have a list of news sources in order to ignore such geographic terms automatically.

This is only a small fraction of issues that would have to be addressed in a geo-tagging algorithm based on the use of a gazetteer. Which is why LITMUS implements an alternative approach that employs a natural language processing technique called named entity recognition (NER).

NER implementations locate and classify elements in a text into pre-defined categories, including names of persons, organizations, dates and locations. For geo-tagging purposes LITMUS extracts sequences of words recognized as locations from text. Then it checks the found geo-terms against a local gazetteer. There is an open source project called GeoNames that provides a free gazetteer dump with more than 10 million places.[3] If the geo term is not found there, LITMUS makes a remote call to the Google Geocoding API[4] to obtain corresponding geographic coordinates, i.e. latitude and longitude values.

See Experimental Evaluation section for the results of the geo-tagging analysis performed by LITMUS during the evaluation period.

Stop words and phrases. During the process of building the ground truth dataset described below, we noticed that we could almost instantly tell whether a given social item was irrelevant to landslide as a natural disaster or not. There were several common irrelevant topics discussed in Social Media that were easy to spot due to the use of specific words, including "election", "vote", "parliament" and "Fleetwoodmac", e.g.:

> What does the Republican election landslide mean?: VIRGINIA (WAVY) — What does the Republican landslide in the… http://t.co/2Alrs48SwK

> Landslide… and every woman in the Tacoma Dome wept with the beautiful @StevieNicks @fleetwoodmac #fleetwoodmacworldtour

Another common irrelevant topic is the use of the lyrics from a popular rock song from the 70's to describe a user's mood at the moment, e.g.:

> Well I've been afraid of changing cause I built my life around you #LandSlide

In this case instead of a particular stop word, we use excerpts from the lyrics of a popular song as a stop phrase instead.

---

[3]http://www.geonames.org/.

[4]https://developers.google.com/maps/documentation/geocoding/.

Stop words and phrases are easy to understand and fast to execute. So, LITMUS attempts to filter out items using stop words and phrases first before applying classification algorithm described next on the remaining items.

Classification algorithm. To decide whether an item from Social Media is relevant or irrelevant to landslide as a natural disaster, we propose the following approach. The textual description of each item is compared against the texts of relevant Wikipedia articles and the texts of irrelevant articles. Then we use the relevance of the article that is most similar to the given item as our decision.

For a list of relevant articles, we use the landslide keywords as Wikipedia concepts, namely landslide, landslip, mudslide, rockfall, and rockslide. These articles are downloaded, parsed and all HTML markup is removed, so that only their content is used for analysis. In addition to these articles, we also use a set of articles describing actual occurrences of landslides, mudslides, and rockslides, including 2014 Pune landslide, 2014 Oso mudslide, and Frank Slide. For a list of irrelevant articles, we use the landslide stop words to download the corresponding Wikipedia articles, namely Landslide victory, Blowout (sports), Election, Landslide (song), and Politics. Similarly, these articles are downloaded, parsed and all HTML markup is removed, so that only their texts are used for analysis.

To compute the distance between social items and these Wikipedia articles we use a formula named after Swiss Professor Paul Jaccard. He compared how similar different regions were based on the following formula:

$$\frac{Number\ of\ species\ common\ to\ the\ two\ regions}{Total\ number\ of\ species\ in\ the\ two\ regions}$$

This formula gives 0 if the sets have no common elements and 1 if they are the same. This is the opposite of what we need as a similarity measure, so we use the following formula instead:

$$Jaccard\ distance = 1 - \frac{Intersection(A, B)}{Union(A, B)},$$

where A and B are the sets that we want to compare.

Each article is converted to a bag of words representation or more precisely a set of words. Each incoming item from Social Media is also converted to a set of words representation. Now these sets can be used to compute the Jaccard distance between them.

Using this approach we were able to successfully classify items in November 2014. Table 1 lists the examples of items from Social Media together with the smallest Jaccard distance values and corresponding Wikipedia concepts. See the Experimental Evaluation section for more details on the experiment.

2.3 Integration Component

Previously the items from social sources have been geo-tagged and classified as either relevant or irrelevant to landslide as a natural disaster. The items from physical

Table 1 Examples of classification of items

Text	Jaccard distance	Wikipedia concept	Decision
Bad weather hampers rescue operations at Sri Lanka's landslide http://t.co/vYYgwRL1S6 #ANN	0.9916317991631799	2014 Pune landslide	1
Bertam Valley still deadly: After a mudslide claimed four lives and left 100 homeless, the danger is far from… http://t.co/ZiauH2YVvJ	0.9913366336633663	2014 Oso mudslide	1
#bjpdrama World's knowledge in 1 hand site: BJP got landslide Will India become a 1 party state like China Russia http://t.co/jGhp1j84az	0.9847715736040609	Landslide victory, wave election	0

sources are already geo-tagged and there is no need to classify them, as they are all considered relevant to landslide as a natural disaster. Now that we have the items' geographic coordinates, namely their latitude and longitude values, we want to integrate the data based on those values. One possible way of doing it is to divide the surface of the planet into cells of a grid. Items from each source are mapped to the cells in this grid based on their latitude/longitude values. Obviously, the size of these cells is important, because it can range from the smallest possible size to the one covering the whole planet. The smaller the cells, the less the chance that related items will be mapped to the same cell. But the bigger the cells, the more events are mapped to the same cell making it virtually impossible to distinguish one event from another.

Currently we use a 2.5-min grid both in latitude and longitude, which corresponds to the resolution of the Global Landslide Hazard Distribution described above. This is the maximum resolution of an event supported by the system at the moment.

The total number of cells in our grid is huge as cells are 2.5 min in both latitude and longitude, there are 60 min per degree, latitude values range from $-90°$ to $+90°$ and longitude values range from $-180°$ to $+180°$. But the actual number of cells under consideration is much smaller, because LITMUS only analyzes non-empty cells. For example, there are only 1192 candidate cells during the evaluation month of November 2014 as you can see in the Experimental Evaluation section below.

Next we consider each non-empty cell to decide whether there was a landslide event there. To calculate the probability of a landslide event w in cell x, we use the following weighted sum formula as the strategy to integrate data from multiple sources:

$$P(w|x) = \sum_i R_i \frac{\sum_j POS_{ij}^x - \sum_j NEG_{ij}^x - \sum_j STOP_{ij}^x}{\sum_i N_i^x}$$

Here, R_i denotes ith sensor's weight or confidence; POS_{ij}^x denotes positively classified items from sensor i in cell x, NEG_{ij}^x denotes negatively classified items from sensor i in cell x, $STOP_{ij}^x$ denotes the items from sensor i in cell x that have been labeled as irrelevant based on stop words and stop phrases, and N_i^x denotes the total number of items from sensor i in cell x.

In our prototype, we use prior F-measure R as the confidence for each sensor, since F-measure provides a balance between precision and recall, namely $F\text{-measure} = 2 * \frac{precision*recall}{precision+recall}$. To generate results in the range from 0 to 1, we normalize the values of F-measure into a scale between 0 and 1.

Finally, it should be noted that the given formula generates a score between 0 and 1 that can be used to rank all location cells based on the probability of a landslide occurrence there.

3 Experimental Evaluation

In this section, we perform an evaluation of LITMUS using real-world data. In particular, we design an experiment to compare the performance of landslide detection by LITMUS versus an authoritative source. We show that LITMUS manages to detect 41 out of 45 events reported by the authoritative source during evaluation period as well as 165 additional locations. We also describe the collection of the ground truth dataset and provide the details of the dataset collected by LITMUS during this period.

3.1 Evaluation Dataset

We select the month of November 2014 as the evaluation period. Here is an overview of the data collected by LITMUS during this period—see Table 2.

For each geo-tagged item, LITMUS also computes its cell based on its latitude and longitude. The total number of cells during the evaluation period is equal to 1192. Hence, there are 1192 candidate locations that LITMUS has to mark as either relevant or irrelevant to landslide as a natural disaster.

Table 2 Overview of evaluation dataset

Social media	Raw data	Geo-tagged data
Twitter	83,909	13,335
Instagram	2026	460
YouTube	7186	2312

3.2 Ground Truth Dataset

In order to collect the ground truth dataset for the month of November, we consider all items that are successfully geo-tagged during this month. For each such geo-tagged item, we compute its cell based on its latitude and longitude values. All cells during November represent a set of candidate events, which is 1192 as shown above. Next we group all geo-tagged items from Social Media by their cell values. For each cell we look at each item to see whether it is relevant to landslide as a natural disaster or not. If the item's textual description contains URL, then we look at the URL to confirm the candidate item's relevance to landslides. If the item does not contain a URL, then we try to find confirmation of the described event on the Internet using the textual description as our search query. If another trustworthy source confirms the landslide occurrence in that area then we mark the corresponding cell as relevant. Otherwise we mark it as irrelevant. It should be noted that we consider all events reported by USGS as ground truth as well.

Overall, there are 212 cells that we marked as relevant. The following are a few examples of social activity related to the events in those cells:

> Landslide on route to Genting Highlands: PETALING JAYA: A landslide occurred at 4.2KM heading towards Genting... http://t.co/AYfCKy6H2n

> Major back up on HWY 403 Toronto bound in Hamilton due to mudslide. ALL lanes closed at 403 between Main & York. http://t.co/QcRJdjydR1

> Trains cancelled between Par and Newquay due to landslip http://t.co/IcGsdS3y5r

3.3 Comparison of Landslide Detection Versus Authoritative Source

In November 2014 USGS posted links to 45 articles related to landslides.[5] LITMUS detects events described in 41 of them, i.e. over 90 % of events reported by the authoritative source were detected by our system. In addition to 41 locations described in these articles, LITMUS managed to detect 165 locations unreported by USGS during this period.

Hence, there are only 4 events reported by USGS that were missed by LITMUS during this period. Next we provide explanation why LITMUS did not detect the events described in these articles.

Out of these 4 articles, 2 did not report recent natural disasters. In particular, one article suggests that Bilayat grass, also called trap grass, can be used to prevent landslides in the hills of Uttarakhand.[6] The other article describes the reopening of

---

[5]http://landslides.usgs.gov/recent/index.php?year=2014&month=Nov.

[6]http://timesofindia.indiatimes.com/city/dehradun/Now-a-grass-that-could-prevent-landslides/articleshow/45196678.cms.

the Haast Pass in New Zealand.[7] It was closed nightly since a major slip last year and it will stay open due to a three-net system that protects the pass against rock fall.

The third article describes a minor event that did not receive much attention in Twitter, Instagram or YouTube. In particular, this article is a link to an image in Wikipedia of a minor rock fall on Angeles Crest Highway in California.[8]

Finally, the fourth article is about a route in Costa Rica that remains closed due to recent landslides in that area.[9] There were many tweets on this subject in Spanish, but not much activity in English. LITMUS currently supports English language only, which is why it missed this event. We are already working on adding support for other languages, including Spanish. See Conclusion and Future Work section for more details.

As we mentioned earlier, LITMUS detected 165 locations unreported by the authoritative source during this period. The reasons why LITMUS manages to detect more landslide events than the authoritative source are twofold. On the one hand we claim that our approach is comprehensive as it is fully automated, so it processes all items from each supported data source as opposed to a manual approach where an expert may miss an event due to a human error or human limits. On the other hand LITMUS integrates multiple sources in its analysis, both physical and social, and we plan to add more sources over time. See Conclusion and Future Work section for more details.

Overall, LITMUS detected 41 locations reported by USGS and 165 locations more, which is 206 locations out of 212 total ground truth locations, i.e. a landslide detection rate of over 97 % during this period.

4 Related Work

Event analysis using Social Media received a lot of attention from the research community recently. Guy et al. [14] introduced Twitter Earthquake Dispatcher (TED) that gauges public's interest in a particular earthquake using bursts in social activity on Twitter. Sakaki et al. [1] applied machine learning techniques to detect earthquakes by considering each Twitter user as a sensor. Cameron et al. [15] developed platform and client tools to identify relevant Twitter messages that can be used to inform the situation awareness of an emergency incident as it unfolds. Musaev et al. [5–7] introduced a landslide detection system LITMUS based on integration of multiple social and physical sources. We provide an overview of LITMUS implementation in this work, demonstrate its advantages using a recent evaluation period and describe enhancements made.

---

[7]http://www.radionz.co.nz/news/regional/258610/pass-reopens-with-rock-fall-protection.

[8]http://en.wikipedia.org/wiki/File:Minor_rockfall_on_Angeles_Crest_Highway_2014-11-05.jpg.

[9]http://thecostaricanews.com/route-27-remains-closed-due-to-landslides.

Document classification or document categorization is one of the most studied areas in computer science due to its importance. The problem is to assign a document to one or more classes or categories from a predefined set. Sakaki et al. [1] described a real-time earthquake detection system where they classified tweets into relevant and irrelevant categories using a support vector machine based on features such as keywords in a tweet, the number of words, and their context. Musaev et al. [6] improved the overall accuracy of supervised classification of tweets by converting the filtering problem of each item to the filtering problem of the aggregation of items assigned to each event location. Gabrilovich and Markovitch [16, 17] proposed to enhance text categorization with encyclopedia knowledge, such as Wikipedia. Each Wikipedia article represents a concept, and documents are represented in the feature space of words and relevant Wikipedia concepts. Their Explicit Semantic Analysis (ESA) method explicitly represents the meaning of any text as a weighted vector of Wikipedia-based concepts and identifies the most relevant encyclopedia articles across a diverse collection of datasets. In our work we identify two classes of Wikipedia articles that contain either relevant or irrelevant to landslides articles. Then we use Jaccard distance instead of a weighted vector to find the most similar article to a given social item. Finally we use the article's class as a decision for the social item's relevance to landslides.

Accurate identification of disaster event locations is an important aspect for disaster detection systems. The challenge for Social Media based analysis is that users do not disclose their location when reporting disaster events or that they may use alias or location names in different granularities in messages resulting in inaccurate location information. Cheng et al. [18] proposed and evaluated a probabilistic framework for estimating a Twitter user's city-level location based on the content of tweets, even in the absence of any other geospatial cues. Hecht et al. [19] showed that 34 % of users did not provide real location information, and they also demonstrated that a classifier could be used to make predictions about users' locations. Sultanik and Fink [20] used an indexed gazetteer for rapid geo-tagging and disambiguation of Social Media texts. Musaev et al. [7] evaluated three geo-tagging algorithms based on the use of gazetteer and named entity recognition approaches. In our work we employ the named entity recognition approach to identify all location entities mentioned in Social Media first. Then we use a public gazetteer to retrieve geographic coordinates for the found locations. If there is no match in the gazetteer, then LITMUS uses the Google Geocoding API to convert locations into geographic coordinates.

5 Conclusion and Future Work

In this chapter, we described and evaluated a prototype implementation of a landslide detection system called LITMUS, which combines multiple physical sensors and Social Media to handle the inherent varied origins and composition of multi-hazards. LITMUS integrates near real-time data from USGS seismic network,

NASA TRMM rainfall network, Twitter, YouTube, Instagram as well as a global landslide hazards map. The landslide detection process consists of several stages of Social Media filtering and integration with physical sensor data, with a final ranking of relevance by integrated signal strength. Our results demonstrate that with such approach LITMUS detects 41 out of 45 reported events as well as 165 events that were unreported by the authoritative source during the evaluation period.

As we showed in the Experimental Evaluation section, LITMUS missed four events reported by USGS in November 2014. One of the events did not have much activity in English, but it did receive more attention in Spanish as it occurred in Costa Rica. That is why we are already working on adding support to LITMUS for event detection in other languages, including Spanish and Chinese. The data from Social Media in different languages can be considered as additional data sources, which will increase the coverage of event detection by LITMUS. It should also be noted that different languages have varying amounts of noise depending on the used keywords. For example, a "mudslide" in Russian is "оползень". We were surprised to find that the overwhelming majority of items in Social Media containing this word are relevant to mudslide as a natural hazard, which is an interesting fact that we plan to explore.

One of our objectives in this project is to analyze the possibility of predicting landslides in LITMUS. We have been collecting data in LITMUS since August 2013. Our plan is to eventually be able to predict landslide events based on the data from multiple sources, both physical and social. Landslides are an illustrative example of a multi-hazard disaster and we plan to study the possibility of predicting landslides in LITMUS using not only real-time data feeds from multiple sources, but also historical data that we collected.

We also believe that comprehensive and real-time information about landslide events can be useful not only to government agencies, but also research and journalism communities. That is why we are developing an automated notification system that people and organizations can subscribe to in order to receive real-time information on major landslides. This service will provide all relevant information collected by LITMUS, including tweets, images and videos related to each detected event.

Finally, the prototype landslide detection system LITMUS is live and openly accessible,[10] collecting data and displaying detection results in real-time for continued evaluation and improvement of the system.

Acknowledgements This research has been partially funded by National Science Foundation by CNS/SAVI (1250260, 1402266), IUCRC/FRP (1127904), CISE/CNS (1138666, 1421561), NetSE (0905493) programs, and gifts, grants, or contracts from Fujitsu, Singapore Government, and Georgia Tech Foundation through the John P. Imlay, Jr. Chair endowment. Any opinions, findings, and conclusions or recommendations expressed in this material are those of the author(s) and do not necessarily reflect the views of the National Science Foundation or other funding agencies and companies mentioned above.

---

[10]https://grait-dm.gatech.edu/demo-multi-source-integration/.

References

1. Sakaki, T., Okazaki, M., & Matsuo, Y. (2010). Earthquake shakes twitter users: Real-time event detection by social sensors. In *19th International Conference on World Wide Web (WWW)*. Raleigh, North Carolina.
2. Wang, D., Irani, D., & Pu, C. (2011). A social-spam detection framework. In *8th Annual Collaboration, Electronic Messaging, Anti-Abuse and Spam Conference*. Perth, Australia.
3. Wang, D., Irani, D., & Pu, C. (2013). A study on evolution of email spam over fifteen years. In *9th International Conference Conference on Collaborative Computing: Networking, Applications and Worksharing (CollaborateCom)*. Austin, Texas.
4. Wang, D. (2014). Analysis and detection of low quality information in social networks. In *IEEE 30th International Conference on Data Engineering Workshops (ICDEW)*. Chicago, Illinois.
5. Musaev, A., Wang, D., & Pu, C. (2014). LITMUS: Landslide detection by integrating multiple sources. In *11th International Conference Information Systems for Crisis Response and Management (ISCRAM)*. Pennsylvania: University Park.
6. Musaev, A., Wang, D., Cho, C.-A., & Pu, C. (2014). Landslide detection service based on composition of physical and social information services. In *21st IEEE International Conference on Web Services (ICWS)*. Anchorage, Alaska.
7. Musaev, A., Wang, D., & Pu, C. (2014). LITMUS: A multi-service composition system for landslide detection. In *IEEE Transactions on Services Computing* (No. 99).
8. Ran, S. (2003). A model for web services discovery with QoS. In *ACM SIGecom Exchanges* (Vol. 4, no. 1).
9. Gangadharan, G., Weiss, M., DAndrea, V., & Iannella, R. (2007). Service license composition and compatibility analysis. In *5th International Conference on Service Oriented Computing (ICSOC)*. Vienna, Austria.
10. Redis: An open-source advanced key-value store. http://redis.io. Accessed January 1, 2015.
11. Tropical Rainfall Measuring Mission (TRMM). http://trmm.gsfc.nasa.gov. Accessed January 1, 2015.
12. Earthquakes Hazards Program, United States Geological Survey. http://earthquake.usgs.gov. Accessed January 1, 2015.
13. Center for Hazards and Risk Research—CHRR—Columbia University, Center for International Earth Science Information Network—CIESIN—Columbia University, and Norwegian Geotechnical Institute—NGI. (2005). *Global Landslide Hazard Distribution*. Palisades, NY: NASA Socioeconomic Data and Applications Center (SEDAC). http://dx.doi.org/10.7927/H4P848VZ. Accessed January 1, 2015.
14. Guy, M., Earle, P., Ostrum, C., Gruchalla, K., & Horvath, S. (2010). Integration and dissemination of citizen reported and seismically derived earthquake information via social network technologies. In *Intelligent Data Analysis IX*. Tucson, Arizona.
15. Cameron, M. A., Power, R., Robinson, B., & Yin, J. (2012). Emergency situation awareness from twitter for crisis management. In *1st Workshop on Social Web for Disaster Management (SWDM)*. Lyon, France.
16. Gabrilovich, E., & Markovitch, S. (2006). Overcoming the brittleness bottleneck using Wikipedia: Enhancing text categorization with encyclopedic knowledge. In *National Conference on Artificial Intelligence (AAAI)*. Boston, Massachusetts.
17. Gabrilovich, E., & Markovich, S. (2007). Computing semantic relatedness using Wikipedia-based explicit semantic analysis. In *20th International Joint Conference on Artificial Intelligence (IJCAI)*. Hyderabad, India.
18. Cheng, Z., Caverlee, J., & Lee, K. (2010). You are where you tweet: A content-based approach to geo-locating twitter users. In *19th ACM international conference on Information and Knowledge Management (CIKM)*. Toronto, Ontario, Canada.

19. Hecht, B., Hong, L., Suh, B., & Chi, E. H. (2011). Tweets from Justin Bieber's heart: The dynamics of the "location" field in user profiles. In *Conference on Human Factors in Computing Systems (CHI)*. Vancouver, Canada.
20. Sultanik, E. A., & Fink, C. (2012). Rapid geotagging and disambiguation of social media text via an indexed gazetteer. In *9th International Conference Information Systems for Crisis Response and Management (ISCRAM)*. Vancouver, Canada.

Printed in the United States
By Bookmasters